WAR AND SECESSION

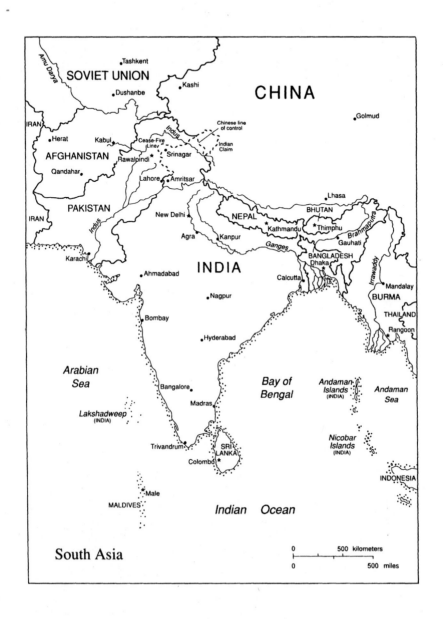

South Asia

WAR AND SECESSION

PAKISTAN,

INDIA,

AND THE CREATION OF

BANGLADESH

RICHARD SISSON and LEO E. ROSE

University of California Press

Berkeley • *Los Angeles* • *Oxford*

954.9205
562w

University of California Press
Berkeley and Los Angeles, California

University of California Press, Ltd.
Oxford, England

© 1990 by
The Regents of the University of California

Library of Congress Cataloging-in-Publication Data

Sisson, Richard.
    War and secession : Pakistan, India, and the creation of
Bangladesh / Richard Sisson and Leo E. Rose.
        p.   cm.
    Bibliography: p.
    Includes index.
    ISBN 0-520-07665-6 (alk. paper)
    1. Bangladesh—History—Revolution, 1971. 2. India-
Pakistan Conflict, 1971.   3. South Asia—Politics and gov-
ernment.   I. Rose, Leo E.   II. Title.
DS395.5.S59   1990
954.9205—dc20   89-32545
                                                    CIP

Printed in the United States of America

The paper used in this publication meets the minimum
requirements of American National Standard for Information Sciences—Permanence of Paper for Printed Library
Materials, ANSI Z39.48–1984.   ∞

Contents

Preface

This reconstruction of the events and decisions leading to the creation of the new independent nation of Bangladesh in 1971 draws upon many sources, many previously unavailable. We have based our analysis primarily on interviews with key political leaders and their principal advisers and associates in each of the countries immediately involved—Pakistan, India, and Bangladesh. In addition, we have used numerous reports published by participants and observers of the grim events of 1971 and accounts by others with greater distance in terms of involvement, if not emotion. In several instances, these reports constituted primary data. We have, however, extended them and modified their interpretations in light of extensive new primary evidence.

Given the complexity of the accounts, our commitment to reconstructing the decision-making process and sequence of events as closely and accurately as possible, and our concern to elicit and record to the fullest extent possible every nuance of sentiment and perception, we decided from the outset that whenever possible we would conduct the interviews together. We believe that the joint interviews created an easier atmosphere for the participants, which often resulted in our being allowed more time for our inquiries. In addition, "observer reliability" was considerably enhanced, and we were able to obtain almost verbatim accounts of the recollections of those interviewed.

Our meetings ranged from one to two-and-one-half hours. Nearly half of those involved were interviewed twice, and several key figures were interviewed three or more times. Between interviews with one person we met with other participants, which allowed us in the follow-up interviews to present respondents with new interpretations and episodically countervailing evidence and in some cases to pursue new avenues that might otherwise have gone unexplored. In all cases we had unrestricted access to the people we interviewed, and we were able to interview everyone alone, except for Gen. Agha Mohammed Yahya Khan (president of Pakistan from 1969 to 1971), whose son was with him because of the general's physical infirmity at the time.

We interviewed as wide a range of participants in the decisions affecting war and peace in South Asia in 1971 as time, reason, and accessibility allowed. We did most of our interviews in India from June to September 1978 and in Bangladesh in July 1978. In April and May 1979 we interviewed people in Pakistan, England, and Washington, D.C. In India we met with the prime minister and principal ministers privy to decision making and senior civil servants intimately involved in affairs concerning Bangladesh, including major figures in key ministries as well as in the Prime Minister's Secretariat. In Pakistan and Bangladesh we interviewed not only important figures in the President's Office and the Office of the Chief Martial Law Administrator, their counterparts in East Pakistan, and general officers commanding at the time, but also leaders of political parties who were central participants or intermediaries in the early negotiations to reach a constitutional agreement.

We were unfortunately unable to interview several important leaders: Zulfiqar Ali Bhutto, who was hanged the morning we arrived in Pakistan to start conducting our research; Gen. Tikka Khan, who was under confinement when we were in Pakistan; and several leaders of the Awami League, including the two most dominant—Sheikh Mujibur Rahman, who had been assassinated, and Tajuddin Ahmed, who had been murdered in the Dhaka Central Jail along with several other leaders before we began our study.

Before we began our interviewing, we developed a framework for a more focused and refined exploration by researching the generally accessible public documents. We spent more time in joint preparation for a particular interview than in the interview itself. We were fortunate at the outset of our research to be able to use records of international radio newscasts in the Archives of the Institute of Defence Studies and Analyses in New Delhi. We are indebted to the institute's directors, K. Subrahmanyam and P. R. Chari, who made its facilities available to us, and to the research scholars affiliated with the institute, whose lively interest in our work made our periods of research there much more challenging than they would otherwise have been. The newscasts of special utility to our inquiry were those of Radio Pakistan (in Bengali, Dari, English, Kashmiri, Punjabi, and Pushto) and All-India Radio (Bengali, English, and Hindi), together with newscasts of the Australian Broadcasting Corporation, the BBC, Radio Moscow, and the Voice of America. The newspaper archives of the Indian Council on World Affairs in Sapru House next door to the institute were most useful in refining the sequence of events. The members of the staff there were ever willing to help us locate materials.

Our analysis is also based on documents from the U.S. Department of State, Central Intelligence Agency, National Security Council, and Executive Office of the President released to us under the Freedom of Information Act. In addition we used testimony on file at the Carnegie Endowment for International Peace. Since these recollections were given, and are held, in confidence, we have not presented them in our analysis in any manner that is directly attributable to their sources.

We wish to express our deepest appreciation to those who supported our project. Our gratitude goes to the Canada Council and the International Crisis Behavior Project at McGill University, whose director, Michael Brecher, extended support to the project during the early stages. We are also grateful for the assistance of the American Institute of Pakistan Studies in our research in Pakistan. Both the International Crisis Behavior Project, under whose auspices our study was launched, and the American Institute of Pakistan Studies supported our ideas for the interviews. Richard Sisson extends his appreciation to the Council on Foreign Relations and to the Research Committee of the Academic Senate and the Council on International and Comparative Studies of the University of California, Los Angeles. Leo Rose expresses his appreciation to the Institute of International Studies, University of California, Berkeley. Our gratitude also goes to Celia Carrera, without whose patience and expert word-processing skills, this study would have been even longer coming to closure.

Finally, we want to thank all the people we interviewed for giving so freely of their time in recalling particulars of critical decisions and events and for sharing their feelings about them, the motivations behind decisions they made, and their perceptions and sentiments about the motivations and calculations of others. In many cases these recollections were as intense and vivid as if the speakers were reliving their experiences—released after having been frozen in time.

Abbreviations

BSF	Border Security Force
CENTO	Central Treaty Organization
CIA	Central Intelligence Agency
CMLA	Chief Martial Law Administrator
CPM	Communist Party of India (Marxist)
CPML	Communist Party of India (Marxist-Leninist)
DOD	Department of Defense
DOS	Department of State
EPCAF	East Pakistan Civil Affairs Force
FOI	Freedom of Information Act
GHQ	General Headquarters
GOBD	Government of Bangladesh
GOP	Government of Pakistan
INR	Intelligence and Research
ISF	Internal Security Force
LFO	Legal Framework Order
NSC	National Security Council
PAF	Pakistan Air Force
PPP	Pakistan People's Party
PRC	People's Republic of China
RAW	Research and Analysis Wing
SEATO	Southeast Asia Treaty Organization
UDI	Unilateral Declaration of Independence
UNESCO	United Nations Educational, Social, and Cultural Organization
UNHCR	United Nations High Commission for Refugees
USAID	United States Agency for International Development
WSAG	Washington Special Action Group

1

Prologue and Overview

Nineteen seventy-one was a year of national and international crisis in South Asia. The year commenced with two historic elections; the first national election ever held on the basis of universal franchise in Pakistan, where the incumbent martial law regime was endeavoring to transfer power to civilian authority; the return of Prime Minister Indira Gandhi with an overwhelming parliamentary majority in an election with a massive turnout in India. By year's end there had been two wars; as a consequence of the first, millions of refugees from East Pakistan sought exile in the politically unsettled and economically impoverished eastern provinces of India; as a consequence of the second, most of the refugees returned to their homes in the new and sovereign state of Bangladesh, and the political contours of contemporary South Asia were given shape.

Pakistan fought both wars; India one. The first, a civil war, deprived the Pakistani government of legitimacy in its eastern province; the second, the Bangladesh War with India and various Bangladesh liberation movements, resulted in the dismemberment of Pakistan. Each war came at the end of a complex political process in which all the players hoped for and expected an outcome that would satisfactorily accommodate their interests and that would be reached nonviolently—by negotiation prior to the commencement of the civil war in the first, by international pressure and rational conciliation prior to declarations of war in the second. Our purpose in this study is to reconstruct as best we can the decisional structures and processes that characterized these two major crises as a matter of historical record; our purpose also is to understand the relations between motivation, calculation, and context in explaining why two wars were fought when at the outset the principals neither anticipated nor wanted them.[1]

The first crisis and war were the outcome of the efforts of Pakistan's military regime to arrange for the creation of a liberal constitutional order and to withdraw from power. Upon assumption of power through an "invited" military coup on 26 March 1969, Gen. Agha Mohammed Yahya Khan indicated his intention of arranging a return to a representative form of government with a constitution to be devised by "representatives of the people elected freely and impartially on the basis of adult franchise."[2] Within six months, general guidelines had been decided upon; they were made public in November 1969, and were formulated in legally binding fashion in the Legal Framework Order (LFO) of 1970, promulgated four days after the first anniversary of the coup, with a call for general elections at both the national and provincial levels to be held in October of that year. The newly elected National Assembly would then be convened to draft a constitution within 120 days of its first sitting as a constituent body.

The LFO set forth a number of basic principles and arrangements that would have to be honored in the new constitution. It stipulated that the new constitution would have to provide for an Islamic republic in which laws repugnant to the Quran and Sunnah would not be admissible, though guarantees of religious freedom would be extended to minorities; the constitution was also to include constitutionally guaranteed fundamental rights of the citizen, together with an independent judiciary. The new order would be organized as a federal system that would allow for the "maximum" provincial autonomy concerning legislative, administrative, and financial powers, and, in a formal expression of concern to East Pakistan, stipulated a commitment to the removal of interprovincial "economic and all other disparities" within a "specified period."[3] Direct elections were to be held from territorial constituencies on the basis of a universal franchise, with no "separate electorates" for religious minorities or functional groups, thus giving East Pakistan an absolute majority in the National Assembly for the first time. In order to encourage expeditiousness in the drafting of the constitution, rules governing the transfer of power required that before the National Assembly could sit as a legislative body, provincial assemblies convened, and representatives from among them called upon to form governments, a constitution had to be completed and had to have received the "authentication" of the president.

In the elections to the 300-seat National Assembly held on 7

December 1970, the regionally oriented Awami League led by Sheikh Mujibur Rahman was elected with an absolute majority, all its seats being in East Pakistan. The Pakistan People's Party (PPP) led by Zulfiqar Ali Bhutto won the majority of the seats in the newly reconstituted provinces of West Pakistan, but none from East Pakistan. The elections resulted in the creation of two regionally dominant parties, each bent upon wielding power at the national level, the former asserting its right to govern as a consequence of its predominance under majoritarian rule, the latter asserting its claim to participate in governance on the basis of the necessity of a "concurrent majority" of broader regional representation to assure governmental legitimacy in Pakistan's consociational polity. Each threatened to make governance difficult, if not impossible, were its claim not honored.

In the political games and formal negotiations that followed, each of the players was committed at the outset to reaching a constitutional consensus and a transfer of power under the rules set forth in the Legal Framework Order.[4] Yet during the two weeks before civil war commenced on 25 March 1971 with a military crackdown in East Pakistan, the rules governing the transfer of power were abrogated by each of the three major actors. While the initial conflict between the Awami League and the People's Party was joined over the substance of the former's Six-Point Demand (first advanced in 1966), which provided for substantial decentralization of power and provincial autonomy and had served as the core of the party's election manifestos, agreement on a revised version of these points had been reached two days before a "military solution" was imposed.[5]

After the elections, as before, leaders of the martial law regime were committed to withdrawing from governance and transferring power to an elected civilian government. Increasingly during the negotiations, however, as their suspicions of the fidelity and trustworthiness of the Awami League leadership were aroused, a core group of army officers started to think in terms of a "military solution according to plan." With groups within the Awami League also preparing for armed resistance, and Bhutto threatening a revolution from the "Khyber to Karachi" if the interests of West Pakistan as defined by his People's Party were not conceded, this "solution" was imposed on 25 March.

Thus although each party to the negotiations commenced its labors with the expectation that a negotiated settlement of outstanding differences would be achieved, they ended them engaged in or prepared for armed combat. In the wake of the military crackdown, most of the leaders of the Awami League, except Sheikh Mujibur Rahman, who was taken prisoner, went underground and fled to India, where they established the Government of Bangladesh (GOBD) in "Mujibnagar," the "City of Mujib" (in reality 7 Theatre Road, Calcutta).

Similarly, the Bangladesh war, the third between India and Pakistan during their first quarter century of independence, was neither expected nor judged necessary by any of the major players before early fall of 1971. This is not to say that war was entirely unanticipated or, indeed, that it came as much of a surprise. India and Pakistan both had long-standing contingency plans for war, and as the crisis escalated in the summer of 1971, the possibility of war was openly referred to by leaders of both states. Each side, however, endeavored to seek the satisfaction of its "interests of state," as it perceived them, in a manner short of war. Furthermore, in a rare instance of confluent interest and intent, the international patrons of each exerted pressure on their respective regional "clients" to exercise restraint, defuse the crisis, and avoid war. Other states likewise urged restraint, although with less vigor and involvement. Perception of viable options and appropriate strategy with respect to outside powers varied among the Awami League leaders, both those who went into exile in India and those who remained behind in Bangladesh, until the fall of 1971. Yet a war was fought, a state divided, and one created.

Indian decision makers expected that Pakistan's leaders would find a political solution to the country's domestic problems; solutions to such internal conflicts had always been found in the past, imperfect perhaps, but sufficient to reestablish political stability. With the expected political reconciliation, the refugees streaming into India to escape state and social violence in East Pakistan would return to their homes, encouraged also by the firm hand of the Indian government, which from the outset, and without lengthy deliberation, had decided that not under any circumstances would the refugees be allowed to settle in India. Pakistani decision makers at the outset neither desired this particular war with India nor anticipated that it would occur. Given that the defense of East Pakistan under circumstances of such severe domestic dissent was problematic, the question was not whether to escalate tension to a state of war, but to avoid providing India with the occasion to commence one. It was also a commonly shared perception on the part of the Pakistani governing elite that the international community would constrain any Indian propensity for aggression, and that if hostilities were to commence, they would be halted before either side won a "victory." This had been the pattern in Indo-Pakistani wars in the past; there was no reason to believe, so they thought, that international peacekeepers would abandon their long-standing commitment to the international state system now. To leaders of the martial law regime, such an eventuality was unthinkable. India, too, during the first months of the crisis sought to impress upon the international community the threat of the massive influx of refugees from East Pakistan on the country's domestic tranquility and to persuade major states to bring their influence to bear on Pakistan to persuade it to reach an accommodation with the Awami League so that political stability, and the refugees, would return to East Pakistan. Neither side communicated directly with the other; both chose to speak through intermediaries or through national forums.

At another level of temperament, Pakistani military leaders commonly believed that the armies of "Hindu India," as they were referred to in common parlance, were no match for those of "Islamic Pakistan." Pakistan had been created in the face of Hindu opposition; its independence had been successfully defended against Indian "machinations"; and the larger Indian armies had been unable to defeat the smaller ones of Pakistan in battle. Any effort on the part of India to take territory in East Pakistan would be countered by Pakistani occupation of Indian soil in the west; and the Indian army had to labor under the control of a civilian government headed by a woman.

Notwithstanding all this, on 21 November Indian troops moved to assert control over territory in East Pakistan by force. Pakistan responded with a declaration of war on 3 December and Pakistani troops surrendered in East Pakistan on 16 December. India's unilateral ceasefire declaration of 16 December was accepted the following day by the Pakistani government, which had lost all control over its eastern province and its credibility in the west. It is ironic that political power was ultimately transferred to a civilian elite in Pakistan after defeat in war, and was forced by way of a mini military coup, rather than transferred voluntarily or by a "general consensus" among political parties and the martial law regime as had originally been planned and intended.

This book is devoted to explaining why things turned out that way. It analyzes the process by which perceptions became increasingly rigid and information more restricted and frequently distorted, so that options for the successful prosecution of the political game were reduced to those based upon collective withdrawal and ultimately the use of force. The book falls into two parts, each encompassing one of the subcontinent's two wars of 1971. In part 1 we analyze the efforts on the part of the military regime and political parties to reach a negotiated agreement between what ultimately became two sovereignties—the military regime in West Pakistan, and the Awami League in East Pakistan, or Bangladesh—together with their abortion in the military crackdown of 25 March and the beginning of civil war. The process is as complex as it is fascinating, and it is necessarily understood in terms of the political context from which the major figures in the drama derived much of their understanding of the situation in 1971, as well as of the intentions of their allies and adversaries. Chapter 2 examines the context provided by political conflict and development in Pakistan, including the crucial elections of December 1970, and chapter 3 reviews the images and legacies in Indo-Pakistani relations that were critical in shaping the perceptions that each held of the other in the 1971 crisis. In chapter 4 we analyze the first phase of negotiations and the definitions of interest and perceptions of distrust that attended them. Chapter 5 concerns the negotiations between two "domestic sovereignties"—the military regime centered in Rawalpindi and the Awami League centered in Dhaka—after the collapse of central authority in East Pakistan that attended the postponement of the convening of the National Assembly and the ineffective employment of military force to quell dissent and reassert central authority in the eastern province. Chapter 6 constitutes an analysis of the negotiations toward constitutional agreement by the civil side of the state, the preparation and imposition of a "military solution" to political conflict by the military side of the state, and the commencement of civil war.

In part 2 we analyze the war of liberation and the relationships between context, perception, and decision that led to the outbreak of the Bangladesh war. Chapter 7 analyzes the Indian response to the military crackdown by the Pakistani government, and chapter 8 reviews the strategies and timing of the military regime in attempting to recreate the state in East Pakistan and in pursuing a different political settlement in the context of the developing international crisis with India. Chapter 9 discusses the development of Indian policy toward the crisis in East Pakistan, and chapters 10–12 analyze the process of decision making that led to war between India and Pakistan, as well as the role of external powers in ameliorating the crisis and as witnesses to its close. We conclude in chapter 13 with a discussion of our findings and their implications for issues of war and peace in the region.

2

Pakistani Politics: Image and Legacy

The wars of 1971 in Pakistan and the critical events immediately preceding them must be analyzed and understood in the context of the country's disjunctive political development. The issues that precipitated the wars had induced national crises in the past, but these had always been resolved; interested parties, domestically and internationally, anticipated that the same would be true in 1971. Similarly, wars between India and Pakistan in 1947–49 and 1965 had been brought to a stalemate and mediated through international intervention. Some principals in the 1971 conflicts had been involved directly in those crises and had remained affected by them. In addition the public had attended or learned about the earlier political and constitutional dramas and had developed strong feelings about them. The events and attitudes of the past thus colored the reactions of the participants to the new conflicts.

REGIONALISM, POLITICAL
FRAGMENTATION, AND DISTRUST

East Pakistani political leaders in 1970 and 1971 firmly believed that powerful interests in West Pakistan, whether through connivance or force, had been blocking the efforts of East Pakistanis to fully participate in the political and economic life of Pakistan. They felt their belief was supported by the failed attempts to devise a constitution and by a series of actions by civilian and military leaders at the national level to displace duly elected Bengali governments whose concerns were incongruent with those of the dominant elite in West Pakistan. The East Pakistani elite felt that when West Pakistan promoted national symbols and national development as a measure of progress, this was for its own (and particularly Punjabi) aggrandizement.

Conversely, politically influential groups in the west perceived the Bengalis as latter-day Muslim converts still corrupted by Hindu practices, unlike descendants of the founders of Islam or conquerors like themselves, and as secessionists in league with their "coculturists" in India. East Pakistanis were suspect for not sharing the west's perception of the threat from India and for their lack of emotional attachment to the meaning of "Kashmir" in Pakistani nationalism. (Most of the Muhajirs [refugees] from Muslim minority provinces in preindependence India who had been among the first to support the demand for the creation of Pakistan had fled to West Pakistan and had witnessed the horrors of communal violence in a measure that East Bengalis had not.) The military tended to ally itself politically with the western wing and also had unquestioned confidence in its already proven ability to control any form of political resistance by the temperamental Bengalis.[1] What were perceived as fundamental and rightful claims by one side were seen as threats to core values and rights by the other.

Regional Conflict and the Fragmentation
of Political Support, 1947–1957

The Bengali claim to greater recognition and participation in the national polity began soon after independence with demands that Bengali be accepted along with Urdu as the national language of Pakistan. Indeed, language and its cultural manifestation in poetry and other expressive arts was to be continually a matter of deep concern to the Bengalis and of suspicion to West Pakistani and refugee groups. Mohammed Ali Jinnah's Dhaka declaration in early 1948 that Urdu was to be the only national language in Pakistan was met in East Bengal with dismay; the reaffirmation of Urdu by the country's second prime minister, Khwaja Nazimuddin, himself a Bengali, in February 1952 resulted in language riots, police shootings, deaths, and the creation of the first martyrs for a Bengali movement.[2] The 1952 riots, although the most dramatic, had been anticipated by several others. Shortly after independence, for example, riots broke out in East Bengal in protest against the recommendation of a national educational conference that Urdu be the official language of Pakistan and be made compulsory in schools. All meetings, processions, and assemblies of more than five persons were banned for fifteen days under provisions of the

East Bengal Special Powers Ordinance.[3] These language protests not only asserted the Bengali need for cultural identity, but also expressed a fear that lack of fluency in a "foreign" tongue would inhibit the entry of Bengalis into the administrative services.

Another conflict concerned the basis of representation in the national parliament to be created in the constitution of Pakistan being drafted by the Constituent Assembly, the interim national legislative body composed of representatives elected to a predecessor assembly in undivided Indian from those areas that became Pakistan.[4] The interests of East Bengal and of the provinces of West Pakistan, especially its majority province, Punjab, differed fundamentally. West Pakistan feared constitutional domination by the Bengalis in a federal system that provided majority representation to a single province, 20 percent of whose population was Hindu.[5] To relieve this concern, groups in the west advanced the concepts of "parity" in representation between the two wings and of "separate electorates" for different religious populations, which the Bengalis perceived as sinister arrangements to reduce their representation and legislative influence.

For Bengalis, whose numbers in the civil service and the military were severely limited, representation in the national legislature was extremely important. Of some 101 Muslim members of the Indian Civil Service and Indian Police Service at the time of partition, for example, only 18 had been from Bengal, and 35 had been from areas that became part of West Pakistan, with the others coming from areas that had remained part of India. A total of 95 of the 101 had opted for Pakistan, thus making the Bengali members of the successor national administrative service in Pakistan a distinct minority. Even by the mid-1950s, of 741 top civil servants, only 51 were Bengali, none of whom had the rank of secretary. Of 41 joint secretaries, only 3 were Bengali; of 133 deputy secretaries 10 were Bengali.[6] With respect to the military, in 1955 there was only 1 Bengali brigadier, 1 colonel, and 2 lieutenant colonels out of 308 of equivalent or higher rank. As late as 1963 only 5 percent of the officer corps of the Pakistani army and 7 percent of the other ranks were Bengali. In the air force, Bengalis constituted 17 percent of commissioned officers and 30 percent of other ranks, and in the navy they constituted 10 percent of the commissioned officers and 29 percent of other ranks.[7]

As early as 1950, regionalist sentiment with respect to constitu-tional order was made public in deliberations and formal recom-mendations of the Working Committee of the East Bengal Muslim League, which emphasized that it was "strongly of the opinion" that although a federal constitution was necessary for Pakistan, "in setting up the actual federal structure the geographical position of East Pakistan, its detachment and distance from other units and also from the federal capital itself has to be seriously considered and provisions made in the Constitution to accord *maximum auton-omy to East Pakistan and to that effect it is essential that a separate list of subjects to be administered by East Pakistan be incorporated in the Consti-tution and the residuary powers should rest in the units.*" The committee was further of the emphatic opinion "that since the railways and navigation system of the eastern wing were separate from those of the west," communications "cannot and should not be a central subject." The committee declared "*that so far as the export and import trade of East Pakistan is concerned adequate provision should be made subject to the least possible control of the center for the administration of this subject by the Government of East Pakistan.*" These very same issues were to be at the heart of the political conflict twenty years later.[8]

Disagreement over what made up a legitimate constitutional order was paralleled by conflict over how the government should be formed and who should control it. The first incident at the national level was the dismissal of Khwaja Nazimuddin, a domi-nant Muslim League leader from East Bengal, as prime minister by the governor-general, Ghulam Mohammed, a strong-willed Pun-jabi civil servant who was later instrumental in arranging Paki-stan's military alliance with the United States—an alliance that would be publicly opposed by a large number of the members of the provincial assembly in East Bengal. There had been no public demand for Nazimuddin's removal, and he enjoyed majority sup-port in the Constituent Assembly, where he had recently received a vote of confidence. But as had been the case in the ousting of several provincial ministers, no public opposition was aroused by his dismissal and replacement by Pakistan's ambassador to the United States, Mohammed Ali Bogra; nor were attempts made at mobilizing opinion within or outside the Assembly or the Muslim League against the governor-general's action.[9]

Popular discontent with the constitution-making process and the developing political identity in the eastern wing were reflected in elections to the East Bengal Provincial Assembly in May 1954. In these elections, the first held on the basis of universal suffrage, the Muslim League was routed by the United Front, a coalition of parties that enjoyed support exclusively in East Bengal. The United Front won 223 of the 237 seats reserved for Muslims, with Muslim League candidates winning only 10.[10]

The two dominant leaders of the United Front were H. S. Suhrawardy and A. K. Fazlul Huq, both of whom at one time had been members of the Muslim League. Suhrawardy had been the Muslim League premier in Bengal just before independence, and Huq had held the same position nearly ten years before. Suhrawardy had become active in postindependence politics with his founding of the Awami League in 1953. Huq, who, ironically, had moved the historic Lahore Resolution in 1940, had left the Muslim League the same year and founded the peasant-oriented Krishak Sramik Party, a revival of a party with the same political base that he had started and led during the preindependence period.[11]

Notable in the campaign were the twenty-one points agreed upon by the partners in the front, which emphasized the necessity of a more broadly distributive public policy and an expanded role for East Bengal in national concerns.[12] The first point, for example, called for Bengali to be declared a national language, and another called for a student's mother tongue to be the language of instruction. Point 19 was the most prophetic: "East Bengal will get complete autonomy according to the Lahore Resolution. Our defence, currency and foreign policy will be joint subjects with the Centre. Army headquarters will be in West Pakistan and Naval headquarters are to be set up in East Pakistan, so that this wing can become strong enough to safeguard her freedom. The ansars [constabulary] will be equipped with arms."[13]

The 1954 elections permanently changed the structure of party politics in Pakistan. Political parties were organized along the lines of basic regional cleavages in Pakistani society, and efforts to establish a coherent national political leadership and national political symbols progressively diminished and became ineffectual.

Shortly after the United Front ministry assumed power, two events occurred that led to its dismissal. First, the new chief minister, A. K. Fazlul Huq, made several emotional statements while visiting Calcutta concerning the inviolability of Bengali unity, which the central leadership judged to be evidence of his secessionist inclinations. In a speech at the Surat Bose Academy in Calcutta, Huq had declared that he could not accept the idea of two Bengals: "We are fellow workers in a common cause. If we have the common cause in view it is idle to say that I am a Bengali, someone is a Bihari, someone is a Pakistani and someone is a something else. . . . India exists as a whole. . . . I shall dedicate my service to the cause of the motherland and work with those who will try to win for India—Hindustan and Pakistan—a place among the countries of the world."[14] Second, reports that some five hundred persons had been killed during major rioting at the Adamjee Jute Mills in Narayanganj took on an east-versus-west tone, since Bengali workers were pitted against non-Bengali management.[15] The governor-general argued that each of these events was cause to remove the provincial government from power. He dismissed the Huq ministry, imposed "governor's rule," and dispatched Iskander Mirza to East Bengal as the new governor with a contingent of ten thousand troops to ensure public order.[16]

In response the Constituent Assembly in Karachi made several attempts to establish legal restraints on the authority of the governor-general. These efforts enjoyed strong support among Bengali representatives, who suspected that the government was about to launch charges of public malfeasance against officials in East Bengal. The assembly enacted a number of provisions that brought current practice into conformity with what had been agreed on in the Constituent Assembly for the new constitution. It placed several minor restrictions on the office of governor-general, but appeared to direct several major ones against the incumbent himself. The governor-general retaliated by dismissing the Constituent Assembly on 7 October 1954. He created a "ministry of talent," whose tenure was abbreviated, however, by a restraining constitutional judgment of the federal court. Charles Burton Marshall, a U.S. adviser on Pakistan at the time, has described the dismissal of the assembly:

> The determining motivation behind all this seems to have been Ghulam Mohammad's desire to redress an offense to a sick man's pride. I say this in full awareness of the pattern of the rationalizations

subsequently produced by various persons privy to the preparation of the action, such as: the need to refresh the mandate of the National Assembly before completing a constitution; the desire to circumvent a draft constitution which would have fastened on the country excessive elements of theocracy; Bengali ascendancy in the popular branch of a bicameral legislature, and subordination of the West to East Pakistan; the desire to bring the two wings into parity by consolidating the diverse provinces of West Pakistan into one unit as a condition precedent to the constitution; and the desire to clear the way for a constitution along presidential rather than parliamentary lines. The fact seems to have been that the action was taken passionately, without much, if any, consideration of what to do in the sequel.[17]

The members of the assembly, the political parties, and the public received the governor-general's actions with their customary silent acquiescence.[18]

The judgment of the federal court mandated a return to civilian governance, and the Constituent Assembly was reconvened in November 1955. During the interregnum, however, two major issues were decided upon by the interim government. The first was the merging of the western provinces of Baluchistan, Northwest Frontier, Punjab, and Sind into "One Unit" named the province of West Pakistan. This new province, although with less than half the national population, was to have "parity" with the renamed eastern province, East Pakistan, in terms of representation in a new National Assembly. The second major decision made during the interim was the preparation of a penultimate draft of a new constitution, which was adopted by the reconvened Constituent Assembly in 1956 after the return to civilian governance, but only after two walkouts by the Awami League members. The new constitution provided for a cabinet form of government with a president, as the titular head of state, elected by the combined votes of the national and provincial assemblies. Provincial governments were organized along the same lines, with the governor being a presidential appointee but governmental authority organized on the Westminster model.

During the period under the 1956 constitution, Pakistan lacked a political elite with an interprovincial base of political support. The Muslim League had essentially become a party of the western wing of the country, and the other parties had only minimal support outside their own provinces. (See Table 1 for the party composition

Table 1   Seats Held in the Pakistani Provincial Legislative
Assemblies, September 1957

Party	East Pakistan	West Pakistan
Republican party	2	178
Awami League	115	3
Muslim League	13	107
National Awami party	36	12
Krishak Sramik party	54	0
Pakistan National Congress	28	0
Scheduled Castes Federation	26	0
Nizam-i-Islam	21	0
United Progressive party	13	0
Total	308	300

Source: Muftaque Ahmed, Government and Politics in Pakistan (New York: Praeger, 1963), p. 295.

of the two provincial legislative assemblies in October 1957). Parties and political leaders became largely responsive to provincial sentiments and groups, from which they drew their support and to which they ultimately had to appeal in elections.

The 1956 constitution imposed the preferences of West Pakistani groups over those of the east. The East Bengali Awami League and parties deriving support primarily from minority communities opposed separate electorates, the provincial council of the league having supported "joint electorates" by a vote of six hundred to five at a meeting in October 1955. These parties also opposed parity, the one-unit scheme, and the presidential form of government. Abdul Mansur Ahmad, an East Pakistani who had participated in the 1956 constitutional debates in the Constituent Assembly, had made an extreme statement on the distinctiveness of the provinces, particularly East Pakistan, and the differences among them:

Pakistan is a unique country having two wings which are separated by a distance of more than a thousand miles. . . . These two wings differ in all matters, excepting two things, namely, that they have a common religion, barring a section of the people in East Pakistan, and that we achieved our independence by a common struggle. These are the only two points which are common to both the wings of Pakistan. With the exception of these two things, all other factors, viz, the language, the tradition, the culture, the costume, the custom, the dietary, the calendar, the standard time, practically everything is different. There is, in fact, nothing common in the two wings, particularly in respect to those [things] which are the sine qua non to form a nation.[19]

The parties of the two wings disagreed about political goals. The two major parties that dominated West Pakistan—the Republican Party and the Muslim League—agreed on many matters of policy, but shared few of the goals of either of the two major parties in East Pakistan, the Awami League and the Krishak Sramik. But the pairs of parties were also competing within their regions for support, and the intensity of the conflicts within their respective provinces inhibited their collaboration at the national level. The absence of a cohesive national leadership and a consensus on constitutional norms made the political system susceptible to incursions of administrative and military power in decision making and to governmental instability. Fragmentation of the political body and provincialization became permanent features of Pakistani politics that divided east and west.

The Ayub Regime, 1958–1969

The Ayub regime was created piecemeal after a military coup in October 1958. The coup was triggered by a riot in the East Pakistan Assembly in which the deputy speaker was killed and by mass demonstrations in West Pakistan organized by the Muslim League. It was encouraged, however, by the wider context of political instability and the army's fear that its interests would not be adequately attended to by a political elite committed to nonalignment and a rapprochement with India.

The military takeover occurred at the invitation of the president, Iskander Mirza. On 7 October 1958 Mirza declared that "the Constitution which was brought into being on March 23, 1956, after so many tribulations, is unworkable. It is so full of dangerous compromises that Pakistan will soon degenerate internally if the inherent malaise is not removed. To rectify them, the country must first be taken to sanity by a peaceful revolution."[20] Mirza abrogated the constitution, dismissed the central and provincial governments, dissolved the national parliament and provincial assemblies, and abolished all political parties. He declared martial law and invited the military to "clean up the mess and set things right." Ultimately, a new constitution would be devised "more suitable to the genius of the Muslim people" and at the appropriate time would be submitted to popular referendum.[21]

Mirza appointed Mohammed Ayub Khan chief martial law administrator. In his initial broadcast to the nation on 7 October 1958, Ayub Khan was more explicit about the purposes of the coup and the martial law regime. He declared that the coup was to preserve the nation from disintegration and protect the people from the uncontrolled machinations of dishonest politicians. This "revolution" on the part of the army, he asserted, was not directed against the people, or toward the radical transformation of Pakistan society, but against the "disruptionists, political opportunists, smugglers, black-marketeers and other such social vermin, sharks and leeches." The new regime had three major aims. First, immediate social and economic ills such as "malingering or inefficiency among officials, any form of bribery or corruption, hoarding, smuggling or black-marketeering, or any form of antisocial and anti-State activity" would be corrected. Second, certain long-range changes and reforms would be made to create the conditions for political stability. Finally, the regime would restore democracy, "but of the type that people can understand and work."[22]

That the new regime would not be a brief one became evident when the military ousted President Mirza after he publicly declared that the martial law regime would exist for only a short period and that he was soon going to set up a national council of "bright young chaps" to draw up a new constitution.[23] Several senior general officers had feared that Mirza, who had been involved in the making of parties and the unmaking of governments as president, would attempt to use the army for partisan political purposes and would involve himself in military matters. According to Fazal Muqueem Khan, after becoming aware of the generals' intentions, Mirza attempted to divide the army and instigate a countercoup. Muqueem Khan reports that after the coup the president

tried unsuccessfully to sound out a few of the most senior (officers) with a view of creating a rift within the armed forces. Before long he became desp· ate and, taking advantage of General Ayub's absence in East Pakistan, he redoubled his efforts. At 2:30 P.M. on 21 October, President Mirza had a long telephone conversation with a well-placed senior officer. Playing on the sentiments and loyalties of this officer, he ordered him to arrest all the general officers on the staff of

the Senior Martial Law administrator. The officer was completely
flabbergasted and finally requested written orders. He promptly
reported the conversation to the Chief of the General Staff. When
questioned as to how he knew the man talking to him on the
telephone was the President, the officer said that he could not have
mistaken the voice of a man with whom he had played bridge
regularly for the last ten years.[24]

Within a week, escorted by an infantry battalion, Mirza was put on
a flight to London.

While the new regime initially directed its energies at solving
immediate public problems in an attempt to fulfill the promises of
the coup, it also had to face the problem of its legitimation. The
military leaders judged essential the establishment of accessible
political channels to induce a sense of national consciousness and
identity by closing the gap between society and the state. This, they
felt, would also help prepare for democratization and the eventual
replacement of the regime. They were also committed to the creation of public institutions that would encourage the development of
a new political class unfettered by the imbroglios of the past and
oriented toward a strong new national political center. Third, the
martial law authorities expressed commitment to involving East
Pakistanis more fully in national and administrative affairs and to
diminishing the economic inequities between the two wings of the
country.

To prepare for a return to civilian rule, Ayub Khan appointed a
constitutional commission to study the earlier collapse of constitutional government and to make recommendations to ensure "a
democracy adapted to changing circumstances and based on the
Islamic principles of justice, equality and tolerance; the consolidation of national unity; and a firm and stable system of government."[25] In early 1962 the commission submitted its report, and
immediately thereafter Ayub promulgated a new constitution that
provided for indirectly elected national and provincial assemblies
with limited legislative powers and an indirectly elected president
with substantial executive power.[26] The constitution, however,
disregarded public opinion. The commission had circulated ques-
tionnaires and conducted formal interviews to find out what people
wanted. The public, especially in East Pakistan, strongly favored a
parliamentary system, a decentralized federal structure, and direct

elections. Many of Ayub's constitutional "reforms" had actually already appeared in a document written by him in London in 1954.[27]

The Ayub regime encountered opposition from the outset. Politicians in and outside of the newly constituted National Assembly started to convene in "like-minded" groups, one coalition in East Pakistan calling for the creation of another Constituent Assembly to draft a new constitution.[28] Student protests in both East and West Pakistan led to police shootings and in East Pakistan to suspension of classes at the University of Dhaka.[29] In an effort to defuse opposition, the government introduced a bill, ultimately made law, allowing the formation and activity of political parties and subsequently acceded to a demand for the enumeration, definition, and justiciability of fundamental rights.[30]

In January 1965 presidential elections were held, and opposition to Ayub's regime was again registered. A combined opposition party with Fatima Jinnah, sister of the Quaid-i-Azam (Founder of the Nation), Mohammed Ali Jinnah, as its candidate won a majority in three of the country's sixteen administrative divisions— Chittagong, Dhaka, and Karachi. Despite a concerted political campaign on the part of the government, Fatima Jinnah received 36 percent of the national vote and 47 percent of the vote in East Pakistan.[31]

In 1965 war broke out between India and Pakistan. Opposition to Ayub was further encouraged by what was perceived, particularly in West Pakistan, as the bartering away of Pakistan's military successes at the cease-fire negotiations, mediated by the Soviet Union in Tashkent.[32] The eastern province was cut off from the world during most of the war and saw itself as defenseless in the event that India had decided to move its armies against East Pakistan.

In March 1966, less than six months after the war ended, Sheikh Mujibur Rahman, the new leader of the Awami League in East Pakistan, advanced a six-point program to resounding public response. This "Six-Point Demand," which would become the political battle cry of the Awami League in elections in 1970 and constitutional negotiations in 1971, distilled the various Bengali claims and frustrations over East Pakistan's perceived mistreatment in economic and national affairs:

1: The Constitution should provide for a Federation of Pakistan in the true sense on the basis of the Lahore Resolution and for a parliamentary form of government based on the supremacy of a directly elected legislature on the basis of universal adult franchise. The representation in the federal legislature shall be on the basis of population.

2: The federal government shall be responsible only for defence and foreign affairs, and currency subject to the conditions provided in Point no. 3.

3: There shall be two separate currencies mutually or freely convertible in each wing for each region, or in the alternative, a single currency, subject to the establishment of a federal reserve system in which there will be regional federal reserve banks which shall devise measures to prevent the transfer of resources and flight of capital from one region to another.

4: Fiscal policy shall be the responsibility of the federating units. The federal government shall be provided with requisite revenue resources for meeting the requirements of defence and foreign affairs, which revenue resources would be automatically appropriable by the federal government in the manner provided and on the basis of the ratio to be determined by the procedure laid down in the Constitution. Such constitutional provisions would ensure that the federal government's revenue requirements are met consistently with the objective of ensuring control over the fiscal policy by the governments of the federating units.

5: Constitutional provisions shall be made to enable separate accounts to be maintained of the foreign exchange earnings of each of the federating units, under the control of the respective governments of the federating units. The foreign exchange requirement of the federal government shall be met by the governments of the federating units on the basis of a ratio to be determined in accordance with the procedure laid down in the Constitution. The regional governments shall have the power under the constitution to negotiate foreign trade and aid within the framework of the foreign policy of the country, which shall be the responsibility of the federal government.

6: The government of the federating units shall be empowered to maintain a militia or para-military force in order to contribute effectively towards national security.[33]

Within a year of the enunciation of the six points, five opposition parties, largely based in East Pakistan, formed a coalition (the Pakistan Democratic Alliance). They issued an eight-point program demanding creation of a parliamentary form of government founded on universal suffrage, a federal system that would augment the power of the provinces and provide for parity in representation in the civil and military services, and the removal of economic disparity within ten years.[34] These demands for political reform and economic redistribution were made in the context of increasingly frequent urban labor unrest.

POPULISM AND THE DEMISE OF THE AYUB REGIME

The promise and the efforts of Ayub Khan after the military coup of October 1958 to create a lasting constitutional order collapsed in the rise of a mass movement that commenced in West Pakistan in the fall of 1968 and that grew even stronger in East Pakistan immediately thereafter. The electorate that was mobilized by 1970 was an extension of this widespread antiregime movement, a concentrated upsurge of dissent that until then had been episodic. In both wings the movement was spearheaded by students and by a young, aspiring, urban middle class alienated from the indirect election process of Ayub's constitution.

In East Pakistan the revolt was driven by a desire to redress the extreme politically and economically disadvantaged position of the province within the country. Economic growth in the east had increased during the ten years of the Ayub regime, but the disparity between east and west continued to grow, though at a slower rate than it had during the first decade after independence.[35] Furthermore, those East Pakistanis taken into the national cabinet during the Ayub regime had not enjoyed a popular political base, thus inhibiting any sense of effective representation on the part of the attentive, and particularly the urban, Bengali public. Four were drawn, for example, from the administrative services, one was a journalist, and eight were erstwhile members of the Muslim League defeated in their bids for election in 1954.[36] Of the four governors of East Pakistan under Ayub, one was an East Pakistani police officer, one a Pathan general, another a Punjabi civil servant, and the fourth, a Bengali, had also lost by a wide margin in the 1954 elections. And even though the government had publicly pledged to honor regional equity in the military and civil services, East Pakistanis still constituted only 5 percent of the officer corps in the army, 15 percent in the air force, and 20 percent in the navy. In the elite Civil Service of Pakistan, successor to the Indian Civil Service of the British Raj, as well as in important positions in the central and provincial governments, Bengali representation continued to be limited during the Ayub decade, with greater demands for entry encouraged by a 162 percent increase in college enrollment in East Pakistan during the Ayub era.[37]

The sense of alienation was augmented by what was called the "Agartala conspiracy." In 1966 Sheikh Mujibur Rahman was charged, along with three Bengali members of the civil service and twenty-four Bengali junior officers in the armed forces, with collaborating with India through meetings in the town of Agartala to bring about the secession of East Pakistan. They were still behind bars and were standing trial when the political uprising against Ayub began in 1968.[38]

In West Pakistan the revolt commenced in district towns in areas bypassed by the general "economic miracle" in the west during the Ayub decade; it was concentrated in towns with comparatively large refugee populations.[39] The movement was joined by the disaffected leaders of various political parties in West Pakistan, most notably Zulfiqar Ali Bhutto of the Pakistan People's Party, which had been created as a reformist opposition force just one year earlier.[40]

In an effort to contain the revolt, Ayub announced his decision to withdraw as a candidate from the presidential elections scheduled for 1970 and agreed to the release of political prisoners. In anticipation of an "All-Parties Round Table Conference" he had summoned for February 1969, Ayub also dropped charges against Sheikh Mujib and his alleged coconspirators in the Agartala conspiracy because of the refusal of several of West Pakistan's leaders to attend the conference unless Mujib was granted parole.[41] After it became known that Mujib was to be released to attend the Round Table Conference, there was a huge outpouring of public support, with thousands of people making their way to receive him. Reportedly when Mujib realized how much public support he had, he demanded that he be unconditionally released and that all charges against him be dropped as a condition of his attending the conference. These demands were conceded, much to the chagrin of those prosecuting the case and of non-Bengali administrative officers in the east.[42] Ayub also conceded to opposition demands for a return to parliamentary democracy based on a universal franchise, but he refused to agree to the breakup of West Pakistan into its constituent "provincial" units or to the severe decentralization of federal power envisaged in the six-point program forcefully urged by Sheikh Mujib. The Round Table Conference adjourned without agreement among political parties on guidelines for Pakistan's constitutional future.

It was in this context that Ayub began negotiations with the top command of the Pakistani army to prepare to intervene and quiet the unrest. Ayub first approached the commander in chief of the army, Gen. Agha Mohammed Yahya Khan, in late February 1969 after the abortive Round Table talks. He reportedly intimated to Yahya that there were few people he could trust and that it might be necessary for the army to do something to restore public order.[43] In mid March Ayub called Yahya and declared that Pakistan was "going up in flames"; the army had to be prepared to assist the civil authorities in "bringing the country back on track," he said. After consulting with his military associates and a key member of the cabinet, Yahya informed Ayub that the military could not limit its intervention and imposition of martial law to only those areas of most intense political ferment; if it did so, he argued, the opposition would only move outside any areas under martial law and would continue to harass the government in other locales and the military around its perimeter. Martial law would have to be imposed throughout the country. Furthermore, if Ayub were merely to step aside without a full declaration of martial law, the next in line for the presidency would be the speaker of the National Assembly, Abdul Jabbar Khan, a Bengali. The constitution would also therefore have to be abrogated.[44]

At the latter suggestion the ailing president reportedly threw up his arms and exclaimed: "My God, that's impossible! It's my creation, my legacy. It has my blood in it!" Yahya then suggested that as an alternative the president again talk with the politicians in an attempt to still the dissent and once again pursue political reforms. Ayub reportedly responded by saying: "The politicians are all swine and won't listen to me." On the evening of 25 March 1969, an order from Ayub in his capacity as field marshal was delivered to Yahya, as the commander in chief of the senior armed service, requesting that he impose martial law and assume power. The imposition of martial law was quite simple; in the words of one general officer central to its operation, it merely required "brushing off a few old orders and documents and imposing them anew."[45]

DESIGNING THE TRANSFER OF POWER

The new martial law regime was designed as a temporary expedient sufficient for interim governance and for the time necessary to arrange a prompt transfer of power to a popularly elected government housed in representative institutions. The intent was to limit military involvement in politics while maintaining order and managing public affairs through the administrative structures of the state.

General Yahya, now president and chief martial law administrator (CMLA), quickly established his own administration. The center of this transitional regime was the Headquarters of the Chief Martial Law Administrator, set up in the President's House in Rawalpindi separate from the military command, but headed by Lt. Gen. S. M. G. Peerzada as principal staff officer.[46] Yahya reestablished the Commander-in-Chiefs' Committee, an old colonial institution, and gave it responsibility for final decisions on military affairs and for handling normal communication between himself and the heads of the armed services. For policy-making a Council on Administration was created, chaired by Yahya, who also assumed charge of the Ministries of Defence and Foreign Affairs. The council included the chief of staff of the army, Gen. Hamid Khan, who had responsibility for the Ministries of the Interior and of Kashmir Affairs; Vice Air Marshal Nur Khan, who was responsible for Labor, Education, Health, and Social Welfare; and Vice Admiral S. M. Ahsan, who was responsible for Finance, Planning, Industries, Commerce, and Food and Agriculture. The council operated informally, meeting once weekly for a couple of hours, largely as an ad hoc body with no set agenda, and ceased to exist when Yahya appointed a civilian cabinet in August 1969. Another central institution was the National Security Council, also chaired by Yahya as CMLA, which included the director of Inter-Services Intelligence, Gen. Akbar Khan; Maj. Gen. Ghulam Umar, who served as secretary of the National Security Council; the director of the Intelligence Bureau, who was responsible for political intelligence; and the home minister. Yahya managed the relationships between all these institutions; there was neither overlapping membership nor any explicit effort at coordinating their activities or sharing information. Although major issues were initially aired in the Council on Administration, after the appointment of the civilian cabinet, policies and political strategies were discussed in the Commander-in-Chief's Committee and the National Security Council with the advice of the Headquarters of the CMLA.[47] The principal staff officer, Lt. Gen. Peerzada, sometimes attended meetings of the Council on Administration and later of the cabinet, but only upon invitation. By all reports, however, he had great influence in the administration of the martial law regime and in the development of political strategy.

Access to Yahya, other than through the occasional meetings of the above organizations, was only through Peerzada; Peerzada's two assistants, each a brigadier, with responsibility for civilian affairs and martial law affairs respectively; and the president's personal military secretary, a position that had continued from the days of the British Raj. Officers with a long and informal association with Yahya could reach him through the military secretary as a consequence of their relationship. This arrangement existed throughout the Yahya regime. Civil service secretaries of the various civilian cabinet ministries could also contact the president–chief martial law administrator through these channels, circumventing the ministers under whose charge they served.

From the outset Yahya's intentions were to preside over the creation of a new constitutional order and arrange for the withdrawal of the military from power. Soon after the coup he decided upon three major principles for the transfer of power: (1) to the extent possible, the issues that had caused political discord in the past would have to be removed from the constitution-making process; (2) political activity and the new constitution would both have to honor the Islamic nature and integrative character of the state, while providing for as much secular participation as possible; and (3) he would have ultimate authority over constitution making by continuing martial law until an elected National Assembly had drafted a constitution and he had approved it. Because the military leadership was committed to an early transfer of power, but also wanted to keep the attention and energies of the opposition "pointed away" from the interim regime, Yahya immediately began discussions with the leaders of the major political parties to encourage their participation in containing the political unrest that had triggered the coup and to explore mutually acceptable and viable routes for creating a stable constitutional government that would ameliorate the deep political conflicts and antagonisms that had been so divisive in Pakistan's public life ever since independence.

These discussions focused on the structure and accountability of authority and the organization of power. Both the leaders of the political parties and the officials in the interim government favored a parliamentary system based on the Westminster model, with a president as head of state but with effective power in the hands of a prime minister and cabinet collectively responsible to a National Assembly from which they would be selected. There was broad consensus on the necessity of maintaining a federal system, but one decentralized in consonance with the maintenance of national integrity. Party leaders also agreed on the breakup of West Pakistan into its constituent provinces and, in some circles, on the recommendation that East Pakistan likewise be divided into several provinces to alleviate the fear in the west, primarily in the Punjab, of Bengali domination.[48] Finally, there was consensus on universal suffrage, with representation based on population distribution and territorially delimited constituencies. The Islamic nature of the Pakistani state was never at issue, although some secular-minded party leaders from East Pakistan mildly opposed this principle.

Based on the outcome of these talks, Yahya formed a drafting committee to work on providing the legal basis and guidelines for holding elections and for creating a new constitution. The drafting committee and some of the military were most concerned with breaking up West Pakistan into its constituent provinces and instituting representation based on population distribution. Both previous constitutions (the first one in 1956 and later Ayub's in 1962) had included the "principle of parity" in representation between East and West Pakistan in the National Assembly. If the guidelines were to resolve such fundamental issues as these, why should they not also stipulate how much autonomy the provinces would have? Yahya was unmoved by their concerns, however, and said that the rules governing the constitution-making process should reflect a broad political consensus from the outset. He also argued for the creation of four provinces in West Pakistan and for direct elections based on universal franchise, otherwise the major political leaders and parties would not participate in elections. In response to the observation that these were all only provincial leaders, Yahya reportedly replied by asking who the leaders of national stature were: "Let them come forward, I want to see them and talk with them."[49]

Within six months of the coup, the drafting committee had decided on general guidelines; in November 1969 these were made public; and on 29 March 1970, four days after the first anniversary of the coup, Yahya promulgated these guidelines in the Legal Framework Order (LFO), with a call for general elections at both the national and provincial levels to be held in October of that year.[50] The newly elected National Assembly would then be convened to draft a constitution, which would have to be completed within 120 days of the Assembly's first sitting as a constituent body and receive the president's "authentication."

The LFO set forth a number of basic principles and arrangements that the new constitution would have to honor. The new constitution would have to provide for an Islamic republic in which laws repugnant to the Quran and Sunnah would not be admissible, although minorities would be guaranteed religious freedom; it would also specify guaranteed fundamental rights of the citizen and establish an independent judiciary. The new government would be organized as a federal system that would allow for the "maximum" provincial autonomy in legislative, administrative, and financial affairs. In a formal acknowledgment of East Pakistani concerns, the LFO also stipulated a commitment to the removal of interprovincial "economic and all other disparities" within a "specified period."[51]

Direct elections were to be held from territorial constituencies on the basis of universal franchise, with no "separate electorates" for religious minorities or functional groups. To encourage expeditiousness in the drafting of the constitution, rules governing the transfer of power required that a constitution had to be completed and approved by Yahya before the national and provincial assemblies could sit as legislative bodies and before their members could be called upon to form governments.

Actually, the full range of principles incorporated in the Legal

Framework Order had been substantially agreed upon four months before its promulgation. The major parties were aware of the arrangements stipulated in the document by the time the ban on political activity was lifted on 1 January 1970 and had begun preparing for the elections to be held in October.

THE TWO ELECTION CAMPAIGNS, 1970

Because of a natural catastrophe in the east, elections were postponed. They were held on 7 December 1970. The participants agree that there was minimal interference by the authorities during the election campaign, which extended over the better part of a year. Some parties, however, thought the government should have taken a stronger hand in curbing what they claimed to be the excesses of their opponents, who they believed were receiving greater governmental largesse than they.[52]

Twenty-five different parties participated in the national elections. Seventeen parties had arisen out of East Pakistan, although five contested seats only in that province.[53] A total of 1,570 candidates—769 in East Pakistan and 801 in West Pakistan—vied for the 300 seats in the National Assembly. Neither the Pakistan People's Party nor the Jamiat-ul-Ulema-i-Pakistan of West Pakistan, however, contested any seats in the east, and the western branch of the Awami League contested only 7 of 138 seats in the four provinces of West Pakistan. Those parties that ran candidates in both wings of the country derived their leadership and support almost exclusively from a particular province. The elections in essence thus involved two separate campaigns—one in the east, one in the west. The leaders of the two parties most successful in the elections—the Awami League and the People's Party—had devoted their energies to one wing only of the country. Efforts to create electoral alliances were unsuccessful both between the parties of east and west and among the parties of the different western provinces, which thus continued the regionalism of party organization and support that had commenced in the mid 1950s. For example, in the west, efforts to create a coalition of the Muslim League parties—the Convention Muslim League, the Council Muslim League, and the Muslim League (Qayyum)—had foundered on regional division and suspicion.[54] The Council Muslim League had rejected an overture from

the Pakistan People's Party because it felt itself much better organized and positioned in the campaign than the People's Party.[55] An
attempt by the Jamiat-ul-Ulema-i-Islam, Nizam-i-Islam, Jamiat-i-
Islami, Council Muslim League, and Pakistan Democratic Party to
maintain an electoral alliance had collapsed in early November.[56]

Negotiations for an alliance between the National Awami Party
(Wali Khan), which had its primary base of support in the North-
West Frontier Province and Baluchistan, and the Awami League
and National Awami Party (Bhashani), both based almost exclusively in East Pakistan, had broken down in late September.[57] Khan
Abdul Wali Khan, leader of the West Pakistani National Awami
Party, subsequently indicated, however, that his party would cooperate with the Awami League, the Council Muslim League, and
the Jamiat-ul-Ulema-i-Islam (Hazarvi Group) in the National Assembly, which it had done in the All-Parties Round Table Conference in 1969.[58]

In East Pakistan the statements of different party leaders and the
manifestos of parties whose support was principally located in that
province strongly expressed Bengali sentiments. They favored a
foreign policy of nonalignment; none called for the "liberation" of
Kashmir, although some did ask for a resolution of the issue. They
wanted a substantial devolution of power in the new constitutional
order, with all referring to the Lahore Resolution as the legitimating standard; party leaders substantially agreed on the principles
behind the six-point program of the Awami League. They called for
the eradication of disparities in economic distribution between east
and west within a specified period of time. Just as in the west, all
the major parties in the east accepted the principle of Pakistan as an
Islamic republic with provisions for the impermissibility of laws
repugnant to the Quran or Sunnah.[59]

As the election campaign progressed, the decentralizationist
demands of East Pakistani parties became increasingly intense,
encouraged by natural catastrophes in the eastern province and the
response of the central government and West Pakistani leaders to
the havoc that they wrought, as well as by the requirements of
competing for the votes of an aroused Bengali electorate. The
elections had been originally scheduled for October, but were
postponed, largely as a consequence of severe monsoon flooding in
East Pakistan. The floods were followed in late October by a

horribly destructive cyclone that tore through coastal districts accompanied by a thirty-foot tidal wave that laid waste the land and claimed untold lives.

What East Pakistanis considered a lack of sufficient aid for those disasters further magnified their perception of the insensitivity of the West Pakistani elite to the welfare and interest of Bengalis. Maulana Bhashani, the venerable radical leader of the East Pakistani National Awami Party, had declared as early as September that if concrete steps were not taken to correct interregional inequities and to protect Bengal against the destructive vagaries of nature, East Pakistan would be forced to separate from the western wing and develop friendly relations with whomever it wanted.[60] He had also called for "complete financial autonomy" for East Pakistan. By the end of the campaign in early December, the Maulana had declared his determination to work for the establishment of an independent state of East Pakistan organized on the basis of the Lahore Resolution.[61]

The Awami League declarations were less dramatic than those of the irrepressible Maulana, though the commitment to the Six-Point Demand became firmer as the campaign heated up and suspicion developed that there were "forces at work" in West Pakistan to subvert the elections. In response to criticism from opponents Sheikh Mujibur Rahman had declared in September that the six points in no way jeopardized the integrity of either Islam or Pakistan. He also castigated the leaders of two political parties in the west for claiming that Bengali Muslims were not really true followers of the Prophet by suggesting that they were fundamentally worshipers of the Hindu goddess Kali, and thus more Bengali than Muslim. Mujib warned anyone who might want to delay or distort the forthcoming elections that the people's aspirations would be realized even through struggle. The possibility of a mass movement to achieve the six points was a consistent refrain during the remainder of the campaign.[62]

In West Pakistan, even though the political parties were primarily devoted to securing seats in the four provinces there, they also focused upon the questions raised by the Awami League concerning the organization of the state. The Muslim League (Qayyum) was the most critical and alarmist of the West Pakistani parties in this regard. Its president, Khan Abdul Qayyum Khan, declared in early September that Mujib and the Awami League had launched "a campaign of hatred against West Pakistan" and had to be opposed.[63] Qayyum's sentiments reflected those of several senior army officers, who felt that Mujib was getting away with too much and needed to be "muzzled."[64] Qayyum later accused Mujib of trying to create a "greater Bengal" by currying favor with India without attempting to resolve fundamental antagonisms between India and Pakistan. He also charged various party leaders in West Pakistan with flirting with the Awami League and endeavoring to reach an agreement with the East Pakistanis that would lead to the disintegration of the country. He further charged Wali Khan, his opponent of long standing in the North-West Frontier Province, of playing into the hands of the Indians in his efforts to reach an understanding with Mujib. If the Awami League and Wali Khan's party, the National Awami Party, were to win the elections, he claimed, they would forget Kashmir and enter a joint defense pact with India. Members of the Jamiat-i-Islami in both West and East Pakistan declared early in the campaign that an Awami League victory would mean the disintegration of Pakistan through secession. However, with the exception of the Muslim League (Qayyum) and the Convention Muslim League, both of which included important political leaders from the Ayub regime, West Pakistani party leaders emphasized the need to change the organization of power and redress economic inequities within the framework of a united Pakistan.

The results of the elections on 7 December 1970 (see Table 2), were unanticipated by winners, losers, and government alike. The elections dramatically changed the composition of political leadership in the country, creating conditions that would profoundly affect the strategies of the major figures in the political drama that was to ensue. Even though most observers had expected the Awami League to be returned as the dominant party in the eastern province, no one expected it to win 160 of 162 seats, most by substantial margins. The central government's military and civilian intelligence services had consistently underestimated the appeal of the Awami League, magnifying suspected weaknesses and exaggerating the estimates and claims of activists from other parties.[65] Central intelligence reports, derived largely from "pro-Pakistani" and non-Bengali sources, were consistently at variance with those

Table 2   Results of the Pakistani National Elections, 7 December 1970

	No. of Seats Won (% Vote)				Total	Voter Turnout (%)	Total No. of Valid Votes (millions)
	Awami League	Pakistan People's Party	Other Parties	Independents			
East Pakistan	160 (75%)	0 (0%)	1 (22%)	1 (3%)	162	56	16.5
West Pakistan							
Punjab	0 (0%)	62 (42%)	15 (45%)	5 (12%)	82	66	10.9
Sind	0 (0%)	18 (45%)	6 (44%)	3 (11%)	27	58	3.1
North West Frontier	0 (0%)	1 (14%)	17 (80%)	7 (6%)	25	47	1.4
Baluchistan	0 (1%)	0 (2%)	4 (91%)	0 (7%)	4	39	.4
Total West Pakistan	0	81	42	15	138		
TOTAL (% vote nationwide)	160 (38%)	81 (20%)	43 (35%)	16 (7%)	300	59	32.3

Sources: Craig Baxter, "Pakistan Votes—1970," Asian Survey (March 1971): 197:218; and G. W. Choudhury, The Last Days of United Pakistan (Bloomington: Indiana University Press, 1974), p. 129.

Note: Total percentages greater than 100 are because of rounding.

from the government of the eastern province, which maintained access to a wider range of social and political groups and had estimated a substantial victory for the Awami League.

The leaders of the Awami League themselves were surprised by the magnitude of their victory. Early in the election campaign, the Awami League high command had been prepared to enter agreements with other parties in the east not to contest the elections against one another. The other parties had all declined, however, because of their own expectations of electoral success, which were supported by financial assistance and other inducements from advocates within the regime.[66] After the national elections more than 500 candidates withdrew from the Provincial Assembly elections to be held on 17 December and several eminent leaders who had held top positions in previous regimes decided to retire from political life.

Although the magnitude of the Pakistan People's Party's victory in West Pakistan was not as great as that of the Awami League in East Pakistan, the measure of surprise was even higher in the west. The number of seats won by the PPP, as one leader put it, was "greater than even Bhutto's wildest dreams would have ever allowed."[67] The People's Party, within three years of its founding and with a loosely contrived organizational structure, won 83 of the 138 seats for the National Assembly in the western provinces—64 of 82 in the Punjab, 18 of 27 in Sind, and one other in the North-West Frontier Province. Like the Awami League, the People's Party had proposed no-contest agreements to other parties but just as in the east, the other parties in the west were confident that their financial and political resources would enable them to sell the virtues of their candidates and programs to an electorate that had been supportive in the past.[68] Leaders of all parties, however, underestimated the passions of a mass electorate that was participating in a national election for the first time and that in no province had voted in anything but village-level elections for a decade and a half.

The other unanticipated consequence of the elections was the profound change in the composition of political leadership. Most of the successful candidates were newcomers to public life; most of the older generation had been defeated. Except for a few political notables in the west, *none* of the newly elected members of the National Assembly had been active in all-Pakistan arenas previously.[69] Although he had served as Ayub's foreign minister, Bhutto had never been engaged in party politics; nor had he ever previously contested an election. Sheikh Mujib, who had apprenticed under the redoubtable H. S. Suhrawardy, had oriented his organizational activities toward East Pakistan; he, too, had never before been elected to public office. Transregional leadership in Pakistan, always limited and fragile, was reduced to marginal participants who had served intermittently as intermediaries between government and leaders of the major parties, but with little consequence. The elections thus continued the provincialization of politics in Pakistan.

Political relationships during the election period under the Yahya regime reflected those of the past. The elections revealed a party system that was still fragmented. The structure of political support that had emerged with the East Bengali elections of 1954, had continued to characterize the party system through the military coup of 1958, and had been reflected in political organization during the Ayub era as well, continued to break down. As had happened in the past, with the exception of the presidential election of 1965, the primary attention of the political parties and their leaders and their principal bases of support in 1970 were concentrated in one or the other wing of the country. The leaders of the three Muslim Leagues and of the several religious parties had campaigned elsewhere in Pakistan, but had spent the largest fraction of their time in their "home" provinces. Since campaigns were directed primarily at the particular appetites of the electorates of the individual provinces, party declarations and actions in other provinces were perceived in terms of existing sentiments and served to feed distrust.

Nonetheless, preparation for elections and the transfer of power resulted in important breaks with the past. First, leaders of the various factions agreed on fundamental issues of representative government, a matter that previously had been severely divisive. But while there was consensus on the character of the regime in terms of the structure of representation and participation, differences remained with respect to the distribution of economic benefits. Second, the dominance of a single political party in each wing shifted concern about regional domination in terms of constitutional structure to concern about regional domination in terms of actual governmental power.

3

Indo-Pakistani
Relations: Image and Legacy

The relationship between India and Pakistan since 1947 has been troubled and hostile, marked by wholesale communal massacres at the time of the partition of British India and three wars and innumerable minor conflicts and disputes subsequently. One critical factor in this history has been the prepartition heritage of the two political movements that dominated the political environment in the subcontinent both before and after independence—the Indian National Congress and the Muslim League. Most of the political and social concepts that dominated the ideology and psychology of the narrow elites that controlled these two movements survived into the independence period and have not disappeared. This has been particularly true of their intensely negative perceptions of each other, which, moreover, were retained in most respects by a younger generation that otherwise rejected much of the ideology of the older elite.

The importance of this prepartition heritage is evident in the rhetoric Indians and Pakistanis used in reference to each other a quarter-century after independence. Political literature from both sides, for instance, continues to be filled with discussions of the relevance of the "two-nation" theory, first advanced by Muslim League theorists as a major political theme in the 1930s.[1] At that time Muslim Leaguers merely argued that the Hindu and Muslim communities in British India constituted two different "nations," in the sense that they were divided by cultural and social values that made it impossible for them to live together peacefully in a common political system. As first expressed, this was not a demand for a *single* Muslim state in those areas of British India in which the Muslims formed the majority or were the ruling class; indeed, it was assumed virtually up to the time of partition that there would be at least two Muslim states, in consonance with the Lahore

Resolution—one in the northwest and another in the section of Bengal in the northeast in which the Muslims formed the majority of the population. A series of unplanned and, at times, accidental developments led to the creation of the unified Islamic state of Pakistan in 1947 that included both Muslim majority areas of British India—divided by nearly a thousand miles of Indian territory.

Under the two-nation theory as originally expounded, it would have been quite plausible to have had two or more Islamic states in those sections of the subcontinent in which Muslims constituted the majority. But that is not how the debate on this issue developed in the postindependence period, as both Pakistanis and Indians acted on the assumption that the validity of the two-nation theory was directly related to the viability and national integrity of Pakistan as constituted in 1947. When Pakistan was later divided into two Muslim majority states in 1971, some Indians argued that this provided incontrovertible proof that the two-nation concept had been ill conceived all along and that the principle upon which British India had been partitioned had been fallacious. For Pakistan, the 1971 civil war was thus a national crisis both psychologically and physically. For Indian Hindus it was a source of deep satisfaction, even though relatively few of them moved to the logical conclusion—namely, that if the principle upon which partition was based was illegitimately conceived, the act of partition itself should be reversed.

Another important aspect of communal politics in British India that has substantially affected postindependence politics has been the disagreement between the Indian National Congress and the Muslim League on the relationship between religion and the state. The Congress made secularism a basic principle virtually from the time of its founding in the late nineteenth century and adopted it as a constitutional principle in independent India. This was more easily said than done, however, as Hindus predominated in the Congress and in most postindependence governments in India at both the central and state levels—an inevitable consequence of the large Hindu majority in the population—with even larger Hindu proportions in various elite categories, both official and political. The result has been an extensive use of Hindu values, concepts, and symbols; this may be more subconscious than intentional, but it is nevertheless noted by the non-Hindu minorities, who, in many cases, would concur with the Pakistani assessment that India is a Hindu state.

The Muslim League, in contrast to the Congress, commenced its existence in 1906 as a strictly Muslim organization, excluding non-Muslims from membership. It specifically rejected the concept of secularism, both before 1947 and in postindependence Pakistan.[2] This was not too important in West Pakistan, where no significant non-Muslim minorities were left after the mass exchange of populations that accompanied partition. But secularism became a critical issue in East Pakistan, where approximately 20 percent of the population was non-Muslim, primarily Hindu. West Pakistani views of East Pakistan were strongly influenced by this factor. The various protest movements in East Pakistan that started erupting in the early 1950s were invariably denounced by West Pakistanis as the handiwork of "wily Hindus," who allegedly manipulated such activities from behind the scenes, whether internally from within East Pakistan or externally from Calcutta or New Delhi. This attitude prevailed in West Pakistan throughout the 1960s, long after the emergence of a Bengali Muslim political leadership in East Pakistan that was scarcely susceptible to Hindu manipulation.

A third factor that had long-term political consequences was the large proportion of key political figures in both Pakistan and India who were either refugees themselves or had been emotionally involved in the partition in ways that strongly influenced them. Most of the Muslim League leaders who dominated Pakistani politics in the first decade after independence had fled from areas that had remained part of India. They were thus refugees in the country they governed, with a strong residue of bitterness about the "barbaric" behavior of the Hindus and Sikhs toward Muslims in India. Only a few of the leaders of the Indian National Congress party were refugees, but many were from areas of India adjacent to Pakistan that had been the scene of gruesome communal riots in the partition period and then became the residence of millions of Hindu and Sikh refugees who had fled Pakistan bringing their own horrifying accounts of Muslim "barbarism." Moreover, many of India's new bureaucratic officials were from the northwestern border states or from Bengal—the areas most beset by the atrocities that accompanied partition. It would thus have been remarkable had the governing elites in both countries not developed a strong distrust and suspicion of each other. Both governments made strenuous efforts for humanitarian and practical political purposes to contain the communal upheavals in their own territories, which threatened the very existence of their two fragile new states; but their deep hostility and propensity to think the worst of each other frustrated attempts to resolve the differences between them.

INDO-PAKISTANI RELATIONS, 1947–1970

The partition of British India was hastily devised and extremely sloppy, and it is not surprising that the new governments of India and Pakistan faced a host of complex territorial problems and disputes. The most critical for their relationship were the disagreements over three of the "princely states"—Kashmir (Jammu and Kashmir), Junagadh, and Hyderabad. The principles upon which the partition had been based were rather ambiguous, particularly with respect to the princely states. British "paramountcy" over them had lapsed, and in theory each of them could have opted for independence. The political circumstances were such, however, that most had no other option than to negotiate accession to either India or Pakistan. But the British had also never precisely defined the terms of accession. Contiguity to India or Pakistan was assumed to be a decisive factor, but it was also expected that the "will of the ruler" and the "will of the people" would be heeded.

For most of the princely states, the issue was not whether they should accede to India or Pakistan but rather under what terms they should do so.[3] For Kashmir, Junagadh, and Hyderabad, however, the situation was more complicated. In each, the ruling family belonged to one religious community and the great majority of the population to the other. The two successor governments used arguments of convenience in defining their respective claims to these principalities. With respect to Junagadh and Hyderabad, for example, which were not contiguous to Pakistan, but where Muslim princes ruled over Hindu majorities, Pakistan argued, in essence, that the contiguity principle should be waived and that the will of the ruler should prevail. In claiming Kashmir, where a Hindu ruling family governed a state in which Muslims formed a large majority, Pakistan used the will of the people as the controlling and legitimating principle.

India's position in each case directly opposed that of Pakistan. In Junagadh and Hyderabad, India used military intervention against the Muslim rulers, justifying the forced incorporation of these states into the Indian Union on the grounds that this conformed to the will of their Hindu majorities. India also used military force to support the maharaja's government when tribal (Pakhtoon and Afghan) raiders, allegedly instigated and supported by Pakistan, invaded Kashmir—presumably to force its accession to Pakistan, though it is not at all clear that this was the intention·of the invaders, who seemed to be more interested in looting and pillaging.

There are two important differences between the Kashmir and the Junagadh and Hyderabad cases. First, neither of the latter two states were contiguous to Pakistan and, thus, under the imprecise principles of partition, they had no alternative but to accede to India. Kashmir, in contrast, bordered on both states, and the contiguity principle thus did not apply. Second, India based its claim to Kashmir on both the will of the ruler and the will of the people, which was possible because a major Muslim political organization in the state, the Kashmir National Conference, opposed accession to Pakistan.[4] Some of the National Conference leaders would probably have preferred independence combined with the deposition of the Hindu ruling family, but when that proved unattainable they chose to join India. Indeed, India's first prime minister, Jawaharlal Nehru, insisted that *both* the Hindu ruler and the leader of the National Conference, Sheikh Abdullah, had to agree to the accession of Kashmir before he would accept it on the part of the Indian government.

The dispute over Kashmir led in 1948 to the first Indo-Pakistani war, which was halted, but not resolved, by the United Nations. The dispute continued to plague relations between the two states, and clashes across the cease-fire line that divided Kashmir were common. But what had initially been a conflict based strictly on communal issues was transformed by the late 1950s into one based on fundamentally different strategic interests in Kashmir. Pakistan, citing India's allegedly aggressive intentions, had opted for inclusion in Western-supported military alliances—the Central Treaty Organization (CENTO) and the Southeast Asia Treaty Organization (SEATO)—thus bringing in the United States as an active participant in South Asian regional politics. India had adopted nonalignment as the basis of its foreign policy for sound practical reasons, prefering to limit the involvement of all major external powers in South Asia as far as possible. In response to Pakistan's alignment with the West, however, India compromised its non-alignment principles and involved the Soviet Union—and, for a few years in the 1950s, China—in South Asia as a counterforce to the United States. Kashmir was by no means the only critical issue in these developments, but it assumed a major symbolic role for both the Indian and Pakistani governments.

The second "Kashmir War" was fought in September and October 1965, with Pakistan initiating the hostilities in what was, in essence, its final effort to resolve the dispute by the use of force. The results, however, were a stalemate on the battlefield and another cease-fire. The Soviet Union, with the endorsement of the United States, offered to serve as a nonpartisan mediator. India and Pakistan both had some misgivings on this, but they finally agreed, and a bilateral conference under Soviet supervision was convened at Tashkent in the U.S.S.R. in February 1966 with Prime Minister Lal Bahadur Shastri of India, President Ayub Khan of Pakistan, and the Soviet leader Leonid Brezhnev attending. After considerable Soviet prodding, the two sides agreed to restore the international boundary between them and also the 1949 cease-fire line in Kashmir—the latter to India's distress, as the Indian army had seized several strategic areas in Kashmir that improved its security and its control over access to the Kashmir valley from Pakistani-controlled areas.[5]

Between the Tashkent Agreement of February 1966 and the December 1970 elections in Pakistan, domestic politics dominated in both India and Pakistan. On occasion relations between the two countries or with the major external powers assumed some importance, but usually only when either the government or the opposition forces in India and/or Pakistan were seeking to use foreign policy issues to serve domestic political objectives. Bhutto, for example, bitterly criticized the "sellout" at Tashkent and the Ayub government's relatively moderate policy toward India during 1966–69, but this was part of a concerted campaign to overthrow Ayub rather than an attempt to confront India. Similarly, some opposition parties in India used Prime Minister Indira Gandhi's alleged weakness in "handling Pakistan" in their attempt to topple her government after a split in the Congress party in 1969. Although there were several significant developments in Indian and Pakistani foreign policy strategies in the late 1960s—for example, a determined effort by Pakistan to expand relations with the Soviet Union while maintaining close ties with both China and the United States—these were generally considered incidental to the far more urgent domestic confrontations in both India and Pakistan that involved diverse and basically incompatible social and political forces.

India and Pakistan became highly vocal over several issues in the late 1960s, but these were comparatively minor disputes and never really threatened the peace in the subcontinent, although they complicated the process of expanding ties between the two states. Neither New Delhi nor Rawalpindi had been fully satisfied with the Tashkent Agreement, but both abided by it. There was even some progress made in improving relations between them. Mainly at India's instigation, the two sides met to discuss several difficult subjects: "enclaves" on the East Pakistani–Indian border, a ban on trade and visitation rights that had been imposed during the 1965 war, and the distribution of the waters of the Ganges between India and East Pakistan. The only significant agreement reached, however, was on overflight rights across each other's territory, that is, between West and East Pakistan for Pakistani civil and military aircraft along a specified corridor, and between India and Afghanistan in the west and between Calcutta and northeastern India in the east. This agreement was more important to Pakistan than to India, because the alternative route between West and East Pakistan was by way of Sri Lanka—approximately three times the length of the route over India. New Delhi considered the overflight agreement (concluded shortly after the Tashkent Conference) as only the first in a series that would expand relations between the two states in the "Tashkent spirit"; Rawalpindi, however, demonstrated little interest in settling the other issues once it had secured air transit rights to East Pakistan.[6] New Delhi became increasingly unhappy with the overflight arrangement, but even in late 1970, when a disastrous cyclone struck East Pakistan, India allowed unlimited overflights between the two wings of Pakistan on a temporary basis. The extra flights were supposed to be for relief purposes, but New Delhi suspected that Pakistan also used them to reinforce its security forces in East Pakistan. If this happened, it was on a very limited scale, but the belief that it did contributed to an already general sense of dissatisfaction with the overflight agreement in New Delhi.

The issue of the so-called enclaves was more persistent. These were small areas on the Indian–East Pakistani border that intruded into territory claimed by the other power. (The actual line of demarcation had been the subject of dispute since 1947.)[7] There were a number of minor armed clashes in these enclaves, the most serious occurring in late 1970 in the Batrigach enclave jutting into the West Bengali district of Cooch-Behar. The Pakistani government tried to bring this dispute before the United Nations—throwing in the perennial Kashmir issue in the bargain—but to no avail.

More serious, potentially at least, were Pakistani accusations of Indian involvement in the 1968 Agartala conspiracy, for which Sheikh Mujibur Rahman and several East Pakistani officials and political leaders were tried on charges of plotting with India to secure the separation of East and West Pakistan. Undoubtedly, Mujib and other Bengali political leaders had contacts in Indian diplomatic and intelligence circles; indeed, both Mujib and the Indians later admitted this once Bangladesh had achieved independence. Diplomatic missions, including intelligence officers, normally maintain contacts with political leaders and organizations in the countries to which they are deputed, so it is highly unlikely that Indian intelligence in its Deputy High Commission Office in Dhaka was derelict in its duties in this respect. But no solid evidence of a Mujib-Indian conspiracy that had an independent Bangladesh as its objective has yet emerged, even in the post-1971 period, during which Pakistan could have produced such proof without any serious political consequences, domestic or international.[8] We can assume that New Delhi encouraged political unrest in East Pakistan when this served Indian purposes, but it is much less clear that India's small foreign policy decision-making elite widely agreed that an independent East Pakistan was in India's interests, or, indeed, that it was possible. Most Indian officials appear to have been as skeptical about the capacity of East Pakistan to mount a successful "national liberation movement" as their counterparts in West Pakistan up to—and indeed through—1971.[9]

Another important irritant in Indo-Pakistani relations in the late

1960s were the policies of both governments that provided limited support to "rebel" groups in the territory of the other state. Pakistan gave various forms of assistance to dissident elements in the Indian section of Kashmir and in 1969 allowed the establishment of Chinese-operated training camps in East Pakistan for Naga and Mizo rebels from India's northeast frontier.[10] India, in turn, continued to provide political and material (primarily financial) support to Pakhtoon dissidents on Pakistan's northwest frontier and also to encourage Afghanistan to maintain a hard-line policy on its dispute with Pakistan over the "Azad Pakhtoonistan" question—even after Moscow had modified its position on this issue after Tashkent.[11]

A less specific, but still major, complication in relations between New Delhi and Rawalpindi were their basically different positions on most foreign policy and regional issues. Although Pakistan began disengaging from the Western military alliances it had joined in the 1950s and moving toward adoption of at least the principles of nonalignment, it still remained out of step with India, except on the more ritualistic Third World issues in global politics—(for example, anticolonialism, antiracism, anti-Israel attitudes, and the redistribution of world resources to the "have-not" states). On the critical regional issues that affected both of them, however, India and Pakistan were fundamentally opposed. Thus, even though foreign policy rhetoric emanating from both capitals after 1966 was closer than at any other time since 1950, their foreign and regional policies continued to be competitive and hostile in most respects.

A LEGACY OF MISPERCEPTION

Pakistan and India "understood" each other in terms of the policies adopted and views expressed in the periods immediately before and after partition, and neither had substantially modified its perceptions by 1971. Pakistanis frequently cited the initial response to partition made by responsible Indian leaders, who had described it as "temporary"—allegedly the outcome of Britain's "divide and rule" policies. Prime Minister Nehru and some of his colleagues had commented in the immediate postpartition period that the reunion of the two successor states of British India was necessary and inevitable, inasmuch as the inhabitants of the subcontinent were one people whatever their religion, language, culture, and so on.[12] In response the first prime minister of Pakistan, Liaquat Ali Khan, expressed a widely held view in 1950 when he declared: "I charge the Government of India: first, it has never wholeheartedly accepted the Partition scheme, but her leaders paid lip service to it merely to get British troops out of the country. Secondly, India is out to destroy the State of Pakistan which Indian Leaders persistently continue to regard as part of India itself."[13] This perception of Indian objectives was still predominant in Pakistan two decades later.

Pakistani elite opinion had thus largely ignored or discounted what would appear to have been a significant, if gradual, shift in Indian elite attitudes on the partition question. By the late 1960s at least, the prevailing view in most Indian political and intellectual circles, though there were important exceptions, was that a democratic, centralized Indian political system was possible *because* of partition and that the incorporation of another hundred million Pakistani Muslims into the system would constitute an unbearable burden that could only lead to the disintegration of the Indian Union. No Indian official expressed such a view publicly, as it would have been interpreted as a communal—that is, anti-Muslim—sentiment, which might antagonize the large Indian Muslim minority, as well as running against the government's "secular" policy. But some rather subtle changes in official Indian statements and in the private outlook of a wide range of officials, political leaders, and intellectuals indicated this shift in attitude.[14] But all this made virtually no impression on Pakistan, which remained suspicious of India's objectives in the region.

Indians have also had difficulty in comprehending Pakistani opinions and apprehensions of the Indo-Pakistani relationship. They have tended to be paternalistic and often sarcastically condescending toward Pakistani concerns about India. Few Indian officials or intellectuals, for instance, seriously tried to understand why Pakistan felt compelled to join military pacts in the 1950s or later to support China. The common response was to dismiss Pakistani fears of Indian expansionist ambitions as totally misplaced—after all, had not Nehru verbally reassured Pakistan on this issue! That India's use of military force in Junagadh, Hyderabad, Goa, and Kashmir made Pakistan skeptical of the reliability of Nehruian reassurances was usually dismissed as indicative of the

Pakistani incapacity to understand the moral basis of Indian foreign policy.

The normally antagonistic character of Indo-Pakistani relations could have been altered in 1959 when President Ayub Khan of Pakistan proposed cooperation between the two countries in a regional security system—just when Sino-Indian relations were seriously deteriorating. Nehru rejected this offer, which was understandable from a narrow Indian perspective, since Ayub appeared to connect a regional security system for South Asia with a resolution of the Kashmir issue, presumably on Pakistani terms. But the contemptuous way in which the proposal was declined without any serious consideration of long-term Indian (and Pakistani) interests elicited a negative reaction in Pakistan and further strengthened its suspicions of India's ultimate goals in the area. While this may have been more an instance of ineptness on the part of India's decision makers rather than a deliberate denigration of Pakistan's importance to India's regional and security policies, that is not how it was interpreted in Rawalpindi. The Ayub government responded by reconsidering its relations with China, which had, until then, been formally correct, but distant and cool. The result was that a tacit Sino-Pakistani alliance emerged in the early 1960s, directed against their common antagonist—India. New Delhi, concerned with the possibility of Chinese and Pakistani collusion in hostilities on the disputed Kashmir and Himalayan frontiers, had to devise expensive counterstrategies that involved both the U.S.S.R. and the United States.

Both Pakistanis and Indians thus had standard negative interpretations of each other's motives and objectives. Even though their perceptions were wrong, or at least inadequate, in some critical respects, they were never modified by the course of events prior to 1971. Developments that reinforced old stereotypes were given great prominence; those that did not were ignored. Communication between the two countries through the exchange of newspapers, books, conferences, and so on was extremely poor after 1947 and, in any case, could never have overcome the confidence with which both groups adhered to their biases. Both sides seemed to be affected by a self-fulfilling prophecy, assuming the worst about each other, acting and reacting accordingly, and thus usually triggering further animosity. It is unlikely that the policies pursued by either side in 1971 would have differed very much even without these mutual misperceptions since many other important factors influenced their decisions at the time. But their unwillingness to even make an effort to understand each other's positions on a broad series of issues and events no doubt contributed to the outbreak of the war.

THE INTERNATIONAL DIMENSION

The differing Indian and Pakistani perceptions of the external world led the two governments to assume different foreign policies internationally as well as regionally. India's basic policy toward the major nonregional powers since 1947 has been to exclude them as much as possible from a significant influence in South Asian affairs. In disputes with other South Asian nations New Delhi has consistently argued for *bilateral* resolutions. Total exclusion of the major powers has not always been feasible, of course, and in several instances India has accepted their involvement as unavoidable, and even potentially helpful—for example, in the Kashmir issue in 1949 (though not thereafter), the 1960 Indus Valley development project, and the Tashkent conference after the 1965 Indo-Pakistani war. New Delhi viewed the outcomes of these as harmful to Indian interests, however, which strengthened its preference for bilateral approaches to regional issues.

When it has not been possible to exclude the major powers, India has sought to manipulate their involvement in South Asia to achieve its own regional objectives. This has proved an elusive goal, since the major powers usually identify their interests in the region quite differently. New Delhi's only consistent success since 1955 has been with the Soviet Union, but even the relationship with Moscow has had periods of trauma, disappointment, and, occasionally, quietly oppositionist roles. With China, the United States, and the West Asian Islamic states India has had less success, but has at least extracted a price for their support of other countries in the region.

Pakistan between 1947 and 1971 based its foreign policy on the assumption that India threatened its national existence, and that it therefore needed to use external powers as a counterforce to New Delhi. In the immediate postindependence period, the Pakistanis turned to the Islamic nations of Southwest Asia for support. This was ideologically attractive, as at that time Pakistan took its Islamic status much more seriously than did most of its neighbors to the west; moreover, it seemed to hold the promise of Pakistan's inclusion in an Islamic system that would allow Pakistan to limit its involvement in South Asia. But this policy collapsed by 1950 because of basic differences within the Islamic bloc of states in Southwest Asia, and Pakistan then began to look to other external powers for support. The Pakistanis were open-minded, but their choices were limited. The Soviet Union was regarded then, as now, as the principal extraregional threat because of its hostile gestures in the early 1950s toward Iran, Turkey, and Iraq—Pakistan's most important Southwest Asian neighbors. China was weak and seemingly uninterested in a relationship with Pakistan. Moreover, during 1952–56 China and India began moving toward an accommodation, symbolized by the 1954 Sino-Indian agreement on Tibet. Pakistan looked on these developments as a tacit Sino-Indian alliance and generally considered China an unfriendly power in those days. Carefully worded Chinese statements on Kashmir prior to 1959, although not explicit, seemingly backed India, and were interpreted by Pakistan as pro-Indian on this critical issue.[15]

By the early 1950s the Pakistanis had come to the conclusion that the United States was the only viable external ally. Pakistan was responsive to a U.S. alliance for two quite different reasons. First, at that time, containment of the Soviet Union and China served Pakistan's interests since both powers had been virulently critical of the Pakistani government and were supporting, rhetorically at least, antiregime "revolutionary" forces in the country. In this respect, there was basic congruity between U.S. and Pakistani policy objectives. Far more important to Pakistan, however, was the support an alliance with the United States would provide against its regional antagonists—India and Afghanistan. The alliance provided Pakistan with the option of a military solution in both of these disputes, something it would otherwise have lacked.

In this respect, however, Pakistani and U.S. objectives ran along quite diverse lines. Pakistan was indeed potentially important to American containment policy directed at the Soviet Union in Southwest Asia and at China in Southeast Asia. But Washington was not interested in backing Pakistan against either India or

Afghanistan, although the United States considered that Pakistan's role in containment, particularly in support of Iran and Turkey, a much higher priority than the maintenance of good relations with New Delhi or Kabul.[16] To attain the former, Washington had to make concessions on the latter, which New Delhi interpreted as motivated by anti-Indian objectives. Although India was wrong on the motivation, it was right about the consequences: the U.S.–Pakistani alliance played only an incidental role in containing communism—and then only into the early 1960s—while allowing Pakistan to take much stronger positions in its disputes with India and Afghanistan than would otherwise have been possible.

Pakistani and Indian foreign policies thus ran directly counter to each other on most global and regional issues. India opted for nonalignment in the East-West Cold War. This was ideologically satisfying to most of the Indian elite, who viewed major-power "meddling" in Asia as neocolonialism. Nehru's concept of non-alignment excluded both the East (i.e., the Soviet Union) and the West from any influence in Asia, but in the 1950s it was the Western powers that were seen as most capable of intervention—at least in areas of critical importance to India. China played a key role in India's foreign policy in Asia in this period, since Beijing's cooperation was required, or so Nehru believed, if the Cold War was to be kept out of Asia.[17] Obviously, China could play such a role only if it were prepared to reduce its ties with the Soviet bloc (for example, under the terms of the Sino-Soviet alliance). It was also essential for Beijing to reassure neighboring states in Southeast Asia about its intentions if they were to be deterred from joining U.S.-sponsored military alliances. The five principles (Panchshila) of "peaceful coexistence," first defined in the 1954 Sino-Indian agreement, were considered to be particularly useful in this respect, and India encouraged China to sign similar treaties with other Asian countries as an important step in isolating Asia from Cold War confrontations.

India's China policy in the 1950s thus had an implicit anti-Soviet tinge by reason of its efforts to persuade Beijing to identify primarily with Asia rather than with the Soviet bloc. But New Delhi felt constrained from pushing this aspect of its foreign policy too assiduously because of Pakistan's decision to join the U.S.-sponsored military alliance systems. The Indians concluded that they had no alternative but to expand their relationship with the Soviet Union, compromising both their nonalignment and China policies in the process. But there were other factors as well that convinced New Delhi of the utility of a close relationship with Moscow. For one thing, the Soviet Union was the only major external power capable of direct intervention in the vital strategic areas to the northwest of India, and New Delhi had to devise policies with this threat in mind. But rather than seeking containment of the U.S.S.R., Nehru sought to deter the Soviets from adopting expansionist policies by providing alternatives that would serve Soviet (and Indian) interests at a comparatively low price. Nehru's policy of accommodation bore fruit in 1955, when the two Soviet leaders Khrushchev and Bulganin, on a visit to India, declared their unequivocal support of New Delhi on the Kashmir issue and endorsed nonalignment. For a few years India thus became the primary channel of communication for *both* the U.S.S.R. and China in their efforts to expand relations with noncommunist states in the Third World.

Pakistan viewed the emerging Indian relationship with the Soviet Union and China in the mid 1950s as an abetment of New Delhi's alleged expansionist ambitions in South Asia. The Pakistanis concluded that they could not compete with India for Soviet and Chinese support; the only option that seemed viable was to cling to and expand their alliances with the United States and its Southwest Asian allies, Iran and Turkey.

Thus, in trying to meet their "felt needs" on regional security— that is, security against each other—both India and Pakistan had invited the intrusion of external powers into the subcontinent on a scale that would have been implausible under other circumstances. The Indians blamed the Pakistanis for creating this situation by joining CENTO and SEATO. But that, of course, ignored New Delhi's insensitivity to Pakistan's security concerns, as well as its unwillingness to reassure Pakistan in such a way that participation in military alliances might have seemed less attractive. India provides an example here—of many that could be cited—of a large power with vast human and material resources that is unable to comprehend the concerns of a comparatively small power with more limited resources. That the latter's apprehensions may at times have been exaggerated did not, under the circumstances, also make them unreasonable, but this rarely seemed to impress New Delhi.

STRATEGIES OF COPING AND EXPLOITING

Pakistani and Indian officials and intellectuals have generally portrayed their countries as the "victims" of external intrusions into the subcontinent, and not without considerable justification. But in most instances the external powers were also there by invitation from one or more of the South Asian states as a support to the regional or extraregional foreign policies. What the regional nations desired, of course, was to manipulate and direct external involvement in South Asia to their own advantage. The results, by and large, were mixed, but both India and Pakistan demonstrated considerable skill in these endeavors.

Pakistan's *principal* motivation in joining the U.S.-sponsored military alliances had been to develop a military capacity equal to or greater than India's. It had some initial successes in this effort in the late 1950s, when the Pakistani army was transformed from the dilapidated and truncated remnant of a colonial army into a relatively modern, well-equipped military force.[18] The results, however, were less than satisfactory to Pakistan, the gap in whose strength comparative to India was not completely filled. To some extent this was because of U.S. policy toward the alliance. On 5 March 1959, Pakistan and the United States had signed the Ankara Defense Cooperation Agreement. Under this agreement, according to the Pakistanis, the United States was committed to assist them against aggression from any source, that is, India, Afghanistan, the U.S.S.R., or China. The official American interpretation, however, was that the United States was only obligated to *consult* with Rawalpindi in the event of aggression and to provide support that would be "mutually agreed upon." Moreover, a reference in this bilateral agreement to the "Joint Resolution to Promote Peace and Stability in the Middle East," adopted in Ankara earlier in 1959 by the United States, Turkey, Iran, and Pakistan, had the effect of limiting U.S. obligations to "armed aggression from any country controlled by international communism" according to the American interpretation.

But although the legal obligations of the United States under the

Ankara agreement were clear, Pakistani confusion on this issue may well have reflected some confusion within the U.S. government on its commitments. On 6 November 1962, for instance, when the United States tried to "persuade" Pakistan to remain neutral in the ongoing Sino-Indian border war, the U.S. Ambassador to Pakistan, McConaughly, sent an aide-mémoire to President Ayub in which he said that the "Government of the United States of America reaffirms its previous assurances to the Government of Pakistan that it will come to Pakistan's assistance in the event of aggression from India against Pakistan."[19] Whether this was a reference to the Ankara agreement is unclear, but it would have been reasonable for the Pakistanis to assume that it was. Later, in the 1965 and 1971 Indo-Pakistan wars, Pakistan complained bitterly that Washington had not fulfilled its obligations to an "ally," but the United States responded in both instances that it had no commitment to Pakistan's security in conflicts with India under the 1959 or other agreements. Since security in Pakistan was generally equated with security against India, the value of the U.S. alliance was significantly diminished.

The United States had also proved unwilling to extend full political and economic backing to Pakistan in its dispute with India. Pakistanis interpreted the massive American economic aid program to India starting in the mid 1950s as a threat, since it allowed New Delhi to divert its own financial and other resources to rearmament. As far as Rawalpindi was concerned, the United States was providing *direct* military aid to Pakistan and *indirect* military aid to India. The limitations imposed by the United States on the use of arms provided to Pakistan were also considered too restrictive by the Pakistanis. Under the terms of the U.S.-Pakistan agreement, arms aid received by Pakistan was to be used only against communist aggressors. Even more important perhaps were restrictions on the provision of ammunition and spare parts, which were limited under U.S. regulations to enough supplies for one month of military operations. Pakistan could avoid strict adherence to the U.S.-imposed limitations on arms aid—which it did in both 1965 and 1971—but these policies seriously inhibited the Pakistanis in defining objectives and strategies in hostilities with India.

Thus, its participation in military alliances strengthened Pakistan, but not to the extent that it could achieve its basic foreign policy goals in South Asia. In 1959, with the first outbreak of a Sino-Indian dispute, U.S. strategic interests in South Asia also began to shift from Pakistan to India. Following the 1962 Sino-Indian border war, U.S. military and economic assistance was balanced slightly in favor of India. Washington introduced a direct military aid program to India, and although the Pakistan program was continued, it was considerably reduced in size and in the kinds of equipment provided. The United States strongly supported India in its disputes with China on the Himalayan frontier and disapproved of Pakistan's policy, which generally supported China. The United States also quietly refused to condone the periodic Pakistani efforts to revive the Kashmir dispute in the United Nations, in effect taking a pro-Indian position, since New Delhi also opposed any further international intervention in that issue.

These were the conditions in the early 1960s that persuaded Pakistan to introduce a fundamental shift in its foreign policy. The close alignment with the United States was replaced by a "trilateral" policy in which Islamabad sought to achieve equidistant relationships with the United States, China, and the Soviet Union.[20] Although the primary goal was to elicit the support of all three major powers for Pakistani foreign policy objectives, Pakistan also hoped at least to neutralize their influence in South Asian regional developments. Pakistan attained only limited success with its new policy, which, in any case, was never really trilateral. The People's Republic of China was prepared to help Pakistan as much as possible in the context of its own confrontations with India, the Soviet Union, and the United States. But its assistance was never sufficient to ensure success in Pakistan's disputes with India, which was clearly evident in both the 1965 and the 1971 wars. The United States tried to assume a balance in its relations with India and Pakistan but only managed to antagonize both governments. Moscow was interested in an "opening" to Pakistan to counter what it considered excessive Chinese and American influence in that country. The U.S.S.R. was, as we have noted, a nonpartisan mediator in the 1966 Tashkent negotiations that followed the 1965 Indo-Pakistani war. It also expanded its economic aid to Pakistan and even introduced a military aid program in the late 1960s. But eventually Moscow had to choose between India and Pakistan, and it decided to retain its old policy of giving primacy to India in its involvement in South Asia. In view of the basically unfavorable international environment in and around South Asia after 1960, Pakistan probably did as well as could be expected in using outside powers to its own advantage. But the results were not satisfactory to the political, military, and intellectual elites of that country.

India was no less active in its efforts to manipulate the involvement of the major external powers in South Asia. In most instances from the mid 1950s on, the Soviet Union followed along rather tamely in accommodating itself to Indian policies and objectives in South Asia—so much so that the other South Asian countries sometimes perceived the U.S.S.R. as an Indian "client state." China was also generally responsive to Indian objectives in South Asia until its own dispute with India in 1962 led it to take a confrontational stance against New Delhi in South Asia. Thereafter, New Delhi was remarkably successful for nearly a decade in using that dispute to elicit support from both the superpowers by cooperating with their separate, but mutually supportive, China containment policies. India was able to use its ties with the Soviet Union and the United States not only against the Chinese "threat" but also in its difficult relations in the 1960s with both Pakistan and Nepal.

The Indian record in manipulating the external powers in South Asia was better than that of Pakistan; even for New Delhi, however, there were almost as many failures as there were successes. India and Pakistan easily arranged for the intervention of the major external powers in South Asian developments; but their alliances did not always work to their advantage, since Moscow, Beijing, and Washington usually had objectives of their own when making commitments to the nations of the subcontinent. Thus, the dynamics of the relations between India and Pakistan as these evolved in the 1950s and 1960s made another conflict between them likely, and the limited obligations accepted by the major external powers in South Asia deprived them of the capacity—or will—to impose "peaceful" methods for the resolution of disputes on their supposed "client states."

4

A Culture of Distrust

The results of the 1970 Pakistan elections had surprised government and party leaders alike and had changed the roles each had
expected to play in the negotiations for a transfer of power and the
creation of a constitution that would accommodate the interests
and allay the fears of all. Some who had expected to play leading
parts were relegated by the electorate to comprimario roles; others
had surpassed their already grandiose dreams. This unforeseen
outcome prompted everyone to reevaluate how to realize their
goals in an environment less amenable to negotiation and compromise than anticipated with a larger number of parties more equal in
power. The expectations of the Awami League and the Pakistan
People's Party were especially heightened.

After the elections there was still consensus within the military
elite that power should be transferred to a civilian government.
Some officers had reservations about the wisdom of such a radical
change after twelve years of having a military man, Field Marshal
Ayub Khan, as chief executive, but most were concerned about the
real issues—to whom power should be transferred and with what
understandings and guarantees.

The military had two central concerns. The first was the integrity
of Pakistan under a central government with effective power; this
was thought to be satisfied by the fundamental principles of the
constitution specified in the Legal Framework Order.[1] The second
concern was for a military budget at current levels and the autonomy of the armed services from political interference in promotion,
posting, and recruitment. These critical matters had not been stipulated by the LFO and would have to be part of a negotiated political
settlement after the elections.[2]

The martial law regime had anticipated that the elections would
result in a party configuration that would facilitate the protection of
these interests. Given its information about voter sentiment and its

efforts to assist the parties that it felt best represented its concerns, the government expected the elections to produce a multiplicity of parties, with none being dominant; this would then encourage a marketplace of interests and power that would result in a coalition government and thus temper extremist demands in terms of both constitutional design and policy-making. Consensus would require an expansion, rather than a reduction, of areas open to negotiation; party leaders would now have to address one another rather than their constituents in their negotiations, and such a distribution of party power and the urge to govern would encourage compromise.

Bargaining and compromise, the government felt, would be encouraged by yet another condition. The Legal Framework Order stipulated that any agreement would have to receive presidential "authentication"; thus, political parties would need to present formulations acceptable to the president. If agreements were not forthcoming within the stipulated 120-day period, new elections would have to be held, a prospect that no party would find attractive given the lengthy, costly, and exhausting campaign just finished and the uncertainties that elections would hold for party cohesion.

The government had not rigorously thought about alternative strategies to be pursued given different electoral outcomes. Neither had it thoroughly appreciated the constitutional and policy consequences of the Six-Point Demand, although memoranda on potential political consequences had been drafted by the intelligence services and on economic consequences by M. M. Ahmed, economic adviser to the president and effective head of the Planning Commission.[3] The development of a strategy on the part of the government would wait; and it would prove to be reactive rather than engaged.

Although certain issues may have been inviolable, prior to the elections politics were not simply perceived in zero-sum terms. Party leaders in the western provinces anticipated the revival of a multiparty system and expected that issues of power and constitutional order would be resolved through negotiation and coalition formation; in short, they, like the government, had expected the elections to create a party distribution like that of the past. The Awami League, in contrast, had expected a substantial victory— not an absolute majority, but a plurality that would enable it to ensure a constitutional settlement based substantially on its six-point program.[4] However, because of the emergence of a two-party system in which the parties were divided by strong ideologies and personalities, were regionally based, and were fearful of each other's designs, party solidarity was emphasized, which inhibited efforts at compromise. After the elections, as time went on, mutual suspicion and distrust intensified, and the demands of each side became more rigid. Party headquarters ultimately resembled fortresses preparing for siege more than brokerage houses preparing to make deals.

Shortly after the elections the Awami League made known its intention to use its absolute majority to ensure the creation of a constitution following its six-point program as closely as possible.[5] What was seen as the grudging acknowledgment of its majority by political leaders in the west and an insistence upon pre-Assembly efforts to reach a consensus were taken as an opening gambit on the part of politicians in the western provinces to once again deprive an eastern-based party of the fruits of electoral victory. Furthermore, a radical secondary group within the Awami League, ranging from those who wished to exact retribution from the west in compensation for past grievances and inequities to those advocating secession, made a political free market difficult. The Awami League's position was "no compromise on principles, but accommodation in their application," that is, no compromise on the principle of majority rule, although certain accommodations to other parties would be possible, but only by majority party consent.[6] For most Awami Leaguers this position was taken as a matter of conviction; for all, it was seen as necessary to maintain the integrity of the party, without which victory would be transformed into defeat.

The major objective of the leadership of the Pakistan People's Party was to keep the loyalty of the diverse body of members elected to the National Assembly on the party ticket. Both party loyalty and organizational scaffolding were as yet untested.[7] Top party leaders were united by a general commitment to the idea of Islamic socialism and the prospect of power. But since many had been elected by virtue of the charismatic mass appeal of Zulfiqar Ali Bhutto and had not previously been involved in common political endeavors, they had not developed an accepted set of reciprocal status and power relationships among themselves. For a viable and permanent party to be created, a share in power at the center was essential. This was evident to the PPP, but its anxieties were intensified by reminders from members of the government of the party's precarious position, as well as by observations to this effect by opposition leaders in the west.[8]

The issue of power sharing among parties and the transfer of power was further complicated by Bhutto's aspirations to national prominence. If power were transferred to a civilian government, those who had resources to distribute within the People's Party would be members of cabinets in the provincial capitals. It was commonly accepted by PPP leaders that were Bhutto to stay at the center and sit in opposition, he would have nothing to distribute; those with resources would find him at best unnecessary to their political welfare and at worst a threat to their positions through his mastery of intrigue. In contrast, if he were to become active at the provincial level, he would forfeit any opportunity of developing a lasting national constituency, becoming in the process merely one of several provincial potentates. Because of the divisions within the PPP over the viability and legitimacy of the six points, Bhutto and his dominant group feared that the party would become factionalized and divided in a National Assembly in which the Awami League could extend positions and favors to selected groups in the opposition, even within the PPP. Thus the top leadership of the PPP early on decided that it could not participate in the National Assembly without a guarantee of a share of governmental power.

Although this calculus of political necessity was by itself compelling, Bhutto's definition of the situation and his actions were also fired by a raw and elemental urge for power. He saw himself as the rightful "heir to the throne" after the Ayub regency. It was he who had led the movement that had unseated "the king" and who had guided a mass movement for the restoration of representative institutions; it must thus be he who would exercise ultimate executive authority. One of the president's senior ministers observed to Yahya just after the elections that if Bhutto did not assume power within a year he would literally go mad. Bhutto confided to Yahya in one of their political discussions that he had to accede to power "now," for his family "died young," and, he added, in a cruelly prophetic vein, "violently." He could not wait; he was destined to lead Pakistan, and he would not brook any delay.[9]

For all parties the principal concern immediately after the national elections was to do no worse in the provincial elections of 17 December than they had in the elections held ten days earlier. Except for passing reference to constitutional issues and the transfer of power, political debate continued to address regional issues. For the leadership of the Pakistan People's Party it was a time spent discussing the most expedient strategy for exacting a share of power at the national level. All politicians, however, became more attentive and sensitive to the statements and claims of others than they had been prior to the national elections. Casual comments by leaders in one region were perceived as serious statements of intent by leaders in the other regions.

Immediately after the national elections, the Awami League started to change its rhetoric from a demand for a "Six-Point" constitution to a commitment to its realization. In one of his first postelection speeches, Sheikh Mujib observed that the national elections had constituted a referendum on the six-point program. He called upon all members of the National Assembly elected on the Awami League ticket to join him in making a solemn pledge to devote their collective energies and resources "to save our people from the exploitation of the vested interests and from the scourge of nature." He welcomed the political awakening in the west, but refrained from calling upon the People's Party for cooperation and assistance, instead calling upon the "awakening masses" of West Pakistan to join their Bengali brethren in an effort to realize their common aspirations.[10]

TESTING AND PREPARATION
FOR NEGOTIATION

Yahya did not choose to participate in the drawing up of the new constitution; indeed, there was no one among the president's advisers working on the more controversial of the six points, much less upon constitutional drafts.[11] Rather, Yahya endeavored to encourage the leaders of the Awami League and the Pakistan People's Party to meet and despatched an emissary to Dhaka to invite Sheikh Mujib to Rawalpindi so that talks might begin in the capital. The emissary also sounded out Mujib on his preference for a venue and date for the inaugural session of the National Assembly. Through the same emissary, the president made the same inquiry of the leader of the PPP, Zulfiqar Ali Bhutto.[12]

As was to occur several times subsequently, Mujib's response was unexpected and did not please Yahya. Mujib declined the invitation to go to Rawalpindi and insisted that the appropriate place for discussing constitutional issues was in the National Assembly. To this end he urged that the Assembly be called for early January and that it be held in Dhaka. Bhutto indicated that he was prepared to attend the talks, but preferred a meeting of the Assembly in West Pakistan, with a later, unspecified date for its inauguration.

Disturbed by Mujib's remarks that the election constituted a referendum on the six points and that a constitution would be framed on these principles, and by his reluctance to engage in political discussions before the convening of the National Assembly, the People's Party decided to challenge the Awami League publicly by raising doubts about the six points, by questioning the right of a party from one region to speak for the entirety of a territorially and culturally plural Pakistan, and by insisting that the PPP have a place in the government.[13] Despite its minority position within the National Assembly, the PPP launched a campaign to establish itself as one of two "majority parties" in Pakistan, attempted to deny the Awami League coalitions with parties in the west, and endeavored to discredit the Awami League's constitutional principles and its commitment to the integrity of Pakistan.

Throughout the negotiations toward a political settlement that ensued until the military crackdown in late March, Bhutto was to be aggressive and confrontative. No better description of his style can be provided than from his own definition of politics, later elaborated in his fascinating "confrontation" with the Italian writer Oriana Fallaci.

Politics is movement per se—a politician should be mobile. He should sway now to right and now to left; he should come up with contradictions, doubts. He should change continually, test things, attack from every side so as to single out his opponent's weak point and strike at it. Woe to him if he focuses immediately on his basic concept, woe if he reveals and crystallizes it. Woe if he blocks the maneuver by which to throw his opponent on the carpet. Apparent inconsistency is the prime virtue of the intelligent man and the astute politician.[14]

Bhutto's first sally came in a speech on 20 December in Lahore in which he declared that no constitution could be framed, nor any government formed at the national level, without the cooperation of the PPP. He stated bluntly that the Peoples' Party was not prepared to occupy the opposition benches, and that it could not wait another five years to come to power; it had to share power now.[15] He went on to argue that "a majority alone doesn't count in national politics," and that the PPP, which had played a central role in bringing down the Ayub regime, had the right to participate in the governance of the country under a parliamentary system that its commitment and sacrifices had been so critical in bringing about. He supplemented his argument with the observation that real power at the center rested in the Punjab and Sind, and that no central government could thus function without the cooperation of the PPP.

Bhutto suggested his conception of the new constitutional order and means of approaching it in a speech to party workers in Lahore the following day.[16] He stated that the "quantum of power" (a phrase picked up by the government and press alike) and the "quantum of autonomy" devolved to the provinces had to be determined in a context of "national solidarity" and had to have the consent of all the federating provinces. First, however, a constitution had to be framed by mutual agreement between the Awami League and the Pakistan People's Party. There would be no difficulty in doing this if the two parties and Yahya could agree on the "quantum of autonomy." If only the Awami League and PPP agreed, however, there would be some difficulty; if they could not agree, then the situation was most unpromising. He reiterated that in pursuit of a constitutional consensus, the PPP and the Awami League would have to share authority at the national level, and that under no circumstance could the PPP be forced into opposition—it would only go there by its own choice. The Awami League and PPP should form a "grand coalition" such as that between the Social Democratic and Free Democratic parties in West Germany. In a speech in Hyderabad on 24 December, Bhutto declared that the PPP was "the sole representative of the people of West Pakistan like the Awami League in East Pakistan, and therefore it cannot be deprived of sharing power in the government.[17]

While the PPP was aggressive and confrontative, the Awami League was reactive and ameliorative, though firm. It is ironic that although Bhutto claimed to represent a single wing of the country, but possessed a national program, Mujib claimed to represent a national majority, but had a program that emphasized the grievances and demands of a single region. Being reactive, the Awami League increasingly turned inward, and as the six points came under attack, it tried harder to develop a more intense internal commitment to them to resist outside efforts to abort them.

This reactive style of the Awami League is reflected in the reply of Tajuddin Ahmed, second in command and principal party strategist, to Bhutto's initial demands that the PPP participate in the framing of the constitution and be included in a national government:

> The statement attributed to Mr. Zulfiqar Ali Bhutto that neither the country's Constitution could be framed nor a Central Government could be formed without active co-operation of his party cannot be correct. The Punjab and Sind can no longer aspire to be "bastions of power." The democratic struggle of the people has been aimed against such "bastions of power." The people have voted to establish a real democracy in which power vests with the people, and the legislature is constituted on the basis of the "one man one vote" principle. In such a system a party enjoying a comfortable[,] indeed an absolute[,] majority as the Awami League does[,] with a clear electoral mandate[,] is quite competent to frame the Constitution and to form the Central Government. This can be done with or without any other party. Such co-operation as may be obtained will be for the Awami League to choose and will be sought on the basis of adherence to and acceptance of the principles and the programme of the Awami League, which seeks to establish a new economic and social order, free from exploitation.
>
> An elected representative of a province cannot claim any special or superior status over that of any other province. To make such a claim is to hark back to the parochialism of the past, when the Central Government was seen as the preserve of a ruling coterie drawn only from certain parts of West Pakistan. The people of Pakistan have rejected the past. If we are to move towards a better future, such claims should be avoided as they generate unnecessary and harmful controversy. The Awami League is fully aware of its reponsibility to implement the will of the people of Pakistan and will spare no effort to do so.[18]

Sheikh Mujib's response to Bhutto was given in his famous Ramna Race Course speech of 3 January 1971, in which he declared in unequivocal terms that the constitution would be based on the six points and that "none can stop it."[19] He took care to note, however, that he would be responsive to the interests of the people of West Pakistan in the constitution-making process. He also reminded what was now a national as well as a regional audience that the Awami League was the majority party for the entirety of Pakistan—there were not two "majority parties"—and that his party would act with the authority and responsibility that was customary for majority parties in representative systems. The Awami League would frame the constitution with the cooperation of representatives from West Pakistan. Mujib also observed that conspiracies that had commenced even before the elections were continuing in a number of disturbing forms. (For example, in addition to the shifting stratagems of the PPP and suggestions by emissaries of the government that Mujib be more accommodating to the PPP, a newly elected Awami League member of the Provincial Assembly was murdered in Pabna on 22 December, a few days after the murder of a party worker in Khulna.) He made a dramatic call to all Awami League national and provincial assembly members to sign a public oath that would bind them to the realization of the six-point program regardless of the cost. All signed.[20]

The martial law authorities had not set a date before the elections for holding the National Assembly, although Yahya had indicated that he would summon the Assembly "as soon as possible" after the elections had been held. In a broadcast to the nation four days before the elections, he had suggested that the "elected representatives and particularly the party leaders . . . usefully employ the period between their election and the first session of the National Assembly in getting together and arriving at a consensus on the main provisions of our future constitution."[21] Yahya had continually indicated that he would not become directly involved in the constitution-making process, although he emphasized that any constitution presented to him for approval would have to be within the guidelines of the Legal Framework Order or martial law would continue.

Because of the apparent inability of party leaders to agree to meet to discuss constitutional issues and the drift of debate between the Awami League and the People's Party toward public acrimony, Yahya felt compelled by early January to initiate a more direct, and what he hoped would be more constructive, dialogue.[22] It was announced on 10 January that he would visit Dhaka two days later to talk with the Awami League. The announcement came as a surprise. Only a week earlier the government had reported that the president planned to visit several countries in Southeast Asia in mid January. The urgency of the talks was also indicated by the announcement that Sheikh Mujib would cut short his tour through coastal districts of East Pakistan, where by-elections were being held on 17 January.[23]

Two meetings were held during the president's three-day stay in Dhaka. The first was a private meeting between Yahya and Mujib, after which each expressed sincere hopes for the prompt return of civilian rule. The second, which lasted three hours, included the two principals and representatives of the government and the Awami League high command. At the end of his stay, Yahya referred to Sheikh Mujib as the next prime minister of Pakistan, adding that his own job was finished, that he was preparing to leave office, and that the transfer of power would occur soon. Both leaders independently indicated their satisfaction with the talks and optimism about the future.

Such public testimony suggested an emerging consensus between the Awami League and the regime, but it masked several misperceptions that had resulted from the talks. The meetings had focused upon two subjects: (1) the substance of the six points and Awami League intentions regarding their implementation and (2), more obliquely, the composition of the new civilian government. Although the six points had constituted the essence of the Awami League's election program and had provided the rhetoric of its campaign, the central government was unclear as to their substance and had not thought through the consequences of their implementation. On the day of their arrival, the members of the presidential party had requested a copy of the Six-Point Demand from the East Pakistani government in order to prepare for the following day's meeting, in which they wished to elicit "clarifications," a request met with surprise and concern by Awami League leaders given the wide currency the program had received.[24]

In the second meeting, Yahya invited Sheikh Mujib to present the six-point program, which Mujib reportedly did quite crisply, observing that there was nothing new or mysterious about it—the six points had been a matter of public knowledge and debate since the latter days of the Ayub regime.[25] After his recitation, Mujib asked the president what objections he might have to the six points as he had outlined them. Yahya replied that he had none, but counseled Mujib that the Awami League would have to convince the leaders of the West Pakistani parties of the virtues and workability of the program. Members of the presidential party recall that Mujib responded openly and solicitously, affirming that he had every intention of enlisting the cooperation of the leaders from the western provinces. He further indicated that there was flexibility in the six points, observing that they were the "word of men, not the word of God," and that they could be molded to accommodate the views of non-Bengali groups. Mujib insisted, however, that it was only appropriate that any deliberations take place on the floor of the National Assembly and not in either private or unstructured public forums. It was absolutely essential as well, he argued, that the Assembly be called immediately. The electorate had returned a single party with an absolute majority, and therefore with a mandate to govern. Also since a date had not been set for convening the National Assembly, many Bengalis were starting to doubt the sincerity of the government's avowed intentions.

The president's group was not openly quizzical of the six points or of the intentions of the Awami League, although it distrusted both. The government's hesitation in probing and confronting the Awami League program was owing to several circumstances. It had not developed a constitutional plan of its own, had not explored the ramifications of the Awami League's proposals, had expected political leaders to commence negotiations as a matter of course, and was uncomfortable with what seemed to it to be the anomaly of a Bengali majority (which, although it hoped it was transitory, the government did not want to antagonize). The hesitancy and latent skepticism of the president's group in the second meeting were evident in some comments made by the governor of East Pakistan, Adm. S. M. Ahsan, to Mujib. Ahsan intimated that because of the absolute majority the Awami League enjoyed, Mujib might conceivably attempt to force a constitution through the

Assembly regardless of assurances given in the privacy of meetings and negotiating sessions. After expressing a deep sense of hurt and indignation at this questioning of his integrity by an official he saw as an impartial advocate, if not a friend, Mujib heatedly insisted that he was the leader of all of Pakistan, not just of its eastern wing, and that he was bound to act in good faith and abide by his assurances by virtue not only of Pakistani opinion but of international opinion as well. He then proposed that to facilitate a constitutional consensus, the members of the National Assembly should meet in Dhaka to discuss a draft constitution several days before the convening of the Assembly. The draft, incorporating suggestions from West Pakistani leaders, would then be prepared for Yahya to present to the National Assembly.

Also during the second meeting, in an effort to assuage the fears of the military, Mujib indicated that he would accommodate the corporate interests of the Pakistani army as well as the personal political interests of President Yahya. In addition, he stated explicitly that he intended to make Yahya the next "elected" president of Pakistan; he would not reduce the size of the army; and he assured Yahya that no one from West Pakistan would be dismissed from either the military or civil services. The president finally raised the question of the involvement of West Pakistani parties in the government and indicated to Mujib the necessity of working closely with the major party of West Pakistan, the Pakistan People's Party. Although he did not commit himself to any form of coalition government, Mujib reportedly affirmed to Yahya that he would not impose any unwanted constitutional arrangements on the western provinces. The meeting concluded with Mujib once more urging that the National Assembly be summoned early, certainly no later than 15 February.

That important officials within the government were less than enthusiastic about the Awami League assuming power became evident in an informal meeting held later that evening at the President's House in Dhaka. Rather than placating their fears at the earlier meeting, Mujib's assurances had induced doubts.[26] They were concerned over what they perceived to be the hard line taken by the Awami League, which enjoyed enough of a majority to enable it to do just about anything that it wanted once the Assembly was called. Once power was transferred, there would be no leverage against the Awami League without constitutional guarantees and the effective participation of a dependable counterpoise in the government. The situation appeared anomalous, if not absurd, with Bengalis telling the army what it could and could not do, and with the army being in the position of supplicant. After a decade of protection under Ayub, it was difficult enough to contemplate the uncertainties of power being transferred into the hands of politicians from the west, much less into those of eastern ones. Rather than alleviating concerns about the protection of military interests, the Awami League had drawn attention to what *could* happen—limits on defense spending, enforced expansion of Bengali representation in the officer corps, rapid promotions of Bengali officers to eliminate old inequities, an accommodative stance with respect to India, and the ultimate possibility of a permanently reduced stature and function for the military with the expansion of provincial militias specified in the six points. These reservations raised the specter of planned military impotence and political interference in military affairs, issues that had not been raised and addressed, much less answered, in the second meeting with the Awami League. The representatives of the regime had been as ambivalent and reluctant about bringing up the questions directly as they were fearful of what the answers might be in reality, if not at the conference table.

Another fear concerned the role of the president. Although Mujib had declared that he intended to make Yahya the first president, there was no way of ensuring this, and it might involve an electoral contest with an opposition leader even if the Awami League stood by its word. Regardless of this eventuality, the president's party felt that the prize might not be worth the taking. The office of president under the new constitution would in all probability have neither effective power nor attractive status, with the incumbent being nothing more than "the Queen Elizabeth of Pakistan"—a role spokesmen for the regime said Yahya had no intention of assuming.

On 17–18 January 1971, within three days of leaving Dhaka, Yahya was a guest at Bhutto's family's baronial estate, Al-Murtaza, in Larkana. Ostensibly he was there for a duck shoot at nearby Drigh Lake, but in fact Yahya went to renew political discussions and to report on what had transpired between himself and Mujib.

Also present were Lt. Gen. S. M. G. Peerzada, the principal staff officer, who had accompanied the president to Dhaka, and Gen. Abdul Hamid Khan, the army chief of staff and a close friend of Yahya's since their company-grade officer days. From the Pakistan People's Party there were Ghulam Mustafa Khar, who had served as Bhutto's emissary to Dhaka in early January to get a sense of Awami League sentiment, and Mumtaz Ali Bhutto, Zulfiqar's cousin. For the most part Bhutto and Yahya met privately, joined by General Peerzada later. Afterward, they reported the substance of their discussions to their advisers.[27]

Not long after the opening civilities, Bhutto registered his undisguised anger with Yahya for having unnecessarily and prematurely "made Mujib prime minister" without consulting any other political leaders. Bhutto insisted that the prime minister could be named only after the convening of the National Assembly and the demonstration of majority support. No one had a majority in the National Assembly before it was summoned, he insisted. The naming of Mujib thus prejudiced his own chances of developing a majority coalition by means of defections from the Awami League. He discerned that even though the president claimed to be only a facilitator and not an actual participant in any of the political deliberations, Yahya was in fact becoming an active participant, and in ways inimical to the interests of West Pakistan and the People's Party.

Yahya replied that he had not made Mujib prime minister; Mujib's majority had. And even though it was a substantial majority, and appeared to be firm, it would still have to be tested in the National Assembly. Chiding Bhutto, Yahya said that unless Bhutto could work out an arrangement between himself and Mujib, he would have to sit in opposition. He also reminded Bhutto of the fragility of his own party organization, the lack of a strong sense of attachment to the PPP by the newly elected members of the National Assembly, and the possibility that the party might collapse under him if he did not succeed in securing participation in the government.

Congruent with the doubts already expressed by some of the military officers, Bhutto told Yahya that Mujib was "a clever bastard" who wanted an early date set for the National Assembly so that he could "bulldoze" his constitution and programs through, which would be impossible to prevent. Assurances from Mujib before the summoning of the National Assembly were one thing; his actions afterward would be quite another, and there was no reason to trust him to do what he need not do, and what it would not necessarily be in his interests to do. Yahya reminded Bhutto of the provision in the Legal Framework Order for a presidential veto of any constitution that did not abide by the guidelines set forth in that document. Bhutto argued that if a constitution were passed by the National Assembly, it would be politically impossible for Yahya to veto it. Because of these considerations, Bhutto strongly maintained that a consensus on a constitution must be reached *before* a meeting of the National Assembly, that in this process the Awami League might weaken, and that he, Bhutto, would forcefully advocate the interests of West Pakistan and could be trusted to attend to the interests of the armed forces as well. To develop a consensus, however, he needed time, although he did not spell out how much time or what kind of consensus he hoped to obtain. The president found Bhutto's arguments compelling.

Bhutto then asked Yahya what he really felt about Mujib's intentions, whether he had confidence in Mujib's "loyalty," whether he thought Mujib could "really be trusted." If Mujib were a "true Pakistani," he would not react adversely to a delay in convening the National Assembly provided that delay served the larger interest of arriving at a truly national constitutional consensus. Indeed, Bhutto intimated that postponement, if for no other purpose, would itself constitute a test of Mujib's loyalty: If he responded responsibly, he could be trusted, and even Bhutto would be prepared to accept him as leader of the government; if he responded wildly, then this would be a sign that he had ideas in mind other than the integrity and well-being of Pakistan. Yahya made no commitment to Bhutto on a date or the timing for the convening of the Assembly. The talks concluded with Bhutto reiterating his plea for time and Yahya again suggesting the wisdom of Bhutto's going to Dhaka for talks with Mujib.

Bhutto informed the Awami League that he and a delegation of leaders from the PPP were ready to visit Dhaka for discussions on the six points and the transfer of power. Mujib responded that he welcomed any leader from West Pakistan who wanted to discuss these issues, indicated that the end of January would be workable and that he would arrange his schedule accordingly. The timing was acceptable to Bhutto and the People's Party.

The talks in Dhaka on 27–30 January 1971 between the Awami League and the People's Party were held at two levels and focused on two separate concerns.[28] Two meetings that were attended by party delegations centered on both constitutional and substantive political issues, although each side came with a different agenda. J. A. Rahim, the party's general secretary and author of the party election manifesto, led the PPP delegation. He insisted on discussing the transformation of socialist programs into public policy. The "underdevelopment" of East Pakistan, he argued, was not a function of inadequate constitutional design, as the Awami League complained, but of "internal colonialism," of a rapacious Pakistani capitalist class, which, if deprived of its protection by the government and relieved of its substantial assets, would wither away, erasing not only regional inequalities but class inequalities as well. According to Rahim, regional inequalities were a form of class inequality. The role of the state was to contain and dismantle this class and at the same time rigorously pursue a policy of redistribution in both investment and welfare.

Although sympathetic to the objectives of the PPP delegation, the Awami League was staunchly committed to discussing only constitutional means for eradicating both economic inequalities and inequalities of cultural status and political effectiveness. It was skeptical of the PPP's obsession with a socialist model alone and considered this yet another West Pakistani ploy to maintain Bengali dependency. The Awami League defined the situation of the country in distinctly regional and ethnic, not in class, terms. It felt that the certainty of change was much greater if power were to be reorganized by means of fundamental law instead of by a political elite with an easily diluted will working against an entrenched economic class that had a web of alliances in an equally strong and well-entrenched government bureaucracy. Rather than play an old game with a changed strategy against powerful and skillful opponents, it was better to redesign the game in such a way that the power and skill of those opponents would be neutralized. The Awami League thought economic redistribution could be pursued under its six-point constitution, which would have the advantage of constitutional assistance.

The PPP delegation was surprised by the Awami League's tough stance. This was not how West Pakistani were accustomed to perceiving their Bengali brethren. The Awami League team did not waver in its conception of what needed to be done, and at one juncture one of its members politely but pointedly asked Rahim to stop talking about socialism and address the central issues at hand—the six points and the issue of autonomy within a federal constitutional structure. The two sides thus faced the future with substantially different ideas of what needed to be done; their conceptions, however, could in principle accommodate each other—an observation not lost on some of the participants on both sides.

The other dialogue was between Mujib and Bhutto.[29] Mujib, like his party delegation, was concerned with constitutional arrangements and the convening of the National Assembly. Bhutto in contrast was interested in more immediate and tangible matters. He wanted to determine the place that he and his party would have in a new government and expressed little interest in discussing the details of the six points other than to indicate that he was prepared to accept them—with the exception of the provision to place foreign trade under provincial control—in exchange for four of the ten cabinet positions, with the deputy prime ministership and the foreign affairs portfolio reserved for himself. As an alternative to the deputy prime ministership, he proposed the possibility of the presidency. Mujib's response was reportedly just as blunt as Bhutto's demand. He indicated that the formation of the cabinet would be decided by the majority party and those parties that the majority party might choose to invite into a coalition and said that Bhutto could not be guaranteed a position in the ministry, much less the deputy prime ministership. Without specifying to whom, he also informed Bhutto that the presidency had already been promised to "someone else."

Afterward Mujib reported to several leaders of other parties from the west that he was incensed at Bhutto's arrogance and presumptuousness, at his cavalier attitude toward a constitutional solution, and at his apparent sense that Mujib's majority was in fact nothing more than a minority of respectable size.[30] He indicated that he was disillusioned; he had thought Bhutto had come to discuss constitutional issues, but all Bhutto had wanted was to discuss ministerial posts, which he demanded to share as a matter of right. Mujib's suspicions had also been aroused by Bhutto's insinuations that the military regime would never transfer power to a Bengali government—the implication being that a deal with Bhutto was an essential precondition to the transfer of power.

The response of the People's Party delegation to the discussions in Dhaka was mixed.[31] One group came away more convinced than before that holding the talks had been pointless, since the Awami League was bent upon secession, and that to become seriously engaged in discussions with the Awami League was to become an accomplice in its ultimate design. The lessons to be learned from the talks were the same as those to be learned from the Agartala conspiracy, from Mujib's incessant fiery speeches during the election campaign, and from what was perceived to be his particularly "inflammatory" speech in Dhaka immediately after the 7 December elections.

Another faction, however, saw the discussions and the possibility of a constitutional consensus quite differently. Although the Awami League delegation had been adamant on the six points in the two formal meetings, in informal meetings with members of the People's Party delegation who were particularly conversant with the technicalities and with the theory behind the constitution, it appeared that there was a common meeting ground between the parties. The PPP could accept the Awami League's explanation of most of the six points, except the decentralization of foreign aid and international trade, and because of the marginal differences of opinion among the Awami Leaguers themselves and a sense that they genuinely desired some kind of agreement, it was felt that an acceptable compromise on those two matters could also be negotiated.

Bhutto's reaction to the meetings in Dhaka was less sanguine than that of the latter, but not as rigid as that of the former. After his discussions with Mujib, he realized that his gambit of toughness and his expectation that the Awami League would be willing to compromise on the formation of a government in exchange for substantial agreement on the six points and an immediate transfer of power had been ill-founded. Mujib's intentions with respect to devising a constitution and forming a government had been made quite clear; his commitment and will to do so had been no less clear and had been unexpectedly intense.

Bhutto is reported to have realized that he needed time to forestall the fait accompli that would turn his party into an eroding minority at both the national and the provincial levels. He needed time to accomplish three tasks. First, Bhutto had to get the other West Pakistani parties to agree on an alternative set of constitutional principles to those of the Awami League and to resist attending a meeting of the National Assembly until a prior consensus on constitutional issues had been worked out. Second, he needed to establish the Pakistan People's Party in the public mind as the sole representative and advocate of West Pakistani interests in the face of Bengali intransigence, while portraying Mujib as nothing more than a regional leader. Delays would induce friction within the Awami League and encourage either greater extremism in its position, fragmentation of the party, or an inclination to meet the terms of the PPP. The Awami League would have to move in some direction in response to initiatives taken by the PPP in the west. Finally, Bhutto had to exact a commitment from Yahya not to summon the National Assembly until he could develop a counterpoise to what he came to call a despotic East Pakistani majority intent on subverting collective West Pakistani interests, even though in his Dhaka press conference he indicated that he would not seek a delay in convening the Assembly.[32]

The Awami League responded to the talks differently. It thought that opposition to the six points was not intractable and that it could reach an accommodation with the PPP, which had neither strongly opposed the program nor presented an alternative constitution for consideration.[33] The Six-Point Demand was the only constitutional agenda available for discussion, but differences between the two sides on constitutional matters appeared resolvable. The Awami League also felt that once constitutional issues had been settled, no major differences between east and west on matters of public policy would remain. In any event, once the National Assembly was convened Bhutto could do little with the support of less than 30 percent of the membership. Bhutto, of course, was also aware of this.

There was, however, some suspicion within the Awami League that Bhutto was only a pawn in the hands of generals opposed to power being transferred to the east. This feeling had been compounded by Yahya's visit to Larkana just after his meetings in Dhaka. The Awami League suspected that Yahya and Bhutto had reached an understanding inimical to the interests of the League. Moreover, they had done so in a manner that depreciated the status of the majority leader. Mujib had gone to the President's House to meet Yahya when he was in Dhaka, and it enhanced the image of Bhutto, the minority leader, to be visited by the president at his opulent family estate. Because neither the reasons for the visit nor the substance of the discussions had been conveyed to the Awami League, its speculations centered on collusion.

By the end of January, however, Sheikh Mujib and the other leaders of the Awami League had the impression that an announcement of the date for convening the National Assembly was imminent and that the actual date of the first meeting could not be far off. Yahya had indicated before as well as during his journey to Dhaka that he favored holding the Assembly promptly, although he had said that Mujib would have to get Bhutto to agree and that it would be important to have a general consensus on constitutional and political matters before the Assembly met. The Awami League understood that Bhutto and the People's Party leadership were also prepared for a reasonably early opening of the Assembly. At the press conference in Dhaka on 30 January, after his meetings with the Awami League, Bhutto had declared that he was not going to ask the president for a delay in convening the Assembly and that all issues did not have to be resolved before it met.[34]

On 1 February, at a press conference in Lahore, Hafeez Pirzada, Bhutto's press secretary and close adviser, reiterated that although the Pakistan People's Party preferred early March as the date for convening the Assembly, it would not stand in the way if the Awami League wanted an earlier date. In talks with Mujib in Dhaka during the first days of February, Shaukat Hayat Khan, a leader of the Council Muslim League who had just met with Yahya, indicated to Mujib that an Assembly session by 15 February, the date Mujib desired, was completely out of the question since, even if Bhutto's concurrence could be secured, the East Pakistani Assembly Hall, where the National Assembly was to meet, would not be ready until the end of the month.[35] Shaukat noted that the end of February or 1 March would be much more reasonable and likely.

Mujib said that this would be acceptable, if not optimal, but that the announcement of a date should be made before 15 February. On 13 February Yahya announced that the National Assembly would be convened in Dhaka on 3 March 1971.

The Awami League leadership thus felt that the issue of holding the Assembly had been settled. It would be physically possible; the PPP, by its public pronouncements, had indicated that it would not insist upon delay; and the lag time before the convening of the Assembly would be ample to allow for the negotiations in West Pakistan that the PPP so much desired. For the next fortnight the Awami League thus busied itself in preparing a draft constitution and in attempting to develop support among the other West Pakistani parties.

POLITICAL FEARS AND STRATEGIES
OF POLARIZATION

The clarity of the Awami League's goals with respect to governance and the constitution and the intensity of its commitment to them led the PPP to devise a strategy aimed at diminishing the league's capacity to gain its objectives effectively, in the hope that this would compromise both its intentions and its collective will. A dual strategy was pursued. The first prong was to develop a reliable and effective counterbalance to the league by asserting control over the elected representatives of the People's Party and to build a common front among all the West Pakistani parties against the six points and for the inclusion of the PPP in the central government. The second prong was devoted to destroying the Awami League's credibility in West Pakistan by raising public doubt about its commitment to national and West Pakistani, as opposed to East Pakistani, interests.

After their return from Dhaka, Bhutto lost no time in attempting to assert control over the members of both the National and Provincial assemblies elected on the PPP ticket. By 10 February he had met with almost all the party representatives with the exception of those elected in the North-West Frontier Province. In each of the four meetings held, party members gave Bhutto a mandate to seek adjustments with the Awami League on the six points.

From 12 to 15 February Peshawar became the center of negotiations between leaders of the major political parties in the west.[36] Bhutto held meetings with Khan Abdul Qayyum Khan, leader of the Pakistan Muslim League (Qayyum); Maulana Mufti Mehmood and Maulana Hazarvi, leaders of the Jamiat-ul-Ulema-i-Islam (Hazarvi); Khan Abdul Wali Khan, leader of the National Awami Party (Wali Khan); and Air Marshal (retired) Nur Khan, organizing secretary of the Council Muslim League. Bhutto's goal in these talks was to develop a West Pakistani consensus on constitutional issues, common opposition to certain of the six points, and a commitment not to agree to the transfer of power until the Awami League agreed to modify the six points to accommodate West Pakistani views. Another element of Bhutto's strategy was to deny Mujib access to the support of any West Pakistani party. Mujib would thus become increasingly vulnerable to the charge among West Pakistanis of being nothing more than the leader of the majority party in East Pakistan, and he, Bhutto, would emerge as the leader of the majority party from West Pakistan and the spokesman for common interests there.

Although these leaders sympathized, albeit in differing degrees, with Bhutto's pleas, agreement on a constitutional format and the timing of the transfer of power proved elusive. No party had developed a constitutional plan, and the agenda for talks was still the six points, with the response to these points ranging from substantial rejection by the Muslim League (Qayyum) to near acceptance by the National Awami Party (Wali Khan). With the exception of Qayyum Khan, party leaders favored a prompt convening of the National Assembly, which was judged the appropriate arena for framing a constitution. Thus Bhutto's strategy to develop a common front did not succeed (indeed, it provided the Awami League with information about what Bhutto's current efforts in fact were). Toward the end of Bhutto's stay in Peshawar, to prepare for a new stratagem and add to the developing sense of crisis, Hayat Khan Sherpao, an important People's Party leader in the North-West Frontier Province, announced that after a Karachi meeting of all PPP National Assembly members scheduled for 20 and 21 February, Bhutto would hold a public meeting in Lahore and that it would be a historic one.[37]

The "Indian question" was to become increasingly important in Bhutto's drive to develop an image for himself and the Pakistan

People's Party as the only true representatives of West Pakistani interests. He was able fortuitously to dramatize his policy of confrontation with India and to encourage a perception in the west of Mujib's untrustworthiness with respect to their neighbor because of the "Ganga incident," in which an Indian Airlines flight from Srinagar to Jammu was hijacked by two young Kashmiri "freedom fighters" on 30 January 1971 and forced to land in Lahore. Bhutto visited the hijackers, applauded their heroism, and supported their request for asylum. He declared that this heroic action was a sign that no power on earth could stop the Kashmiri struggle and that the PPP would contact the Kashmiri National Liberation Front to offer its cooperation and assistance, which would also be given to the hijackers. Mujib, in contrast, expressed his abhorrence of the hijacking and urged the government to take "effective measures to prevent interested quarters from exploiting the situation for their nefarious ends."[38] It was, he said, an attempt to distort the process of the transfer of power.

During the first week of February, meanwhile, the president, in an effort to continue discussions, remove Mujib from the pressures of his party, and "test" his good faith and national commitment, had invited Mujib and some of his associates to come to Rawalpindi as his personal guests. Although both Governor Ahsan and members of the martial law administration in East Pakistan had urged Mujib to accept, he had declined, indicating that there was an upcoming meeting of Awami League members of both the National and Provincial assemblies and that the draft constitution had to be completed.[39] The government officers had advised Mujib that it would be wiser for him to accept the invitation, since a visit to the west would enhance his visibility as a national leader, enable him to elicit support there, and allow him to discuss problems with Yahya away from the heavy everyday demands of public life. His refusal to go might be taken by Yahya as an affront and an act of extreme discourtesy. Despite these pleas, Mujib had said that he could see no immediate need for him to disrupt his schedule by going, but that he would perhaps be prepared to go after the party meetings in mid month. He was in any event unable to depart right away. The president was then so informed.

A few days later Ahsan received a telegram from Yahya directing him to inform Mujib of his dissatisfaction with his refusal to visit

Rawalpindi and say that if Mujib did not do so as soon as possible, he would be entirely responsible for the serious consequences that would follow.[40] The governor was instructed to read the telegram to Mujib in the presence of Gen. Yaqub Khan, the martial law administrator and general officer commanding the Eastern Command. Ahsan called Mujib and met him together with Gen. Yaqub and Maj. Gen. Rao Farman Ali Khan. Just as they were meeting, the governor received a telephone call from the President's House instructing him to withhold the message. Ahsan then merely renewed his plea that Mujib visit Rawalpindi. The following morning he was told to burn the telegram. Ultimately, Mujib was prevailed upon to plan a short visit to the west, but the plan was dropped because of subsequent events.

In the context of the Ganga hijacking and amid reports that Bhutto was endeavoring to develop a united front of West Pakistani parties against the Awami League and the six points, the president's unexpected invitation, with no indication of the substantive issues to be discussed, produced a sense of foreboding among the Bengali elite.[41] The leaders of the Awami League perceived the failure to set a date for the meeting of the National Assembly as a violation of the intentions expressed by the president in January; moreover, they saw Bhutto's actions as incongruous with the sentiments he had expressed in Dhaka.

In talks with visiting West Pakistani political leaders in early February, Mujib had expressed fear that Yahya would neither summon the Assembly nor transfer power to the Awami League. He believed that Yahya, Bhutto, and certain generals were in collusion, with Bhutto functioning as the president's stalking-horse by creating conditions that would offer an excuse not to transfer power (the risk to Bhutto being minimal, since he would not gain power under present circumstances but might hope to if they were fundamentally changed).[42] The evidence—reluctance to fix a date for the Assembly, insistence on prior agreement on constitutional issues, suggestions that the Awami League rule in concert with the People's Party, and the pressure certain generals were bringing to bear on party leaders in West Pakistan to cooperate with Bhutto and avoid the overtures of the Awami League—certainly suggested that this was true, Mujib observed. He told at least one major party leader from the west that he had solid private evidence of this collusion, substantiating what publicly seemed to be the case. He had further commented that if the results of the elections were not honored and power were not transferred to the Awami League in consonance with accepted democratic practice, he could not be held responsible for the political consequences.

The Awami League responded to events in the west by renewing its affirmation of the six points to the Bengali public and at the same time calling for a meeting of the National Assembly and continuing to seek agreement with West Pakistani parties. After a meeting of the League's working committee on 14 February, party leaders expressed their pleasure with the president's announcement that the National Assembly would be convened on 3 March in Dhaka, while Tajuddin indicated that the League would continue to seek a broad consensus with other parties and that he was "more than optimistic" about the ultimate success of the quest. If it should not prove possible, he added, "the forces of democracy should be allowed to take care of the situation."[43] In an address to a meeting of the Awami League National and Provincial assembly members the following day, Mujib declared that the six points were now "public" and not "personal or party property"; they were not susceptible to "adjustment and expansion," and he warned his adversaries that the current situation was far different from those in the 1950s when the threat of force had been used to silence Bengali protest. At the conclusion of this meeting Mujib was voted carte blanche to use whatever strategy was appropriate to reestablish representative government and implement the party program.[44]

After his unsuccessful meetings with the other West Pakistani political leaders in Peshawar and the president's call for the inauguration of the National Assembly, Bhutto announced on 15 February that the People's Party would not go to Dhaka for the opening of the Assembly on 3 March. First he stated that PPP representatives could not attend "only to endorse the constitution already prepared by a party and return humiliated. If we are not heard and even reasonable proposals put up by us are not considered, I don't see the purpose to go there."[45] He asserted that the Awami League had not offered "reciprocity," which was essential on its part if the PPP were ever to attend. He declared that the PPP had gone as far as it could possibly go on the six points: he accepted the first and sixth points and was not without hope for the points on trade and taxation, but under no circumstances would he accept a West Pakistani subfederation. He also noted that the requisites for holding a meeting of the Assembly were not complete. He had not had enough time to create the necessary consensus. He further reminded his listeners that Mujib had not visited West Pakistan, supposedly because he found the atmosphere there "uncongenial," whereas both he and Yahya had gone to Dhaka. If it was difficult for Mujib to come to West Pakistan, it was doubly difficult for him and the PPP to go to East Pakistan given the Awami League's ingratiating attitude toward India and the increasingly threatening posture of Indira Gandhi's government toward Pakistan. He could not, he declared, put his party members in the position of being a "double hostage" in Dhaka, to Indian hostility on the one hand and Awami League intransigence on the other.[46] As had been the case in the past, however, the possibility of compromise accompanied tough positions stated in harsh terms. Bhutto indicated that he would accept any assurance from Mujib, even through private channels, that there would be reciprocity in constitutional deliberation. He would give a final decision on whether he would participate or not at a PPP meeting scheduled to be held in Karachi.

This speech elicited only mild rebuke from the Awami League leaders, who described it as being at once aggressive and derogatory and surprising since it was not in character with the temper of the PPP–Awami League talks in Dhaka. Other East Pakistani leaders responded more harshly. Nurul Amin, president of the Pakistan Democratic Party, a former chief minister of East Pakistan, and one of the two opposition National Assembly members elected from the eastern province, deplored Bhutto's "double hostage" comment and urged all members to attend the first session; Ataur Rahman Khan, president of the Pakistan National League and also a former chief minister of East Pakistan, declared that Bhutto's stand was nothing less than an attempt to divide Pakistan.[47]

Bhutto's political offensive did not stop. In a speech on 17 February he declared that conditions of hostility between India and Pakistan as they currently existed had in the past led to war, and that in a situation so fraught with crisis it was imperative that his party members be with their own people. He further insisted that there were only three political forces in the country—the Awami League, the Pakistan People's Party, and the armed forces—and that they had to come to an agreement if a way was to be found out of the present impasse. In a reference to talks between Mujib and the leaders of other parties, he observed that he did not recognize any "fourth power," and that attempts to mediate and arbitrate would only complicate matters—there was no room for further negotiation with the Awami League. A National Assembly meeting in Dhaka would be a "slaughter house," he declared.[48]

Not long after Bhutto's speech, Mujib visited a high-ranking member of the government in Dhaka and informed him with finality that he would not go to West Pakistan—if Dhaka would be a slaughterhouse for Bhutto, then West Pakistan would most certainly be the same for him.[49]

Late on 18 February, Bhutto was summoned by Yahya to Rawalpindi for a meeting. In a statement to the press upon his arrival at the Rawalpindi airport, Bhutto presented a less rigid attitude than he had the day before by suggesting the possibility of his going to Dhaka if substantive adjustments were made by the Awami League concerning foreign trade, currency, and taxation.[50] Portraying the current crisis as something from the theater of the absurd, he observed that framing a constitution for Pakistan without the participation of the PPP would be "like staging Hamlet without the Prince of Denmark." After his meeting with Yahya, Bhutto informed the press that he had told the president that the current crisis was neither of his nor of the People's Party's making. He had gone from one end of the country to the other in an effort to develop a consensus. He noted that he and the president had agreed that there was a serious crisis and said that they were both aware of its "implications." He also indirectly suggested what was ultimately to unfold when he observed that the PPP had a political approach to the crisis, but that the military regime could not, since it was not a political party. Finally, continuing what was to become a repeated refrain, Bhutto emphasized the severity of the tensions between Pakistan and India. He declared: "[My] primary duty is with the people, the peasants and the working class. My place today is in villages and I call upon my partymen to go to the people, to give them leadership, to stand by them and to be a source of strength in case there is an attempt by the predatory aggressor."[51]

PREPARATION FOR MILITARY ACTION

The government's worst fear at this time was that convening the National Assembly in Dhaka would severely diminish its control and would place the armed forces in a precarious position. Given the Awami League's overwhelming majority, the east for all practical purposes would be under alien control; and if Bhutto were true to his word, the west might be in a state of upheaval and perhaps ungovernable. The prospect of military action in the two most politically active provinces—Punjab and Sind, where the PPP had demonstrated its popular support—was not attractive; nor could the military handle enemies on two fronts.

First and foremost, Yahya wanted to put Mujib in his place, to reestablish the supremacy of the president's office, which he sensed was being ignored by people in the east. The government needed to assert itself as an active participant in the resolution of the developing stalemate in negotiations. According to one able military officer in the regime, Yahya declared in an important meeting on 20 February that Mujib was not "behaving," that he needed to "sort this bastard out," and that he wanted "to test his loyalty." Some kind of action would have to be taken against Mujib unless he were made "to see sense."[52] It was decided that to deal with the situation the government needed to think seriously about new options, including taking limited military action in the east. The question was what action to take and when.

The same day, at a meeting of several officers in the martial law administration from both Rawalpindi and Dhaka, Yahya was presented with four plausible scenarios for taking action against Mujib and the Awami League.[53] The first involved an immediate show of military force, much in line with what had happened with the dismissal of the United Front government of A. K. Fazlul Huq in 1954, but with a firmer use of force to quell any opposition. In the second scenario, the military could step in after the constitution was presented to the National Assembly. If West Pakistani leaders found it totally unacceptable and saw little chance of a workable compromise, they could request the president to act on behalf of national integrity. A third possibility would be to allow the National Assembly to convene, but for the president to put new teeth in the administration of martial law and to refrain from approving the constitution if the Awami League were bent on ramming one through based on the Six-Point Demand. A fourth option was to allow Mujib to assume power—he could do no harm, it was argued, and within six months he would become the most unpopular man in East Pakistan. He would endeavor to centralize power in his hands and would find the six points alien to his personal style and unworkable. Yahya emphatically rejected the last scenario, although an officer from Dhaka asked him to reconsider.

On 21 February Yahya instructed the civilian cabinet he had appointed to replace his Council on Administration in 1969 to resign. Its usefulness as a civilianizing feature of the regime had passed, and it would either be "a nuisance" if military action followed or would be replaced by a new elected government if negotiations resulted in consensus. Moreover, because five of its members were Bengali, discussing East Pakistan in the cabinet was impossible for fear of a breach of confidence. The work of government could easily be carried on by the secretaries of the ministries, who had been the effective managers all along, having had direct access to Yahya through his military secretary without going through the ministers under whom they formally served. The military had in any case always doubted the usefulness of the civilian cabinet. One high-ranking general officer called the ministers "a bunch of smart alecks"—an unnecessary bottleneck to efficient administration.[54] The president accordingly decided that he would govern through advisers until the National Assembly met and a new government, whatever shape it might take, was formed. He called the cabinet to his house for what one officer attending called a formal "champagne, slosh-up dinner," thanked them for their assistance, and bid them good-bye.[55]

On 20 and 21 February the People's Party members of the National and Provincial assemblies met in Karachi. They unanimously accepted Bhutto's appeal not to attend the first National Assembly session.[56] Adding to the intensity of the drama, Bhutto on the eve of the meetings named his successors—Miraj Mohammed Khan and Ghulam Mustafa Khar—in case anything should happen to him. In an effort to ensure the support of his party's Assembly members, Bhutto was able to convince the president to amend article 11(1) of the Legal Framework Order to allow any National Assembly member to resign his seat before the opening of the Assembly.[57] This led East and West Pakistanis alike to believe that Bhutto enjoyed special access to and influence with Yahya.

The following day, all the PPP Assembly members assured Bhutto that they would resign en bloc if the National Assembly convened without them and also swore an oath on the Quran that they would support Bhutto without reservation in his negotiation of a political settlement with the Awami League. The representatives in addition unanimously passed a party declaration that confirmed the darkest suspicions the Awami League had of the PPP leadership. It began by "taking note of the grave national crisis arising out of the different approaches to the constitutional problem, of the chauvinist designs of the Indian Government in massing troops on the borders of West Pakistan, of the increasing machinations of anti-national obscurantists and capitalist elements as well as of the imperialist and neo-colonialist powers." Among other things it then went on to reject "the authoritarian principle of elected despotism," offered support to the people of Jammu and Kashmir until they finally achieved self-determination, and declared that the best form of government for Pakistan was a federation "in its truest sense" that would include "the necessary institution at the centre in which each federating unit will be represented on an equal basis and have the right to be heard in matters affecting its interests and in which the units can coordinate their planning and policy." The resolution also stated that the central government must have the right to raise necessary revenues directly and that "the subjects of foreign trade and aid should be assigned to the federal government and the Constitution must ensure free movement of goods and services and of Pakistani citizens between the Provinces." The Awami League rejected the declaration as a return to the imperial patterns of the past and as patently unacceptable.[58]

It was in this context that the president, in his role as chief martial law administrator, presided over a meeting on 22 February—the same day that the resignation of the civilian cabinet became effective—of all governors and martial law administrators, who had been called to discuss the crisis. The meeting was also attended by the heads of the military and civilian intelligence services.[59] At the outset Yahya noted the difficulty of getting the PPP to attend the National Assembly because of the Awami League's "uncompromising and rigid" stand on the six points. He therefore gave it as his opinion that a meeting of the National Assembly would serve no useful purpose.

A number of those present then firmly expressed their opposition to the six points and declared that the irascibility of Mujib was the cause of the country's present political woes. One martial law administrator said that unless pressure were brought to bear on the National Assembly members in his province, they were likely to attend the National Assembly and seek a compromise with Mujib. One governor, in an effort to enable the political process to continue, suggested that Yahya should appeal to the West Pakistani Assembly members to attend the National Assembly by assuring them that he would never authenticate a constitution that did not safeguard the integrity of Pakistan. The participants further recommended that the president issue a like appeal to the East Pakistani members for a commitment that they not use their "brute majority" against West Pakistani interests. Admiral Ahsan, the governor of East Pakistan, reminded those in attendance that the six points were not new and that the president had been at least neutral concerning them during his talks in Dhaka in January. The preaching of the six points had been tolerated for a year—they had never been denounced by the government as transgressions of the martial law regulations. He also observed that whatever flexibility there might be in the six-points scheme, Mujib was not likely to announce it beforehand.

After this general meeting Yahya beckoned several officers—Generals Hamid, Peerzada, and Yaqub and Admiral Ahsan—to a separate room. He told them that he intended to postpone the meeting of the National Assembly to give the parties more time to resolve their differences. Yahya dismissed suggestions that he instead cancel the 120-day limit for framing the constitution after the first meeting of the Assembly.

Ahsan advised the president that the reaction in the east to postponement would be adverse and immediate. Public order would be difficult to maintain. The provincial civil service and police were largely Bengali, as were the majority of the East Pakistan Rifles. Many of those employed by the government had supported the Awami League in the elections and had long suffered what they felt to be the stifling of their careers because of West Pakistani dominance. Furthermore, those who had been born since independence did not feel the ties of nationhood that the older political generation shared. If politics were turned into the streets, the participants would not be as dedicated as the political elite to the integrity of the state.

Those who did not hold positions in the eastern province judged Ahsan's view needlessly alarmist and as representing a continuation of a policy that had proved bankrupt. Yahya then indicated that he had also decided to take two additional steps: he was going to combine the posts of governor and martial law administrator in East Pakistan and impose stricter press censorship and tighter enforcement of martial law. He intended to announce the postponement on 1 March and directed Ahsan to inform Mujib twenty-four hours in advance.

The top governmental and martial law administrators stationed in Dhaka thought the decision to postpone the Assembly and take military action, if necessary, in the east was ill advised. On 23 February, the day after the meeting of the martial law administrators, a delegation attempted to persuade Yahya that the postponement and a stiffening of martial law to discourage public disturbances did not represent an appropriate course of action by any stretch of the imagination.[60] Dissent there certainly would be, and it would be difficult to control. Nor could the possibility of armed resistance be discounted, and the reliability of the Bengali police and constabulary units was not at all assured. Once disrupted in such fashion, the political process would be hard to begin again, and the Indian government could exacerbate the situation by encouraging antigovernment and anti–West Pakistani attitudes and actions in the east. The president replied that they could convince him, but that they should just try to convince Bhutto.

Late on 25 February, Governor Ahsan and Maj. Gen. Rao Farman Ali Khan, in charge of civil affairs in the martial law administration of East Pakistan, went to Karachi to meet with Bhutto to convey these concerns and to persuade him of their views. Bhutto told them that they should not be so concerned and that they certainly should not worry about a guerrilla war. The Awami League, he advised them, was a bourgeois party, and such parties were as incapable of governing Pakistan now as they had been in the past; they were even far less able to launch and sustain a guerrilla war. The delegation returned to Rawalpindi and informed

Yahya of Bhutto's position. Yahya then indicated with finality his decision to announce postponement of the National Assembly on 1 March and reaffirmed his directive to Governor Ahsan that Mujib be informed twenty-four hours before.

While the representatives of the Pakistan People's Party were meeting in Karachi and the martial law administrators were meeting in Rawalpindi, Mujib and other Awami League leaders were meeting with Maulana Mufti Mehmood and Maulana Hazarvi of the Jamiat-ul-Ulema-i-Islam party in Dhaka. The Awami League used the talks to signal West Pakistani leaders, and particularly the PPP, that once the Assembly met the Awami League would be responsive in the constitution-making process to the interests and suggestions of the members from the provinces of West Pakistan.[61] In these meetings Mujib reiterated his call for representatives to come to Dhaka four or five days before the convening of the Assembly to discuss the constitution; he also invited economic experts from West Pakistan to take part. He claimed that the fears of some West Pakistani leaders about the distribution of the taxing power as proposed by the Awami League were unfounded, since the central government would have first call on a proportion of all tax revenues collected by the provincial governments; this arrangement would have constitutional sanction, and a constitutionally authorized national financial commission would review and revise the arrangement as necessary. Foreign trade and aid, he argued, would not be handled autonomously by each province, but would be administered within the larger framework of foreign policy.

The leaders of the smaller West Pakistani parties accepted these statements as signs of Mujib's sincerity and commitment to show "reciprocity" and to accommodate alternative points of view in the constitution-making process. Yet neither the PPP nor the martial law administrators acknowledged Mujib's conciliatory efforts in their meetings.[62]

The Awami League leaders were deeply concerned about the dismissal of the cabinet on 21 February, and they could barely control their anger over the reports of the meetings of the PPP representatives and the martial law administrators. In a statement read to the press on 24 February, Mujib declared that powerful groups in West Pakistan were bent upon returning to the practices of the 1950s and had been deliberately fabricating an "artificial crisis" to "sabotage the making of a constitution by the elected representatives of the people and the transfer of power to them." He noted that the Awami League had purposely remained silent to "avoid poisoning the atmosphere by bitter controversy." He then reviewed the series of discussions that he had held with party leaders from the west, who had included members of all parties with any appreciable representation in the National Assembly. The Awami League had been encouraged by the announcement of a date for the National Assembly, since this seemed to indicate a departure from the tradition of conspiratorial politics that had dominated the 1950s—the dismissal of the East Bengal government in 1954, the dissolution of the Constituent Assembly in 1955, and the imposition of military rule in 1958. Yet it appeared that conspiratorial elements were preparing to strike again. Bhutto and the PPP in particular were taking positions aimed at subverting the constitutional process. Given the background of economic domination by the west, "the insistence upon the retention of foreign trade and aid in the Centre appears all too clearly to be designed not to secure the interest of national integrity but to ensure the retention in the hands of the Centre of the principal instruments required for the colonial exploitation of Bangladesh." The proposal to "share" power at the center was similarly a move to reduce the Bengali majority in the national community to the position of a perpetual minority. Other objections raised by the PPP, Mujib declared, were gross distortions of the meaning and intent of the six points, which he had been elaborating and clarifying to a wide range of West Pakistani leaders.[63]

After his return to Dhaka, Governor Ahsan met with Mujib to inform him that Yahya was under immense pressure to postpone the Assembly. He strongly urged Mujib to go to Rawalpindi to help break the deadlock.[64] Although visibly shaken by this unfolding of events, Mujib replied that because of the resistance in the west to eastern interests in the past, additional overtures on his part would make no difference and might even give the western groups reason to believe that their strategies were finally achieving success.

Communications between Rawalpindi and Dhaka came to a standstill during the last few days of February, and the government in East Pakistan was unaware of what was transpiring in the President's House. On 27 February, therefore, Ahsan sent an urgent telegram to Yahya reviewing the situation and advising him that if the Assembly was postponed, there would be an outbreak of lawlessness that could not be controlled by the civil administration. The economy, which was already disrupted and fragile, would come to a grinding halt. There was no reply.[65]

As late as 28 February there was still hope among some Awami Leaguers that the National Assembly would be convened as scheduled.[66] Mujib had observed to Ahsan the day before that Yahya had reserved space on a PIA flight to Dhaka. By 27 February all the parties in the western provinces, with the notable exceptions of the Pakistan People's Party and the Muslim League (Qayyum), had decided to attend the opening session, though several party leaders had made it clear that their participation was not to be construed as concurrence with the six-point program in toto and that they expected certain accommodations to be worked out on the floor of the Assembly.

Attention in the west was focused on the speech that Bhutto was to make in Lahore. The choice of Lahore for the historic declaration that Hayat Mohammed Khan Sherpao had promised Bhutto would deliver was made for symbolic as well as more immediate political reasons. In Lahore, as Bhutto was to remind his listeners, Jinnah had made his demand for Pakistan thirty years before, and it was thus only fitting that Bhutto should appeal for a renewed commitment to maintaining the existence and life of the child of that dream there. Furthermore, the PPP had won the bulk of its seats to the National Assembly in the Punjab, of which Lahore was the provincial capital. Representatives from this province in the PPP were also the staunchest advocates of a strong central government and were the most resistant to a transfer of power to the Awami League, especially without some guarantee of leverage and control.[67] As anticipated, the turnout at the rally was immense, the crowd enthusiastic.

In his speech on 28 February, Bhutto threatened personal as well as public harm if he were denied control of the political situation. At the same time, he endeavored to exonerate himself from charges of responsibility for the present crisis and the suspicion, misunderstanding, and rancor that attended it. In his customary earthy language and style, Bhutto promised to "break the legs" of any member of his party brazen enough to go to Dhaka. He told the other Assembly members that they had better go on a "one-way ticket," suggesting that they would be traitors to the cause of the people of West Pakistan and would never be welcome home again. If the Assembly were held without his conditions being met, he would call a general strike and launch political agitation "from the Khyber to Karachi." Bhutto's comments were unsettling to members of the government because of current public unrest over inflation and the scarcity of essential commodities as well as their almost obsessive concern with maintaining public order.[68] They felt confident, however, that they could handle public unrest in the east, but only with continued public support in the west. Widespread public unrest in the west would make the central government's position untenable.

On the evening of 28 February, following the president's directive of a few days earlier, Ahsan called Mujib and Tajuddin to the Governor's House to inform them that Yahya was going to announce the postponement of the National Assembly in his address to the nation the following day.[69] Ahsan tried to assure them that it would be only for a short time, but Mujib was not to be mollified. He said that the authorities were bent on destroying not only him but also Pakistan. Tajuddin observed that this confirmed their darkest suspicions that West Pakistan would never hand over power to a party from the east. After the formal meeting, Mujib asked Ahsan if they could meet briefly in private. He pleaded that a new date for the convening of the Assembly be given in the president's speech announcing the postponement. Mujib would then have some flexibility and would be able to control the reaction to the announcement. Otherwise he could not.

After the Awami League leaders had left, Ahsan and Generals Yaqub and Farman Ali discussed what was to be done. Between 9 and 10 P.M. they tried to reach Yahya by telephone. The president's personal staff officer in Rawalpindi suggested the governor call the president in Karachi, where Ahsan spoke with Maj. Gen. Ghulam Umar, the head of the National Security Council. Umar informed him that the president was "otherwise indisposed," but that he would relay the message expressing the concern of the officers in the east. Ahsan then spoke with General Hamid, the army chief of staff, in Sialkot, in the Punjab, urging him to inform the president of the gravity of the situation. Hamid replied that he was not conversant with political matters but that he would try to get in touch with Yahya. The governor then drafted and sent a telex to Yahya in Karachi, which concluded: "I beg you even at this late hour to give a new date for the summoning of the Assembly and not to postpone it sine die, otherwise . . . we will have reached the point of no return."[70]

Then, at 10:30 P.M., Ahsan received a telegram informing him that he was being relieved of his duties as governor of East Pakistan and being replaced by Yaqub.

5

Crisis Bargaining

Negotiations to save Pakistan after the postponement of the National Assembly approximated those between sovereign states. Postponement changed the context radically. Central authority in East Pakistan collapsed completely. Government offices ceased to function, and the authority of the martial law administrator, in the words of one senior army officer, "extended no further than his Headquarters."[1] Regulations imposing stricter censorship went unheeded, and curfews were purposefully violated, resulting in shootings by the army and police. In Dhaka troops had returned to their barracks by 5 March, with an accompanying statement from the martial law authorities that lawlessness had been contained largely because of an appeal by Mujib for nonviolent resistance.[2]

Although hoping that the decision to postpone the Assembly sine die might be rescinded before it was announced, the Awami League leadership had been duly informed by Governor Ahsan of the projected announcement. The Bengali public had not and was unprepared for postponement. Upon hearing the announcement on 1 March, people filled the streets of Dhaka and the district towns with what was described by government, journalistic, and diplomatic sources alike as a demonstration of collective anguish rather than of anger.[3] The spontaneity and intensity of this response, like the electoral verdict three months before, surprised many political leaders in both east and west. The Awami League leadership was able to capitalize on the tension, although it was also to become a captive of it. Units of the Pakistan army in the east, whether because of surprise, inadequate forces, or design, were unable to control this public upsurge, and they became increasingly constrained in their movements and even in their procurement of supplies.

The Awami League assumed authority, although by default rather than by design, and after a period of uncertainty the party proceeded to effectively exercise the powers of a legitimate government. Political leaders in the west were taken aback by the hostility, long held in sublimation, unleashed against people from the west, whether they were government servants, men in uniform, or the non-Bengali Urdu-speaking "Biharis" who had settled as refugees at the cultural margins of Bengali society after partition and now paid the price for their marginality and their support for a succession of West Pakistani–dominated regimes. Authority emanating from the west could not contain the public outcry; it could only be guided and its excesses ameliorated somewhat by political leaders in the east.

REACTION AND REDEPLOYMENT

The first response of the Awami League was given by Sheikh Mujib on 1 March after a meeting of the Awami League parliamentary party at the Hotel Purbani in Dhaka. Mujib told the waiting press corps that he was prepared to make any sacrifice necessary for the emancipation of his people. He alleged that the postponement was yet another manifestation of a conspiracy against the Awami League and the people of Bengal on the part of vested economic and bureaucratic interests in the west. He advised his listeners that they would "see history made if the conspirators fail to come to their senses" and declared that the action to postpone, taken without inviting the advice of the majority party, would not go "unchallenged."[4]

On the following day Mujib outlined the initial Awami League plan of action at a public meeting organized by student groups.[5] A strike that was to take effect in Dhaka on 3 March would be expanded into a provincewide *hartal* (a nonviolent noncooperation movement), during which time all governmental and commercial activities were to cease from early morning until mid afternoon. The *hartal* was to affect all government offices; the courts; semi-governmental and autonomous corporations; the airlines, railways, and other public and private transport; communication services; and mills, factories, and all other industrial and commercial establishments.[6] The day the National Assembly was to have been convened, 3 March, was also declared a "Day of Mourning." Mujib announced that a mass rally would be held at the Ramna Race

Course on 7 March, at which time he would issue and elaborate on further directives. Mujib also then urged, as he was to the following day, that the *hartal* be conducted as a "peaceful *satyagraha*" and declared that everyone living in Bangladesh regardless of language or place of origin was a Bengali whose life and property were to be honored and protected.[7] He and the other speakers asked for communal harmony between Hindu and Muslim and between Bengali and non-Bengali. Since the postponement people had been killed and injured by the police and army as well as in vengeance taken by Bengalis against non-Bengalis.[8] In this speech Mujib also first voiced a premonition of death, observing that this might be his "last speech," but said that if he were not present at the 7 March rally, others would be able to provide direction in his place.[9]

The *hartal* was successful beyond expectation. East Pakistan was cut off from the world, as it had been during the 1965 Indo-Pakistani war. This time, however, it was by East Pakistani choice and design. Awami League directives were treated as authoritative writ, while the authority of the martial law administration was limited exclusively to military movement and logistics.[10] Between the postponement of the National Assembly and the military crackdown four weeks later, two systems of authority prevailed in East Pakistan. One was civil and political, with the Awami League governing a new self-proclaimed "Bangladesh"; the other was military, its control confined to cantonments, with the martial law administration constituting the functional equivalent of a diplomatic legation in a hostile land.

Bhutto and the Pakistan People's Party expressed surprise at the reaction in East Pakistan to the postponement and disclaimed any responsibility for what had occurred. In a press conference on 2 March, Bhutto insisted that his party had never rejected the six points, but had worked tirelessly to come as close to them as possible, both within the PPP and in conjunction with public opinion in the west. In his inimitable fashion, he also repeated again that while he did not reject the six points, he did not accept them either, but was prepared to negotiate about them. The postponement was merely designed to "provide the two major parties with an opportunity to have another dialogue." He indicated that he was prepared to meet with the "other majority party" anywhere, anytime, to attempt to break the deadlock. If the Awami

League was not prepared to meet, then he observed "the onus for the consequences will not be on us."[11]

In contrast to the image of reasonableness with which he sought to characterize his intentions and behavior, Bhutto portrayed the response of the Awami League as excessive, self-serving, and disloyal to the integrity of Pakistan, saying:

> It is most unfortunate that a necessary postponement of the National Assembly Session should have incited a disproportionate reaction in the East Pakistan Awami League. Surely, nothing is lost, if the promise of United Pakistan is accepted, by the delay of a few days to enable the major parties of the whole of Pakistan to come to an agreement upon the nature of (the) constitution that ought to last for years and years to come. The constitution should not be made the excuse to break up Pakistan.[12]

The response of the People's Party to the new crisis in East Pakistan was consistent with its previous strategy and in part a fulfillment of it. By announcing the postponement, President Yahya had overtly accepted the PPP as the majority party of West Pakistan, with political standing equal to that of the Awami League. The PPP remained committed to a transfer of power, but only if it could force the Awami League into negotiating with it and accepting a coalition with it as the price for forming a government and framing a constitution. Bhutto had been able to magnify doubts within the army as well as among the West Pakistani public about the fidelity of the Awami League to the integrity of Pakistan. By pushing Mujib into extremist positions, the PPP appeared politically dependable and rational in contrast. And, finally, Bhutto had successfully managed to reassert his image as the victor in a contest against opponents much stronger, though less clever and virtuous, than he.[13]

Although they had been forewarned of it by officers in the east, the core decision makers in the central government and the army had not anticipated the intensity of the resistance with which the postponement was met in East Pakistan, and they were angered by the inability of the army to restore order in the province.[14] The expectation had been that the postponement, together with the firm hand of the army discouraging dissent, would force the Awami League leadership to realize that prior agreement on outstanding political and constitutional issues was mandatory before the convening of the National Assembly, and that this would require serious negotiation among the major parties. The government had neither developed nor even considered alternative strategies to meet the potential response in the east. The accepted dogma was that, regardless of its protestations, the Awami League would be awakened to the power of the central government to control the direction of political affairs as it had in the past. It was felt that the Bengalis would "knuckle under" when confronted with West Pakistani military force, and that not much more would be required than the usual "company in Chittagong and battalion in Dhaka."[15]

The army high command had been prepared to provide the troops necessary to restore "order" in East Pakistan. The commander in chief of the army, Gen. Abdul Hamid Khan, had told General Yaqub at the time of the meeting of the martial law administrators in February that two divisions were in reserve near Karachi ready to be used if "a military solution according to plan" was pursued and indicated that they were available to Yaqub if he needed reinforcements to carry out the more limited objective of reasserting central authority. Yaqub had indicated that the forces at his command were sufficient for the task, and that in any event the transporting of troops would be unnecessarily alarming in the existing circumstances. Within twenty-four hours after his return to Dhaka, however, General Yaqub wired that limited reinforcements were essential. The equivalent of one-and-a-half battalions was sent the next day.

Given the resources that they were prepared to commit, the president and his military advisers judged that only mismanagement or a lack of will on the part of the Eastern Command could account for its lack of success.[16] But the contradictory judgments of what was militarily possible after the postponement were a function of different perceptions of the political situation in the east and of what the consequences of different forms of military involvement would be. The military command in the west saw the operational orders to reinstate public order as meaning the utilization of the minimum force necessary. The military command in the east, after returning from the February meetings in West Pakistan, judged that nothing short of military action throughout the province would allow it to accomplish its mission, which, even if possible, would result in a situation that would preclude a return to

political negotiation.[17] A rigorous enforcement of martial law
would have completed the alienation of the Bengalis and endan-
gered the physical safety of the army as well. The implementation
of orders was defined as a police function—curbing riots and
preventing the destruction of life and property. The army found its
task more difficult than it had previously because of strong resistance to its authority in district towns as well as in Dhaka, but its
situation was also eased by Mujib's pleas for nonviolence.[18]

In an effort to bring coherence between what was expected in
the west and what was judged to be possible by those in authority
in the east, Yaqub wired Yahya on the morning of 3 March explaining the urgency of the situation and insisting that since it was
changing from "minute to minute," it was essential that Yahya
come to Dhaka. At approximately 10:00 P.M. General Peerzada
telephoned Yaqub to inform him that the president was not coming. Later that night Yaqub submitted his resignation as governor
and martial law administrator of East Pakistan, and with his resignation curfews were lifted and troops in most areas were returned
to their barracks.[19]

THE GOVERNMENT'S CONCESSION

Immediately after announcing the postponement of the assembly,
the government sought to reopen political negotiations as it had
planned. The timing was accelerated by the events in the east and
the army's inability, for whatever reason, to thwart the public
turbulence, which the government perceived to be induced and
abetted by the Awami League. The central issue for the government was the creation of an appropriate forum, short of a meeting
of the National Assembly, that would be conducive to party leaders
forging a political solution. The institutional vehicle was decided
upon in a meeting on 2 March between President Yahya and
Bhutto, accompanied by several of his key advisers—J. A. Rahim,
Hafeez Pirzada, Mustafa Khar, and Mumtaz Ali Bhutto. The latter
agreed to participate in a roundtable conference of all parties
represented in the National Assembly; they had urged just such a
meeting in the past so that they could face the Awami League in a
situation that would be morally, though not legally, binding.[20] The
following day Yahya called for a conference of party leaders to be

held 10 March in Dhaka, to be followed by the convening of the National Assembly within a couple of weeks.[21]

The decision to call an all-party conference, like the decision to postpone the National Assembly, was made without consulting the Awami League. Although party leaders in the west were initially receptive to the idea of such a conference, the Awami League leadership firmly opposed participation, and on 3 March Mujib announced that he would not attend:

> The radio announcement of the proposed invitation to the political leaders to sit with the President of Pakistan in conference in Dacca on March 10, coming as it does in the wake of widespread killing of the unarmed civilian population in Dacca, Chittagong and other places in Bangladesh, while the blood of the martyrs on the streets is hardly dry, while some of the dead are still lying unburied and hundreds are fighting death in hospitals comes as a cruel joke. This is more so since we are being called upon to sit with certain elements whose devious machinations are responsible for the death of innocent and unarmed peasants, workers and students. With the military build-up continuing [and] with [the] harsh language of weapons still ringing in our ears[,] the invitation to such a conference is in effect being made at gun point. Under these circumstances, the question of accepting such invitations does not arise. I, therefore, reject such an invitation.[22]

He was also unprepared, as leader of the majority party in the National Assembly, to sit as an equal with other party leaders, all but one of whom were from West Pakistan. Not only would the Awami League be placed in the position of a minority party at such a conference, but the province of East Pakistan would also be relegated to a minority position, even though it held a majority of the elected representatives and the citizenry of Pakistan.[23] The president and his advisers, encouraged by commentary from the PPP, perceived this as yet another affront to the government and to West Pakistan on the part of Mujib and the Awami League that suggested at best an insensitivity to the interests of the west and at worst a commitment to the breakup of the state.[24]

On 5 March, in an effort to reestablish more direct communication between the government in the east and the authorities in the west after Yahya's refusal to go to Dhaka and Mujib's refusal to participate in an all-party conference, Maj. Gen. Rao Farman Ali Khan went to Rawalpindi, as he had two weeks earlier, to stress the gravity of the situation and the need for Yahya to communicate with Mujib. Late in the evening of 4 March, Farman Ali had gone to meet Mujib at his home in Dhan Mandi and had asked, "Can Pakistan be saved?" Mujib had replied without hesitation that it could, but then, as was his wont, began a recitation of the historical grievances of the Bengalis and remarked on the apparent inability of West Pakistanis to accept a Bengali-dominated government.[25] Given the present situation, Farman Ali then asked, what precisely could be done to salvage the situation? Mujib replied that first of all there should be no opposition to the six points. Bhutto had not opposed any of their provisions during their private talks in January, but had been interested only in cabinet positions for his party leaders and in the presidency for himself.[26] But the current situation, Mujib said, also required that the government make commitments beyond the six points, among them abrogation of martial law and the transfer of power.

Tajuddin joined the conversation at this juncture and insisted that the only solution to the present impasse was to have the National Assembly convene as two separate constituent assemblies, one for the east and one for the west, to prepare constitutional drafts, and then to meet as one to complete the final document. Tajuddin indicated that representatives of the Awami League could not sit in the same room with Bhutto, who was "murderer number one" as far as the Bengalis were concerned, but they would be able to talk with Yahya, although he had unwittingly become "murderer number two."[27] Negotiating directly with Bhutto was impossible after his unilateral "veto" of the convening of the National Assembly and after he had so viciously and publicly impugned the character and motives of the Bengali people and the Awami League.

The following morning Farman Ali conveyed these sentiments to Yahya at the President's House in Rawalpindi. The president responded that he planned to make a statement the next day and that he was committed to finding a political solution, but from a position of strength. He indicated that he was prepared to talk directly with Mujib and other political leaders. He also expressed his extreme displeasure with the behavior of the army in Dhaka by commenting that if he had his way he would court-martial Generals Yaqub and Farman Ali, or anyone else who refused to obey his orders.[28] He said that he had called upon Gen. Tikka Khan and was "sending him over to do the job."[29]

In his speech of 6 March Yahya offered his perceptions and analysis of the dilemma. He singled out Mujib as being primarily responsible, since he had rejected his call for an all-party conference, just as he had rejected Yahya's other invitations "to come and discuss the situation with me on more than one occasion with a view to working out an acceptable method of moving forward. . . . We thus lost the opportunity of avoiding misunderstandings and of working out an amicable solution." He also indicated that his decision to postpone the National Assembly had been "completely misunderstood" and that "instead of accepting the decision in the spirit in which it was taken, our East Pakistan leadership reacted in a manner which resulted in destructive elements coming out in the streets and destroying life and property." The decision to postpone had been made because a large number of West Pakistan's representatives were not going to attend the inaugural session, thus rendering it a futile exercise and likely to result in the dissolution of the Assembly. He had wanted, he noted, to save the Assembly and to allow passions to cool. He then called for the inaugural session of the National Assembly to take place on 25 March and advised that he could not "wait indefinitely" for the impasse to be resolved. His speech concluded as follows:

> Finally, let me make it absolutely clear that no matter what happens, as long as I am in command of the Pakistan Armed Forces and Head of the State, I will ensure complete and absolute integrity of Pakistan. Let there be no doubt or mistake on this point. I have a duty towards millions of people of East and West Pakistan to preserve this country. They expect this from me and I shall not fail them. I will not allow a handful of people to destroy the homeland of millions of innocent Pakistanis. It is the duty of the Pakistan Armed Forces to ensure the integrity, solidarity and security of Pakistan, a duty in which they have never failed.[30]

Yahya's statement suggested that the impasse was a consequence of misunderstandings between the major political parties, and that these had been caused by a lack of cooperation by the Awami League leadership, which he also held responsible for the ferment in the east. He mentioned the political leaders in the west matter-of-factly and without the opprobrium that characterized his references to the Awami League. His firmly stated observations toward the end of his speech implied both the threat of secession in the east and consideration of the military option that had been used in the past.

At the mass rally at the Ramna Race Course on 7 March, the day after Yahya's speech, Mujib gave a masterful demonstration of oratorical skill. He satisfied the crowd with his toughest public stand against the west and the unshakeable commitment of his party to the emancipation of the Bengali people.[31] He declared that he would not attend the National Assembly on 25 March unless four demands were met by the martial law authorities.[32] First, martial law had to be abrogated; second, the troops had to be returned to their barracks; third, an inquiry had to be launched into shootings by the police and army during the period since the postponement of the Assembly; and fourth, power had to be immediately transferred to elected representatives. He also enumerated ten additional points or principles that were to be translated into a series of directives to guide the continuing noncooperation movement.

Mujib also recounted events, both recent and historical, that appeared to be calculated efforts on the part of West Pakistani interests to deprive the Bengalis of the right to govern. The Awami League's choice of a date for the first meeting of the National Assembly had been 15 February, but that of the People's Party had been 3 March; the latter date was chosen. The Awami League had given public assurances to all parties on 24 and 27 February that any and all suggestions concerning the drafting of the constitution would be heard and that those judged "just and reasonable" would be accepted, but on 27 February Bhutto had threatened grave bodily harm to anyone from the west who attended and had promised a mass strike from the Khyber to Karachi if the Assembly were held. He, the leader of the majority party, had not even been asked about the postponement of the Assembly, Mujib observed, but Bhutto had demanded it and had been able to exercise an effective veto. Also without consulting with the Awami League, Yahya had amended the Legal Framework Order after a meeting with Bhutto to allow members of the National Assembly to resign before the inaugural session. The current decision to set a new date for the Assembly was a continuation of this pattern; the date had been set without seeking the advice of Mujib and the Awami

League and had been announced after a five-hour meeting between the president and Bhutto. The decision to hold a ten-party conference had also been made without explicitly seeking his counsel, and the public had been misled by the president, who had indicated that Mujib had pledged to attend the meeting, when in fact, Mujib exclaimed, he had merely invited the president to come to Dhaka to see the situation for himself, to gain an appreciation of the deep feelings of the Bengalis about recent events, and to understand the need for immediate corrective action. He also recounted the dismissal of governments in the 1950s when West Pakistani interests had been threatened by the assertion of Bengali political power. Because of what Mujib called the current military buildup in East Pakistan, it appeared that "political confrontation was soon to be followed by military confrontation, if the majority did not submit to the dictation of the minority."[33]

Toward the end of his oration, using the evocative symbols that were increasingly becoming the norm among Pakistani leaders as they addressed their various publics, Mujib declared emotionally: "If the ruling coteries seek to frustrate these aspirations, the people are ready for a long and sustained struggle for their emancipation. We pledge to lead this struggle and ultimately to attain for the people their cherished goal of emancipation for which so many martyrs have shed their blood and made the supreme sacrifice of their lives. The blood of these martyrs shall not go in vain."[34] Mujib's declaration was no less confrontational than Yahya's the day before had been.

One issue that Mujib did not mention in his speech was the independence of East Pakistan, even though some officers in the government of the east and in the martial law administration had expected him to declare Bangladesh an independent state.[35] "UDI" (unilateral declaration of independence) had become something of an incantation, the letters themselves replacing the reality they presumably were reflecting. But the incantation did not lack support. Student leaders had demanded independence, and some Awami League leaders had started to discuss it as an increasingly sensible option.[36]

If there had been any question about the authority accorded the Awami League by the Bengali public before 7 March, there certainly was none thereafter. The public directives of the league during the ensuing days were complied with almost completely; and as one senior officer recollected with mixed astonishment and admiration, they were "formulated by Tajuddin Ahmed with the help of a single clerk-typist."[37] The supply of water to the President's House, the symbol of central authority in East Pakistan, was cut off, not to be restored until Yahya arrived on 15 March as a "guest" of Bangladesh. The success of the noncooperation movement and the disassociation of the Bengali public from the formally constituted government was made powerfully evident on 8 March when the chief justice of the East Pakistani High Court refused to administer the oath of office to the newly appointed governor, Lt. Gen. Tikka Khan.[38]

STRATAGEMS IN THE WEST

The role of the leaders of the smaller political parties through February had been limited, as their influence had been marginal. Prior to the postponement of the National Assembly, leaders of these parties had dealt with Mujib and Bhutto individually and autonomously. In the case of Bhutto, he had made the overtures, in keeping with his desire to develop a common strategy among all the parties in the four western provinces for negotiating with the Awami League. Between the smaller parties and the Awami League there had been greater mutuality of interest in exploring the ministerial representation that would accompany the transfer of power. Coalitions among the smaller parties were inhibited because they were competing among one another for access to executive power both at the center and in the provincial governments in the west.

With the influence of the Pakistan People's Party made manifest by the postponement of the Assembly, the leaders of the smaller parties in both the east and west at once became critical of the activities of Bhutto and the PPP and collectively supportive of Mujib's position on the transfer of power. Although several of those leaders invited to the all-party conference had initially indicated they would attend, with the exception of the PPP and the Muslim League (Qayyum), they decided against attending within a day of Mujib's announcement and called instead for the immediate convening of the National Assembly. During the first week of

March opposition leaders in East Pakistan, all but two of whom either had been defeated or had not run in the 1970 elections, declared support for the Awami League. Nurul Amin, one of the two opposition members elected to the National Assembly in the east, refused to attend the all-party conference. Maulana Bhashani and Ataur Rahman Khan pledged support to Mujib at a mass meeting on 9 March, with the Maulana declaring that only the majority party, the Awami League, had the authority to frame a constitution for Pakistan.[39]

The most significant and concentrated effort urging the government to seize the initiative in seeking a negotiated solution was taken by Maulana Mufti Mehmood, general secretary of the Jamiat-ul-Ulema-i-Islam, the day following Mujib's Ramna Race Course speech, when he called for a meeting of the leaders of the smaller political parties in West Pakistan to be held in Lahore on 13 March.[40] The meeting was attended by dominant figures from the Council Muslim League, Convention Muslim League, Jamiat-ul-Ulema-i-Islam, Jamiat-i-Islami, and Jamiat-ul-Ulema-i-Pakistan, plus two important Independent members elected to the National Assembly. Those present conceived their role primarily as providing a moderating influence in the tense political situation and as constituting a collective alternative to the PPP in the west.[41]

Everyone at this meeting accepted Mujib's four demands in principle and called for interim governments to be established both at the center and in the provinces with the convening of the National Assembly on 25 March. In a formal press release those present also declared that since the elected representatives of the people had not even had "an inaugural opportunity to meet much less to identify, discuss and thrash out issues of their common and agreed destiny," it was inappropriate to speak of a constitutional crisis. In an effort to contain Bhutto's insistence on a prior agreement on constitutional principles, the group proposed that "compromises insisted upon and arrived at outside the floor of the house and concealed from the scrutiny and vigilance of the people can have no relevance to constitutional settlement, although they may have to arrangements for sharing power." The group also indicated that in its judgment "a great part of the present crisis is due to misunderstanding" and urged President Yahya to proceed to Dhaka to remove any "misunderstandings, apprehensions and suspicions in frank and cordial talks with Sheikh Mujibur Rahman."[42]

At this meeting the leaders of the smaller parties in the west, while not overtly critical of the government or the PPP, unequivocally backed Mujib and the Awami League. The group publicly declared that Mujib had given the "clearest assurance" that in constitutional debates in the National Assembly there would be "an atmosphere of free unprejudiced discussion" and responsiveness on the part of the majority party to constitutional suggestions. In another extension of support to the Awami League and in an effort to help erase perceptions within the party leadership that a conspiracy was afoot, the leaders of the smaller parties indicated that if there was such collusion, they would stand solidly with the Awami League to defeat it.[43] They also moved to petition the president for an immediate interview in which they could discuss the transfer of power and constitutional negotiation, but were able to see Yahya only after the negotiations between the government and the Awami League concerning the transfer of power had been judged by the government to have failed.

Bhutto and the PPP leadership had anticipated that negotiations among party leaders would take place prior to the convening of the National Assembly on 25 March and that these would, in some way, also result in face-to-face discussions between Bhutto and Mujib. Such a meeting would fulfill the commitment that Bhutto had made to the West Pakistani public to do all in his power to develop a consensus on constitutional issues, and it would establish the wisdom of his refusal to attend the 3 March session of the National Assembly, which had resulted in its postponement. It would serve also to disarm his increasingly vocal detractors among the smaller parties in the west, and it would feed claims of unusual sagacity and power on his part if he could bring the Awami League to the negotiating table on his terms.

After Mujib's rejection of an all-party conference and the announcement of a new inaugural date, Bhutto pursued his strategy further by making an overture to Mujib on 10 March in the form of a telegram indicating that he was prepared to go to Dhaka to continue their talks before the convening of the National Assembly. Bhutto informed the public that he had told Mujib: "We have come to a stage when the two wings of Pakistan must immediately reach a common understanding if the country is to be saved; and it must be saved whatever the cost. The future of our country stands in the balance and the leaders of the two major parties carry an extremely heavy responsibility and everything humanly possible must be done to arrest the disaster that threatens us."[44] Bhutto's statement, like Yahya's on 6 March, suggested the grave possibility of the division of the country and also suggested, as had the president's, that any means necessary must be used to prevent this eventuality. To reject such an overture as this, given the situation portrayed, would be tantamount to furthering the prophesied disaster.

The reasons that made a meeting with the Awami League so attractive to the PPP were judged pernicious by the league, which perceived Bhutto as untrustworthy. He had not acted in good faith after the January meetings and had not been responsive to the league's assurances of fair treatment. He was described by Mujib to a senior army officer as a "Trojan horse" bent upon sowing political havoc, who could never be satisfied and who would make and take concessions toward an agreement only then to destroy it.[45] Finally, the animosities of an aroused Bengali public would not allow talks with Bhutto or any other discussions that would imply a dilution of the Awami League program or a compromise of the league's commanding position among the members of the National Assembly. In a response to a reporter's query on 12 March, Tajuddin replied that rumors that the Awami League was seriously considering the message in Bhutto's telegram were groundless.[46] Thus, as of that date, if any discussions were to occur, they could only be held between the Awami League, parties other than the PPP, and the government, with the first order of business being the substance of the four new demands, later followed by constitutional issues.

With this change in the agenda and with information concerning what the Awami League might demand and what the government was prepared to do, the focus of the PPP shifted from the Six-Point Demand to the terms of the transfer of power. While the PPP was more isolated than other parties as a result of the president's decision to go to Dhaka, it had a more advantageous position than either the Awami League or the smaller parties by virtue of its access to the government and the military. This was in large part because of Bhutto's political cunning and the military's fear of becoming politically isolated in the western provinces as it had in the east. One of the senior officers in the regime, who at this juncture enjoyed particularly close ties with Bhutto, has observed that Bhutto was masterful at eliciting information from the government.[47] He was at once provocative and disarming, would play upon uncertainties, and could hint at possibilities in such a way as to evoke confirmation or correction.

In an address at a public meeting on 14 March, much to the alarm of most other West Pakistani leaders, Bhutto announced that if there were to be a transfer of power before the framing of the constitution, it must be transferred to the Awami League in the east and to the People's Party in the west, after which the majority parties would have to come to a consensus on the constitution.[48] In an important press conference the following day, Bhutto indicated that if power were transferred to the PPP in the western wing, he would ensure that the provinces of Baluchistan and the North-West Frontier, in which the PPP had done poorly in the elections, would have representation.[49] He did not, however, say that the representatives would come from the smaller political parties—the "defeated parties" as Bhutto referred to them.[50]

Bhutto's demand elicited intense criticism from party leaders in the east as well as in the west. While the demand was clear, the terms were vague. First, it was unclear how power would be transferred to parties in West Pakistan. There were four provinces in the west, and the leaders of the smaller parties vociferously insisted that "one unit"—the integration of the four western provinces into one—not be reinstituted. Second, without consideration of constitutional issues concerning the federal division of powers between the center and the provinces, the demand implied the creation of two autonomous sovereignties. When queried about his intent during his press conference of 15 March, Bhutto blamed the media and vested interests for misrepresenting his call for a transfer of power to the two wings; the common man, he asserted, understood very well what he meant.[51]

The common man understood his demand, Bhutto argued, in the context of the unjust attacks on himself and his party for being the only advocates of West Pakistani interests and for allegedly causing the postponement of the Assembly. He declared that neither he nor the PPP wanted power at any cost, as his opponents had charged, but that the West Pakistani people insisted that they have power in order to change the lot of the oppressed. A report that he had discussed the sharing of power with Mujib in January rather than constitutional matters was "a total lie."[52] The current crisis was neither new nor caused by his or anyone else's action; it was an "inherent crisis," in which the Awami League wanted "more or less independence" while the PPP wanted to eradicate exploitation and achieve economic equality. If the six points were accepted, not only would the Bengalis attain dominance but the PPP would also have to forgo its policy of confrontation with India over Kashmir. He insisted that he had not set any preconditions for attendance at the National Assembly, but had only asked for assurances that his voice would be heard.[53]

Thus Bhutto's portrayal of the situation and of recent events—a portrayal that would haunt some West Pakistani leaders when they later went to Dhaka—was that only he and the PPP had stood fast to their commitments to the electorate and to the maintenance of the integrity of Pakistan, and that they had done so in the face of adversity. While his detractors accused him of being mad for power, it was they who were willing to compromise their own and the country's integrity to deprive the PPP, and thus the West Pakistani people, of power. No better evidence was needed than their unwillingness to cooperate with the PPP and their inclination to capitulate to the Bengalis, said Bhutto.

A NEW CONTEXT

From the latter part of February on, as it became increasingly distrustful of the reporting of affairs in the east by the martial law authorities there, the government relied more heavily on military and civilian intelligence services. The central governmental and martial law authorities in East Pakistan were perceived as being pro-Bengali and pro–Awami League, serving more as advocates of Awami League interests than as conveyors of valid information.[54] The government also distrusted the rapport that several military officials had with the Awami League, and this distrust was intensified by the inability of the military officials to get Mujib to consent to visit West Pakistan as the president had requested. Furthermore, leaders of the martial law regime thought that the advice of the governor of East Pakistan, Admiral Ahsan, had been largely responsible for the electoral successes of the Awami League over more pro–West Pakistan parties. They felt they should now place more confidence in alternative sources of information and advice.

The government from this point on started to rely completely on information provided by intelligence services headed by Generals Akbar Khan and Ghulam Umar, both of whom were also active in the political drama. The former was one of the officers advocating a hard line against the Awami League, the latter was a conduit between the government and the opposition parties, particularly in the west. Information concerning the political situation was not authenticated, screened, or evaluated, but was placed directly before Yahya by important figures in the martial law regime.

Regardless of the way intelligence was evaluated and presented, it still did not adequately reflect the intensity of Bengali sentiment or the scope of the public support enjoyed by the Awami League. Government intelligence services had poor access to the Awami League and relied increasingly on non-Bengali groups. Government leaders deduced that the Awami League phenomenon was inflated and temporary, something that could be countered by a show of force. The stereotype firmly held by military leaders in the west was that although brave in front of a mob, Bengali leaders turned coward when faced with a gun. Thus, when confronted with force, they would become respectful and obedient, while their supporters quietly faded into their *mohallas*. Their appraisal of information from the intelligence services was congruent with such long-standing perceptions—or misperceptions—of Bengali "character."

Just as the sources and substance of political intelligence were confused, decision making within the government was unstructured. With the dismissal of the cabinet on 21 February, there was no longer any forum for collective deliberation, and no substitute for the cabinet was sought, in the form either of a military cabinet or a council of civil servants. The composition of those groups with access to the president also changed. Yahya met with advisers and political leaders separately and in an ad hoc manner; Bhutto was the political leader he most often consulted. Access to the president was at once intermittent and obtrusive. When officials in the east tried urgently to reach Yahya, their requests were intercepted or deflected by interested parties around the president. This had also been true earlier for the leaders of the smaller political parties in the west.[55] In contrast Bhutto and certain groups within the military regime had immediate and "unfiltered" access. Because of the loosely structured decisional framework and the monopoly of interested parties on political intelligence, it proved impossible for the president to check the validity of information and to monitor the activities of those close to him.

The ad hoc style and limited instruments of influence and control available to the president made the development of alternative options difficult. Greater emphasis came to be placed on the military "solution," the option subject to most control. Little effort was expended on developing contingency plans.

The decision to postpone convening the National Assembly produced a new political environment, much different from what the government had envisioned. The strategy of "arranged" consultations among party leaders that the government had hoped to pursue was unworkable. Government leaders felt themselves losing control, unable to be the influential arbiters they had desired to be. The government had become impotent and merely one of several equal participants because of forces outside its control. The new context was defined by an expanded political agenda with altered priorities, and the agenda was defined by the Awami League, not the government. The government had not anticipated the east's demands, the changed power relationships, or the reduced flexibility among the different leaders. The Awami League's power and its will to persevere had been augmented as a consequence of the government's decision; concomitant with the increase in its power, the flexibility that the Awami League leadership could show in negotiations diminished. The league could not negotiate with the PPP after the postponement and still maintain its integrity.

Leaders of the smaller political parties of West Pakistan, which the government had pressured to support postponement, distrusted the motives behind Bhutto's activities in late February. All the parties except the Muslim League (Qayyum) were prepared to attend the Assembly, resisting government pressure and the pleas and threats of the PPP. A strategy of disassociation from Bhutto and the PPP not only held the possibility of political gain, but also seemed vital to provide a medium of communication between east and west in order to maintain the integrity of Pakistan.

The People's Party had become politically isolated by mid March and thus reactive, while the Awami League became more aggressive and confrontative. The PPP was not going to be actively involved in negotiations; the smaller parties were converging on a strategy of support for the Awami League and were increasingly critical of Bhutto, though *not* of the PPP. The government had become active in the negotiations, assuming the position that both Bhutto and the government had desired for the PPP, though for different reasons. The PPP, however, still held the power of veto, since the president had indicated that no agreement would be validated without its consent. This was to prove critical in the days ahead.

6

Constitutional Consensus
and Civil War

The president and his principal military aides arrived in Dhaka for a final effort to resolve the political crisis in mid afternoon on 15 March. Those present recall the sharp contrast between the somber mood of the men greeting the arriving delegation and Yahya's jovial, confident manner. One observer described the scene as follows:

> All entries to the airport were sealed. Steel-helmeted guards were posted on the roof-top of the terminal building. Every inmate of the airport building was scrupulously screened. A heavy contingent was posted at the P.A.F. Gate—the only entrance to the tarmac. A company (nearly one hundred men) of an infantry battalion (18 Punjab) mounted on trucks fitted with machine guns waited outside the gate to escort the President to the city. Only a handful of officers, carefully picked, were allowed inside the airport. . . .
> There were no bouquets of flowers, no civil officials, no rows of "city elite," no hustling of journalists, and no clicking of cameras. Even the official photographer was not admitted. It was a strange eerie atmosphere charged with a deadly stillness.[1]

Upon Yahya's arrival at the President's House, a meeting of top military officers was held to discuss the political and military situation in the province. Those attending included Generals Tikka Khan, Ghulam Umar, Rao Farman Ali Khan, A. O. Mitha, S. M. G. Peerzada, and Air Commodore Masood. General Hamid Khan, a close friend and confident of Yahya's, did not accompany the president to Dhaka at the latter's order, since Yahya feared that Hamid's arrival would be interpreted as a sign of greater military involvement.[2] The meeting started uneasily with perfunctory observations on sundry matters. No one seemed to want to broach the central question on their minds—"What could be done to save Pakistan?" Several officers stationed in the province soon used the meeting, though briefly, to express their grave concern about a military solution to the crisis. The first to address the issue reportedly did so forcefully and, as remembered by one participant, with an eloquence unusual in military councils. He argued that military efforts to suppress the Bengalis would be an "act of madness." Instead of restoring public tranquility, such action would cause deep and permanent hostility toward both the army and the west that no amount of negotiation could erase. Nor would it resolve the present conflict; it would merely create new and more intractable ones. This position was supported by General Farman Ali, who had previously presented similar sentiments to the president. He observed that military action would not only make a political solution more improbable, but would further disrupt an already fragile economy and severely interrupt interregional trade. Prudence in both the short and the long run required a political, rather than a military, solution.

The president did not respond negatively to these arguments and even observed that since the Quaid-i-Azam himself had not opposed the idea of provincial autonomy in Pakistan, who was he, Yahya, to oppose decentralization now? While he was noncommittal and his comments did not reflect a full appreciation of Jinnah's changing conception of the appropriate organization of the state in Pakistan, some took the president's observations as indicating a serious commitment on his part to seek a negotiated settlement. He also gave the impression, however, that he would negotiate only from a position of strength afforded by his incumbency as president and chief martial law administrator and that he would take a tough stand toward Mujib and "bring him around."

PRELIMINARY TALKS BETWEEN
YAHYA KHAN AND SHEIKH MUJIB

Negotiations between the government and the Awami League began the following day, 16 March. After an early morning meeting with his senior colleagues, Mujib arrived at the President's House in a white car flying a black flag that symbolized the public's mourning for those who had died under army and police fire after the postponement of the National Assembly. The first decision to be made was where the two leaders were to confer.[3] Mujib strongly objected to meeting in the drawing room for fear that it might be bugged and insisted that Yahya and he hold their discussions in a room that was more private and secure. After some deliberation, and with Mujib's concurrence, the president ordered two chairs brought to the bathroom off the main bedroom of the President's House. It was there that the final negotiations to save Pakistan began.

At this meeting Mujib formally presented the four demands enunciated in his speech of 7 March as the initial agenda for discussion. He observed that the demands were not new since they were essentially demands for de jure recognition of a de facto situation. He also insisted that the participants in deliberations would have to be different. Substantive agreements as well as procedures for their implementation would have to be worked out between the government and the Awami League, without any participation by the Pakistan People's Party. Mujib also proposed, as Tajuddin had suggested and as Bhutto had advocated before (though for different reasons), that the constitution-making process would be made much simpler if there were two meetings of the National Assembly—one east and one west—instead of a common meeting at the outset. The office of the president, he suggested, should continue during the interim, as should its incumbent, who would exercise executive authority until such time as a national constitution was finally framed.

Yahya indicated that he was committed to transferring power and to ending martial law and that he would consider Mujib's suggestions seriously and carefully. He reminded Mujib, however, that he had a responsibility to oversee the development of an agreement that would enjoy a national consensus and that he was not prepared to submit to populist threats. A government that represented both wings of the country would also have to be formed, and in this regard he advised Mujib that he would have to come to terms with the major party in the west. He finally observed that as president and chief martial law administrator he had other options, just as the parties did, and that any arrangement would have to meet with his approval.[4]

At their next meeting, on the following day (17 March), Yahya conceded all but one of the four points. He consented to a prompt inquiry into the police and army firings, to restriction of troops to their barracks as long as there were no civil disturbances, and to revocation of the proclamation of martial law, which would be part of an interim constitutional instrument that would be promulgated and continue in effect until the creation of a new constitution. On the fourth point, an immediate transfer of power, Yahya responded that this was precisely what everyone was coming to Dhaka to talk about and that it would be both presumptuous and premature for him to commit to either the terms or the timing of this demand. This had to be negotiated. He assured Mujib that just as he was committed to lifting martial law, he was also committed to the transfer of power, but the details had to be agreed upon by all interested parties, including the PPP.

Yahya and Mujib agreed that negotiations should proceed along two tracks. First, the provisions, both substantive and procedural, to be included in an interim constitutional arrangement would be discussed by "negotiating teams" representing the Awami League and the government, and these provisions would be prepared as a "draft proclamation." Second, Yahya and Mujib would separately continue their deliberations on the transfer of power and the formation of an interim government.

After their private meeting, the president was joined by two senior military aides and Mujib by Tajuddin, Kamal Hossain, and Syed Nazrul Islam to discuss an agenda and procedures for negotiating the interim constitution. They agreed on the following: (1) the lifting of martial law; (2) the continuance of Yahya as president during the interim; (3) the creation of two constituent committees, one for West Pakistan and one for East Pakistan, to resolve provincial issues; and (4) the drafting of a constitution in the National Assembly sitting as one body after the regional committees had completed the preliminary work. They further agreed that the negotiating teams would work out the details of implementation and that they would also decide upon the powers to be exercised by the center and by the provinces in the interim. Each side was to study these matters before meeting again on 19 March.

A third meeting between Yahya and Mujib took place on the morning of 19 March. Each expressed disillusionment concerning an event that had occurred the previous day, and each advanced a new issue for negotiation. Their disillusionment resulted from the creation of the commission to inquire into the actions of the police and army during early March. On 18 March, Gen. Tikka Khan, in his role as martial law administrator of East Pakistan, had appointed a "commission of inquiry" to be headed by a judge of the High Court of East Pakistan named by the chief justice and to include four additional members, selected from the civil service, the police, the Pakistani army, and the East Pakistan Rifles. The army would nominate its own representative, and the chief secretary of the East Pakistani government would select the other three. This commission would report to the martial law administrator.

Mujib rejected the commission outright. He felt that it would be incapable of conducting an unbiased inquiry because while the perpetrators of violence were well represented, no representation was provided for the aggrieved. The mandate given the commission—"to go into the circumstances which led to the calling of the army in aid of civil power in various parts of East Pakistan between March 2 and March 9"[5]—was also biased. The commission was authorized to inquire into the wrong thing. Mujib declared that both the composition and the role of the commission thus violated the spirit and intent of the Awami League demand and his understanding of Yahya's agreement to an inquiry. It was thus yet another demonstration of West Pakistani insensitivity to the concerns and rights of the Bengali people. Yahya was, however, disillusioned by Mujib's rejection of the commission. He was under pressure from army officers and the civil service to inquire into the larger social conflict during early March rather than just the shootings alone.[6] He defended the proposed composition of the commission, indicating that it would prevent the commission from being used for political purposes and would ensure the protection of the army, which felt itself much abused and had, in the opinion of many senior officers, acted less forcefully than it should have given the duties it was assigned and the provocations it faced.

Yahya and Mujib nonetheless chiefly focused on the agenda for the deliberations between the negotiating teams to be held that evening and on the composition of the interim government.[7] Each side advanced a change of agenda. Mujib indicated that the Awami League now wanted provisions included in the draft proclamation that would grant full legislative powers to the civilian governments at both the national and provincial levels upon the transfer of power. Yahya indicated that this could be discussed, even though it had not been agreed upon as part of the original agenda, but countered by asserting that while the transfer of power appeared possible, his constitutional adviser, Justice A. R. Cornelius, had said that there was a serious question about the legality of a complete abrogation of martial law before the meeting of the National Assembly and the promulgation of a new constitution. The matter, therefore, had to be placed on the agenda and reopened for discussion.

The two leaders also continued their discussions about the formation of an interim government. It was after this meeting that Mujib informed a senior military officer that he and Yahya had tentatively agreed on the formation of a national government composed of eleven ministers. Six of these, including the prime minister, were to come from East Pakistan, and five, three from the PPP and two from the National Awami Party (Wali Khan), were to come from West Pakistan.[8]

TOWARD A CONSTITUTIONAL
SETTLEMENT

The meeting of the negotiating teams on the evening of 19 March began with Justice Cornelius presenting his argument concerning the illegality of the lifting of martial law. He did this in a manner that the Awami League found condescending. Cornelius proposed that the removal of martial law before the adoption of a constitution would leave the country in a legal void, since all governmental authority derived from the proclamation of martial law made on 25 March 1969. The constitution had at that time been abrogated. The office of president had been created under the supreme authority of martial law, which was also the basis for the proclamation of constitutional procedure and the promulgation of the Legal Framework Order. The lifting of martial law would thus also abolish the presidency and these other basic laws under which the country was being governed and from which existing institutions derived their legitimacy. The justice was interrupted by a member of the Awami League team, who expressed his surprise and dismay that this should be an issue at this stage of the negotiations, inasmuch as the president had already explicitly committed himself to the lifting of martial law (a fact Yahya had neglected to mention to Cornelius). The issue, therefore, was moot. Another Awami League representative observed that the question was immaterial in any event, since the issues being discussed were political, and not strictly constitutional, matters. The assumption of power by the military and the abrogation of the 1962 constitution, this participant wryly observed, had not been accomplished according to the canons of constitutional law and practice.

The teams also addressed the questions of the organization of power at the center and the distribution of power between the central and provincial governments during the interregnum. Proposals were advanced on behalf of the Awami League by Kamal Hossain and were discussed in substantial detail. They were in essence an explication of the six-point scheme. The central government was to oversee defense, foreign affairs (excluding foreign aid and trade), and finance and commerce (excluding currency) and was to receive a fixed proportion of revenue from each province. The provincial governments were to enjoy powers to be specifically granted by the interim instrument, which would include authority to negotiate for and receive foreign aid directly and to trade with any country. Each province would have a reserve bank, and any interprovincial currency transfers would have to be approved by the government of the province from which the transfer was being made. Provincial governments alone were to be empowered to levy income tax. The government team, while agreeing that an interim constitution should address these substantive issues, reserved judgment on the Awami League's more specific proposals, indicating that it needed to study them further.

The meeting, described by one government negotiator as extremely long, involved, and exhausting, was continued the next morning. The Awami League began by explicitly summarizing the points it had enumerated orally the previous evening. The teams then decided that the draft proclamation should be prepared, which, once a consensus was reached on all items, would serve as the vehicle for the transfer of power. The government team encouraged its Awami League counterpart to prepare the original drafts, including what had been agreed upon as well as its more specific demands with respect to the distribution of power. The Awami League refused, insisting that since the proclamation would derive its authority from the existing regime and would be promulgated by the president, it was appropriate that the president's team prepare the drafts. The league was fearful that anything it committed to paper and submitted for ratification would immediately be declared unacceptable, and could be leaked and used for propaganda purposes by its foes. Its representatives wanted the provisions, regardless of their origin, to appear as though they had the sanction of the governmental team. The league would then prepare amendments and propose editorial changes in "revised" drafts as necessary.

The presidential team prepared a draft the same day, incorporating those items suggested by the Awami League with which they felt comfortable and including a provision for presidential emergency powers, since the authority of martial law was to be removed. The principle elements of the draft proclamation were as follows: (1) martial law would be ended effective with the administration of the oath of office to provincial cabinets; (2) the Provisional Constitutional Order of 4 April 1969 would serve as the fundamental law until a new constitution became effective; (3) Yahya would continue as president during the interim period; (4) the president would exercise power as authorized by the Provisional Constitutional Order and the 1962 constitution; (5) a central cabinet would be selected from among the representatives of East and West Pakistan; (6) the National Assembly was to function as prescribed under the 1962 constitution except for "limitations and modifications to be agreed upon with respect to the Province of East Pakistan"; (7) the functions of the provincial assemblies would be the same as under the 1962 constitution, again with exceptions made for East Pakistan; (8) provincial governors would be appointed by the president in consultation with the leaders of parliamentary groups of the provinces and were to hold office during his pleasure, while a cabinet of ministers was to be appointed with a chief minister at its head to "aid and advise the Governor in the exercise of his functions"; (9) within seven days of the creation of the provincial governments, two constitutional committees would be established—one in Dhaka and one in Islamabad—for the purpose of "formulating special provisions and requirements of each province of Pakistan to be incorporated in the constitution to be framed by the National Assembly," which would be convened by the president after the committees had completed their work; and (10) "whenever it is made to appear to the President on a report from the Governor of a Province or otherwise, that a situation has arisen in which the Government of the Province cannot be carried on, the President may by Proclamation assume to himself all or any of the functions of the executive government of the Province."[9]

The seriousness and the authenticity of the negotiations were emphasized by two responses. First, the leaders of all the West Pakistani political parties decided to journey to Dhaka. Second, and most important, the president summoned his chief economic adviser, M. M. Ahmed, and two of his associates to Dhaka to help the presidential negotiating team establish what was economically feasible in the division of economic power between the central and provincial governments—the next step in the negotiations. Among the first party leaders to arrive, on the evening of 19 March, were Mian Mumtaz Daultana and Shaukat Hayat Khan of the Council Muslim League and Maulana Mufti Mehmood of the Jamiat-ul-Ulema-i-Islam. Wali Khan and Ghaus Bux Bizenjo of the National Awami Party (Wali Khan) had already been in Dhaka since 13 March. Qayyum Khan, leader of the Muslim League (Qayyum) and Maulana Shah Ahmed Noorani of the Jamiat-ul-Ulema-i-Pakistan arrived on 23 March.

On 20 March, after the talks between Yahya and Mujib and those between the two negotiating teams, Bhutto announced that he had received "clarifications" that he had requested from the president concerning his role in the negotiations and that he and a team of constitutional and economic experts would depart for Dhaka the next day. Bhutto had rejected previous invitations from Yahya to come to Dhaka. In his published account of this period, Bhutto recalled that he had received a message on the night of 16 March from Yahya asking him to come to Dhaka on 19 March. Bhutto replied that he would come if he could negotiate face to face with Mujib, and he requested a response on this point. On 18 March he received a message from General Peerzada, the president's principal staff officer, to the effect that he should come to Dhaka for discussions with the president. Bhutto again refused. As the discussions appeared to be taking a serious turn, with the president's economic advisers being summoned to Dhaka, the attention of the PPP leadership focused on the next invitation. Bhutto wired the president to remind him that he was closely following the course of events and that the PPP could in no way be left out of a governing coalition, be it interim or permanent. On the evening of 19 March, he received a message from Yahya indicating that Mujib was prepared to discuss things.

The Awami League became concerned, however, about "clarifications" that Bhutto claimed to have received from Yahya, which prompted the former's immediate departure from Karachi with fifteen of his top party associates after observing that his presence in Dhaka would serve no useful purpose. In an unscheduled meeting Yahya told Mujib and Tajuddin that Bhutto had been informed that agreements in principle—one on the formation of a central cabinet among them—had been reached and that he should be present for discussion of the interim constitutional instrument and cabinet formation. Mujib then told Yahya that if Bhutto were going to become involved in the discussions, the Awami League no longer wanted a cabinet at the national level, although the appointment of a council of presidential advisers would be acceptable. He also indicated that forming a cabinet with Bhutto's participation would prove an insurmountable obstacle given the extreme opposition in the Awami League to his being a part of the government and the distrust that Mujib and other senior leaders in the party had of Bhutto's intentions. Leaders of the Awami League also remained skeptical about the relationship between Bhutto and core military decision makers.

The arrival of Bhutto and his associates on 21 March excited an already aroused public. The delegation was greeted by crowds of Awami League volunteers, who insisted on performing the customary functions of a sovereign government. The newly arrived entourage was also met by a police escort who, like the Awami League activists, were wearing black arm bands and waving Bangladesh flags. Ultimately, this effort at protection broke down, and the delegation was taken to the Intercontinental Hotel under heavy military guard. At the hotel Bhutto and his advisers were greeted by silence within and shouting without. Workers refused them service of any kind. They were finally taken to the top floor, where they spent all of their time except for excursions under armed guard to meet with Yahya and the presidential negotiating team.[10]

That same day, shortly after his arrival, Bhutto met with the president, who briefed him on the substantive and procedural agreements reached in the negotiations. Yahya also informed

Bhutto that a letter of consent to the agreement would be required from all party leaders in an effort on the part of the president to forestall any public demurrers after an agreement was announced. Bhutto registered his continued opposition to the Awami League's position on the issues of aid and trade and asked for time to discuss the other issues with his advisers. Yahya told him that Mujib was coming to the President's House for a meeting the next morning and that he should be there if he wanted to meet Mujib.

The closeness of consensus between the presidential team and the Awami League was not lost on Bhutto and the PPP leadership. The difficulties of managing a constitutional committee in West Pakistan would undermine the position that he had so skillfully built for himself and the PPP. Antagonism between provinces would be intense and directed primarily against the Punjab, the bastion of PPP strength. Conflicts between the PPP and the smaller parties would deepen, decreasing the likelihood of agreement in a West Pakistani constitutional committee, and thus removing the possibility of a common front in the National Assembly and raising the probability that a constitution would indeed be drafted on the Awami League's terms. Bhutto's claim to represent West Pakistan would be tarnished, if not destroyed. Parliamentary fratricide would also encourage divisions within the PPP—divisions that had already required a mixture of physical threat and communal exhortation to bridge.

Finally, the appointment of provincial ministries would place Bhutto in the position of having to choose to be either governor or chief minister of a single province, and thus risk the provincialization of the PPP elite, or to remain as head of a party with little regular organization in a context in which effective power would be in the hands of the provincial governments. Either choice would hasten the processes of division within the PPP—divisions that would make a common stand in the National Assembly and the probability of inclusion in a national government no more than a vivid, receding dream. The PPP now shifted its attention from the six points and representation within what would now be a council of presidential advisers to the conditions of the transfer of power— it opposed separate meetings of the National Assembly and the lifting of martial law before the convening of the Assembly as a whole.

The meeting on 22 March was the first in the protracted negotiations after the December elections in which Yahya, Mujib, and Bhutto had met together face to face. It began and ended with misunderstandings. Each of the participants felt that he had been manipulated and deprived of the opportunity to control or manipulate the others. Mujib was annoyed that Bhutto was present, since he had told Yahya that direct negotiations with the PPP or tripartite talks were out of the question, inasmuch as any hint of his negotiating with Bhutto would threaten his credibility in his party. Bhutto was disturbed that negotiations were not possible, since he had understood from the "clarifications" sent by Yahya that such talks would be arranged once he was in Dhaka.

By all accounts the meeting was no more conducive to agreement than were the January discussions held between each pair separately. Upon their first encounter at the President's House neither Mujib nor Bhutto would look more than obliquely at the other, and at first they refused to converse, each sitting half turned away from the other. The president chided them about their behavior, indicating that they appeared to be bashful newlyweds rather than contenders for leadership of an important country. Yahya took them by the hand and encouraged them to honor the rules of courtesy that such situations required.[11] The two leaders then moved to the veranda for a private talk. In his published account of this episode, Bhutto recalled that Mujib argued strongly for his acceptance of the constitutional proposals, saying that he recognized the PPP as the dominant party in the west and that the leaders of the other parties were good-for-nothings.[12] He reported that Mujib warned him not to trust the military, which, if it destroyed him first, would certainly then move to destroy Bhutto. Awami League leaders and those from the opposition parties with which they were holding intermittent discussions recall, however, that it was Bhutto who attempted to encourage Mujib's suspicions and distrust of the military by telling him that he was a fool for negotiating with the military, since they were not prepared to hand over power, most certainly not to a Bengali. Upon leaving the President's House that day, Mujib noted publicly that he had had discussions with Yahya and that Bhutto had also happened to be there.

The turning point in the negotiations came on 23 March—

Independence Day, renamed Resistance Day by Bangladeshis. The events of the day made a deep impact on representatives from the west and encouraged the belief, particularly within the army, that the East Pakistanis were not committed to a negotiated solution that would be acceptable to the west. The day was filled with demonstrations, parades, and students demanding independence and calling for armed resistance, marching in military formation with the Bangladesh flag ever in view, while that of Pakistan was only to be seen being trampled in the streets or flying behind armed guards at military installations. On the eve of Resistance Day, Radio Pakistan in Dhaka started to refer to itself as Radio Dhaka; the Dhaka TV Centre ceased broadcasting altogether the following day because of alleged military harassment.

The army command was deeply concerned over a meeting of ex-servicemen that was addressed by two retired Bengali officers, Maj. Gen. M. U. Majid and Col. M. A. G. Osmani, who urged support of the Bangladesh movement and led a procession to Dhan Mandi for Mujib's blessing. Similarly, the Joi Bangla Brigade, a student militia, staged a parade at Paltan Maidan, where four leaders of the Awami League–affiliated student organizations saluted and raised the Bangladesh flag before proceeding to Dhan Mandi for Mujib's blessing as well. Taken as the ultimate affront, however, was the arrival at the President's House of the Awami League team flying the Bangladesh flag. Military personnel in particular felt this to be a deliberate insult at a time when many still considered a political solution possible.

While the mood of the day did not bode well for negotiations, agreement on the implementation of the principles embodied in the six points was ultimately achieved. At the first meeting of the negotiating teams, the Awami League representatives presented a memorandum that constituted an amended version of the presidential team's draft proclamation. The differences between the two, according to two members of the presidential team, were not substantial and most of the issues had been discussed in previous meetings. Given the importance and content of the document, the first session of the day was devoted primarily to discussions of foreign aid, trade, and the other economic dimensions of the Awami League proposals. The meeting was then recessed until the government team could absorb the changes into an amended draft.

This draft would then be studied by both teams and presented for consultation with the PPP.

The government's position on the difficult issues of economic and fiscal policy and power was by all accounts ably and creatively presented by M. M. Ahmed, the president's chief economic adviser. Ahmed argued that the provision that foreign aid and trade be under provincial control without significant qualification was unacceptable, unworkable, and was in fact unnecessary to realization of Awami League objectives—the equitable distribution of foreign exchange earnings and foreign aid and the ability to seek imported goods at the most favorable terms available. Foreign aid, he argued, was a political process involving sovereign states and international lending agencies, whether they be states, consortia of states, or the World Bank. If policies were not coordinated, it would be impossible for any Pakistani province to bargain effectively. The World Bank, for example, would deal with only one government—under the constitution anticipated there would be four "sovereignties" in the west and one in the east. It would jeopardize all of their interests to expect international lenders to change their policies in this regard.

A second problem was that policies with respect to foreign affairs and foreign aid could be contradictory. Conceivably a province might wish to negotiate aid or trade with a country with which the central government had no formal diplomatic relations, or a province might conceivably deny aid from a country with which the federal government wished to be more friendly. At a minimum this would unnecessarily inhibit the foreign policy of the central government.

The government team proposed an alternative that was acceptable to the Awami League. A constitutional provision would stipulate a set percentage of all foreign aid for East Pakistan; it was suggested that this be 55 percent, plus a temporary additional percentage to compensate for past inequities. Under this arrangement, as appropriate, particular projects could be negotiated for different provinces, with the provinces themselves playing an influential role in aid acquisition. In addition, the government proposed that a foreign aid portfolio in the central government be created and be held by an East Pakistani for five years, with the civil service head of the ministry also being a Bengali. Thus, those charged with negotiating foreign aid would be Bengali, and the majority of all aid negotiated would be constitutionally guaranteed for the east. The central government, not the provincial governments, however, would conduct all negotiations.

Ahmed also opposed the suggestion that the provincial governments collect all customs and taxes. He insisted that the central government had to have autonomous sources of revenue to support federal projects. In the case of customs, for example, the administrative problems in the west would be particularly complex. With one port in West Pakistan, how would the ultimate destination of all imported goods be determined so that the officials of the appropriate provincial government could levy and collect the payment of duty? Would there be common duties or variable duties? How would accounts be kept and payments of duty made on interprovincial trade in goods of foreign origin? Ahmed again proposed that in principle a formula guaranteeing revenues to the central government be adopted for the allocation of taxes and customs, but that the existing arrangements continue in the interim.

The government agreed to the Awami League demand for the establishment of separate provincial accounts of foreign exchange earnings, a simple enough task, and indicated that an appropriate agency of the provincial government could monitor disbursements from them. The government team also accepted the Awami League proposal for a separate reserve bank for East Pakistan, but noted that because of the commitment to a common currency and monetary policy a federal reserve board would be necessary. These arrangements on economic policy were agreed to by *both* the government and the Awami League teams, and there is no indication that they were opposed by the People's Party. The PPP's reservations about the six points, especially those concerning aid and trade, had in fact been met.

The subsequent meeting between the negotiating teams ultimately yielded a historic irony: the issues that had prompted postponement of the National Assembly were resolved before it would have met. Agreement was reached on the provisions of the draft proclamation that involved the six points. Two days prior to the date initially set for the convening of the National Assembly, there was consensus in this respect. The crucial differences con-

cerning those items of the draft encompassing the four demands
had surfaced as a *consequence* of the postponement. The opposition
to these arrangements, primarily over the terms of the lifting of
martial law and the transfer of power, came from the PPP and
several senior army officers. The PPP feared exclusion from power;
the military feared ethnic division in its ranks and an unsympathetic government beholden to a hostile public.

The Awami League draft, like the government's, called for a
lifting of martial law, but on different terms. The government had
proposed its abrogation on the day provincial cabinets took office,
while the Awami League proposed that martial law be revoked in
a province when its governor took the oath of office, but in no event
later than seven days after the presidential proclamation was
made. The Awami League's proposal would thus make the withdrawal of martial law effective immediately, inasmuch as the government could not leave the provinces without any political authority at all. The government's draft had allowed the continuation of
martial law by providing that provincial ministries need not be
appointed under certain conditions. The Awami League draft also
included the abolition of all martial law regulations and orders, as
well as of the provisional constitutional order. The new presidential proclamation would serve as the source of constitutional
authority in the interim, with government conducted as closely as
possible in accordance with the 1962 constitution.

Both drafts kept Yahya as president in the interim, and under
the Awami League draft he would also be commander in chief of
the army and the supreme commander of all armed forces until a
new head of state "by whatever name called" was selected under
the new constitution. The Awami League draft also proposed that
the president be assisted by advisers appointed by him as he saw
fit, rather than by a cabinet composed of representatives from the
political parties of the various provinces as the government draft
suggested.

The powers of the executive, however, were more constrained
under the Awami League plan than they were under the government's. The league's draft proclamation deprived the president of
the "emergency powers" enjoyed under the 1962 constitution. The
president would also be unable to prorogue or dissolve either the
National Assembly or any Provincial Assembly; he would be di-

rected to appoint provincial governors on the "advice of the majority parliamentary party of the state," rather than after "consultation with leaders of political groups," as the government plan proposed, with the governors formally bound to act on the advice of the provincial ministries.

Three provisions in the Awami League draft caused considerable consternation among the government team, one in particular because of both its substance and its timing. Each of these provisions held important symbolic meaning for the members of the government team, if not for the Awami League as well. First, the teams had agreed that members of the National Assembly would meet initially in two "Constituent Committees for the purpose of formulating special provisions and requirements of each province of Pakistan after which they would convene as the National Assembly to draft a national constitution." In its draft the Awami League had substituted "Constituent Conventions" for "Constituent Committees" though their purpose was unchanged. The second provision concerned the nature of the oath under which members of the National Assembly were to be sworn into office. The government's oath emphasized sovereignty and obligation to the state, but the Awami League's version emphasized obligation to the constitution.

Each of these changes became magnified in the judgment of the government team as a consequence of a third and final change. At what appeared to be the end of the discussions, a member of the Awami League team indicated that he had been instructed by Mujib to change "Federation of Pakistan" to "Confederation of Pakistan." At this suggestion one distinguished member of the government team temporarily lost his usually calm demeanor. Jumping from his seat, he exclaimed that a confederation was in essence an agreement between two sovereign states, and that such an arrangement had not even been intimated, much less discussed, before.[13] He said that the word "Union"—if the Awami League was so intent upon using the Indian constitution as a model—was acceptable, but that "Confederation" was inimical to the welfare of the Pakistani state and was completely out of the question. Another member of the government team observed, however, that the Awami League could amend its own draft in any way that it saw fit and that the government then had the prerogative of either agreeing or disagreeing. For a third member, this change, timed as it was in the context of the other proposals, served as final confirmation of a long-held suspicion that the Awami League was not negotiating in good faith. Instead of seeking clarification, he accepted the meaning of "Confederation" as defined by the first government member. The third member furthermore felt that his own team was too exhausted to reopen the issues or further contemplate the Awami League's motives and intent.

Although the PPP did not object to the six-point provisions as encompassed by the amended draft, the party took strong exception to the provisions for transfer of power. In their next meeting with the president's team, Bhutto and his aides argued that the lifting of martial law without a meeting of the National Assembly would deprive the central government and its officers of authority and could lead to "constitutional secession." Such an arrangement would be tantamount to yielding to a demand for two Pakistans. The argument was the same as that of Justice Cornelius, though Bhutto emphasized the possible consequence of such an outcome in terms of the army's deepest fears. Bhutto later recalled his position as follows:

> Martial Law was the source of law then obtaining in Pakistan and the very basis of the President's authority; with the Proclamation lifting Martial Law, the President and the Central Government would have lost their legal authority and sanction. There would thus be a vacuum unless the National Assembly was called into being to establish a new source of sovereign power on the national level. If, in the absence of any such national source, power were transferred as proposed in the provinces, the government of each province could acquire de facto and de jure sovereign status.[14]

The Awami League's draft also entailed the removal of one form of institutional veto that the PPP had felt it enjoyed and presented the party with a local arena that could provide its detractors with the same advantages that it had with respect to the Awami League in the national arena. First, the repeal of the Legal Framework Order and the weak "authentication" authority of the president under the draft proclamation removed a constraint that the PPP would have had at its disposal in negotiations with the Awami League in a legislative forum. Second, because of the creation of separate constituent committees or conventions for the four provinces of the western wing without reinstitution of a single province of West Pakistan, the PPP would be hard pressed to reach a controlled constitutional consensus and would run the risk of its majorities in the Punjab and Sind dissolving into segments that would join other parties in coalition. The creation of provincial ministries would likewise serve to decentralize power. Without the prospect of an early end to constitutional deliberations in the west and a call for the convening of the National Assembly, Bhutto would be reduced to being either chief minister merely of a province or the leader of a loosely held together political party. The latter position would make him dependent upon the resources and goodwill of those wielding power in the provincial ministries. It was in this context that Yahya finally called upon the leaders of the smaller parties to discuss the contentious issues between the Awami League and the PPP with them.

Although they were meeting periodically with Mujib, he was not giving the leaders of the smaller parties full details of the negotiations on the grounds that some aspects might be misconstrued or become distorted when they found their way into the media. All signals during the first days of the negotiations indicated that discussions were proceeding in a positive and fruitful fashion, but the minority leaders had been left out of the formal deliberations and were unable to see the president until 22 March (three of the leaders had threatened to return to West Pakistan unless such a meeting were held). At this meeting Yahya informed them that progress was being made, but that Mujib was becoming difficult and adamant on the matter of cabinet formation. He requested that they urge upon Mujib the importance of the creation of a government with PPP participation. The president also told the representatives that Mujib was being irascible and unpredictable, agreeing to certain things and then coming back to ask for something different or more. For example, he had changed his demand for a transfer of power to a national ministry to a transfer of power to a national council of advisers; and instead of an initial convocation of the National Assembly in the form of a meeting of regional constituent committees, he now wanted constituent conventions to which the members of the National Assembly would swear their oaths. The representatives shared the president's concern over the demand for constituent conventions to meet separately before the convening of the National Assembly, and the president suggested that the leaders go to Mujib and "try to make him see sense."

When the delegation met later with Mujib, they indicated that they could not understand the Awami League's position on the initial meeting of separate constituent conventions, which departed from the positive search for accommodation that had seemed to characterize the Dhaka negotiations thus far. Such an arrangement would make things impossible for minority party leaders in the west at this juncture, especially if the PPP did not go along. Their credibility would be permanently diminished, and they would be assaulted from all sides as traitors. They told Mujib that a convocational meeting of the National Assembly would have to be held first and that he could be assured of their support in addition to that of his own autonomous majority. In addition, they urged Mujib to take Bhutto and his colleagues into his cabinet. Mujib replied that it was impossible to change the plan and that it was in essence no different from what had already been agreed to by the negotiating teams representing the government and the Awami League. He also vigorously opposed taking Bhutto, a "Trojan horse," into his cabinet. Later these representatives met with a delegation of the PPP, and with the exception of the representatives of the National Awami Party (Wali Khan) they concurred on the unacceptability of meetings of separate conventions or committees before the initial convening of the National Assembly.

Later, on the night of 23 March, the president summoned the minority party leaders to inquire about the results of their discussions with Mujib. They reported that Mujib appeared committed to the position asserted by the Awami League team, a stubbornness some indicated they could not understand, given their previous sense of Mujib's willingness to accommodate. Yahya then asked what he was supposed to do—he was being made to appear "a fool in the eyes of the world"; "the whole world was laughing at him." They suggested that the president himself might show more sensitivity in his dealings with Mujib and that this would perhaps induce a change. They also suggested a meeting of the West Pakistani parties with the president's team to attempt to reach an accommodation. Yahya replied, however, that it was too late.

Those attending this meeting also remember cautioning against the use of military force, but government representatives recall no party leaders present opposing the use of force to reassert government authority. Several leaders present remember that Peerzada watched Yahya like a hawk, much as they felt Mujib had been watched by Tajuddin in the exploratory meetings they had held in Dhan Mandi. The following morning minority party leaders were informed that they would be leaving for Karachi that afternoon on "the last plane out."[15]

Discussions continued on 24 March, but with a sense of distance and foreboding. Wali Khan and Ghaus Bux Bizenjo met briefly with Mujib in the morning, reportedly in an effort to encourage him to withdraw the proposal for two separate constituent conventions and the reference to the state as a "Confederation." Sardar Shaukat Hayat Khan of the Council Muslim League met with Khondikar Mushtaq, a senior leader of the Awami League with personal ties to Muslim League leaders in the west, who indicated a meeting was being held at Mujib's house. He shared Shaukat's premonitions about military action and pleaded that the West Pakistani leaders make Yahya "see sense." Shaukat also spoke with Mujib by phone several hours prior to the scheduled departure of the leaders for Karachi to inquire if a delegation might not again meet with him to discuss matters. Mujib responded that it would not be worthwhile; he could not guarantee its safety, he had "lost" in a vote to compromise on constitutional issues, and he was not sanguine about the outcome of the efforts to reach an acceptable constitutional settlement. They should leave, he said, since it would be difficult to distinguish between friend and foe if force were resorted to. In his dramatic way Mujib told Shaukat "we might not meet again in this world, but we surely will in heaven."[16]

The last meeting of the negotiating teams was held on the evening of 24 March. Afterward Tajuddin said that the Awami League had presented a final plan to the president and that it had done all that it could at the level of the negotiating teams to resolve the constitutional and political crisis. He stated that no more meetings at this level would be necessary, although the teams might have to meet for clarification. He observed that the political situation was extremely tense and might deteriorate further if the announcement of a presidential proclamation was delayed.

THE ASCENDANCY OF THE ARMY

Given the toughness that Mujib had displayed in their initial talks, the impotence of the central authority, and pressure from the hawkish group within the army high command, Yahya called Generals Tikka Khan and Rao Farman Ali Khan shortly after the negotiations with the Awami League began and instructed them to finalize the drafting of operational orders for military action to reinstate public order and central authority in East Pakistan. Generals Farman Ali and Khadim Raja, however, had already started drafting preliminary orders on the morning of 18 March. With slight modifications, these orders had been approved on 20 March by the army command, though no decision on implementing them was made. Three provisions were given highest priority: (1) the Awami League and its supporters were to be treated as rebels; (2) East Pakistani units of the military forces were to be disarmed along with the police; and (3) the top leaders of the Awami League and antigovernment student leaders were to be arrested.

Preparation for military action was prompted by serious concern about the security of the armed forces and by mistrust of the Awami League's commitment to a united Pakistan. The senior officers, including Yahya, felt that the army had lacked leadership and direction in East Pakistan. This had begun, in their view, with Gen. Yaqub Khan's unwillingness to use sufficient force to implement his own plan to reinstitute law and order in the east and his subsequent resignation on 7 March. In their judgment, it was this softness and lack of will that had encouraged the Awami League and its supporters in the excesses to which they had gone. The lack of central direction had also been accompanied by the development of a siege mentality within army units. When the troops returned to their barracks after the abortive crackdown in early March, cantonments had become increasingly isolated in pockets cut off from rations and supplies, without central command providing focus and direction. Because of their physical and emotional isolation, the military command feared, the forces in East Pakistan would at best become prisoners in their cantonments and ultimately be forced to leave East Pakistan without a fight unless preemptive action were taken; at worst they would have to fight a civil war in which they were pitted against Bengali troops, police, and guerrillas while lacking effective centralized command and lines of supply. Such an eventuality was unthinkable to the military.

On 23 March the reports on the progress of the negotiations and the Awami League's demand that "Confederation" be used to describe the Pakistani state were met in the army command with alarm. They were accepted as final confirmation of the suspicions that many in the top command had of the intentions of the Awami League, giving credence to their fear of the army becoming isolated in East Pakistan and erasing any remaining confidence that the corporate interests of the armed forces would be protected under the existing provisions for the transfer of power as Mujib had assured they would be protected more than two months before. The decision to take military action to suppress what was termed a rebellion unless the Awami League could be made "to see sense," was made at teatime on 23 March by the army command and was recommended to Yahya that evening shortly before his meeting with leaders of the smaller parties from the west about their discussions with Mujib. Preparations were to commence the following day in such a way as not to arouse suspicion.

As the West Pakistani leaders were leaving Dhaka for Karachi to report that progress was being made in the negotiations, Generals Farman Ali and Khadim Raja were boarding helicopters to visit brigade commanders to inform them of the planned military action and to instruct them to make preparations according to the operational orders delivered to them orally. Negotiations on a constitutional transition and a transfer of power had ended, and with that ending the thin sinews that bound the nation were severed. Pakistan's first war of 1971 began on the night of 25 March.

7

The Indian Response

The Indian government was as surprised by the December 1970 Pakistani election results as the Pakistani government, but was, of course, infinitely more pleased about them, since they raised at least the possibility of a reasonably friendly government in Islamabad headed by the Awami League. An East Pakistani–dominated central cabinet, it was assumed, would be less inclined to raise the issue of Kashmir than the previous governments of Pakistan, although it was accepted that an actual resolution of that dispute would still probably not be possible.[1] On several occasions both before and after the elections, the Awami League, and specifically Mujib, expressed the view that Pakistan must learn to deal realistically with India in the subcontinent, and in particular to expand economic relations with the major regional power, a position that New Delhi appreciated and Islamabad held in suspicion.

But while New Delhi would have welcomed an Awami League–led government in Rawalpindi (particularly if it was in a coalition with the "dissident" Pakhtoon political party, the National Awami Party led by Wali Khan in the North-West Frontier Province, some officials doubted that the benefits for India would be as substantial as the Indian public generally expected. The Indian government knew that the Awami League was highly factionalized, and it had serious reservations about the younger, more radical elements in the party. At this time New Delhi was experiencing major problems in West Bengal with the so-called Maoist Naxalite terrorist organizations of the Communist party (Marxist-Leninist) and was concerned that pro-Maoist groups on the two sides of the Bengali border might strengthen their ties in the context of an Awami League provincial government in East Pakistan and an Awami League–dominated central government in Rawalpindi. Nor was the Indian government complacent about the capacity of an Awami

League government in Pakistan to control policy-making in the face of strong pressure from the military and some West Pakistani parties on a wide range of issues. It also doubted whether the Awami League could remain united if confronted by enticements or threats from the military or West Pakistani economic interest groups; the inner group around Prime Minister Indira Gandhi had a reasonably favorable opinion of Mujib, but had reservations about several of his colleagues in the party. Moreover, New Delhi realized that the Awami League was more hard-line than Rawalpindi on one important issue in dispute—the redistribution of the Ganges River waters—because East Pakistan was the area most seriously affected.

New Delhi preferred to maintain a low profile while negotiations were under way to form a government in Pakistan based on the 1970 election results. The Indian government reportedly even quietly sought to discourage the Indian media from being overtly pro–Awami League, since it realized that evidence of support from either official or private sources in India could embarrass Mujib in his negotiations with the Pakistani martial law regime and the West Pakistani political parties. Moreover, from mid January to early March, the entire political leadership in India was heavily involved in its own election campaign, with both the government and opposition party leaders on almost constant tours of their own constituencies and the country. They had neither the time nor the inclination to follow events in Pakistan in any depth. Even the External Affairs and Defence ministries and Mrs. Gandhi's private secretariat were rather perfunctory in their analysis of developments before 25 March. No top-level in-depth discussions of Indian policy toward Pakistan took place from February to early March, the critical period, except indirectly in some consideration of developments in West Bengal.[2] Although the Government of India held strong views on how its interests were affected by the political negotiations in Pakistan, the available evidence suggests that New Delhi preferred to await the course of developments there before defining its own policy.

This view of India's role in the events leading up to the 25 March crackdown in Pakistan has, of course, been strongly challenged by most Pakistani sources, official and otherwise, in part on the basis of what came to be known as the "Ganga incident." On 30 January

1971 an Indian Airlines flight from Srinagar to Jammu and Kashmir was hijacked by two Kashmiris, forced to land in Lahore, and later blown up by the hijackers after the passengers and crew had been allowed to disembark and return to India. There was a great deal of publicity on both sides and official statements, rather cautious initially, became increasingly intemperate. The Pakistani government and press lauded the brave Kashmiri "freedom fighters" for their daring act of resistance to the "illegal" government in Srinagar;[3] the Indian government and press denounced the "dastardly crime" committed by "criminals."

The Indian government saw the Ganga hijacking as evidence of divisions within the Pakistani elite. The best Indian intelligence suggested that extremists within the military regime had manufactured the incident, without the knowledge of the central government, to remind Pakistanis of India's control over most of Kashmir. Several members of the Indian decision-making elite at that time have observed that Gen. Akbar Khan, the chief of military intelligence in Pakistan, was, as one put it, used to "taking the bit in his teeth."[4] The incident, exploited as it was by Bhutto after his return from Dhaka, was also taken as proof of the intensity of the conflict between the contending parties over the conditions of the transfer of power.

The dispute assumed more serious proportions on 4 February, when the Indian government used the incident as the stated reason for banning all Pakistani overflights of Indian territory.[5] The immediate Pakistani response was relatively moderate, merely protesting the violation of an international agreement for an act over which the Pakistan government had had no control and that it had not instigated. Later, however, the Pakistanis were to interpret the incident differently. On 15 April a commission of inquiry presented a report to President Yahya that claimed that the two erstwhile freedom fighters were actually Indian intelligence agents, and that the Indian government had arranged the hijacking. This was accepted in the standard Pakistani view of Indian policy on the East Pakistan crisis, which held that the hijacking was part of a pre–25 March conspiracy between India and the Awami League. According to this elaborate scenario, New Delhi had ordered the hijacking to have an excuse to ban Pakistani overflights, thus drastically complicating Pakistan's logistical problems in communicating between the two wings, and in this way assisting the separatist movement in East Pakistan.

New Delhi continued to denounce the hijackers as criminals and to demand compensation from the Pakistani government for the destruction of the aircraft. A number of Indian officials admitted in interviews with the authors that the suspension of overflights at that time was convenient, but they also maintained that there was ample justification other than the Ganga incident for this decision, and that, indeed, the government had been considering ending overflights before the hijacking on the grounds that Pakistan had not negotiated in good faith on other issues—the Ganges river, trade, enclaves, and visitation rights. The Ganga incident, they insisted, was an excuse rather than the reason for the ban.

There is no way to verify what really happened. It does seem unlikely, however, that such a complicated and expensive "conspiracy" (India lost a plane as well as important overflight rights for its own military and civilian planes over both East and West Pakistan) was required to "justify" New Delhi's action in this case. Even more persuasive, however, is the fact that the hijackers were released from prison after the 1971 war and in 1982 were still living in Pakistan without any restrictions—hardly possible if they had actually been "Indian agents."

THE FOREIGN POLICY DECISION-MAKING
PROCESS IN INDIA, 1971

In the period following Nehru's death in 1964, the Government of India was very vulnerable to both domestic and external political pressures and had generally been quite indecisive in the handling of foreign affairs, including relations with Pakistan. This was particularly the case after the 1969 split in the Congress party, which had left Mrs. Gandhi head of a minority government in the Indian parliament and dependent upon support from various opposition parties to remain in office. All this changed drastically after the overwhelming victory of Mrs. Gandhi's wing of the Congress party in the March 1971 elections, in which it won approximately two-thirds of the seats in the Lok Sabha, the lower house of parliament. The results were generally described as part of an "Indira wave," and the prime minister was given most of the credit for her party's victory. India had not had as strong a prime minister to deal with recalcitrant elements in both her own party and the opposition since the pre-1960 Nehru era, and Mrs. Gandhi proved as adept and adaptable as her father in using her power base in formulating and implementing policy—especially foreign policy in the context of regional developments in 1971.

These basic changes in the power structure of Indian government and politics could not have been better timed for creating effective policies in the Pakistani crisis. Before the March 1971 elections Mrs. Gandhi would have been under heavy pressure to move quickly and more forcefully—possibly prematurely—on the developments in East Pakistan, but this was not the case from mid March to December 1971, when the Government of India firmly headed by Mrs. Gandhi, could proceed at a pace and in directions carefully selected to meet India's basic objectives at the lowest possible price.[6] The opposition parties had not only been badly defeated in the parliamentary elections but had also in most cases been discredited in the states in which they still controlled the state governments. No effective anti-Congress alliance survived the March elections. The opposition parties were on the defensive in parliament and in public debates on all issues, and the anti-Gandhi elements in the Congress party had either left in the 1969 split or were intimidated by the extent of her victory in the elections. While they still constituted a significant force in the party (and by 1973-74 had regained the capacity to challenge Mrs. Gandhi's leadership), they had little influence in the immediate post-election period in 1971.

Thus, the critical group involved in decision making in India on all subjects—but particularly on foreign policy—from March to December 1971 consisted of a quite small and homogeneous coterie around Mrs. Gandhi that consulted together and reached decisions rather informally.[7] Mrs. Gandhi, the final source of authority, depended extensively on her private secretariat, headed by P. N. Haksar until July 1971 and by P. N. Dhar thereafter, and on a number of other secretaries (G. Ramchandra, M. Malhotra, Sharada Prasad, and B. N. Tandon), who later achieved high posts in the Indian administrative service. This group, supplemented at times by G. Parthasarthy (not an official but a close confidant of Mrs. Gandhi's) and by D. P. Dhar (formerly ambassador to the

U.S.S.R., but in 1971 the head of policy planning in the Ministry of External Affairs), met almost daily with the prime minister.

A more formal consultative institution was the Political Affairs Committee (PAC), composed of several key cabinet ministers: from March to December 1971, Foreign Minister Swaran Singh, Defence Minister Jagjivan Ram, and Finance Minister Y. B. Chavan. Various other ministers and secretaries attended when appropriate in terms of the subjects being discussed. Mrs. Gandhi held the Home Ministry portfolio herself in 1971, but had two ministers of state for home affairs, K. C. Pant and R. N. Mirdha. Pant had responsibility for West Bengal—and hence East Pakistan—under the regional distribution between him and Mirdha, and thus frequently attended PAC meetings at which developments in East Pakistan were being considered. Indeed, since he was both close to Mrs. Gandhi personally and was usually better informed on specific aspects of this subject than his colleagues were, Pant was probably more active in decision making on Pakistan than the higher-ranking cabinet ministers in the PAC.

At the highest bureaucratic level in the Government of India, there was an interministerial committee of key Indian administrative service officials. In 1971 these were V. W. Swaminathan (cabinet secretary); P. N. Haksar and later P. N. Dhar (prime minister's secretary); K. B. Lal (defence secretary); I. G. Patel (economic affairs secretary); T. N. Kaul (foreign secretary); and other top bureaucrats when appropriate. This committee was very important in decision making on East Pakistan, both as a channel of communication to the prime minister and in its policy recommendations. Another interministerial committee was specifically charged with handling the East Pakistani refugee problem, but it primarily implemented policy and usually made little contribution to its formulation.

Following the 1962 Sino-Indian war, the military leadership—primarily the three service chiefs—had assumed an increasingly important role in defense and foreign policy matters. The Defence Committee of the cabinet, the formal institution through which the service chiefs had become involved in decision making, had been abolished by Mrs. Gandhi.[8] On occasion, however, one or all of the service chiefs would be invited to participate in the proceedings of the Political Affairs Committee, but only when their presence was considered necessary, that is, when military or military-related matters were being discussed. General S. F. H. J. (Sam) Manekshaw, the chairman of the Chiefs of Staff Committee, also had informal contact with the prime minister and, more typically, with her secretariat and with D. P. Dhar in the External Affairs Ministry, and could influence policy through these channels to a limited extent. But for the most part the service chiefs had to depend upon Defence Minister Jagjivan Ram to express their views to the decision makers, and because of his own strong views on the subject, which differed from those of General Manekshaw on some major issues, Ram was not always considered a reliable channel by the military. The several intelligence agencies also had input into the decision-making process through a Joint Intelligence Committee consisting of representatives from the Research and Analysis Wing, (RAW), the Intelligence Bureau, and the directors of intelligence of the three armed services, headed by the vice chief of the army staff.

Several nominally important political and bureaucratic institutions were incidental to decision making on East Pakistan in 1971. The cabinet was usually not consulted but merely informed of decisions that had been reached by the prime minister and the Political Affairs Committee; its formal approval, when requested, was automatic and usually given without serious discussion. Similarly, parliament, including the Consultative Committee on External Affairs of the Lok Sabha, played a very minor role in the Bangladesh crisis. On occasion, government leaders used parliament to announce important policy decisions, and there were several debates in which both opposition and Congress members of parliament elicited information or criticized the government (usually for not taking more decisive action in East Pakistan), but given her overwhelming majority in the lower house, Mrs. Gandhi was under no compulsion to pay much attention to their views. On the administrative side, while Foreign Secretary T. N. Kaul and D. P. Dhar (along with P. N. Haksar and P. N. Dhar, members of the Kashmiri Brahman "Mafia" that was very close to Mrs. Gandhi in 1971) were active in decision making on East Pakistan, the External Affairs Ministry was less crucial as an institution than it had been in previous international crises. The leadership in the ministry below the level of secretary was atypically subservient, since several of the higher-ranking officials who did not get along too well with the "Kashmiri Mafia" (for example, Jagat Mehta, later foreign secretary from 1975 to 1979) had been sent off to duties outside New Delhi.

Thus, a small group around Mrs. Gandhi, operating in a highly informal manner—though within a formalized structure—was the key element in decision making on East Pakistan in 1971. Other sources provided input, but were usually of limited importance and easily ignored if it was judged inappropriate. By and large this core group was quite homogeneous, at least in Indian political terms, and there were no major differences among its members on basic policy issues, although minor disagreements did surface on occasion concerning implementation.

FROM CONCERN TO CRISIS

Even though the conflict over formation of a civilian government in Pakistan was intense and the stakes great, the Indian government believed that the contending groups would negotiate a settlement.[9] It was in everyone's interest to find a solution. Indians assumed that the military leaders and Bhutto would cheat Mujib, either by deceiving him or by deflating his expectations and demands through the threat of force. Such had been the pattern in the past; but the general Indian appraisal was that the movement toward a transfer of power had gone too far this time for a new martial law regime to be either viable or appealing. The military would have to come to terms with Mujib and the Awami League. They would have to negotiate; it made sense to negotiate; it was a political tradition in the subcontinent to negotiate. As one Indian leader observed, the British had even negotiated with Mahatma Gandhi, and surely Yahya must negotiate and reach an accommodation with Mujib.[10] Although the Indian government saw that one of the options available to the central government was the use of force, it did not anticipate the break-off of negotiations, the arrest of Mujib, and Yahya's declaration that Mujib was a traitor and that the Awami League was banned "for all time to come."

The initial response of the Indian government to the military action in East Pakistan was circumspect; it wanted neither to arouse greater hostility in Pakistan against India nor to encourage demands for immediate action from political groups in India. The expectations and hopes of the prime minister and her closest advisers in the secretariat and the Ministry of External Affairs were that the military action would be of short duration, after which negotiations toward a political settlement would begin anew. Differences such as these had always been resolved in Pakistan before, and there was no reason to believe that the current situation would differ from those in the past, although the terms of settlement would of necessity be different. Although the Pakistani army could act decisively in the short term, it could not impose a military solution in the long term given the intensity of public support in East Pakistan for Mujib and the Awami League. There was no other political body with which the military governors could negotiate and arrange a peaceful and successful transfer of power, which India felt the martial law authorities were indeed committed to doing. Although the restructuring of provincial political coalitions had been possible in the past, this had occurred in the arena of indirect elections or where the parties were largely Bengali in their support base, and where public sentiment had not been so aroused. The military elite in Pakistan, it was felt, was certainly aware of this.

The Indian response to the Pakistani government's decision to suppress the Awami League and other dissident forces in East Pakistan on 25 March was highly vocal, but rather ambiguous. The crackdown was strongly and unanimously criticized in India, but the statements of support for the Awami League issued by most official sources at the central level were carefully worded to avoid the impression that India would provide material assistance to the East Pakistani "rebels."[11] India granted refuge to Awami League and other political leaders and cadres from East Pakistan as well as elements of the East Pakistan Rifles, the East Bengal Regiment, and the East Pakistani police, but it had followed this policy in similar developments in other neighboring states, for example, the 1959 rebellion in Tibet and the December 1960 royal coup in Nepal.

New Delhi's policy toward the East Pakistani political refugees took a novel form in early April, however, when the Indian government permitted the establishment of an Awami League headquarters, Mujibnagar, on Indian soil—eventually in Calcutta. On 17 April at Baidyanath Tala, just across the border in East Pakistan, the Awami League leaders issued a declaration of independence (drafted by an Indian well schooled in the art of legal writing) announcing the formation of the "Sovereign People's Republic" of Bangladesh. A Bangladesh "government in exile" was established in Calcutta at this time, and training camps for the Bangladesh "liberation forces" were established, with Indian assistance, at a number of places in Indian territory close to the East Pakistani border. A Radio Free Bangla was set up near Calcutta, and on 18 April the Pakistani Deputy High Commission in Calcutta was taken over by an East Bengali defector from the Pakistani Foreign Service, Husain Ali, and functioned thereafter as a Bangladesh mission with India's tacit cooperation.[12]

There were, however, substantial limitations upon what New Delhi was prepared to do to support the Bangladesh liberation movement in this period. The declaration of independence by the Bangladesh government in exile was, in effect, publicly ignored by India, which did not extend official recognition to this "sovereign" body until December. India closely supervised the Government of Bangladesh (GOBD) headquarters in Calcutta. The Awami League leaders issued public statements on occasion, but only after the External Affairs ministry's "representative" in Calcutta had cleared them. Some of the Awami League leaders resented this relationship of dependency to India, but they had no real alternatives available.

New Delhi was equally careful in its establishment of training camps for the Bangladeshi liberation forces. India wished to make sure that these were under the control of reliable, moderate Awami League leaders or officers from the East Pakistan Rifles or police rather than the more radical political elements in the resistance.[13] Initially, primary responsibility for the supervision of these camps was given to the Border Security Force (BSF), but on 30 April the task was transferred to the Indian army. Initially, most of the resistance fighters in these camps were from the Pakistani military, paramilitary, or police forces; thus they did not require extensive military training.[14] By late May, however, a growing number of young East Bengali civilians were being recruited into the principal resistance force—called the Mukti Fauj (liberation army) until July and the Mukti Bahini (liberation force) thereafter—and New Delhi assumed responsibility for the training and arming of this expanded force.[15]

India's BSF had intervened in developments across the border in the first few weeks after 25 March, assisting Awami League and other rebel forces in establishing their control over much of the border region of East Pakistan immediately following the crackdown in Dhaka. But the BSF's role was limited in scope, both in time and in the kind of assistance rendered. By early May the Pakistani army had regained at least tenuous control over most of the border areas with India without encountering any substantial interference by the BSF or the Indian army. Pakistani allegations of massive BSF intervention were completely fictitious.[16] A few BSF men were captured by the Pakistanis on the border and probably in Pakistani territory (the Indians claimed they were kidnapped from Indian territory), but it is clear that the BSF did not pose a serious problem for the Pakistani army in its campaign to reestablish Pakistani authority throughout East Pakistan in the spring of 1971.[17]

There would also appear to be little evidence to support the Pakistani charge that the BSF had arranged the infiltration of Naxalite and other Indian terrorist groups into East Pakistan in the immediate post–25 March period. Reliable reports from Indian and other sources indicate that Indians belonging to such political organizations did enter East Pakistan in April, presumably to assist their "Maoist" brethren across the border, but also reportedly to seek refuge in the "liberated" areas of East Pakistan from the intensive antiterrorist campaign then being waged in West Bengal by India's Central Reserve Police and army.[18] In any case, it is highly unlikely that government circles in New Delhi and Calcutta were interested in providing the Naxalites with another potential source of support in East Pakistan; indeed, it was official policy to *prevent* linkages between the insurgencies by West Bengali and East Pakistani "extremist" elements then under way on either side of the border. Moreover, even if Indian officials had wanted to encourage the Naxalites to move into East Pakistan on the grounds that they would be less troublesome there than in West Bengal, it is scarcely credible that they had the capacity to make such arrangements in the context of their own intensive antiterrorist campaign. There is no doubt that both the Indian and Pakistani governments faced serious problems in controlling their respective sides of the East Pakistani border in the spring of 1971 and that there was movement back and forth for some time; this does not, however, constitute evidence supporting the elaborate conspiracy theory that became integral to the Pakistani analysis of these developments thereafter.

In the latter part of 1970 and early 1971 the Border Security Force in areas adjacent to East Pakistan had been reinforced, and some regular Indian army forces had been sent into West Bengal to contend with the expansion of Naxalite terrorist activity that had followed the removal from office of the coalition government supported by the Communist party (Marxist) and the declaration of "President's Rule" in March 1970. Pakistanis charged that these troop movements were, in fact, part of a military buildup for offensive action in East Pakistan in the event of major disorders there, and thus further evidence of Indian–Awami League collaboration in anti-Pakistani activities. The Indian position was that the BSF and army detachments had been sent in for police duties long before there was a political crisis in East Pakistan; moreover, according to Indian sources, the military brought in only light arms suitable for police actions but none of the heavy equipment that would later be required for offensive action in East Pakistan. This latter point is contested by some Pakistani officials.[19] It should be noted in this respect, however, that when the service chiefs of the Indian military were consulted in late March 1971 about India's capacity for military intervention in East Pakistan, they informed the government that it would take several months before such intervention would be feasible despite the desertion of most of the East Pakistani military, paramilitary, and police units.[20]

In any event, after 25 March India began a gradual, but substantial, buildup of its military forces in West Bengal, Assam, and Tripura. The Indian explanation is that the BSF required assistance in carrying out its border security responsibilities because of the developments in East Pakistan. In April and May the Pakistani army and the rebel forces engaged in numerous clashes in the border area, which on occasion extended into Indian territory. Moreover, refugees had begun streaming out of East Pakistan—a few thousand in early April but over three and a half million by late May—who posed major law and order problems beyond the capacity of the local Indian police and the BSF to handle.[21] In addition, Indian officials were concerned with the prospects both of

Pakistani agents coming across with the refugees and of radical political elements in East Pakistan and India establishing links through this channel. A new coalition government in West Bengal, which excluded the Communist party (Marxist)—the party that had won a plurality in the March state assembly elections—had assumed office in Calcutta on 2 April, raising some concern in New Delhi that this would lead to cooperation between the previously antagonistic Marxist and Marxist-Leninist (i.e., Naxalite) Communist parties, at least on the issue of East Pakistan.

By the middle of May Pakistani military forces had substantially expanded in East Pakistan, particularly in areas bordering on India that had been controlled by the Awami League. This constituted a novel security problem for India, which had never before had to contend with large Pakistani military concentrations in the east. Even during the 1965 Indo-Pakistani war, Pakistani military forces in East Pakistan had been kept at a level sufficient to maintain control in the face of internal disorders, but not large enough to defend the province against an Indian invasion. By mid 1971 the Pakistani army was capable of launching military action on both the eastern and the western frontiers with India. This required major changes in Indian security—including the stationing of a larger military force on the East Pakistani border for ordinary security purposes. Although this provided India with a greater capacity for intervention in East Pakistan in late 1971, the initial decision on the buildup also involved other, more immediate considerations.

Perhaps the most critical issue facing the Government of India in the immediate post–25 March period was not security but the flow of refugees from East Pakistan. New Delhi had decided by early April to attempt to concentrate the refugees in camps close to the East Pakistani border rather than, as in the past, allowing them to move into India as *citizens* of India.[22] Several factors influenced the Indian government in reaching this decision.

The first refugees from East Pakistan were Bengali *Muslims* of diverse backgrounds: Awami League leaders and cadres; Bengali Muslims in the Pakistani army or police in East Pakistan; a substantial number of so-called Bihari Muslims, that is, Muslims from neighboring areas of India who had moved into East Pakistan after partition in 1947; and a few West Pakistani civil and army officials fleeing from Awami League–controlled areas near the border. This refugee flow into India thus differed from previous ones, which had consisted almost exclusively of Bengali Hindus resident in East Pakistan. The Government of India was not disposed to accept the permanent settlement of Muslims from East Pakistan in India, no matter what their politics might be.

New Delhi also perceived very early that the 25 March crackdown in East Pakistan was basically different from earlier, more limited Pakistani government actions directed at suppressing dissident elements in East Pakistan, and that it would have more serious consequences—for India as well as Pakistan. By mid April some high Indian officials were operating on the assumption that a large proportion of the remaining Bengali Hindu population in East Pakistan, some twelve million to thirteen million people, would eventually seek refuge in India—vastly larger than any previous refugee influxes into the country. The government was not prepared to accept such a massive migration into already overcrowded and politically explosive areas in West Bengal and northeastern India. There was also some apprehension in New Delhi that the Pakistani government would actively "encourage" the Hindus in East Pakistan to migrate in order to "solve" what had become both a minority and a political problem in terms of presumed Hindu support of the Awami League. In these circumstances, New Delhi considered it essential to demonstrate to Pakistan that it was not even prepared to accept a large number of Hindu refugees again.

Since it was impossible, physically or politically, for India to halt the tide of refugees from East Pakistan, charges from Rawalpindi that New Delhi had deliberately encouraged the outflow of refugees through radio broadcasts in Bengali about Pakistani atrocities lack plausibility. All-India Radio did denounce repressive actions by the Pakistani army—quite inaccurately termed "genocide"—in April and May, and it also described the battlefield victories of the pro–Awami League forces against the Pakistani army in glowing terms. While these reports were greatly exaggerated, they did have the immediate effect of persuading some East Pakistanis that victory was near and that there was no need to seek refuge in India—some political activists were persuaded of this until it was too late. The Indians may have wanted to encourage East Pakistani resistance, but they did not desire a flood of refugees from the province. *Official* Indian statements on the refugees played down the religious composition of the refugee population, which after the first outflow of Muslim Awami League supporters consisted overwhelmingly (an estimated 80 percent) of Bengali Hindus.[23] The primary consideration in this policy decision was to discourage reactive communal outbreaks against the Muslim minority community in India, but it also complicated any effort by India to depict the conflict in East Pakistan as a communal anti-Hindu crusade by Rawalpindi.

Inadvertently, no doubt, Indian actions and statements encouraged some East Pakistanis to flee into India, but this was neither the consequence of a specific policy nor an objective of New Delhi's. There is no question, however, that Indian policy toward the refugees *once they were in India* was a major obstacle to any political settlement in East Pakistan. Throughout 1971 the Government of India considered any political settlement that did not specifically include provisions for the return of *all* refugees—not merely the Muslims—to East Pakistan to be unacceptable. Islamabad, on the other hand, appeared uninterested in any settlement under which the "traitorous" Hindu Bengali refugees would be allowed to return, at least on a wholesale basis. The refugee question thus became a major barrier to even the initiation of serious negotiations for a political settlement between the two countries, ultimately making a military solution appear to be the only realistic option to both sides.

The public reaction in India to the 25 March events in East Pakistan was voluble, intense, but rather uncertain on the most critical issue—the proper policy response. Initially, most of the official government spokesmen assumed a hands-off position, strongly criticizing the Pakistani government's crackdown, but nevertheless classifying it as an internal affair that was not a matter for Indian intervention.[24] With the growing numbers of refugees placing a heavy strain on Indian resources, however, the official line began to change. By early May some responsible government leaders were beginning to describe the refugee situation as a form of "indirect aggression" against India that was elevating Pakistan's civil conflict into a dispute between Pakistan and India.[25] This was still argued with restraint in the spring of 1971, but it provided a basis for New Delhi's demand for the resolution of the civil war in Pakistan and eventually for Indian intervention.

The Indian political parties were highly vocal, but proposed no specific policies to the government. A few Congress party leaders and members of parliament initially advocated a tough response as a form of pressure upon Pakistan to reverse its policy in East Pakistan. But by the end of May virtually all had fallen into line when Mrs. Gandhi made it clear that her government was on top of the situation and would move at its own time and discretion. There was little public, and reportedly not much private, pressure on the government from the Congress party thereafter. The opposition parties were more critical of the government's "weak" response to the crackdown in Pakistan, and most of them called for direct intervention in East Pakistan in support of the Bangladesh government in exile from the beginning of the crisis. Nevertheless, the opposition was not a serious problem for the government and could be ignored in the formulation of policy, as it generally supported the policies adopted by the government in 1971.[26]

The press was somewhat more divided than the parties on this issue, with some of the major English-language papers calling for moderation. Their editorials and some of the political commentary columns pointed to the dangers, both international and domestic, of overreaction by the Indian government. On the other side the conservative *Motherland* and *Organizer* and the pro-Soviet *Patriot* generally argued for immediate Indian intervention. But most of the press was noncommittal, which fitted in well with the government's position, and generally supported Mrs. Gandhi's carefully orchestrated policy response.

A few public figures in India played significant roles on both sides of the debate on East Pakistan. Undoubtedly the most highly publicized in Pakistan was K. Subrahmanyam, then the director of the Institute of Defence Studies and Analyses in New Delhi. On 31 March, Subrahmanyam participated in a Council of World Affairs seminar on the East Pakistani developments in which, in contrast to most of the other participants, he argued against a policy of restraint by the Indian government.[27] Then on 5 April he published an article in the *National Herald* (a newspaper that had long been closely associated with the Nehru family and strongly supported Indira Gandhi) in which he reiterated his argument that the East Pakistani crisis presented India with "an opportunity the like of which will never come again." This phrase was widely cited by the

Pakistani government, press, and intellectuals as *proof* that the Indian government had decided on an interventionist policy by late March—if not earlier—given Subrahmanyam's "important" position and status in governmental circles.[28] According to Subrahmanyam, however, he had not consulted with any government officials in preparing the article, which was an expression of his personal opinion.[29] Moreover, the *National Herald* refused to publish subsequent articles by Subrahmanyam stating similar views, and he had to turn to the pro–Jana Sangh paper *Motherland* as a medium for publication. Later, he was "advised" by the Defence Ministry to suspend publication of articles on the subject when a report prepared by him for a "closed door" seminar sponsored by his own institute advocating the seizure of sections of East Pakistan and the establishment there of a provisional government of Bangladesh under Indian army protection was acquired by a London *Times* correspondent, published, and even more widely quoted than his earlier statement.[30] While we cannot conclude from all this that the Government of India did not share his views, it raises doubts about Pakistani assertions that Subrahmanyam spoke for New Delhi.

The tendency in both Pakistan and India to look for "worst case" interpretations of each other's behavior is reflected in Pakistan's failure to place Subrahmanyam's contributions to the debate in India in proper perspective. Several other, more prominent Indians who publicly counseled against any form of Indian involvement in East Pakistan were totally ignored in Pakistan. These included C. Rajagopalachari, governor-general of India from 1947 to 1950 and a former chief minister of Tamil Nadu; General Cariappa, the former commanding general of the Indian army; and M. Karunanidhi, the chief minister of Tamil Nadu in 1971, who cited the developments in East Pakistan as a warning to India to avoid creating conditions that would encourage autonomy movements in its own territory.[31]

While only a small number of politicians expressed such views publicly, several key members in the Indian bureaucracy shared their reservations about the ultimate consequences of Indian intervention in a neighboring state. Some were concerned with international reaction, particularly from several Islamic states with whom India had important ties. Others were apprehensive that the "national liberation" movement in East Pakistan would provide a precedent for similar regional separatist political movements in

India. Bangladesh, they noted, meant "country of the Bengalis," and India had a large number of Bengalis in its population who might be attracted by the "Amra Bengali" ("We're Bengalis") concept of a unified, independent Bengal.[32] And on security policy, some officials argued that Indian interests were better served by an East Pakistan that was, in fact, "captive" to India, and thus a complication to decision making in Islamabad, than they would be by a second large Islamic state in the subcontinent.[33] The bureaucrats, of course, usually refrained from expressing such views publicly, but channeled them to Mrs. Gandhi's core group, who then considered them.

The decision-making elite in the Government of India could not totally ignore public views on the East Pakistani situation, but it handled all suggestions and criticisms calmly, rarely rejecting anything out of hand, but also rarely, if ever, revising policies to suit critics. Thus, while East Pakistan was the most widely and intensely debated issue in India throughout 1971, the total effect of all this clamor on decision making was negligible. From 25 March to the end of May, New Delhi discouraged projections of a major Indian role in the resolution of the crisis in East Pakistan, which did not make good political or strategic sense. The Indian army was prepared neither for direct intervention in East Pakistan nor for the inevitable counterthrust from West Pakistan.[34] New Delhi considered it essential to assist in the creation of a resistance movement in East Pakistan as the political and military basis for direct Indian intervention. If military action were unavoidable, India preferred that its moves be interpreted as supportive of a Muslim-led East Pakistani liberation movement rather than just another Indian-Pakistani (i.e., Hindu-Muslim) conflict.

India also sought to set the stage for widespread international support, both official and popular, for intervention prior to the act itself. An interventionist policy in the spring of 1971 would have been condemned by most of the international community, including some of India's friends. In this first stage of the crisis, therefore, New Delhi placed great emphasis on the *duty* of the international community to bring pressure to bear on Pakistan for a political solution that met East Pakistani (and Indian) demands, for example, a popularly elected Awami League government that provided for the return of all the refugees who had fled to India.[35] From the very beginning there was little apparent optimism in New Delhi that other countries would respond effectively to this challenge. Nevertheless, the Government of India considered it necessary to provide the international community with the opportunity to act, particularly since India could not do much itself at this stage of developments.

India's policy during March through May 1971 can thus best be described as a holding operation while New Delhi appraised both the strength of the resistance in East Pakistan and the willingness and capacity of the rest of the world to intervene to resolve the crisis on terms New Delhi could accept. By mid May the Indians were impressed with both the intensity and the breadth of the opposition to the Pakistani government in East Pakistan and had concluded that, with some encouragement and assistance, the resistance could be sustained to the point where the price Islamabad had to pay would become too high and a negotiated settlement might appear the better alternative to the Yahya Khan government. New Delhi had also concluded by the end of May that the major external powers would be only peripheral factors in East Pakistan and would also not place any serious obstacle in the way of direct Indian intervention if this should become necessary.

The magnitude of the refugee crisis was impressed on Mrs. Gandhi during a two-day visit to the states of Assam, Tripura, and West Bengal in mid May prior to the opening of the budget session of parliament. The refugees in some districts of these states outnumbered the local population. The prime minister's concern was reflected in her comments in the Lok Sabha shortly after it convened in the latter part of May. Mrs. Gandhi noted that more than 330 camps had been established to care for the nearly 4 million refugees who had arrived in India by that time and who were continuing to come at an estimated rate of 60,000 a day. "Pakistan cannot be allowed to seek a solution of its political or other problems at the expense of India and on Indian soil," she declared.[36] Subsequently the government reported to parliament that as of 8 June some 4.7 million refugees had arrived, and by mid July the government estimated that 6.9 million were being assisted at over 1,000 camps and reception centers. By the end of May, 900,000 refugees had arrived in the small hill state of Tripura, according to a report to parliament, placing an enormous burden on a state with an indigenous population of only 1.5 million. The budgets of state governments could not meet the cost of refugee support, and the central government had to extend "on-account advances" to help meet deficits.

The severe health problems of the camps and among the general populations where the refugees were concentrated contributed to the sense of impending crisis. The government indicated that by 4 June there had been approximately 9,500 cases of cholera reported, with 1,250 deaths. This toll progressively increased, and the number of cholera cases among the refugees alone was estimated at over 46,000 by the end of September, with nearly 6,000 deaths.[37] Of concern also was the entry of refugees into an already volatile labor market and the problems of social unrest that the density of populations induced.[38]

Mrs. Gandhi reported to parliament that although foreign governments had expressed their sympathy and concern in response to India's request that they press Pakistan to come to terms with those elected in East Pakistan, none of them were prepared to take action to bring about what the Indian government had come to accept as necessary for a settlement that would enable the refugees to return to their homes—an agreement between the central government of Pakistan and the Awami League under the leadership of Mujib. She stated on May 24:

> Conditions must be created to stop any further influx of refugees and to ensure their early return under credible guarantees for their safety and well-being. I say with all sense of responsibility that unless this happens, there can be no lasting stability or peace on this subcontinent. We have pleaded with other powers to recognize this. If the world does not take heed, we shall be constrained to take all measures as may be necessary to ensure our own security and the preservation and development of the structure of our social and economic life.[39]

She also observed that there must be a political, rather than military, solution to Pakistan's problem in its eastern province and that the great powers had a special responsibility to help see such a solution through.

8

Pakistan, 25 March–October 1971

On 26 March Yahya addressed his "fellow countrymen" to explain and justify the military's takeover of East Pakistan. His audience, the "fellow countrymen," were West Pakistanis; East Pakistanis were not encompassed. The speech was delivered in Karachi rather than in Dhaka; those declared culpable were members of the Awami League; no West Pakistani leader or party was judged responsible either wholly or in part for the impasse. The leaders of the east stood charged with treason, and a substantial majority of their Bengali-speaking supporters were perceived as guilty through complicity.

The president commenced his speech by reviewing the efforts he had made to encourage dialogue and agreement among political leaders on the subject of a viable constitutional arrangement for the country. In so doing, he noted that "having consulted West Pakistan leaders it was necessary for me to do the same *over there* so that areas of agreement could be identified and an amicable settlement arrived at."[1] The military action "over there," he argued, was prompted by Mujib's failure to "see reason." Yahya continued by proposing that Mujib's "obstinacy, obduracy and absolute refusal to talk sense can lead to but one conclusion—the man and his party are enemies of Pakistan and they want East Pakistan to break away completely from the country. He has attacked the solidarity and integrity of this country—this crime will not go unpunished."[2] The president suspended all political activity and banned the Awami League. But in an effort to retain options for a future political settlement, the president stated that those elected on the Awami League ticket would not be deprived of their constitutional position by virtue of their party affiliation alone—they would be able to retain their positions in their individual capacities. However, the terms of the decision made at this time and set forth in this declaration were to severely constrain future deliberations and choices concerning constitutional and political settlement.

THE "MILITARY SOLUTION ACCORDING TO PLAN"

As threats to the interests and values important to the army increased and as expectations for a political settlement that could be trusted declined, Yahya, under pressure from his army command, chose to pursue a "military solution according to plan." More than a month previously the army command had argued that the real threats to its security interests had become exceptionally grave. Lines of communication and supplies in East Pakistan had been interrupted. Crowds had successfully disrupted the efforts of military personnel to unload military supply ships in Chittagong after civilian employees had refused to do so. The threat to the non-Bengali Muslims living in the east, who were seen by Bengalis as agents of the west, was also judged by the military authorities to be substantial. Violations of martial law were becoming an unacceptable affront to the military's sense of public propriety and discipline. The army was losing control. As Yahya was to note in his 26 March speech, the Awami League had insulted Pakistan's flag and defiled the photograph of Jinnah, the Father of the Nation; murders had been committed in the name of the movement; and the armed forces located in East Pakistan had been subjected to "taunts and insults of all kinds."[3]

The army especially feared a mutiny of its Bengali units. Yahya had been advised in mid February that a strong sentiment prevailed in the civilian as well as in the military and police services in East Pakistan in support of the Awami League, and that it would be difficult under the current circumstances for Bengali troops and police to fire on their own people.[4] In the view of key army commanders in the west, these observations were given powerful credence by the events that followed the postponement of the National Assembly. On 12 March the president had again been advised that the support of Bengali troops in any military action was doubtful; ten days later it was feared that units of the East Bengal Regiment would be responsive to the directives of the

Awami League rather than those of the army. Given these exigencies, the commanding officers insisted that preemptive action against Bengali military and police units and installations was necessary to forestall mutiny as well as to reassert governmental authority. If action were not taken, the army in East Pakistan might be divided, if not destroyed.

The military also claimed to have evidence that the Awami League itself was planning an insurgency against non-Bengalis, military and civilian alike. This judgment was not based on what one officer referred to as "refined intelligence," but was suggested by the boldness of the paramilitary training organized by student groups, the demonstrations of support for the Awami League on the part of ex-servicemen, the involvement of Col. M. A. G. Osmani as an adviser to the Awami League on military affairs, and the intelligence network and support that the Awami League had evidently developed within Bengali units of the armed forces.[5]

As the threat to the military increased, expectations of an acceptable political settlement declined. The military, in the words of one principal on the government negotiating team, perceived itself as "getting nothing" while "giving in on everything" in the negotiations.[6] The negotiations themselves seemed unending and openended, and the army's distrust was confirmed by the belief that the Awami League was making qualitatively new demands after the members of the government had understood that an agreement had been reached. That the Awami League leadership was not receptive to the accommodative counsel of West Pakistani political leaders was taken as evidence that the league did not want a constitutional agreement conducive to the maintenance of national integrity. Suspicion focused on whether Mujib was being duplicitous or whether he had lost control of his party, but either was judged unacceptable.

The military further noted that the cost of inaction and continuing the political negotiations would be great, first in the slide toward anarchy in the east and second in the alienation of populations in West Pakistan. The costs of military action would be relatively small, and it would have the positive consequence of "cleaning the political stables" in the east, while at the same time creating conditions that would be more conducive to a lasting political solution the military and western political parties could live with. Military action was thus seen as the only means of halting the continuing political crisis and as essential as well to avoid loss of control over the East Pakistani military units.

The military command did not see its action as being constrained by either regional or international considerations. Indeed, each of these contexts was seen as favoring military action. The action contemplated was to be surgical and directed at a problem that was exclusively internal. It was to be carried out in such a way as not to alarm India or provoke the Indian army by carrying military operations close to border areas.[7] Given the above objectives and conditions, Indian military involvement would be difficult to justify and was not considered a serious possibility by the Pakistani command.

That India was involved, and a major cause of the current problem, was not disputed within the military high command. The consensus among top decision makers at the time was summed up in the comments of one central figure, who stated that the Pakistani government had received intelligence reports of Indian involvement in East Pakistani affairs from both civilian and military intelligence services, but that regardless of whether or not verifiable evidence was available, it was accepted as fact that India was involved. India had always been involved in Pakistani affairs, and thus there was no need to monitor or verify such intelligence reports.[8] A continuation of the political dialogue and the deepening of discontent would only encourage Indian interference, but military action would stop it.

While there were differences of opinion within the general officer corps on how to handle the military operation, there was consensus on the objectives to be achieved and the strategy to be employed in what was called "Operation Searchlight."[9] The objectives were to neutralize the political power of the Awami League and to reestablish public order. First, the top leadership of the party had to be captured. The second priority was to neutralize its more radical elements, in particular student leaders and organizations and various cultural organizations that advocated a Bengali renaissance. Several residential halls at the University of Dhaka would need to be cleared of students and checked for arms that were believed to be there in preparation for rebellion. Leaders were to be taken peacefully if possible, but if armed resistance was offered, troops were to respond with force.

Third, the Bengali armed forces had to be disarmed and neutralized. The army assumed that the East Bengal Regiment, the East Pakistan Rifles, the Ansars, and the police would all turn against the military authorities. Finally, the operation called for the establishment of control over all communications media. After taking over the large urban areas, the army was to restore order in the remainder of the province in four phases: (1) clearing all major border towns and sealing routes of infiltration; (2) opening essential river, road, and rail communications; (3) clearing all major towns in the interior and coastal areas; and (4) combing out rebels and infiltrators from the whole of the province.

Although the army was successful in its mission in most major urban centers within ten days of the first strike, it took six weeks before the martial law authorities gained control over the entire province. At the beginning of the crackdown there had been only islands of effective government control. After two days of fighting, for example, the army claimed effective control only in Dhaka, the Comilla cantonment, the Syhlet airport, Rangpur, the Saidpur cantonment, Khulna, and Rajshahi. After two weeks of hostilities the only links between Dhaka and the cantonments of Chittagong, Comilla, Syhlet, Rangpur, Rajshahi, Jessore, and Khulna were by air. Indeed, both the Pakistani and Indian principals we interviewed agreed that through the middle of April it was possible for anyone, friend or foe, to traverse the province from east to west without being detected by the military or anyone else associated with the Pakistani government. Central governmental authority was not reestablished until 10 May, when the army took control of Cox's Bazar, located at the lower extremity of the eastern fringe of the province.

Although the military operation to reassert central authority was considered successful, efforts to arrest the Awami League elite and to disarm the Bengali units of the armed forces were not. The plan of military action was neither carried out in the sequence anticipated nor achieved its main objectives. Nearly all the Awami League leaders escaped, even though prior to the crackdown in Dhaka, government agents had marked their houses with chalk to assist the army units charged with arresting them.[10] The army was able to capture only those leaders who, for whatever reason, had decided not to try to escape into India. Those who sought to avoid arrest were able to do so.

There are several reasons for this outcome. The Awami League leadership had anticipated some form of military action since the early part of the year. Although at the outset such an eventuality had been judged quite unlikely, it was seen as a greater possibility in February and as a distinct threat after the deadly engagements of early March.[11] The Awami League leadership still felt, however, that because of the magnitude of its majority, the intensity of public support in the east, Yahya's apparently genuine commitment to transferring power, and the difficulties that any military action would encounter, a "military solution" would appear to the government as less than a rational choice, especially since other options were clearly available.

The Awami League leaders sensed that something was amiss, however, when Major Mazumdar, a supporter of the party, was summarily relieved of his command in Chittagong and transferred to Dhaka, where he could be monitored more easily by the army.[12] Furthermore, Wing Commander Khondkar, a Bengali officer, saw the president depart from Dhaka and informed Mujib at meetings subsequently held at Mujib's house in Dhan Mandi. On the night of 25 March, it was decided that everyone should disperse to avoid capture. Almost all did so, dressed in the garb of peasants. One leader left after spending almost two weeks bandaged as a casualty in a medical clinic. Almost all went into exile in India.

The problems the army faced in accomplishing its mission once again showed the limitations of its political intelligence and public support, as well as its incapacity to employ selective force against political targets. According to one high-ranking officer stationed in East Pakistan at the time, the troops did not know what the leaders of the Awami League looked like and were unable to discriminate differences in the features of their Bengali brethren. The Bengali police could not be relied upon to take action against the Awami League and had also been scheduled to be disarmed. The chaos in the streets, road blocks, human interference, and other forms of unexpected resistance resulted in more aggressive action than selective search and seizure. While the army was able to carry out the military aspects of the operation with considerable dispatch, it failed completely in its more uncomfortable and unfamiliar police role.

The army also met unexpectedly tough resistance from Bengali units and was unsuccessful in disarming all but a few. In some cases, Bengali troops killed their West Pakistani officers and fought rearguard actions on their way to the Indian border, where they became the core elements of the Mukti Bahini freedom fighters. In other instances, West Pakistani commanders were released or were able to escape to find their way to safety. Indian officials reported that some of the first refugees to arrive in India were West Pakistani officers attempting to escape the wrath of their troops.

AFTER THE CRISIS

The Pakistani army's apparent success in reestablishing order in the eastern province seemed to revalidate the assumption that the unruly Bengalis could be tamed and their radicalism contained by a firm military hand. It also seemed to justify the contention of many senior army officers that the Awami League movement could have been suppressed in early March had the will of leadership been stronger in Dhaka and had orders been executed with fidelity.

By April's end the military elite felt that it had surmounted or at least diminished the crisis. The Awami League, though not eliminated, had been isolated as a political force.[13] The government no longer had to deal with an antagonist demanding a decentralized political system that would place the military's corporate interests and West Pakistani economic interests at unacceptable risk. Time was on the government's side, and rushing into a political settlement was unnecessary. There were still three important considerations, however. First, to inhibit a Bengali revival, India's involvement in Pakistan's affairs had to be dramatized and an effort made to isolate India from international support. Second, the administrative and police apparatus in East Pakistan had to be recreated to maintain government authority and public order. Third, a political settlement had to be approached that would entail the bestowal of a constitution and the cleansing of the political elite of "corrupt and criminal elements" in a fashion similar to that pursued by Ayub Khan in the late 1950s.

Dealing with India

After the military action, rather than pursuing an immediate return to the quest for a constitutional settlement and a transfer of power, Pakistani decision makers focused on Indian actions, intentions, and capabilities. The government became obsessed with dramatizing the alleged collusion of the Indian government and the Awami League and New Delhi's continued involvement in Pakistan's internal affairs and tried to counter India's efforts to marshal international support for the immediate return of refugees in a manner consonant with the terms India espoused. Some leaders of political parties in West Pakistan who had been critical of the government during the negotiations condemned Indian interference in Pakistan's internal affairs within a week of the commencement of the military action. Both Radio Pakistan and the Pakistani press reported Indian incursions into Pakistani territory and the capture of Indian army personnel in substantial numbers, detailed Hindu oppression of Bengali Muslims prior to partition, and alleged an Indian plot for "brahmanical subjugation" of East Pakistan in order to finally establish "Akhand Bharat," a "Greater India" incorporating Pakistan.[14]

The Pakistani elite did not question whether or not India was involved in East Pakistan. Nor did it question India's ultimate aims. As clearly put to us by one principal, "variations in statements by Indian leaders had nothing to do with basic Indian policy; they did not reflect any basic differences in Indian objectives. Different statements may have been made to deflect, to lull, to deceive, much as players in a hockey match, some playing up, some playing back, but all committed to scoring a common goal. The basic and hostile intent of India's goal was the breakup of Pakistan."[15] After the military action, just as before, India was felt to be committed to the bifurcation of Pakistan. It wanted to whittle away at Pakistan territory and sovereignty if it could, just as it had in denying Pakistan its claim to Junagadh, Hyderabad, and Kashmir in 1947–48. A substantial segment of the Awami League, whether consciously or unconsciously, had become powerful instruments of Indian Policy.

Policies were thus developed to constrain Indian action, deny India international support, and dispel any Indian expectation of being able to influence the timing or character of the political solutions to be pursued in East Pakistan. Pakistan perceived India's capacities and alternatives as limited. India was obliged to provide sanctuary for the refugees; it could no more keep them out than it could weather the political consequences of a policy to deny them entry. India could extend limited support and training to the disparate guerrilla groups, but could not initiate massive involvement or intervention. These groups alone, even when organized as the Mukti Bahini, would not constitute a threat to the Pakistani army and the reconstituted East Pakistani constabulary. While India could encourage a favorable portrayal of the Bangladesh movement in the Western media, it would not be able to attract the support of many governments given the protective shield of a state system that mandated the continued integrity of sovereignties that had been extended de jure recognition by the international community. India could not attract support from the Muslim states, and aggressive action on India's part would result in its isolation from the Muslim world and jeopardize its standing in the nonaligned world. The Pakistani government found both pleasure and solace in India's notable lack of success in attracting international support despite its major diplomatic efforts. This contrasted with Pakistan's enjoyment of expressions of support and good wishes for a resolution of its "internal" problems in East Pakistan.[16]

India could thus not do those things that would be necessary to force an "Awami League solution" on East Pakistan. In the judgment of Pakistani military intelligence, India would probably back the Mukti Bahini, but not at a level that would make its containment unmanageable for the Pakistan army. Supported by Indian artillery, however, the Mukti Bahini could endeavor to nibble at the territory of Pakistan in an attempt to carve out a defensible "liberated" area from which a Bangladesh government could seek international recognition. In early June the Pakistani government regarded this as the most threatening goal India could pursue, and an outcome that had to be prevented.[17] Throughout the first part of June the Pakistani government attempted to portray India as committed to the breakup of Pakistan and as a constant meddler in Pakistan's internal affairs. It tried to secure commitments from foreign governments to the effect that the problems in East Pakistan were matters internal to Pakistan that did not admit of outside commentary and interference. By June, in contrast to India's inability to develop international support, Pakistan had received at least tacit support from all, and formal commitments from most, of the major powers and Muslim states on its position.

Reconstruction in East Pakistan

Within a month of the military action, the martial law authorities attempted to recreate the administrative structure in East Pakistan that had dissolved in March. This effort followed fairly quickly upon the restoration of military control over the major population centers. The martial law authorities were inclined by "reason of necessity" to sympathize with civilian administrators who had left their posts during and before the military action, whether out of fear or because they supported the Awami League movement, and as an inducement extended the promise of back pay for the period during which they had been absent from their desks.[18] By late May and before the activity of rebel forces had become more than a periodic nuisance, the civilian administration had been reestablished in elementary form, but it was never reconstructed completely and in many areas it was unable to exert authority or function effectively.

Another critical problem was the reorganization and reconstitution of the police and other internal security services so as to enable the army to withdraw from its police function, for which it was ill prepared, and return to its defense function.[19] In April the government tried to reestablish the East Pakistan Civil Affairs Force (EPCAF) by recruiting West Pakistanis, primarily from the Punjab police, and non-Bengali Muslims, commonly called "Biharis," resident in East Pakistan. The government experienced great difficulty in recruiting and organizing the EPCAF, which ultimately reached a strength of some ten thousand by November. This force, which was to provide security for border outposts, interdict incursions from across the border, and provide internal security after the Pakistan army moved to forward positions in September, never became effective, primarily because of a shortage of weapons and inadequate training. Senior army officers posted in East Pakistan have also reported that upon first contact with Indian troops in December, personnel of this force abandoned their positions with an immediacy unusual for people supposedly born to arms.[20]

Other forces were developed to defend against attacks on strategic communication centers, railroad bridges and transportation networks, and power installations. The first, the Internal Security Force (ISF), consisted of three thousand personnel, also primarily from West Pakistan. Of the twenty-two companies of the ISF, eight were recruited from among ex-servicemen, while the remaining fourteen were composed of raw recruits. It was complemented by the Vulnerable Points Force, also three thousand strong, recruited principally from pro-Pakistani groups in East Pakistan.

Reconstituting the police force was a particularly difficult and sensitive task. After initially disarming the units of the East Pakistan Rifles, the martial law authorities ultimately found it necessary to press those who had not fled to India back into service for duty in the *mofussil,* or hinterland, but augmented and closely monitored by transfers from the West Pakistani police. The military authorities ultimately judged these units ineffective and unreliable during the ensuing months; they often assisted the Mukti Bahini and its local supporters rather than disrupting and curtailing its activities. A new East Pakistani police force with a targeted strength of 11,500 (a number never realized) was also created to supplement and ultimately supplant the "old police force." It performed much more reliably, stimulated by accelerated promotions, monetary incentives, and postings in urban areas. Finally, some 5,000 West Pakistani police arrived in Dhaka toward the end of May for a six-month tour of duty and initially proved to be dependable and effective "rebel fighters." Toward the end of their tour, however, these units threatened to strike because they had not received any travel allowance, had not been provided with family housing, and had not been paid on time. They became particularly defiant upon receiving orders in early November directing that they remain in East Pakistan for another tour of duty.

In an effort to counter increasingly effective guerrilla activity in late summer, the martial law authorities also attempted to raise paramilitary forces of mujahids and razakars. The former were organized in thirteen battalions and forty-seven independent companies, but never became an effective force owing to the absence of trained officer personnel, inadequate facilities for training recruits, and limited availability of arms. In most instances Mujahid units were attached to regular army units both to amass firepower and to inhibit the dissolution of the former. The Razakars were created in an effort to concentrate support among religious youth to protect lines of communication, but in some instances this fostered conflict. Two distinct wings of the Razakars were formed. Al-Shams was charged with protecting bridges in and around urban areas and was relatively lax in recruitment and control. Al-Badr was recruited from public schools and *madrassas* (religious schools) and was used for raids and "special operations."

While the Pakistani government was able to reassert military control over East Pakistan, it was never able to reassert administrative control over the province outside the urban areas. The constraints of military necessity, time, and the availability of personnel inhibited reassertion before the monsoon season (June–September), and the heavy rains that year conspired to limit communication and access in rural areas. After the floods had abated, the Mukti Bahini increasingly demonstrated its capacity to disrupt and to deny the government consistent control. Personnel were also of necessity recruited in a manner that accented the difference between state and society. The reconstituted services were dominated by Punjabis and Pathans from the west and "Bihari" muslims from the east. The government thus became dependent on "alien" personnel for the administration and the maintenance of order among a population that had become estranged from a regime dominated by such aliens, but far less pervasively, in the recent past.

The government encountered insuperable organizational problems in recreating institutions employing personnel who were either on temporary duty or whose allegiance was in doubt. Those recruited from West Pakistan developed a "cantonment" mentality. They were isolated from local populations, who seemed to forget their bazaar Urdu upon the approach of Urdu-speaking government personnel. The armed services moved in large units, always returning to the psychological—and later the physical—protection of the barracks and the cantonments. The government was also faced with the collapse of its sources of information and means of communicating with rural areas.

TOWARD A POLITICAL SETTLEMENT

After the military action in March, the center of decision making in Pakistan shifted from the Office of the President and the headquarters of the chief martial law administrator to the general headquarters of the army. This change reflected Yahya's perception that the central government's problems in the east were primarily military ones and his greater ease among the officers with whom he had spent his career.[21] Those in the military who had been particularly active in searching for a negotiated settlement found their access to the president even more circumscribed during this period than they had in the past. Leaders of political parties did not try to influence policy, and the government did not seek their views. The military would pursue its own agenda and time schedule.

The first efforts to develop a strategy for a transfer of power commenced in late May. Although deliberations were not formulated around formally stated alternatives, four general approaches were proposed by various officers with access to the president. One plan suggested from within the martial law administration, but quickly vetoed and discarded, advocated a return to the status quo ante. It involved culling the most extreme groups from the Awami League before the president called a meeting of the National Assembly, which would then work on framing a constitution based on the tentative understandings reached before the military action. An anticipated benefit of this approach would be the indication that the martial law authorities had indeed been acting in good faith and were truly committed to the transfer of power.

The military viewed this option as both impossible to implement and unthinkable in terms of military "ethics." Such a strategy would require the release of Mujib and the declaration of a general amnesty. Mujib could not be released, however, since he had been declared guilty of crimes against the state. While politicians might be able to shift their positions thus, several senior officers in the martial law administration observed, such behavior went totally against the military grain, and it would have been perceived publicly in West Pakistan as capitulation. Furthermore, most military leaders felt that the Awami League leaders who had gone to India were doubly guilty of treason. Inviting such traitors back to govern was unthinkable. This position was shared, though more for practical than for ethical reasons, by the leaders of the opposition parties in the east.

The experience of the military action had hardened the army's perception of the Awami League as duplicitous and untrustworthy, and if the transfer of power had been fraught with danger before, it now faced even greater uncertainties. Differences still remained with respect to constitutional issues, and the Awami League elite would no doubt by now have become more firmly set in its stance. The Awami League, and particularly Mujib, would have no standing in the west, and the possibility of creating a governing coalition, problematic before, was now even more remote. The military also had neither the energy nor the patience to return to a negotiation process that it had no power to end. It felt that even if the Awami League were to return contrite and agree to military terms for the transfer of power, the army would ultimately become captive of the insurgency led by the Mukti Bahini. In sum, as one high-ranking officer in the regime insisted, almost everyone concerned believed that if the government were to return to the pre-March situation, the army would appear "an insane, but cruel, collection of clowns." The central government for all intents and purposes would be extending independence to Bangladesh without a contest and after justifying military action against the threat of precisely that eventuality. India would also have won a decisive victory without contest or cost. Finally, the pursuit of such an alternative risked a severe division within the officer corps, the consequences of which would be uncertain.

A second option involved calling the National Assembly and simultaneously granting selective amnesty to those who had gone to India or underground in opposition to the central government. It also involved the appointment of a national government by the martial law authorities with Mujib as prime minister and representation from all parties in the west. Several arguments were advanced on behalf of this position. Selective amnesty would divide the Awami League by peeling off the more radical elements, who would, it might be hoped, remain in India rather than risk return. Second, the government could release Mujib by explaining that he had been liberated from the tyranny of the extremists in his party and could now function as a true patriot. Mujib would then be dependent upon the assistance of the military to keep the extremist factions isolated. If Mujib succeeded, it would be on terms not inimical to the military; if he failed, the Awami League would collapse and a new party coalition would be possible. Furthermore, if the military chose this alternative and formed a government before the monsoons, India would have difficulty expanding its military involvement in support of the Mukti Bahini, and the prospects for maintaining the integrity of the country would be dramatically increased. This option, however, like the first, foundered on the release of Mujib and the risks entailed in inviting those already judged traitors to return.

A third option was to start anew. New elections would be called, and a committee appointed by the president would draft a constitution, taking into account interests and agreements that had already been registered and reached, but deciding autonomously on issues that remained unresolved. New elections might not only generate greater plurality of representation in East Pakistan, but also place stress on the fissures within the Pakistan People's Party, with the possibility of it being returned without a majority in any western province. The establishment of a presidential constitutional commission had been considered previously, but rejected during deliberations concerning the Legal Framework Order. Because agreement on a substantial range of issues had been reached in the March negotiations and others were non-negotiable as far as the army was concerned, a promulgated constitution would have the virtues of inhibiting Bhutto's veto role and of reducing the likelihood that new issues would arise to further frustrate the search for a constitutional solution. Like the first two, however, this option was discarded. The risks were too great and it was too uncertain that the electoral outcome would be substantially different from the previous election—and if different, better. The best political estimates had been woefully off the mark in December. Moreover, the PPP had made known its adamant opposition to any new elections, reflecting its fear of losing its majority in the west, and had declared that it would boycott and disrupt them if they were called. The military did not relish the possibility of the disorder in the east spreading to the west.

The fourth option was to extend selective amnesty and to charge a committee with drafting a new constitution. This had all the virtues but fewer of the risks associated with the other suggested plans. Constitutional controversy would be reduced, and the corporate interests of the military could be protected as in option three. Martial law would remain in effect for some time, as had been initially anticipated under the provisions of the Legal Framework Order. Selective amnesty would provide representatives elected in December 1970 with the opportunity to repent and mend their ways. Those who did not return within a specified time would have their election declared void, and by-elections would be held before the convening of the National Assembly for all seats vacated in this fashion.

President Yahya chose to follow essentially this option. On 21 May he offered the first invitation to the refugees to return to their homes, with subsequent statements made on 25 May, 1 June, 10 June, 18 June, and 28 June in a presidential address.[22] In his speech of 28 June, Yahya also announced the appointment of a Bengali, Dr. A. M. Malik, as special assistant to the president for displaced persons and relief and rehabilitation operations in East Pakistan. These appeals, however, were ineffective. They did not result in substantial repatriation, and the magnitude of the refugee flow increased dramatically after the initial appeals had been made, with over half the refugees making their way into India after the presidential statement at the end of June. This alarmed the Indian decision makers as to the intent and the capacity of the Pakistani government to correct the refugee problem and reach a political accommodation with the Awami League, judged essential by New Delhi if the refugees were to return to their homes, as return they eventually must.

Furthermore, in his 28 June statement, much to New Delhi's dismay, Yahya indicated categorically that there would neither be new elections nor a return to the status quo ante. He reiterated the ban on the Awami League and the continued isolation of Mujib from public life because of actions that were "tantamount to secession." The president declared that Mujib's duplicity and untrustworthiness were reflected in his initial indication that the Six-Point Demand was negotiable followed by his indication later that it was not and in his refusal to visit West Pakistan despite repeated invitations. In sum, Mujib "had no intention of acting in a responsible and a patriotic manner as leader of the majority party in the country as a whole. He had already made up his mind that he was going to break the country into two, preferably by trickery and if this did not succeed, by physical violence." Yahya declared that Mujib and the Awami League had also enlisted the assistance of India in their plan. "It is unfortunate," he noted, "that our neighbor, which has never missed an opportunity to weaken or cripple our country, rushed to help the secessionists with men and material to inflame the situation further. This was all pre-planned. As the troops moved forward and fanned out, the whole dark plan of collusion between the Awami League extremists, rebels and our hostile neighbor gradually unfolded itself."[23]

In his plan for a political settlement the president reached to the past, to stratagems of his predecessor, for guidance. The first stratagem was the "cleansing" of the Awami League elite of elements who threatened Pakistan's integrity. In his statement Yahya implied that distinctions had to be made within the Awami League. He referred, for example, to the "unscrupulous and secessionist elements in the defunct Awami League" and stated how his efforts to mediate between parties on a lasting constitutional framework had been "frustrated by certain leaders of the defunct Awami League." He then proposed that those representatives elected on the Awami League ticket who had not engaged in antistate, criminal, or antisocial activities would be allowed to retain "their status as such in their individual capacities." The president would decide who would survive and who would not, with by-elections being held to fill the vacancies created by the disqualification of the latter. This purge was modeled on the Elective Offices (Disqualification) Order of 1959 under which Ayub Khan's martial law administration had been able to prohibit the electoral activity of those found guilty of corrupt political practices. The prohibition had lasted long enough to allow the development of a new political elite and the formation of new political institutions without the participation of those beholden to the old. The provisions of the Ayub regime, however, had applied to politicians from East and West Pakistan alike; those of the Yahya regime were to affect politicians from East Pakistan alone.

Yahya also decided, as had Ayub before him, that a "committee of experts" would draft the new constitution, which would then be promulgated under the rubric of martial law authority, with the possibility of amendment in the National Assembly under provisions that would be included in the draft constitution. He indicated that he had already appointed a constitutional committee, which had started its work. In his discussion of this approach, the president referred to the difficulties experienced by the Constituent Assembly in drafting a constitution during the first nine years after independence, which had ultimately resulted in the creation of one that was short-lived. He noted too the political problems under the Ayub constitution, in which participation had been constrained and found wanting by 1969. It was Yahya's sense that it was necessary to promulgate a constitution sensitive to the demands for popular participation and provincial autonomy and responsive to "responsible" public opinion, yet at the same time to avoid the parochial excesses that public forums for constitutional debate in Pakistan seemed to encourage.

Finally, he declared that the fragmented, provincially based party system made manifest in the 1970 elections was as disruptive to national unity as a similar system had been during the two years prior to the military coup of 1958. Thus, Yahya indicated, he had suggested to the constitutional committee that "in the interest of the integrity of the country, it would be a good thing if we ban any party which is confined to a specific region and is not national in the practical sense."[24] Designed to encourage interprovincial coalitions, this proposal would, of course, have banned all parties as they stood after the 1970 elections.

The martial law authorities gave political settlement secondary priority during July. They were concerned with India's intentions and activities, and they were absorbed with the visit of U.S. Secretary of State Henry Kissinger that month, whose trip to China had been arranged through the good offices of the Pakistani government. Convinced of Indian complicity in Awami League strategy and in backing the Mukti Bahini, the government perceived an escalation on the part of India in July. After a stop in New Delhi, Kissinger reportedly indicated to the Pakistanis that he had found there a "mood of bitterness, hostility and hawkishness."[25] He had reportedly come away with the distinct impression that India was likely to start a war with Pakistan, and while he had firmly warned India against such action, it was his sense that India would not pay heed. He observed as well that the hostile attitude in the U.S. Senate concerning East Pakistan and American policy toward Pakistan might encourage India to invade. Kissinger is also reported to have suggested that it would be helpful if India were to receive a signal from China that it was strongly committed to maintaining the unity of Pakistan and that in the case of hostilities between Pakistan and India, China would "not remain a silent spectator."

In this context Yahya declared on 19 July that any effort on the part of India to take over any territory in East Pakistan would result in a "general war."[26] He announced too that Mujib would be soon tried secretly in a military court for waging war against Pakistan. This declaration of intent was taken by Indian decision makers involved in formulating policy toward Pakistan as an indication of the Pakistani government's intransigence with respect to any workable political accommodation in the east.[27] The Indian government sensed that whatever his talents or lack thereof as a statesman and administrator, Mujib was critical to the leadership of the Awami League. He was the unquestioned leader of the party; the movement it represented had been created around him; without him groups within the Awami League were quarrelsome and lacked coherence. A central and consistently held tenet of Indian policy was that the Pakistani government would have to negotiate with Mujib if a lasting and stable political settlement were to be achieved in East Pakistan.

Two days after India and the Soviet Union signed a Treaty of Peace and Friendship on August 7, Yahya announced that Mujib's trial would begin 11 August. The trial was held in camera, and the government did not break its silence on the proceedings until 28 September, when it announced in a press release that the prosecution had begun presenting its case on 7 September and that twenty witnesses had been called to testify.[28] The trial was to last through the escalation of the crisis between India and Pakistan in the fall, and the results had not been made public by the time war was declared on 3 December.

In its preparation to isolate members of the Awami League from the political process, both the civilian and military intelligence agencies, as well as the martial law administration in East Pakistan, were charged by the president with preparing lists of Awami League members of both the National and Provincial assemblies that detailed their activities since the first of March. These lists were consolidated and used by Yahya to decide who were to be "cleansed" and who were to be "disqualified" from assuming the seats to which they had been elected.[29] The results were announced during the first week of August: 79 of the 160 Awami League National Assembly members were disqualified, 30 of whom were charged with sedition, and 195 of the 228 Provincial Assembly members were disqualified.[30] The others were allowed to sit as members of the assembly to which they had been elected, but not as members of the Awami League. The call for by-elections was not forthcoming until 19 September, one day after Yahya's statement indicating that a constitution was soon to be drafted. An appointed election commission announced that elections for 78 seats to the National Assembly and 105 to the Provincial Assembly would be held between 25 November and 9 December, with elections for the remaining seats to be held at a time to be specified later.[31]

Although there was contact between Mujibnagar and the Pakistani government, Yahya resisted proposals that he negotiate a new political arrangement with the Awami League. A major conduit between the martial law administration in East Pakistan and Mujibnagar was reportedly a Provincial Assembly member from Tajuddin's constituency who had suggested to the martial law authorities as well as to the governor of the province that if negotiations could be held on the basis of full autonomy for East Pakistan, a settlement within the rubric of a united Pakistan could be found.[32] As early as 30 July a representative of the Awami League approached a U.S. consular official in Calcutta reporting that he had been deputed by the Bangladesh foreign minister, Khondikar Mushtaq Ahmed, to indicate that leaders in Mujibnagar were anxious to explore a political settlement with the Government of Pakistan and were prepared to withdraw the demand for independence. This emissary suggested a "summit meeting" between the United States, India, Pakistan, and the Awami League to explore possibilities, although such a meeting would have to include Mujib.[33] In another meeting later in Delhi between representatives of the Awami League and the United States, the Awami League was described as "sharply contradictory" regarding compromise as opposed to independence.[34] Subsequently the Awami League contact from Mujibnagar in Calcutta indicated that a political settlement had the support of the entire "Bangladesh cabinet," information that the U.S. government authorized the Government of Pakistan to receive without comment as to its merits.[35]

The prospects for direct talks between Awami League representatives in Mujibnagar and the Pakistan government were minimal after mid August. In a 19 August meeting with U.S. Ambassador Joseph S. Farland and Maurice Williams, deputy administrator of the U.S. Agency for International Development (USAID), Yahya reaffirmed his refusal to deal with any group, however purged, under the name or banner of the Awami League, although he held out the possibility that additional names of assembly members elected in 1970 might be added to the list of those cleared.[36] In early September the Government of Bangladesh in exile advised all members of the Awami League that they would be disciplined for engaging in contacts with foreigners. On 25 September, one week after the call for by-elections and the Pakistani government's announcement that it was proceeding to draft a constitution, Khondikar Mushtaq, reputed to be the leader of the Awami League most inclined to pursue a political settlement, declared that the aim was now "total independence."[37]

The timetable for the holding of elections and the transfer of power accelerated after mid September, as Mukti Bahini resistance became more effective and India more inclined to use force from across the border. By 12 October, Yahya had announced that a constitution would be made public by 20 December, that elections would be completed by 23 December, and that the National Assembly would be summoned to meet on 27 December.[38]

ELECTIONS AS A MEASURE OF SUPPORT

A new sense of urgency was induced by the government's realization that holding the elections it had called would be physically impossible. The preparations for them were a severe test of its writ of authority; it proved impossible to set up polling stations and provide the protection they required in many areas over which the government had believed it enjoyed control.[39] Other constituencies were located in areas contested by the Mukti Bahini, in which government control could not even be secured. The government thus found it necessary to hold "uncontested" elections in a number of areas.

The government's own "strategy" in the elections was to facilitate the activities of parties that enjoyed popular support in the provinces of the western wing, but had a weak autonomous popular base in East Pakistan, through active cohorts of party elites in that province. The government supported parties opposed to the Pakistan People's party in an effort to encourage an electoral outcome that would preclude a PPP majority in the National Assembly and make possible the creation of a coalition government with Nurul Amin as prime minister and Bhutto as deputy prime minister, as the latter had proposed in his negotiations with Mujib.[40] The government hoped to facilitate a distribution of party strength more congruently with what had been anticipated before the elections of 1970, resulting in a government more amenable to presidential persuasion.

The call for by-elections encouraged renewed activity on the part of the political parties, which had maintained a low profile during the six months after their meeting in Dhaka. Since both National Assembly and Provincial Assembly elections were to be held, and there was the possibility of the National Assembly being convened in West Pakistan and a new constitution being devised regardless of the state of affairs in the east, it was essential for parties to compete. The most vigorous advocate of contesting the elections was Bhutto, who insisted in early September that a return to civilian governance was necessary to solve the crisis, and that the civil war could yet extend to West Pakistan.[41] Later in the month he demanded that power be handed over to him and the PPP by the end of the year and also observed that governments could be changed by parliamentary means, by revolution, or by coups d'état and that the People's party was preparing for all eventualities.[42]

In early October leaders of several political parties other than the Awami League and PPP started to consider merging and creating a United Front that would make possible no-contest agreements in the elections and provide the basis for a parliamentary coalition in the National Assembly. The government was also deeply interested in assisting no-contest arrangements among conservative parties of both secular and religious predilections given their integrationist and anti-Indian orientations.[43] The move toward coalition was furthered by the announcement on 22 October that 201 candidates were running for 78 National Assembly seats and 276 for 81 of the 105 Provincial Assembly seats.[44] Coalitions were also encouraged when it became clear to the martial law authorities later in October that holding bona fide elections in East Pakistan would be impossible because of the tenuous government authority in many constituencies. Protection of voters could not be assured, campaigning could not be conducted without grave risk, and there were not enough officials available to man polling stations.

On 26 October Nurul Amin announced that a coalition of six parties had been created. At the same time the leaders of each party made public statements condemning India's involvement in the disruption of political order in East Pakistan.[45] Amin also stated that agreement had been reached on a list of candidates for 78 National Assembly seats and a list of 178 jointly sponsored candidates for elections to the Provincial Assembly.[46] On 29 October the government announced that 50 National Assembly seats had been filled without contest, a figure that had increased to 58 by 8 November.[47] The following day the government announced that candidates in 105 Provincial Assembly constituencies had been "elected" unopposed as well.

The remaining elections were never held. One senior army officer in East Pakistan spoke of "total administrative paralysis and absence of governmental control" in outlying areas from November on. The election process would clearly have to be brokered through an agreement among the political elite with the good offices of the martial law authorities—elections in drawing rooms rather than in polling stations.[48] On 7 December, in the midst of the war and after military reverses in East Pakistan, the government announced that the remaining elections were being postponed indefinitely. It was like a scene from the theater of the absurd.

9

India and the Prelude to War, June–October 1971

Any hope that the East Pakistan civil war might be resolved without an Indian contribution to the "solution" had virtually disappeared in New Delhi by the end of May 1971. One of the major factors in the Government of India's assessment of these developments was Pakistan's obvious inflexibility toward the "dissident" forces in East Pakistan. The inevitable consequence of this was a massive outpouring of refugees into India from mid April on. By June nearly four million refugees had crossed over, most of them Bengali Hindus likely to become permanent residents of India unless drastic changes in the political, social, and economic environment in East Pakistan would allow India, in effect, to force them to return.

Bengali Hindus in East Pakistan were largely concentrated in several districts bordering on India. They were thus well placed to make their escape when the Pakistani army moved in to occupy these areas in April and May. Although according to reports the military indulged in some anti-Hindu actions, by midsummer these had largely been brought under control. According to several unofficial Indian sources, it was primarily West Pakistani paramilitary units, and in some cases Bengali Muslims, who indulged in anti-Hindu outbursts thereafter, persuading ever larger numbers of Hindus to flee. It would also appear from some reports that pro–Awami League and anti–West Pakistani Bengali Muslims were not prepared to do much to protect the Bengali Hindus in East Pakistan, who might consequently be disinclined to return even to an independent Bangladesh without assurances of Indian support and protection. This was an important factor in Indian decision making on East Pakistan, since New Delhi was not confident that an Awami League government would welcome back the Hindu refugees, who, if allowed to stay in India, would place an unaccept-able burden on the economy and exacerbate social tension.[1]

The theme of economic burden had become prominent in both Indian domestic and international calculations by late spring. The official estimates for supporting several million refugees in camps that had to be constructed and maintained for this purpose were astronomical in terms of India's resources, threatening a serious disruption of the government's budget allocations for development programs and cutting deeply into the country's substantial, but painfully acquired, grain surplus. In the Indian view the interna-tional community was responding slowly and inadequately; other countries eventually assumed only about one-fourth of the esti-mated costs of supporting the refugees in camps and virtually none of the costs for the large number of refugees who found sanctuary outside the camps.[2] There were, moreover, strong doubts in gov-ernment circles that even this level of international assistance would be long maintained unless most of the refugees were kept concentrated in camps rather than allowed to disperse into the broader Indian public as had millions of refugees in the postparti-tion period.

In late May consideration began to be given to proposals to move a large number of the refugees to camps outside the Indian states bordering East Pakistan, and in early June the Indian government reached a decision "in principle" to allow limited dispersal on this basis.[3] Some refugees were moved from the overcrowded camps immediately on the border in the overburdened tribal hill state of Tripura in June and July with the assistance of U.S. and Soviet air forces, chiefly to camps in adjacent areas of Assam and West Bengal.[4] In July the Government of India announced its intention to move 2.5 million of the refugees to camps away from the border,[5] but this plan was never implemented on that scale and most of the refugees remained confined to camps near the border throughout 1971. The cost of relocating them was a major disincentive, but even more important to New Delhi were the possible political consequences, domestic and international, of a removal of the refugees from areas adjacent to the struggle under way in East Pakistan, which might constrain subsequent action to resolve the problem.

THE REFUGEE ISSUE AND DOMESTIC
POLITICS

The refugee influx was not only very expensive; it raised several tricky domestic political problems that complicated decision making. The refugees were concentrated in some of the most trouble-ridden sections of India for the ruling Congress party: West Bengal, Assam, and the "tribal" hill states of northeastern India—primarily Tripura and Meghalaya, but also Mizoram and Nagaland. West Bengal had just gone through several years of political upheaval and violence. In November 1967 the central government in New Delhi had dismissed the state government formed in April of that year, a coalition that had included the Communist party (Marxist), or CPM. The Congress-supported coalition that replaced it proved unable to control a terrorist campaign launched against both local "elites" and government officials and organizations by the Communist party (Marxist-Leninist), or CPML—the so-called Naxalites. "President's rule" was therefore declared in West Bengal on 20 March 1970, and the central government assumed direct control of the state administration. Following the March 1971 state assembly elections in West Bengal, a Congress-supported coalition government once again took office in Calcutta. But it lasted only until 28 June, when "President's rule" was again declared in the state.

The growing controversy in the state over the refugees and the Indian government's policy toward East Pakistan were major factors in India's decision to dismiss the West Bengali coalition government in mid 1971. New Delhi preferred to operate directly rather than through a weak coalition government in which the Congress party was only one constituent. The CPM remained the largest and best-organized party in West Bengal and, still strongly resentful at having been maneuvered out of office in 1967, was disinclined to cooperate with the central government even on vital national security issues. While the CPML terrorist campaigns had been contained through the deputation of Indian army and central police units to West Bengal on internal policing duties in late 1970, there were still areas of the state—some close to the East Pakistani border—in which the Naxalites continued to operate with some success. It was a worrisome problem for Prime Minister Gandhi and her colleagues, with potentially serious consequence for her party, government, and country.

The leftist parties in West Bengal were only too eager to derive the maximum political advantage from the evolving situation in the state and in East Pakistan. The CPM's Politburo met in mid June and adopted a resolution that reflected the views of the West Bengali branch of the party—namely, opposition to armed intervention by India in East Pakistan on the grounds that this would transform a "people's war" into an Indo-Pakistani war but immediate recognition of the Government of Bangladesh in exile (GOBD) and the provision of military assistance to *all*—that is, leftist as well as pro–Awami League—Bangladeshi resistance forces.[6] The CPML was, as usual, badly divided on policy toward East Pakistan and the various Bangladeshi political factions, but it was united in its apprehension that developments across the border would provide New Delhi with a much-enhanced capacity to suppress and control Naxalite activities in West Bengal. This indeed turned out to be correct.[7]

The CPM and the CPML had moved in eagerly and quickly to establish—or, in some cases, expand—ties with various leftist factions in East Pakistan. The CPM was most closely associated with the "regular" East Pakistani communists, in particular the pro-China wing of the Pakistan Communist party, and with the National Awami party (Bhashani), also usually identified as a pro-China party. The various CPML factions, in contrast, had connections with several of the more extremist Bangladeshi resistance groups, most of which remained based in East Pakistan and refused to enter India except occasionally to acquire arms and supplies from their CPML allies. New Delhi's capacity to control or even influence the interventionist activities of the Indian leftist parties was limited, seriously complicating the task of coordinating the Indian response to the crisis in East Pakistan.

The leftist parties were also quick to exploit some of the legitimate complaints in West Bengal and Tripura over the economic impact of the influx of millions of refugees into their territories.[8] Despite the government-imposed ban on refugees taking jobs, nearly three million did not go into the camps, but tried to enter the already badly overcrowded labor market in West Bengal, depressing wages and inflating prices in the process. The allocation of

Indian money and resources to maintain the refugees was also irksome to the local Indian communities, who received no such benefits, for example, free rice, better (if poor) medical facilities, and the like. The CPM's "they're better off than the poor Bengalis" line, although never formally adopted by the party, was widely used by local party units and received a favorable response from broad sections of the public in West Bengal and Tripura, where most of the refugee camps were located. The CPM could also play to popular sentiments by loudly demanding that the government adopt policies that would halt the inflow of refugees, while at the same time insisting that New Delhi refrain from direct military intervention in East Pakistan, since that would interfere with the "people's war" supposedly in the process of developing there. The CPM leadership acknowledged that a "people's war" was likely to be a long-drawn-out affair that would inevitably increase the number of refugees over an extended period of time, but consistency in its policy position was not important when opportunities to use a difficult and complex situation for local political advantage against the ruling party and the central government were there, ready for exploitation.

The developments in East Pakistan raised a different kind of problem for the Government of India in the northeastern hill states of Tripura and Meghalaya. In both states, but particularly in Tripura, the sudden influx of two to three million refugees threatened the internal stability of complex tribal political systems by seriously distorting the tribal-nontribal population ratio, to the former's disadvantage, in the process raising new issues and problems in what had been comparatively quiescent areas. This, of course, enhanced New Delhi's determination to reject any "solution" of the Pakistani crisis that did not specifically include provisions for the return of the refugees to East Pakistan.

INDIA AND THE BANGLADESH
GOVERNMENT IN EXILE

By late July the decision-making group around Mrs. Gandhi had achieved a broad consensus on the issue of Bangladesh, laying the foundations for the domestic and foreign policy of the government thereafter. One of the more immediate consequences was the perceived need to establish more direct supervision of the Bangladesh government in exile and the Mukti Bahini and other Bangladeshi "liberation forces." The Indian army had assumed primary responsibility for the arming and training of the Mukti Bahini forces from the Border Security Force on 30 April. Even occasional participation by Indian military personnel in raids across the border was now permitted. An effort was also made to bring the different autonomous resistance groups under Mukti Bahini (that is, Indian) supervision and direction, but with only limited success.

The Indian government was uncertain of the composition and political temperament of the East Bengali armed groups that came to India. The force from which the Mukti Bahini was ultimately created included personnel from five battalions of the East Bengal Regiment—a unit of the regular Pakistani army in East Pakistan; remnants of the East Pakistan Rifles—a paramilitary force charged with border patrol, policing, and antismuggling functions; and police, ex-servicemen, and students.[9] These units did not come to India en bloc, but in small, straggling groups. Although they supported Bengali autonomy and harbored a sense of injustice at the treatment of their East Pakistani comrades, the personnel of the uniformed services had not been prepared to mutiny on orders from the Awami League, but they had rebelled when West Pakistani troops tried to disarm them.

The impact of the Mukti Bahini prior to the monsoons (June–September), romanticized in the Indian and international press, was minimal. The paramilitary units that found their way to India usually lacked trained regular and noncommissioned officers; police, students, and other recruits lacked arms; regular troops lacked ammunition. Almost all lacked the functional training necessary to conduct a guerrilla war, although few reportedly lacked the spirit to launch one. Although some of its officers had received commando training, members of the East Bengal Regiment were trained for conventional warfare, but they did not have the weapons or manpower to engage the Pakistan army in conventional battle. The East Pakistan Rifles had been trained almost exclusively for police and antismuggling duties rather than military operations. Used to operating in large units, they were not conversant with the small-unit tactics necessary for guerrilla-style combat. Students usually were untrained in the use of firearms and in the coordinated activity that is essential to any military operation, conventional or guerrilla, and were without the weapons to pursue either.

The Indian authorities also discovered that severe rivalries existed among the various groups. The East Bengal Regiment personnel, for example, kept aloof from other armed groups, seeing themselves as professional soldiers and reportedly in many instances expressing disdain for politicians in a fashion similar to their West Pakistani associates. Generational and educational gaps separated the East Pakistan Rifles personnel from student groups. Some groups that had cooperated previously, whether from political persuasion or affinity of locale, insisted on operating autonomously and resisted being folded into a larger, unified command. To protect itself politically in the future, the Awami League, as well as groups in other parties, encouraged this autonomy and the augmentation with men and arms of groups that supported its ambitions, with or without the return of Mujib.[10]

Given its concern about the volatility of its eastern states, particularly West Bengal and Tripura, and its uncertainty about the political persuasion of many of the "freedom fighters," the Indian government sought to maintain a quarantine to separate East Bengali from West Bengali groups. Camps were created initially to establish control over the movement of these would-be guerrilla groups rather than to train them or conduct clandestine operations. The government also had severe reservations about training personnel whose political proclivities might be inimical to India's interests, particularly in the absence of a unified command structure and of Indian control after their return to East Pakistan. Just as compelling were India's reservations about supplying arms that, in a situation where control was limited, might find their way into the black market in West Bengal either as a result of political affinity among groups or as a consequence of economic need. As one central figure noted in retrospect, the government had to know whom it was giving arms to and the long-term purpose to which they would be put, and short-run considerations augured against arming groups that were not under a centralized command and whose activities could not be controlled.[11]

The first effort to create an organized armed force from among these groups was made on 14 April by the Bangladesh government in exile when it appointed Col. M. A. G. Osmani, a military adviser to Mujib and a retired Pakistani army officer, as commander in chief of the Bangladeshi armed forces. Osmani had entered the army prior to independence and had been instrumental in raising and forging the East Bengal Rifles. He was a well-trained senior officer who had had high-level staff, but limited command, experience, and was reported to have felt that his career had been thwarted in the Pakistani army. He had not achieved the rank held by the Indian officers with whom he had to deal.[12] Osmani was instrumental in creating a series of training camps along the Indo-Pakistani border in late April and May, first as centers to receive and temporarily house recruits and armed personnel coming from East Pakistan, but subsequently to impart training in small-unit tactics and in the use of firearms and explosives. Initial training was given by East Pakistani personnel in collaboration with personnel from India's Border Security Force (BSF) established after the 1965 war for policing functions, like the East Pakistan Rifles on the Pakistani side. The BSF was under police command, but included many retired Indian army personnel in its ranks. As the ranks of the Mukti Bahini recruits swelled, however, the Indian army assumed training and organizing functions. By the time serious hostilities commenced in November, Pakistani intelligence reported fifty-nine training camps in operation around the perimeter of East Pakistan.[13] By the end of May a command structure had been created that incorporated a substantial proportion of the Bengali freedom fighters into company units, ultimately organized into three brigades responsible for guerrilla operations, with East Pakistan divided into various sectors, each under the charge of Bengali officers.

According to Pakistani intelligence, the Indian army started a more concerted effort to train Mukti Bahini personnel in June. Three hundred recruits were reportedly sent to Cochin for training as underwater saboteurs, and another three hundred, almost all university students, were trained at Plassy on the Bhagirathi River in West Bengal as frogmen.[14] Student trainees were sorted in terms of their education. Science graduates were given two months' technical training; undergraduates were trained in small arms, mortars, recoilless rifles, rocket launchers, map reading, and commando tactics; non-matrics were trained as saboteurs in the use of explosives, mines, and grenades. Others were trained at artillery-

and signal-training centers in Lucknow and Dehra Dun or selected for short courses in officer training in Dehra Dun. By the end of June some thirty thousand Mukti Bahini recruits had been trained, although in a rather slipshod manner; by November seventy thousand were under arms, with another thirty thousand reportedly undergoing training. According to both Pakistani and Indian sources, the weapons made available to the Mukti Bahini by India were limited and largely obsolete. Modern weapons became available when the Mukti Bahini could purchase them on the international and West Bengali arms markets. Indian political and military leaders considered it prudent to provide some training and weapons to guerrilla activities in East Pakistan; otherwise, the Mukti Bahini would have had to become directly involved in West Bengal in their search for arms—something that New Delhi preferred to discourage. They had to be kept involved in East Pakistan regardless of their military effectiveness.

New Delhi's lack of confidence in the Awami League leadership[15] was clearly demonstrated in late summer, when on 9 September a coalition five-party East Bengali committee was set up to "advise" the Bangladesh government in exile. This followed a series of intensive discussions between D. P. Dhar and T. N. Kaul (two of Mrs. Gandhi's confidants) and the Bangladesh leaders. While both sides preferred to call this a decision of the government in exile, most sources generally agree that Mujibnagar reluctantly gave in to strong Indian pressure. The inclusion of two staunchly pro-Soviet Bangladeshi leaders—Mani Singh and Muzaffar Ahmed, the heads of the pro-Soviet factions of the Pakistan Communist party and the National Awami party (Bhashani), respectively—led to speculation that India had acted under Soviet pressure.[16] But although the Indians may have seen this as a cheap concession to Moscow, New Delhi was apparently still more concerned with expanding the political base of the government in exile in the critical months ahead, as well as with providing itself with another channel of control and supervision over the difficult leftist elements in the Bangladesh movement. Indeed, according to some sources, the Government of India would have liked to have brought several of the other East Bengali leftist factions into the coalition, but these rejected the conditions attached—acceptance of Indian direction and coordination of their resistance activities.

The Government of India also sought to establish more direct contacts with the Bangladesh government in exile and other Bangladeshi factions through the appointment of A. K. Ray, a joint secretary in the External Affairs ministry who had been responsible for Pakistani affairs, as the "adviser" to the West Bengali government on relations with the Bangladeshis. From early September on, Ray was the "guiding light" in Mujibnagar, ably assisted by N. C. Sen Gupta (the chief secretary of the West Bengali government and the dominant administrative official under President's rule), as well as by special units set up in the External Affairs Ministry under Peter Sinai and A. M. Dikshit. While bargaining between India and the government in exile was never discarded, there was little doubt whose views would prevail whenever differences arose.

MOBILIZING INTERNATIONAL SUPPORT

By late May, New Delhi had also concluded that a peaceful resolution of the East Pakistani civil war through a negotiated settlement between the Awami League and the Pakistani government was inconceivable without strong international pressure on Rawalpindi. A general sense of dissatisfaction was felt in the Indian government over both the results of its own comparatively restrained response to the 25 March crackdown and the failure of the international community to exert any real pressure on Pakistan to change its policy. The general reaction in most world capitals had been to remonstrate with Rawalpindi over its excessive use of force in East Pakistan, but then to back off by calling these developments an "internal matter." Washington became the primary target of Indian criticism on this question, particularly after the *New York Times* revealed on 21 June that American "military aid" to Pakistan had not been totally suspended in early April, as had been announced. But India did not find the ambivalent and evasive policy positions adopted by the U.S.S.R. and some Western European and nonaligned powers any more helpful.

From New Delhi's perspective, basic changes were required both in Indian policy and in the position of the major external powers if the East Pakistani crisis was to be resolved and the increasingly heavy flow of refugees to India halted. New Delhi pressured Rawalpindi in various ways, in particular by substantially expanding its support of the Bangladeshi resistance forces and by raising the prospect of direct Indian military intervention. In a series of public statements in June, Indian government leaders clearly indicated that Pakistani policies in East Pakistan were creating a situation in which, in the words of Defence Minister Jagjivan Ram, "war may be thrust on us."[17] Foreign Minister Swaran Singh was even more explicit when he told the Congress parliamentary party on 24 June that if no political solution acceptable to the Awami League was forthcoming, "India will be compelled to take action on its own."[18] To provide substance to these verbal warnings, regular Indian military units were moved into positions near the East Pakistani border in May and June, and Indian artillery occasionally lobbed a few rounds across the border at Pakistani military concentrations in support of Mukti Bahini operations.

By late spring a series of basic decisions on East Pakistan had thus been made by the key group of advisers around Mrs. Gandhi, and the objectives underlying these decisions set the framework for Indian policy thereafter. The first and most fundamental objective was the return of *all* refugees, including the Bengali Hindus; any "peaceful solution" that did not provide for this—either directly or indirectly—would not be acceptable to New Delhi. A second basic objective was the transfer of power to the moderate Awami League leadership in East Pakistan, either within the nominal confines of a Pakistani federation or in a newly independent state; either was acceptable to India as long as conditions were established for the return of the refugees. Third, a decision was made to use force—initially indirectly through increased support to the Mukti Bahini, but, if that proved unavailing, through direct Indian military intervention at an appropriate time. And, finally, it was decided that greater efforts must be made to mobilize the international community and organizations in support of Indian objectives in the Pakistan civil war, or, if that proved impossible, to neutralize their capacity to intervene in ways that countered Indian policy. A variety of policy options were available to the Indian government to achieve its objectives, and New Delhi was intent upon trying all of them to find a solution that met Indian requirements.

At the international level, in late spring India initiated a campaign directed at persuading other governments to pressure Rawalpindi to revise its policy in East Pakistan by suspending their economic and military aid to Pakistan. In a proposal submitted to UNESCO on 17 May, India had noted what it considered the minimum requirements for a peaceful solution: the restoration of human rights and the introduction of rehabilitation measures in "East Bengal"; the creation of a situation there that would allow for the return of the refugees from India; and U.N. aid "as needed" for the refugees as long as they were in India. Mrs. Gandhi told parliament on 24 May that "if the world does not take heed, we shall be constrained to take all measures as may be necessary to insure our own security and the preservation and developments of the structure of our social and economic life"—the first discreet official threat to use force if the "Great Powers, [who had] a special responsibility" to act on this issue, failed to do so.[19]

An intensive Indian diplomatic campaign got under way immediately thereafter, with Foreign Minister Swaran Singh, several other cabinet ministers, and the highly respected "independent" Jayaprakash Narayan leading missions to key countries in Eastern and Western Europe, North America, and Asia. The message carried by all these missions was the same—the need to pressure the Pakistan government into offering a political solution in East Pakistan acceptable to the Awami League if peace and stability were to be preserved in South Asia. The response everywhere was also the same—sympathy and agreement with India, but a sense of helplessness in persuading the Government of Pakistan to change its policies. If New Delhi had had any illusions about the utility of international pressure upon Pakistan when these missions set out, these had disappeared by the time the last of them returned in early July. A second wave of diplomatic missions was sent out in September, but this time primarily to Latin American and African countries to brief them on the position India would press at the U.N. General Assembly session starting in October and prepare them for the direct use of military force by India.

An inherent contradiction existed, however, between the efforts of India to "internationalize" the emerging crisis in the subcontinent and its insistence that this was solely a Pakistani affair. While New Delhi was charging that Pakistan's suppressive policies in East Pakistan constituted "indirect aggression" against India by pushing millions of refugees into its territory, the Government of India also consistently refused to accept the classification of the dispute as Indo-Pakistani in character in response to international initiatives directed at mediating the civil war in East Pakistan. India's relationship with U.N. Secretary-General U Thant and with a number of specialized U.N. agencies, for instance, were strained at times because of New Delhi's unwillingness to cooperate with U.N.-sponsored efforts to settle the dispute, or at least to offer humanitarian aid to its victims. This first became evident in mid June, when India reacted very negatively to the visit of Sadruddin Aga Khan, the head of the U.N. high commission for refugees (UNHCR), to the East Pakistani border area. In particular the Indian Government objected to the Aga Khan's alleged remark that Pakistan had established facilities to receive returned refugees, which, in the words of India's minister of labour and rehabilitation, R. K. Khadilkar, left the "unfortunate impression he was not above bias."[20] The Aga Khan denied that he had made the remarks attributed to him, but he and the UNHCR were "suspect" in the eyes of the Indian government and public from then on.

Foreign Minister Swaran Singh had met with U Thant on 16 June and requested that he use his "tremendous prestige" in restoring "normalcy" in East Pakistan and thus prepare the way for the return of the refugees. From then on, however, New Delhi opposed virtually everything the U.N. secretary-general sought to do on this matter. In early July, U Thant proposed to the Indian representative at the United Nations that the UNHCR "establish a presence" in the refugee camps in India and in the "reception centers" in East Pakistan that had been set up on the border to receive returning refugees to "facilitate" their reentry. The Indian reponse was "categorically negative" on the grounds that no refugees could return to East Pakistan, whatever the policy position of the Government of Pakistan, until a "climate of security" was achieved through the establishment of an Awami League–led government there.[21] Swaran Singh stated the position of the Indian government in parliament on 3 August, when he declared that India was "totally opposed to the posting of any U.N. observers on our territory. So far as posting of observers on the Bangla Desh side is concerned, it is our considered view that mere posting of observers in Bangladesh, particularly on the border, is not likely to create the necessary feeling of confidence among the refugees who are now in India. . . . The refugees can be persuaded to return only when they have confidence that they can do so in safety and without fear, and render credible guarantees for the security of their person and property. This can be ensured only through a political settlement acceptable to the people of East Bengal and their already elected leaders.[22]

According to some sources, however, another factor in India's refusal to allow U.N. observers in the refugee camps in India was its concern that this would provide the United Nations with the opportunity for surveillance of Indian military assistance to the Mukti Bahini operations in East Pakistan. Also at this time, India ordered all foreign volunteers who had been working at several of the refugee campus to withdraw—presumably for the same reason, even though most of these volunteers were sympathetic to the Bangladeshi cause.

New Delhi reacted even more negatively to the secretary-general's suggestion of a mutual withdrawal of Indian and Pakistani military forces from their respective borders and the posting of a team of U.N. observers on each side of the border. The United Nations first raised this idea informally in the summer, and pressed it more seriously in late September–early October, when both India and Pakistan commenced a full-scale mobilization of their military forces on both the eastern and western borders. In a letter dated 20 October to the president of Pakistan and the prime minister of India, U Thant offered "his good offices" in mediating the dispute and called for a mutual withdrawal of forces from the border by both sides.[23] President Yahya Khan responded favorably, but Mrs. Gandhi replied in a thousand-word letter that, in effect, accused the international community, and by implication the secretary-general, of trying to save the military regime in Pakistan. "This is what must be kept in mind instead of the present attempt to save the military regime. To sidetrack this main problem and to convert it into an *Indo-Pakistani dispute* can only aggravate tensions." U Thant was urged to focus his attention on a political settlement in "East Bengal which meets the declared wishes of the people."[24]

New Delhi's unwillingness to concede that Indo-Pakistani relations were a substantive factor in the Pakistani civil war because of Indian support of the Mukti Bahini, while insisting at the same time that Pakistan's policy constituted "indirect aggression" against India, undermined efforts to mediate the crisis by any third power, including the United Nations. The UNHCR and other specialized agencies contributed substantially to refugee food-aid programs in East Pakistan and India in 1971, and through supervision of the distribution of food grains by U.N. personnel in East Pakistan prevented a wide-scale famine in the province under most difficult circumstances. From New Delhi's perspective, however, this did not constitute a humanitarian act to save lives, but was rather another form of external assistance to the military regime in Pakistan. Some Indian sources even attributed the low level of Bengali Muslim participation in the refugee flight to India to the lack of economic incentives to leave because of the relative success of the U.N.-managed food program.[25] Obviously, U Thant and the U.N. agencies could not carry out their assigned tasks to New Delhi's satisfaction and still abide by the basic U.N. principle of noninterference in the internal affairs of member states.

DIFFERENCES WITH THE UNITED STATES

New Delhi's unhappiness with the response of the international community to the East Pakistani crisis was not just limited to the United Nations and its agencies. India also felt that few, if any, of the major international powers were contributing to the peaceful solution of the dispute by applying the maximum possible pressure upon Rawalpindi to abandon its repressive policies in East Pakistan and accept a "popular"—that is, Awami League—government. The Indian government's dissatisfaction with the major international powers was general, including even the Soviet Union for most of the year; but it was specifically and most publicly directed at the United States, which became the primary target of Indian criticism in the latter half of 1971. Washington, in turn, had strong reservations of its own about Indian policy toward Pakistan, which was seen as undermining any possibility, no matter how remote, of a peaceful solution.

The first public strains in U.S.–Indian relations over the Pakistani civil war surfaced in early June, when India responded rather testily to a 27 May U.S. statement counseling "restraint" by both India and Pakistan in the emerging crisis. Foreign Minister Swaran Singh commented that the Indian government resented American efforts to equate India and Pakistan in this respect, since the crisis was solely of Pakistan's making.[26] "Restraint," moreover, applied to India's support of the Bangladeshi side in the civil war, and New Delhi interpreted the U.S. government's position as yet another form of assistance to the Yahya Khan regime in its "war against the people of East Bengal." All subsequent reiterations by Washington that both India and Pakistan exercise restraint always met with a similar response from New Delhi, combined later with allegations that this constituted a tilt toward Pakistan.

In June, India began a broadly based international campaign directed at persuading third governments to "suspend" all military and economic assistance to Pakistan as a form of pressure "to end the agony" in East Pakistan as quickly as possible.[27] On 21 June, India found out that some shipments of American "military supplies" to Pakistan were continuing despite the suspension of such sales in early April. The Political Affairs Committee of the Indian cabinet met on 24 June to consider this revelation, and Swaran Singh made a statement in parliament that same day expressing the government's views:

> We have pointed out to the US Government that any accretion of military strength of Pakistan . . . would not only pose a threat to the peace and security of the subcontinent but the whole region. What is more, it would not only amount to a condonation of these atrocities, but could be construed as an encouragement to their continuation. We have stressed that this is not merely a technical matter, but a matter of grave concern involving social, economic, political and security considerations. We have therefore urged the US Government that they should try to stop the two ships which have already sailed, from delivering military arms to Pakistan and, in any case, to give an assurance that no further shipments of military stores will be allowed even under "past authorisations." The United States Government have promised to give urgent consideration to this matter and we are awaiting their response.[28]

Similar views were repeated by various Indian officials thereafter, who noted rather caustically that the United States was counseling Indian "restraint" while at the same time not exercising restraint itself in its aid to the other side in the Pakistani civil war. The United States, however, had clearly and correctly informed New Delhi of the small quantity of aid provided to Pakistan after 25 March under the U.S. program and also that the aid was not in "lethal weapons," but no mention was made of this in Indian public statements. To the U.S. government's irritation, the Indian government extensively publicized statements by such opposition U.S. politicians as Senators Edward Kennedy and Frank Church that exaggerated the amount of military equipment in the "pipeline" by about a thousand percent (alluding to $50 million rather than $5 million) and referred to it as "arms."

New Delhi also rejected out of hand Washington's contentions that the introduction of a formal and total embargo that included military sales to Pakistan licensed before 25 March would be tantamount to sanctions, and that a government involved in a civil war would not modify its fundamental policies in response to such sanctions—particularly when they involved such a small quantity of assistance.[29] In the Pakistani case, the United States argued, the result would be that Rawalpindi would move closer to China—which was not desired by the United States, the Soviet Union, or India—and would become even less flexible and more resistant to American efforts to persuade Pakistan to accept a political settlement in East Pakistan through "quiet diplomacy."[30] New Delhi, however, had already concluded that neither quiet diplomacy nor sanctions were likely to move Pakistan to change its policies. What the Indians wanted, therefore, were public condemnations of Pakistan that would, in effect, justify Indian intervention, indirect or direct, in the civil war.

When such condemnations were not forthcoming from Washington—or any other government—by the fall of 1971, India assumed an increasingly critical and obstructive position on the efforts made to settle the conflict peacefully through a political solution. This became most evident in August and early September in New Delhi's eventual response to the one hesitant effort made by the United States to mediate between the Yahya Khan government and the Awami League. On 30 July the American consulate general in Calcutta had been approached by an official of the Bangladesh government in exile who claimed to represent his colleagues in requesting the U.S. government to act as an intermediary between Mujibnagar and Rawalpindi. According to one Bangladeshi source, this initiative was taken by the government in exile—or possibly one faction within it—with the tacit approval of the Indian authorities. While this cannot be verified from Indian or American sources, U.S. officials considered it highly unlikely that any representative of the Bangladesh government in exile, which was under close Indian security surveillance, would openly meet American consular officials without Indian permission.[31] Possibly New Delhi had noted the slight liberalization in Pakistan's policy on East Pakistan in July and was interested in determining whether a political settlement that conformed to Indian terms could be negotiated. If so, it was soon disillusioned on this matter, for in the first half of August the Government of Pakistan "disqualified" 79 of the 160 Awami League members elected to the National Assembly and 195 of the 228 Awami Leaguers elected to the East Pakistan Provincial Assembly and announced that Mujib would shortly stand trial on a charge of treason. In India's judgment, this removed any possibility of an Awami League government emerging in East Pakistan out of negotiations with Rawalpindi unless Pakistan was prepared to reverse itself, which was seen as highly unlikely. In early September the Indian authorities instructed the Bangladesh government in exile to terminate all contact with the U.S. consulate-general in Calcutta.[32]

This was all a rather minor incident as far as the U.S. government was concerned. Washington doubted that Yahya Khan could be persuaded to make the concessions necessary for a political settlement that would be acceptable to the government in exile and India. No real efforts to commence mediation had been made by the time Bangladeshi officials, under Indian instructions, removed themselves from the negotiation process. Nevertheless, Washington was somewhat irritated with New Delhi's clampdown on the talks, which was seen as reflecting a lack of interest in peaceful resolution of the conflict.[33]

The Nixon White House decided to pursue this subject in more depth during Mrs. Gandhi's visit to Washington in early November to ascertain her views on a "peaceful political settlement." She had stressed in talks with the Belgian, Austrian, and British governments en route to Washington that the East Pakistani civil war was the result of West Pakistani repression and genocide; that the refugees represented an impossible burden for India; that this was not an Indo-Pakistani dispute; that a negotiated solution taking into account the aspirations of the people of East Pakistan must be found quickly; and that India did not seek war, but could not put up with the refugees indefinitely. She was, however, unwilling even to consider third-party mediation or U.N. involvement in the negotiation of a settlement.[34] This was also, in essence, the position taken by the prime minister in her talks in the United States with Richard Nixon and Henry Kissinger.

In Washington, President Nixon tried to reassure Mrs. Gandhi on several points. First, he stated that the United States would assume full financial responsibility for the refugees' support. Second, he referred to Yahya's recent agreement to unilaterally withdraw Pakistani forces from the East Pakistani–Indian frontier, with only the understanding that India would respond in some way in the near future. Nixon noted that this went "beyond anything we've gotten before," as Pakistan had always insisted on a mutual withdrawal of forces from the border. This concession, Nixon suggested, deserved India's attention. Nixon agreed with Mrs. Gandhi that a political accommodation satisfactory to the people of East Pakistan was necessary and informed her that there had been some significant changes in Rawalpindi's position on this issue as well. Yahya Khan, he stated, had agreed to meet any bona fide Awami League representative, that is, not necessarily someone who had been declared "acceptable" by the Pakistani government. Alternatively, Yahya had said, he would meet with any Awami League leader designated by the Government of India as a "representative of the Bengali cause." It was noted that Yahya was still opposed to including Mujib directly in these discussions, but his "welfare" would necessarily be part of any negotiations. Nixon commented that Yahya considered these terms a "capitulation" rather than an "accommodation," but was prepared to move ahead on this basis.[35]

Mrs. Gandhi was unresponsive to these proposals other than to indicate that India would accept any financial assistance offered for refugee relief. Her answer to Nixon's second point came indirectly after her return to India in a public statement that simultaneously called for the unilateral withdrawal of Pakistani forces from the border and authorized the Indian military to cross the border as far as necessary to counter Pakistani artillery shelling. There was no response at all to the third proposal other than Indian military action in late November that commenced the process of settling the Pakistani civil war by military, rather than political, means. According to American sources, some high American officials were convinced that the Indian government had decided to dismember

Pakistan by force before Mrs. Gandhi came to Washington and that the discussions there had been an exercise in futility.[36] This contributed to the mutual sense of distrust that characterized Indo–U.S. relations in subsequent months. Responsible officials in Washington acknowledged that their efforts to encourage a political solution may have been "too little and too late," but felt that they should not have been ignored and misinterpreted as they had been by the Government of India. The result of all this was a strong dissatisfaction at the highest levels of both the Indian and U.S. governments with each other's policies in the emerging Bangladeshi crisis, which was only intensified by their differences once the war broke out.

THE SOVIET ROLE FROM NEW DELHI'S PERSPECTIVE

Indo-Soviet relations went through a rather troubled period following the Tashkent Conference in early 1966 at which the U.S.S.R. had served as a "neutral" moderator in the negotiation of the agreement that settled the 1965 Indo-Pakistani war. To New Delhi's discomfiture Moscow had modified its policy of total support of India during and after the Tashkent Conference for a more balanced and nonpartisan position between the two major powers in the subcontinent. Later in 1966 the Soviet Union began to expand its economic aid program in Pakistan, and in 1968 it introduced a military aid program second in size only to that of China. Some of the reputedly pro-Soviet personalities inside the clique around Mrs. Gandhi, such as P. N. Haksar and D. P. Dhar, sought to rationalize the change in Soviet policy as being in India's interests, on the grounds that Moscow was seeking to counteract China's "dominant" influence in Pakistan through its aid programs and that, in any case, the balance of military power in South Asia would not be disturbed, since India would continue to receive more Soviet military aid than Pakistan, for example, India would obtain three Soviet tanks for every one Moscow provided to Pakistan.[37]

Nevertheless, even the Haksars and Dhars were disturbed by the change in Soviet policy, which for the first time since the mid 1950s raised serious questions about Moscow's reliability as a source of support for India in both its regional and extraregional disputes. Some of their colleagues in the government noted that under the new Soviet policy, Pakistan would now get substantial military aid from *both* the U.S.S.R. and China in a competitive context that was likely to expand rather than limit the aid available from them.[38] Haksar's reassurances that India would obtain more Soviet military aid than Pakistan were not persuasive, particularly to the Indian military chiefs, who noted that by the late 1960s the U.S.S.R. was almost the sole source of foreign military sales to India, while Pakistan had had ready access to arms from China, several Islamic states, and sources in Western Europe. Furthermore, in 1969–70 Pakistan had been negotiating with the U.S. government for the purchase of some military equipment— including fighter planes more modern than in the Indian air force— under a "one-time exception" to the boycott on arms sales to Pakistan and India imposed by the United States after the 1965 Indo-Pakistani War.

India could do little about the other sources of military assistance except complain, but New Delhi did have some bargaining chips that could be used with Moscow. And while there were some differences within Mrs. Gandhi's inner clique on this subject, by late summer 1969 New Delhi had decided to make a determined effort to outbid Pakistan for Soviet support and, in the process, persuade Moscow to restore its pre-1966 pro-India priorities in South Asia. Several regional economic and international issues (for example, a 1966 Kosygin plan for an "Asian Highway" connecting the U.S.S.R. and India through Afghanistan and Pakistan) were considered in the protracted Indo-Soviet negotiations conducted in 1969 and 1970. But the key issue for both governments was Brezhnev's proposal of an "Asian Collective Security System" on 7 June 1969, as New Delhi's cooperation with this major initiative in Moscow's Asian policy was critical to its success. Three months earlier, in March 1969, the Soviet defense minister, Marshal Andrei Grechko, had brought a draft of a proposed Indo-Soviet treaty to New Delhi. In the negotiations that followed during the next few months, and in particular during Foreign Minister Dinesh Singh's visit to Moscow in September 1969, the Soviets expressed their position clearly, that is, suspension of their military aid to Pakistan depended on India's receptivity to a treaty with Moscow that would, at least, constitute a step in the direction of New Delhi's acceptance of the Brezhnev proposal.[39]

While Mrs. Gandhi was reluctant to endorse the Soviet Asian collective security proposal explicitly, she was prepared to sign a more ambiguous agreement that would primarily emphasize economic cooperation rather than collective security if, in exchange, the Soviet Union terminated its arms sales to Pakistan. By early 1970 the two powers had reached an accommodation on this subject. In the spring of 1970, Moscow "suspended" arms sales to Pakistan, although shipments continued into 1971 under contracts signed before May 1970.[40] By mid 1970 a draft treaty had been prepared that reflected Soviet preferences for a security agreement but was ambiguous enough to be acceptable to India. According to one Indian official involved in these negotiations, the draft text was identical to the treaty finally signed in August 1971, with the important exception of the controversial article nine of the treaty. The treaty was not concluded in mid 1970, according to Indian sources, because at that time Mrs. Gandhi headed a minority government that was scheduled to contest a national election in early 1971. Under these circumstances she preferred to avoid an agreement with the U.S.S.R. that most of the opposition parties other than the pro-Soviet Communist party of India would criticize as a violation of India's sacrosanct nonalignment policy.[41] Moscow was understanding of Mrs. Gandhi's difficult position and raised no objections to postponing the signing of the treaty until after the elections. While the public posture of the Soviet government after mid 1970 continued to reflect a balanced relationship with India and Pakistan, the "primacy of India" principle was actually in the process of being revived.

In part this ambiguity in Soviet policy on Pakistan finally persuaded Mrs. Gandhi and her associates in July 1971 to press for the immediate conclusion of a "Treaty of Peace, Friendship, and Cooperation" with the U.S.S.R. They also felt it would help bolster the morale of the Indian bureaucracy, which was becoming increasingly depressed by India's inability to attract international support for its cause.[42] New Delhi did not want to present the treaty to the Indian public in these rather negative terms, however, so a wonderfully complex scenario was concocted involving alleged threats to Indian security from China and the United States as well as from Pakistan. Most of the opposition political leaders, the press, and the political public bought the line completely. The old China-

Pakistan "collusion" theme—seemingly discredited by Beijing's failure to intervene in support of Pakistan under far more advantageous circumstances during the 1965 Indo-Pakistani war—was revived and even expanded by the addition of an American threat to
the script. Kissinger had visited New Delhi and Rawalpindi in mid
July and then, with the assistance of the Pakistani government, undertaken a secret mission to Beijing that laid the basis for the commencement of negotiations on the normalization of relations between the United States and China—finally formalized in late 1979.
According to carefully contrived Indian leaks to journalists, Kissinger was alleged to have told an Indian official close to Mrs. Gandhi
during his visit to New Delhi that the American commitments to
Indian security against a Chinese "attack"—made in the context of
the 1962 Sino-Indian border war—no longer applied.[43] In certain
sections of the Indian press this false allegation was somehow transformed into a Pakistan–China–U.S. "axis" directed against India
that required an external counterforce, that is, the Soviet Union.

The line used by the Indian authorities to "justify" the treaty
with Moscow had little basis in fact, which the ruling group in New
Delhi clearly understood. By July 1971—and probably earlier—the
Indian government had obtained copies of the letters exchanged
between Beijing and Rawalpindi in April in which the Chinese
government had explicitly stated that although it would support
Pakistan *politically* in the emerging dispute with India, Chinese
military forces would not intervene in another Indo-Pakistani
war.[44] Indeed, New Delhi was so confident that it could safely
ignore China in these developments that, according to Indian
Defence Ministry sources, in late July (that is, *before* the Soviet
treaty) orders were sent to the army commander on the northeastern section of the frontier with China to transfer three of his six
divisions to the East Pakistani front.[45] Obviously, the much publicized Pakistan–China–U.S. "axis" was of no great concern to the
key group in the Indian government, as they knew quite well that
such an "alliance" was inconceivable in the preliminary stages of a
U.S.–China rapprochement, particularly given the nature of the
emerging crisis in South Asia and the continuing basic disagreements between Washington and Beijing over U.S. involvement in
the Vietnam War—a much more critical issue for both than anything going on in South Asia.

But while the threat of external intervention in support of Pakistan was not critical to the Indian decision to seek a treaty with Moscow, the *timing* of the signing of the treaty was affected by developments surrounding the Pakistani civil war. In late July, India took the initiative in pressing Moscow for the *immediate* conclusion of a treaty along the lines of the 1970 draft, but with the addition of a new clause—article nine in the treaty—in which both sides would agree "to abstain from providing any assistance to any third party that engages in armed conflict with the other Party." According to both Indian and American sources, article nine was added at New Delhi's insistence to deter Moscow from reviving its military aid to Pakistan. D. P. Dhar was sent to Moscow on 2 August to persuade the Russians to conclude a treaty immediately. Reportedly, Soviet officials expressed some initial reluctance, particularly to the inclusion of the new article, but finally agreed to the Indian request without too much argument.[46] On 8 August, therefore, Foreign Minister A. A. Gromyko flew to New Delhi, and on the following day the treaty was signed without any further substantive discussions.

Several factors influenced the Indian government's decision to press for the treaty in early August. In domestic political terms the best possible circumstances existed for implementing the decision made in 1970—but never announced to the Indian public or parliament—to conclude a treaty with Moscow, since the growing crisis in relations with Pakistan ensured that criticism of the treaty by the opposition and the press would be muted. The treaty was also seen as a useful form of public reassurance against Chinese intervention in the event of hostilities, in particular to the Indian military leadership that expressed some concern on this matter, since they would be the ones who would pay the price if the civilian leadership's confident assessment of China's role proved incorrect. While the treaty did not commit the U.S.S.R. to counter Chinese intervention in an Indo-Pakistani conflict, several "unofficial" leaks to the press implied, incorrectly, that Moscow had extended such guarantees verbally during the negotiation of the treaty. New Delhi also saw the treaty as an effective way to pressure Moscow to remove the ambiguity in its position on the Pakistani crisis, as well as to pressure Rawalpindi to agree to a political settlement on East

Pakistan that would be acceptable to India, in the process making military action by India unnecessary.

Kissinger's highly publicized "secret" visit to Beijing had ended any hope in New Delhi that the United States might serve as a mediator in settling the East Pakistani crisis, and this also made the Soviet treaty more attractive to New Delhi. The Indian government was very concerned with the U.S. response to the treaty, however, and sought to reassure Washington, both publicly and privately, on this question. Indian statements emphasized that the treaty did not constitute an alliance or even a "tilt" toward the U.S.S.R. and insisted that India's role in the nonalignment movement had not been compromised in any way. India also expressed its willingness to sign similar treaties with other foreign powers, including the United States, to emphasize these points.[47]

In the negotiation of the treaty in early August, the Indians informed the Russians that they intended to use military force to "solve" the East Pakistani problem within a few months if a satisfactory political solution had not been achieved. The Soviet negotiators expressed some concern over this and urged India to continue to explore other options before resorting to force. A joint statement issued by the foreign ministers of the two countries on 11 August reflected the Soviet position, declaring: "both sides . . . reiterated their firm conviction that there can be no military solution and considered it necessary that urgent steps be taken in East Pakistan for the achievement of the political solution." In fact, however, the Indians had stated their strong conviction that a political solution was highly unlikely and that another Indo-Pakistani war was a virtual certainty. They pressured the U.S.S.R. to support India politically in the event of hostilities and in the meantime to provide certain military equipment the Indian armed forces urgently required as quickly as possible.

Moscow agreed to discuss these subjects, if with an apparent lack of enthusiasm, and an intense dialogue ensued between the two governments over the next three months before they finally achieved a "coordination of policies." A senior Soviet diplomat came to New Delhi—shortly before Mrs. Gandhi's visit to Moscow in late September—to explain the uncritical position that the U.S.S.R. had taken on the Pakistani question at the Inter-

Parliamentary Union Conference on 10 September and, ten days later, in the joint communiqué signed on the conclusion of the visit of the king of Afghanistan to the Soviet Union. In Moscow Mrs. Gandhi reportedly was explicit in telling the Russians that hostilities were likely "after the monsoon," but Kosygin continued to repeat the Soviet position that "this basic problem must be solved by peaceful political means and not by military conflict."[48] In a surprise stopover in New Delhi on 1 October enroute to Hanoi, President Nikolai Podgorny repeated the Kosygin line. And on 9 October a Soviet-Algerian joint communiqué called for respect for "the national unity and territorial integrity of Pakistan and India" and urged the two governments "to find a peace settlement for the problems confronting them" in "the spirit of the Tashkent meeting."[49]

Mrs. Gandhi's hard-line position was finally getting through to the Soviet leadership, however, and it became increasingly clear to Moscow that it had to make a choice it would have preferred to avoid. It conceded to India's demands. Deputy Foreign Minister Nikolai Firyubin was sent to New Delhi on 22 October, just thirty-six hours before Mrs. Gandhi's departure for her tour of Western Europe and Washington, to consult with India "under the provision of Article IX" of the treaty. While the Indians would have preferred to have him come either earlier or later, they met with him, and according to an official Indian source "the two sides reached full accord in the assessment of the existing situation"[50] by Firyubin's departure on 25 October. Three days later Soviet Air Marshal P. S. Koutakhov arrived in New Delhi to negotiate the shipment of the arms urgently requested by the Indian army. New Delhi now concluded that it could count on "total support" from the U.S.S.R. as Foreign Minister Swaran Singh expressed it before the parliamentary Consultative Committee on 28 October.[51] This assessment was correct; special shipments of military equipment by air commenced in early November, and Moscow assumed a broadly supportive position toward New Delhi both publicly and privately on developments in South Asia up to and through the 1971 war. Thus, New Delhi's confidence that Moscow would tamely fall in line when it had to make a choice was justified once again.

INDIA AND THE OTHER "CONCERNED"
POWERS

The Soviet Union and the United States virtually monopolized the attention of the Indian government from March to October 1971 on foreign policy issues, for reasons that were persuasive to New Delhi. Washington was seen as the only outside power that might—if it were so inclined—pressure Rawalpindi into accepting a political settlement that met Indian requirements; Moscow was critical to India's efforts to impress upon Yahya Khan and his key advisers the unavailability of any effective external sources of support that could prevent a disastrous defeat in another war with India.

There were, however, several other governments whose views on the Pakistani civil war and its impact on Indo-Pakistani relations had to be taken into consideration in Indian decision making. Public attention on this issue in India was largely focused on China, and the Indian officialdom and press devoted massive amounts of time and space to Beijing's unfriendly attitude and the threat that China allegedly posed to Indian security. Zhou Enlai, in his letter of 11 April to Yahya Khan, had stated that China would "firmly support the Pakistan Government and people in their just struggle for safeguarding national independence and state sovereignty should the Indian expansionists dare to launch aggression against Pakistan,"[52] and this statement was frequently cited in India as proof of China's intention to intervene in support of Pakistan in any conflict with India. What was left unnoted in Indian commentaries—as in Pakistani ones—was that Zhou's letter and other Chinese statements on South Asia issued in 1971 emphasized *foreign* interference—primarily Indian, but by the superpowers as well. What Beijing refused to do, at least publicly, was take a position on the internal crisis in Pakistan—an important qualification of Chinese support of the Pakistani government on the East Pakistani question.

According to several authoritative sources, Zhou Enlai included in his 11 April message to Yahya Khan a statement that "the question of East Pakistan should be settled according to the *wishes of the People of East Pakistan*" (emphasis added). The text of the letter was not published by the *New China News Agency*, very unusual indeed, and was only summarized in broadcasts over Peking Radio without the inclusion of that sentence. The Pakistani government issued the text of the Zhou Enlai letter, but also without that sentence.[53] As noted before, the Indian government obtained copies of important Sino-Pakistani correspondence, including this letter, but of course carefully refrained from mentioning the missing sentence in the Pakistani version, as this would have contradicted the official Indian position that Beijing supported Pakistan's repressive policies in East Pakistan. The Indian government knew from the correspondence that China was quietly pressing Islamabad to settle the East Pakistani conflict peacefully before India intervened militarily. But New Delhi also concluded correctly that China would not pressure Yahya Khan too strongly on this subject and that Pakistan would ignore Beijing's views, just as India was ignoring unsolicited advice from Washington. Thus, in their assessment of China's potential role in this crisis, Mrs. Gandhi's advisers perceived China as no serious obstacle to Indian objectives; hence they could, and did, make policy with little apprehension about Beijing's possible responses.

The views and policies of the Islamic countries of West Asia, Africa, and Southeast Asia were somewhat more of a problem for New Delhi, as these could not be as easily and safely ignored as those of China. India understood that it would never expect open backing from the Islamic states in any dispute with Pakistan. But over the years New Delhi had developed a set of tactics that had been used relatively successfully in earlier disputes with Pakistan. This was directed at dividing Pakistan's support within the Islamic "bloc" by playing upon the serious divisions inherent in this grouping of nations and thus minimizing the support, other than verbal, extended to the government of Pakistan.

During the summer of 1971, Indian diplomatic missions—usually headed by Indian Muslim leaders—were sent to virtually all the major Islamic states to explain the Indian position on the Pakistani civil war. New Delhi insisted that these developments did not constitute another Indo-Pakistani (that is, Hindu versus Muslim) dispute, but rather a conflict between two hostile *Muslim* communities—East and West Pakistan. This was intended to diminish support for Pakistan among the Islamic states and was at least partially successful. While the Islamic states were virtually unanimous in their rhetorical support of Pakistan once the Indo-Pakistani war had broken out, the degree of substantive military and financial assistance extended to Pakistan by them was much less than it might have otherwise been. Moreover, India's military intervention in the Pakistani civil war had almost no impact upon relations between New Delhi and the Islamic states, and indeed several important Islamic countries (for example, Iran) began to give greater importance to relations with India in their own policies following India's victory in the 1971 war.

The other "concerned" power that was of vital importance to Indian decision making on developments in South Asia in 1971 was, of course, Pakistan. But while New Delhi gradually evolved a well-defined policy on the Pakistani civil war during the course of the year, this was done without *any* substantive discussions or negotiations with the Pakistani government. No serious effort was made by either New Delhi or Rawalpindi throughout 1971 to ascertain whether a compromise solution could be achieved through direct negotiations between the two governments without outside interference.[54] The two sides were making decisions on the basis of strongly held preconceptions about each other's behavior and simply assumed that nothing could be accomplished by having Mrs. Gandhi and Yahya meet to discuss their differences. And they may well have been correct. But it is rather curious that India, which had strongly encouraged other governments to negotiate disputes under the principles of nonalignment and peaceful coexistence that it espoused, paid no attention to this advice in its relations with Pakistan. Obviously, in this imperfect world, it is far easier to preach noble principles than to practice them.

10

War: India

The course of events in Pakistan and the evident reluctance of all the external powers, including the Soviet Union, to apply the quantum of pressure upon Rawalpindi that might have persuaded the Yahya Khan regime to seriously consider a political solution in East Pakistan placed the Indian government in a difficult position. By mid July, after four months of rather desultory debate, the key groups around Mrs. Gandhi had made several basic decisions. There was a broad consensus that India should resort to armed intervention in East Pakistan at an appropriate time if a satisfactory political settlement had not been achieved in the Pakistani civil war. Under the strategy adopted, India would move in stages, gradually escalating the degree of direct Indian involvement in the hostilities in East Pakistan. But the first tangible evidence of India's decision was in the international sphere, that is, New Delhi's sudden and unexpected overtures to the Soviet Union in late July for the *immediate* conclusion of a "Treaty of Peace, Friendship, and Cooperation."

Several critical factors influenced Indian decision making on East Pakistan. The refugee issue was certainly important, but probably not decisive; indeed, it is doubtful whether New Delhi would have resorted to direct armed intervention if the refugees had been the only issue.[1] Of greater importance to New Delhi was the potentially destabilizing influence of the conflict in East Pakistan on strife-ridden West Bengal, as well as on the tribal hill states and Assam in northeastern India, in which the basic political alignments pitted the "indigenous" communities against the "outsiders"—mainly Bengalis. The problem for India was not just the "existence" of refugees, but where they existed.

This communal factor in northeastern politics was superimposed on ideological conflicts—in very complex forms—and this was also critical to the Government of India's perceptions of its interests and responsibilities. In New Delhi's view it was not sufficient that East Pakistan gain independence or autonomy if, in the process, a radical government were established in Dhaka that (1) had ties with leftist "extremist" factions in West Bengal and the northeast and (2) carried out internal policies (for example, land nationalization) that would result in another outpouring of refugees to India. What New Delhi wanted in Dhaka was a government that was both democratic and politically moderate—but with emphasis on the moderate.[2] The Indians were skeptical not only of the capacity of the Bangladeshi political groups to win independence on their own but also of the political orientation and stability of any Bangladeshi government not set up under Indian guidance and supervision.[3]

Thus, for crucial Indian political purposes, Bangladesh had to be neutralized to the extent possible as a factor in northeastern Indian politics. This had been most effectively achieved, of course, when the region was part of Pakistan. There were important officials in the Government of India in 1971 who considered the disintegration of Pakistan of doubtful utility to India and who also questioned the usual line of analysis that the loss of East Pakistan would seriously weaken the remnant state of Pakistan. Several commented that East Pakistan had been more of a burden than a boon to Pakistan's military and that economically it was no longer the principal source of foreign exchange as it had been earlier. Indeed, a stage had been reached in which more Pakistani resources would have to go into East Pakistan than could be extracted from the province, whether the Pakistanis realized it or not.[4]

Even the more skeptical Indian leaders, however, generally admitted that India would benefit somewhat both in the region and beyond from what was expected to be a rather easy and humiliating defeat of Pakistan. Pakistan's role in South Asia as a reasonably effective counter to India's status as the dominant power in the region would be seriously undermined, in part because the remnant Pakistan was likely to identify itself more with the Islamic states of Southwest Asia than with South Asia once East Pakistan had been lost. It was a constant irritant to New Delhi throughout 1971 that Sri Lanka ignored India's protests over the use of Colombo airport as the transit point for Pakistani transport planes carrying Pakistani troops—in civilian garb—between East and

West Pakistan.[5] Similarly, Nepal's quiet, but persistent, support of Pakistan in its efforts to maintain its national integrity against Indian-based rebel forces—a very sensitive issue for King Mahendra in Nepal as well—was a constant reminder to New Delhi that no one in the region rendered even symbolic tribute to India's dominant power status.[6] Moreover, Mrs. Gandhi strongly desired to have India recognized as a major Asian power—not just a South Asian power—and a victory over Pakistan was seen as a contribution to this objective.

A successful war would also reap domestic political rewards for Mrs. Gandhi and her party. At the national level, the opposition was so weak and divided as to be easily ignored, but state assembly elections in several key states were scheduled for early 1972, and something was needed to counter the charges that Mrs. Gandhi's government had done nothing to implement the "Garibi hatao" ("Abolish poverty") slogan that the Congress party had campaigned on in the March 1971 parliamentary elections. A victorious war with Pakistan was the answer, and a very effective one.

One subject in the dialogue on Pakistani policy in New Delhi was the timing of a military action in East Pakistan.[7] While there were some initial disagreements on this subject with the foreign policy establishment, these had all been worked out by mid July. Certain climatic factors could not be ignored in planning military operations in East Pakistan. A campaign would have to commence long enough after the monsoon (June–September normally) to allow the rain-swollen river systems in East Pakistan to return to their more normal channels during what passes as a "dry season" there. The Brahmaputra and one of the branches of the Ganges, as well as several smaller rivers, disgorge into the Bay of Bengal south of Dhaka. From about May, with the melting of the snows in the Himalayas, through the monsoon, and for six to eight weeks or more thereafter, the rivers are so high and broad as to make the kind of fast (twenty-one days at the maximum) military campaign New Delhi was planning extremely difficult to execute prior to mid November, since the extensive use of armored forces would have to be precluded. India also preferred to time the conflict with a period when the main passes through the Himalayas on the Sino-Indian border are closed by winter snowfalls, with early to mid December the safe dates to project, to inhibit any possible Chinese temptation to interfere and to allay any residual fear of the army command that their units might end up fighting offensive and defensive actions at the same time.[8]

Several military factors also had to be considered in Indian projections. Chief of Staff General Manekshaw had curtly dismissed proposals by a few Indian leaders in April for immediate military intervention. Manekshaw stated that the Indian army was not prepared for an offensive operation in East Pakistan or to meet the inevitable Pakistani military counterthrust in West Pakistan, and insisted that the army would need six to seven months to prepare for conflict on both fronts. New Delhi also considered it essential to have a Bangladeshi force, the Mukti Bahini, deeply involved in any military action in East Pakistan and recognized that it would take some time to organize and train these units for both guerrilla and conventional warfare.

Certain international considerations also influenced New Delhi's timetable on East Pakistan. Despite its skepticism about the probable results, the Indian government wanted to give the international community and the United Nations sufficient time to attempt to mediate a viable political solution in East Pakistan or, in the process, expose beyond all doubt their inability to do so. Mrs. Gandhi's visits to Moscow in September and to Western Europe and the United States in October and November were intended to serve this purpose.[9] The American government was correct in its assessment that India had already decided to launch a military operation in East Pakistan when Mrs. Gandhi came to Washington in early November pretending that she was still seeking a peaceful solution. But Nixon and Kissinger had had nothing very tangible to offer her either with respect to a more realistic and liberal Pakistani position on the crisis in East Pakistan. Thus, the Indian government's conclusion that no political solution that would meet India's minimum requirements was possible in the foreseeable future was correct. Mrs. Gandhi returned to New Delhi in mid November, and the order went out to initiate another "military solution according to plan" immediately.

The timing was right in all respects, as late November to early December was ideal for a "clinical" military operation that would accomplish India's basic objectives quickly and with a minimal cost in lives and resources. The only negative factor was that the U.N.

General Assembly would be in session at that time. The Government of India was confident that the Soviet Union would forestall, or at least delay through the use of its veto power, any action by the U.N. Security Council, but it also understood that this would embarrass Soviet relations with the Islamic countries and the other South Asian states, as well as affecting its emerging détente with the United States and even relations with a large proportion of countries in the nonaligned movement, which tended to be critical of India on this issue. These factors made it even more important that the Indian army accomplish its tasks as quickly as possible.

While the Government of India operated on the assumption throughout the last half of 1971 that another war with Pakistan was unavoidable, this was not final or irreversible. Any political settlement of Pakistan's civil war that established an environment in East Pakistan under which the refugees could be persuaded to return would be acceptable to India. But from New Delhi's perspective this could occur only if an Awami League government headed by Mujib were formed at the provincial level. India did not insist, however, that Pakistan had to concede full independence to the east. A federal system under which East Pakistan was granted broad autonomy—per the Awami League's Six-Point Demand, for instance—would be sufficient. Nor did India demand at this time that the results of the December 1970 elections in Pakistan be accepted and that the Awami League be allowed to form the central government in Pakistan. But it noted that a martial law regime and a highly decentralized federal system were basically incompatible.

MILITARY TACTICS

Having concluded that India would eventually have to resort to the direct use of force against Pakistan, New Delhi set about devising a strategy that would achieve its objectives on the most cost-effective terms. A decision had been made as early as April to give some assistance to the Bangladeshi resistance forces as a form of pressure upon the Pakistani government to make basic concessions, but by midsummer it was clear that this would not be sufficient. The newly organized Mukti Bahini had not been able to prevent the Pakistani army from regaining control over all the major urban centers on the East Pakistani–Indian border and even establishing a tenuous authority in most of the rural areas.[10]

The next phase in Indian tactics, from July to mid October, involved both much more intensive training of the Mukti Bahini and direct involvement in Mukti Bahini activities by Indian military personnel.[11] This enabled the Mukti Bahini to launch major organizational and sabotage campaigns in East Pakistan at the height of the monsoon season, at a time when the Pakistani army's maneuverability was reduced because of its dependence on vehicles and armored personnel carriers. The Mukti Bahini campaign, with some disguised Indian involvement, was directed—and with some success—at such strategic facilities as bridges, power stations, communication systems, and ships in Chittagong harbor. The destruction of bridges handicapped the Pakistani forces in this period, but it proved to be a major obstacle to the Indian invasion forces in December.[12] Indian artillery stationed on the border was used on occasion to support Mukti Bahini activities in the immediate transborder areas, usually in response to Pakistani army shellings and incursions if the Indian reports are taken seriously.

This sudden expansion of Indian-aided Mukti Bahini activity in July and August aroused strong apprehensions in Pakistan that these were the initial stages of a limited Indian military intervention in East Pakistan in the immediate postmonsoon period that would have as its objective a "liberated zone" in which a Bangladeshi government would be established on Bangladeshi soil under Indian protection. In response the Pakistani government ordered a full mobilization of its own reserve forces in West Pakistan under the tattered Pakistani security policy that the best defense of East Pakistan was an offensive capability in West Pakistan. India was caught by surprise by the Pakistani mobilization and, of course, entertained suspicions of its own that Pakistan would try to "redo 1965" by launching a limited war centered on Kashmir to win concessions or at least reassurances on East Pakistan from India. This made it necessary for India to order an immediate countermobilization, but it also had the positive aspect of allowing India to disguise the mobilization of forces it had intended to carry out on both the eastern and western fronts a few weeks later as a response to Pakistani actions rather than as preparation for its own military campaign in East Pakistan.

The next phase in the preliminaries to open and direct intervention by Indian forces was the period from mid October to 20 November, in which both quantitative and qualitative changes occurred in Indian military support of the Mukti Bahini, particularly in several key strategic border areas.[13] Indian artillery was used much more extensively in support of rebel operations in East Pakistan, and Indian military forces, including tanks and air power on a few occasions, were also used to back up the Mukti Bahini.[14] Indian units were withdrawn to Indian territory once their objectives had been brought under the control of the Mukti Bahini—though at times this was only for short periods, as, to the irritation of the Indians, the Mukti Bahini forces rarely held their ground when the Pakistani army launched a counterattack. Nevertheless, quite substantial, if scattered, areas of East Pakistan had been brought under tenuous Mukti Bahini control by mid November, since the Pakistanis had to concentrate their limited forces on those sections of the border that were considered strategically critical.

India's limited support of the Mukti Bahini raised a difficult question about Indian objectives in East Pakistan for the Pakistani government and military, and one that complicated Pakistani decision making throughout the fall and winter of 1971. Did New Delhi have a limited objective in mind—the establishment of a section of East Pakistan under Mukti Bahini control, with Indian military support, in which a government of Bangladesh could be founded and internationally recognized? Or was all this carefully disguised military intervention by India in fact the prelude to an all-out invasion of East Pakistan that had the defeat and surrender of the Pakistani army as its objective? There was uncertainty on this matter in Pakistan into early December and confusion on how best to respond on the ground.

From April to July there had been a continuing, if sporadic, debate in India on this subject. Some military officers argued that a river-ridden area like East Pakistan was ideal for defensive purposes, and that it would thus be preferable to create a situation in which the Pakistani army would have to launch an offensive against the combined Indian–Mukti Bahini forces in a liberated area of the province. But this kind of strategy would probably have resulted in a long-drawn-out conflict, which was unacceptable to Mrs. Gandhi and her advisers. What they wanted was a quiet war directed at the "liberation of Bangladesh" within a reasonable time frame. This decision had been made by July. While Indian policy and actions through November were deliberately contrived to keep the Pakistanis uncertain as to Indian objectives in East Pakistan and encourage indecision within Pakistan on the appropriate response, there was no confusion in the inner circles in New Delhi on this matter or in Indian military tactics in East Pakistan in the fall and winter months of 1971.

THE CAMPAIGN

The scope of Indian military involvement increased substantially in the first three weeks of November, but in most instances the Indian units would hit their objective in East Pakistan and then withdraw to Indian territory. After the night of 21 November, however, the tactics changed in one significant way—Indian forces did not withdraw. From 21 to 25 November several Indian army divisions, divided into smaller tactical units, launched simultaneous military actions on all of the key border regions of East Pakistan, and from all directions, with both armored and air support. These were, as usual, described as "defensive" responses to Pakistani shellings of Indian (or in a couple of cases, Mukti Bahini–controlled East Pakistani) territory, presumably as part of an attempt to project them as the same kind of crossborder strikes and then withdrawals that had been employed earlier.[15]

From 21 November to 3 December, Indian forces moved into key strategic areas around the principal Pakistani defensive positions on or near the Indian border with the objective of either capturing or neutralizing them.[16] In the process the Indian army, supported by Mukti Bahini units, also established operational bases in Pakistan on the east, west, and north for an assault on Dhaka. But the preparatory tactics used—relatively small units directed at Pakistani army outposts—had the effect of causing uncertainties in Pakistan, for the first week at least, as to whether this was part of an all-out attack directed at Dhaka or a more limited campaign with the seizure of some territory as its goal.

Under the Indian schedule, the formal war would begin on 6 December with the launching of an all-out offensive to capture

Dhaka.[17] The Government of India was greatly relieved and pleas-
antly surprised when Pakistan, after temporizing in its responses
to the Indian military intervention in East Pakistan for nearly two
weeks, ordered the Pakistani air force in West Pakistan to strike at
major Indian air installations in northwestern India on 3 December.
This date is usually cited for the commencement of the third
Indo-Pakistani war, and because of the air strikes, Pakistan is often
depicted as having taken the initiative in starting the war. In more
realistic, rather than formal, terms, however, the war began on 21
November, when Indian military units occupied Pakistani territory
as part of the preliminary phase to the offensive directed at capturing and liberating Dhaka.

The Pakistani air strike and the beginning of armed hostilities on
the West Pakistani–Indian border allowed the Indian commanders
on the eastern front to push their schedule ahead, and the Dhaka
offensive was actually launched on 5 December. The outcome of
the conflict on the eastern front after 6 December was not in doubt,
as the Indian military had all the advantages. Its force was considerably larger, much better armed, more mobile, and had complete
control of the air and sea. It had established excellent logistical
supply lines right up to the border and had ready access to the
rivers and roads in East Pakistan. The Pakistani forces, in contrast,
were cut off from the outside world and had insufficient supplies.
The Pakistanis also had to deal with a basically hostile local populace, while the Indians, acting through the Mukti Bahini and the
Awami League, had excellent local intelligence that gave them a
decided advantage over the Pakistanis. In addition, most Pakistani
units had been involved in a difficult struggle against the rebel
forces for six months and were both physically and emotionally
exhausted.

Nevertheless, despite all these advantages, the war did not go as
smoothly and easily for the Indian army as the Indian civilian
leadership had projected. In the Indian press it was usually termed
a "two-week war" in which India defeated the Pakistani army in a
"lightning campaign" in East Pakistan. But actually it was closer to
a four-week war if the 21 November starting date is used. Virtually
all of the top Indian leaders we interviewed dismissed the highly
eulogistic Indian reporting on the Indian army's performance in the
war, and several were rather caustic in their comments. One, for

instance, noted that the main concentrations of forces were to the east and west of Dhaka, but that it was a division from the north, which met only light Pakistani opposition, that finally captured the city. These criticisms seem a bit curious, since some of these political leaders themselves benefited politically from extolling India's great victory. They also demonstrate a lack of sensitivity about warfare under difficult circumstances. East Pakistan, even in the dry season, is a land of wide rivers, ideal for defensive warfare. The Pakistanis fought hard and well; the Indian army won an impressive victory.

The various ventures in Indian military intervention in East Pakistan during October and November were carried out without any serious discussion of the issues in the cabinet or any decisions emanating from the key cabinet institution on foreign policy—the Political Action Committee.[18] Indeed, the hostilities on the West Pakistani front were the only serious subject debated in the PAC meeting on 4 December, the day after the formal declaration of war. Reportedly, Defence Minister Jagjivan Ram, with rather tepid support from Y. B. Chavan, argued for a major offensive against West Pakistan, with the "liberation" of the Pakistan-held sections of Kashmir as the minimum goal. But Indira Gandhi and her support group held to the decision that had been made earlier on this issue—namely, to fight what would essentially be a defensive war on the western front.[19] Two exceptions to this general rule, however, were accepted—indeed, insisted upon—by Mrs. Gandhi. First, several small but strategic sections on the Pakistani side of the cease-fire line in Kashmir—which had been seized in the 1965 Indo-Pakistani war but restored to Pakistan under Soviet pressure in the 1966 Tashkent Agreement—should be occupied again and this time retained.[20] Second, a limited but very threatening offensive into Sind Province should be launched in the directions of the main communication lines between Lahore and Karachi as a deterrent to a major Pakistani offensive in Kashmir, Punjab, or Rajasthan. Both the Kashmir and the Sind actions were successfully carried out. After the war the Indian forces withdrew from Sind but remained in place in Kashmir. A new "line of control" established in the 1972 Simla Agreement between India and Pakistan replaced the old Kashmir cease-fire line and left these positions under Indian control.

INTERNATIONAL REACTION

The war proceeded almost exactly as projected and did not raise any serious problems for the decision-making elite in New Delhi. Several external powers, however, both in their unilateral policies and in the United Nations, did appear at times to complicate matters for India. Although they were the subject of intensive publicity in the Indian media, New Delhi dealt with these intrusions with a sense of assurance that they would have little or no impact on the outcome of the war—at least if the Indian army performed its duties quickly and efficiently, which everyone expected.

The policies adopted toward China and the United States in December clearly demonstrated India's confidence that both countries could safely be ignored. After several months of authorized leakages to the press on the dangers that a new "U.S.–China axis" held for India in the context of a conflict with Pakistan, Indian strategic policies during the war paid little or no attention to the alleged threat of interference from either country. Six of the ten Indian divisions assigned to the Chinese border in both the eastern and western Himalayas were transferred to one of the Pakistani fronts, clear evidence of New Delhi's confidence that China would sit this one out—as it had the 1965 Indo-Pakistani war.[21] That the main passes in the eastern Himalayas are usually closed in December was one factor in the Indian analysis; but the main Sikkim-Tibet passes and the Ladakh-Tibet border are not as seriously affected by the winter, and the Chinese could at least have made threatening gestures on the sensitive Kashmir and Sikkim fronts. But New Delhi also knew that the Chinese had not undertaken any of the buildup of forces and supplies needed for even a minor military action in the difficult Himalayan terrain and thus were in no position to do much even if ordered. India had also taken note of the severe internal conflict in China suggested by the death of Lin Biao.

The strain in relations between India and the United States that emerged during the course of the war has frequently been defined as a "near confrontation" between the Indian military forces and the small detachment of the U.S. Seventh Fleet, led by the aircraft carrier *Enterprise*, that was dispatched to the Indian Ocean in the last week of the war. As several responsible Indian officials around the prime minister and in the Defence Ministry noted in comments to the authors, there were no apprehensions that the U.S. fleet would intervene in the East Pakistani campaign, or, indeed, that it could do much in that sector.[22] New Delhi recognized that the dispatch of the fleet was a symbolic gesture intended to impress China and the Islamic states in Southwest Asia as well as to counter the reinforced Soviet fleet in the Indian Ocean. The Indians assumed that the United States, deeply involved militarily in Vietnam, would not violate the basic principle of the new Nixon Doctrine by becoming involved in a conflict in South Asia. Given the importance of Pakistan to the CENTO alliance system along the "northern tier" from Turkey to Pakistan, New Delhi was less certain of the U.S. response if India launched an all-out offensive against West Pakistan that could lead to its disintegration into three or four states. But then India did not intend to launch such an attack, so the question was purely theoretical.[23]

Much Indian attention during the war was directed to influencing the public and key political leaders and groups in the West, particularly the United States, to pressure their governments to adopt pro-Indian—or at least refrain from anti-Indian—policies. With the cooperation of most of the Western media, India was spectacularly successful in this endeavor. India had, of course, a good case to make in terms of Pakistani atrocities in East Pakistan, and it found the foreign press incredibly gullible in accepting, without effort at verifying, the substantial exaggerations that were appended to the list of horror stories from Dhaka.[24]

India also made a serious effort to at least minimize support for Pakistan within the Islamic bloc by emphasizing that this was a Muslim versus Muslim (Pakistan versus Bangladesh) war and not another Hindu-Muslim conflict. In Indian presentations to close associates in the nonaligned movement, it also insisted that Pakistan had started the war on 3 December and that India was the victim of aggression. One question that was debated within the inner clique for several days was whether India should invoke the treaty with the U.S.S.R. and ask Moscow for consultations. Some Indian leaders argued that the failure of the Chinese to do anything on the Sino-Indian border made this unnecessary. But finally it was decided that a symbolic response by India to the symbolic dispatch of the *Enterprise* by the United States was necessary, and consultations with the Soviets under the treaty became the obvious choice.

Perhaps the most difficult problems for India emanated from the voluminous discussions within the United Nations on the Indo-Pakistani war from 4 to 23 December, as these posed some possible complications for India's grand strategy. New Delhi knew that it could depend upon the Soviet Union to cast two or three vetoes in the Security Council against proposed resolutions that did not serve India's objectives, but it was uncertain whether Moscow would sustain a totally negative position as the bargaining process went on in the United Nations. The U.S.S.R., India assumed, would prefer to demonstrate a willingness to make some concessions, in part to avoid antagonizing the Islamic states any more than was absolutely necessary. And this, indeed, is what happened—in slightly disguised form.

India's formal declaration of war on 3 December brought on a spate of resolutions in the U.N. Security Council—a total of twenty-four over a two-week period—submitted by individual member states or combinations of members.[25] Debate, however, focused on two submitted separately by the United States and the Soviet Union, and another one submitted by eight of the member states. The entire process surrounding the resolutions was marked by extensive "consultations" outside the Security Council forum in an effort to reach compromises and build coalitions. It was also typified by amendments to amendments of proposed resolutions, the withdrawal of draft resolutions that had been submitted, and by some states deciding not to press for a debate on their resolutions—presumably for tactical and procedural reasons.

The rhetoric flowed in grand and glorious style, of course, but the key issues of the debate can be summarized briefly. First, should there be an immediate cease-fire and the withdrawal of troops from the territory of the other state (which meant, in fact, the withdrawal of Indian troops from East Pakistan, since the incursions on the West Pakistani front had been insignificant as yet)? Second, should the implementation of the cease-fire be linked to a political resolution of the Pakistani civil war—usually interpreted to mean the withdrawal of Pakistani troops from East Pakistan and the establishment of an elected (that is, Awami League) government? And third, should the Bangladesh government in exile be invited to participate in the Security Council proceedings?

The only resolution adopted by the Security Council during the war was one proposed by Somalia on 6 December referring the issue to the U.N. General Assembly for discussion. The General Assembly met on 7 December and by a vote of 104 to 11 (with 10 abstentions) adopted a resolution calling for a cease-fire and a mutual withdrawal of troops from both sides of the border.[26] But General Assembly resolutions are merely recommendatory, and the issue then returned to the Security Council, where the internal debate continued. It was only on 21 December, after India and Pakistan had already signed their own cease-fire agreement, that the Security Council finally passed Resolution 30 demanding that the cease-fire remain in effect until troop withdrawals had taken place and called on both sides to treat prisoners and enemy civilians properly as specified by the Geneva Convention of 1949. The United Nations, in other words, was a forum for discussing, but not resolving, the 1971 conflict.

For the Government of India the most controversial and potentially embarrassing of the resolutions presented to the Security Council was that submitted by Poland, since it was the only resolution that had a high probability of adoption. The Polish resolution, like the earlier Soviet resolutions, called for the transfer of power in East Pakistan to the representatives elected in December 1970— that is, the Awami League—and this was, of course, Indian policy as well. But unlike the Soviet resolutions, the Polish proposal also called for an immediate cease-fire and troop withdrawals by both sides, as well as the renunciation of claims to any territories acquired by force during the war. These provisions aroused considerable distress in New Delhi.[27]

A cease-fire and immediate mutual withdrawal before the capture of Dhaka, as specified in the Polish resolution, would have deprived India of the clear military victory in East Pakistan symbolized by the surrender of the Pakistani armed forces on that front. But even more important, a quick withdrawal of its forces would have vastly complicated India's capacity to assist the Awami League in establishing a stable and moderate regime in Bangladesh once both the Indian and Pakistani forces were withdrawn and the conglomeration of Bangladeshi resistance groups commenced their own civil war for control of the new country under circumstances that would have been difficult for India to influence. New Delhi also disliked the "renunciation of occupied territory" clause in the Polish resolution, which would have obligated India to once again restore the strategic points on the Pakistani side of the cease-fire line in Kashmir that had been seized at some cost.

India did not doubt that the Polish resolution was really Soviet in origin, and New Delhi reluctantly conceded that it would have no option but to accept a Security Council resolution that was approved unanimously, which the Polish resolution would have been. Fortunately for New Delhi, Zulfiqar Ali Bhutto, the head of the Pakistani delegation to the United Nations, came to its rescue. In the Security Council proceedings on 15 December, Bhutto denounced the failure of the United Nations to act promptly, tore up a copy of the Polish resolution, and stormed out of the session, halting all consideration of the subject.[28] Two days later Dhaka fell, the Pakistani army in the east surrendered, and the war was over.

11

War: Pakistan

The reluctance and inability of the external powers to influence the Pakistani government to pursue a political solution in a timely fashion was paralleled by their inability to exert the pressure necessary to dissuade India from increasing its involvement in destabilizing the military regime in East Pakistan and, ultimately, serving as midwife in the birth of Bangladesh through invasion. The probability of war with India did not weigh heavily on the minds of Pakistani decision makers during the first few months after the military crackdown of 25 March. The "miscreants" and "traitors" had either fled or were dispersed; order was restored by a firm military hand; the monsoons soon followed.

Whereas war with India was considered improbable in April and May, it started to seem possible, though unlikely, to military decision makers in August and September; it was judged probable, but still avoidable, in October and early November, but inevitable by the end of the month. The Pakistani air attack on India on 3 December was considered the "option of last resort," an unwanted choice, but the only possible response to India's occupation of Pakistani territory in the east if Pakistan was to maintain national integrity, and the only alternative that might induce the intervention of outside powers to restore the status quo ante.[1]

OBSESSION WITH INDIA

From the outset of the crisis in Pakistan created by the elections and abortive negotiations, there was a strong, universally held belief that India was behind the Awami League and Bengali regionalist sentiment in the east. These views were held across the spectrum of groups within the military—those at the center of power as well as those in outer orbits, those sympathetic to transferring power to a reformist civilian regime as well as those less sanguine and intermittently resistant. Indeed, military decision makers agreed that India had always been and continued to be committed to the destruction of Pakistan and that the disturbances of 1971 were largely a consequence of the latest efforts on the part of "Hindu India," "Bharat" (a Sanskritic name for India), or just "the enemy," as India was variously referred to, to achieve what had not been achieved before partition.

The primary objective in Pakistan's foreign policy-making from May through the December war was to constrain India from acting in ways that threatened the integrity of Pakistan or that would force a political settlement on any terms other than those stipulated by the military regime. With respect to an effective insurgency and secessionist war, Pakistan assumed that "if Indian involvement could be thwarted or curtailed, the Bengalis would just not be able to pull it off."[2] Thus the task was to develop support within the international community, the "international restraint option" as one core decision maker called it, by calling international attention to any involvement, overt or covert, of India in East Pakistan, and to counter any effort on the part of India to solicit international support. The second prong of this strategy was to prepare to suppress insurgency and defend against armed incursion from India, whether it were the occupation of territory in East Pakistan to set up a "Bangladesh" government on East Pakistani soil or "all-out war" to dismember Pakistan. Throughout, Pakistan strategy toward India was to constrain and to defend; and throughout the autumn months Pakistani leaders looked outward to the international community for salvation rather than inward for political accommodation.

A STRATEGY OF CONSTRAINT

Until the Indian "attack in force" on East Pakistan on 21 November, the strategy of constraining India seemed to have been effective. The United States was perceived to be acting to restrain India and strongly supportive of Pakistan's position, with President Nixon warmly praising President Yahya Khan for his statesmanship in personal communications and expressing understanding of the difficult circumstances in which Yahya found himself.[3] The Pakistanis perceived the U.S.S.R. as also committed to restraining India from aggressive behavior, finding evidence both in public statements and in private conversations.[4] The Chinese were believed to be supportive short of military action, and among the core decision makers some hoped for direct Chinese intervention to the point of expecting it.[5]

The Pakistanis also took satisfaction in the failure of India to attract support from the Muslim states, in contrast to the vocal support they gave Pakistan.[6] Rawalpindi firmly believed that aggression against Pakistan would entail unacceptably adverse consequences for India in the Islamic world, as well as in India's own Muslim community, which was seventy million strong.

In terms of the expectation of international support, the past also served as guide and prophet. Major international powers in the past had always intervened promptly to end war in South Asia—in Kashmir in 1948–49, in the Rann of Kutch in 1965, and in the Indo-Pakistani war later that year. Pakistan assumed that if India pursued direct armed involvement, international pressure would be brought to bear to exact a cease-fire, which would place India in the untenable situation of having an army of occupation on Pakistani soil. Such a condition, Pakistan believed, would be unacceptable not only to the wider community of nations but to East Pakistanis as well.

Finally, the refugees, rather than being perceived as a problem that would become intolerable for India, were seen by Pakistan as retribution for India's meddling in Pakistani affairs. The refugees were a consequence of India's own interventionist escapades and "served them right" for the continued and unrelenting Indian involvement in secessionist activity in East Pakistan.[7] India was prone to exaggeration as well in its attempts to embarrass Pakistan. Any contribution the refugees made to the turmoil in West Bengal would constitute a problem for India rather than for Pakistan; and communal tensions, were they to increase, would remind Muslim Bengalis that life in Pakistan was far preferable to Hindu supremacy and domination.

The possibility of a third war between India and Pakistan, an eventuality that Pakistani leaders wanted to avoid even in late November, required the review of long-standing military contingency plans. This renewed military planning, like that of the past, was bolstered by a firm conviction, held even through the end of the December war, that it was impossible for Pakistan to lose a war to India. Such an outcome was inconceivable; in the worst case "some miracle" would intervene to save Pakistan. The belief was also commonly held that "Muslims had never been defeated by the Hindus." Muslims had created Pakistan against great odds and Hindu opposition; Kashmir had not been lost to India, but was an unresolved and continuing conflict; the 1965 war, though imprudently waged, had not been a defeat, even though victories on the battlefield had been sacrificed at Tashkent. As one senior general officer forcefully observed: "Never before had a Muslim sword been handed over to a Hindu. In Islam, surrender is taboo; you either return with the land, or you bathe it in your blood!"[8]

To assist the power of history, however, Rawalpindi adopted two plans for the defense of East Pakistan—one designed to fight the insurgency, the other to defend against Indian aggression. Each was predicated on the long-standing strategic assumption that "the defense of the east is in the west"—that is, that the threat of Pakistani occupation of Indian territory, whether Kashmir, Punjab, or the desert expanses of western Rajasthan on India's western border, would be sufficient to tie down the bulk of the Indian troops, making the defense of East Pakistan possible with a minimum of force. Moreover, if India seized East Pakistan territory, Pakistan would seize territories on India's western front and use these to bargain. This long-standing strategy had received additional credibility with the diversion of ten Indian divisions to the Sino-Indian border after 1962.

Pakistan developed its plans according to standard operating procedure. In the east, Gen. A. A. K. Niazi, commanding general of the Eastern Command, drafted specifications in May with the assistance of his divisional commanders and staff, which were reviewed in June at a commanders' conference and approved by general headquarters in Rawalpindi. Final plans were drafted, approved, and issued in July. The latter were then approved "on the ground" in August by the chief of the general staff, Gen. Hamid Khan.[9] The mission in the east was simple, but difficult—seal the borders, and in the case of aggression "keep the maximum enemy forces involved in East Pakistan and do not allow them to be shifted to face West Pakistan." In accomplishing these tasks, the military command in the east was to "keep regular troops in certain designated towns and defend them as fortresses or strong points." Given the status of forces in the east, the objectives of sealing the border and operating from a "fortress defense" proved incompatible—sealing the borders required that the fortresses be minimally defended, while manning the fortresses would leave wide corridors for easy enemy entry and withdrawal.

THE WAR THAT WOULDN'T HAPPEN

The military situation in East Pakistan in September and October was significantly different than in the months before. First of all, Pakistani intelligence reported in mid August that Gen. S. F. H. J. (Sam) Manekshaw, commander in chief of the Indian army, had received orders to prepare for military action in East Pakistan; it reported a month later that Manekshaw had issued operational orders to Gen. Jagjit Singh Aurora to prepare for more direct Indian involvement in the east.[10] September also witnessed a marked increase in border clashes and a greater ability by the Mukti Bahini units to inflict damage from bases on the Indian side of the border than had been true before and during the heavy rains of the monsoon, including attacks against both oceangoing and coastal vessels.[11] From late August on, Pakistani intelligence reported heavy movement of Indian troops toward the East Pakistani border, which became more pronounced in September—a fact associated in Pakistani appraisal with Manekshaw's orders to Aurora. By mid month, at the time of a general briefing on East Pakistan at general headquarters attended by all chiefs of staff and corps and divisional commanders, it was reported that Pakistan's forces in the east faced seven Indian divisions and an infantry brigade in addition to two Mukti Bahini brigades.[12]

In the view of Pakistani leaders, a new level of escalation had occurred by early October.[13] Efforts to restrain Indian involvement were not working. Mukti Bahini operations were increasing and were increasingly successful, as they would be from then on. Reports of Soviet arms shipments were also a source of concern. Meanwhile, the severity of the political situation had become abundantly clear to both the civilian and martial law authorities when the holding of by-elections was attempted. The collapse of local authority outside large urban areas was found to be virtually complete.

The first public indication of the seriousness of the situation came on 9 October, when the Pakistani government announced that a blackout exercise would be held in Peshawar; it was acknowledged again two days later when Yahya referred to the "serious possibility of aggression by India against Pakistan" and reported new movement of Indian infantry, armor, and artillery units to the East Pakistani border.[14] To allay anxiety at home and abroad and to affirm a sense of movement and commitment to political reform, Yahya announced in a broadcast on the evening of 12 October that a constitution would be made public on 20 December, by-elections in East Pakistan to the National Assembly would be completed by 23 December, and the National Assembly would be convened on 27 December to begin reviewing the draft constitution and prepare for the transfer of power to a civilian government.[15]

After mid October signals were ambiguous on both sides of the border. Yahya proposed a mutual withdrawal of troops from the borders on 17 October, yet five days later placed the Pakistani air force on alert, recalling pilots undergoing training in Saudi Arabia.[16] In addition to blackouts and border evacuations, the government announced on 24 October that sirens would no longer be used in Karachi as a call to prayer.

By the eve of Indira Gandhi's departure for Europe and the United States in late October, there was talk of war in Pakistan. Among party leaders, Qayyum Khan declared on 20 October that India had already launched a war, though undeclared, against Pakistan. Less than a week after Mrs. Gandhi's departure, Radio Pakistan reported that Indian troops were massed for an attack on East Pakistan, observing that the seriousness of the situation was also made evident by India's call up of reserves, the canceling of leaves of the Border Security Force, and the prime minister's meeting with her service chiefs before her departure for the West.[17] In an interview published in *Newsweek*, Yahya declared that he did not want to escalate the level of tension with India, but that if India tried to set up a "puppet" regime in East Pakistan, there would be war.[18] He also informed the American ambassador that he was willing to initiate a unilateral withdrawal as a first step to defusing the crisis and added that "in order to bring normalcy back to the subcontinent I will do anything within my power short of simply turning Pakistan over to India."[19] Yahya was not prepared, however, to release Mujib or to meet with any Awami League National Assembly members facing major criminal charges. He maintained this position to the end.[20]

THE DECISION ON WAR

With the escalation of hostilities on the East Pakistani border and Pakistan's perception of India's evident commitment to escalation, the "international restraint option" became the only viable avenue for the avoidance of war. The Pakistanis continued to attempt to dramatize their case before the international community by emphasizing the gravity of the situation and to convince observers that they were prepared to reduce regional tensions. The severity of the situation was articulated by Pakistan's foreign minister, Sultan Mohammed Khan, who followed in Mrs. Gandhi's wake through Western capitals. The foreign minister declared publicly in New York, Ottawa, and Paris that war was becoming more likely every day and that the situation between India and Pakistan had changed from a state of confrontation to a "virtual state of war"; a political settlement in East Pakistan, he observed, was not India's concern.[21] In his address to the nation on 19 November, Yahya declared that Pakistan was prepared to defend its "honour and territorial integrity at any cost." He also observed, however, that "India and Pakistan have frittered away their resources on arming against each other. These should have been used to reap the real fruits of independence," and indicated that he wanted to extend to India a "hand of friendship," inviting "India to grasp it and let us begin a new era of good neighborly relations."[22] To Indian decision makers this invitation appeared incomprehensible and surreal. It reflected either a lack of seriousness or a misperception on the part of the Pakistanis as to the actions they would have to take and the conditions that would have to be created to alleviate what was to India an unacceptable threat to its security and domestic tranquility in its eastern and northeastern states.[23] The overture was inconsistent with the pattern of action and inaction on the part of the Pakistani government in the crisis as it developed. It made no reference to what would have to be done; India did not trust it, and it did not fit into the image that India had constructed from the activities and the perceived intentions and capabilities of its antagonist.

Differences within the top military leadership became evident on 21 November with India's incursions into Pakistani territory at Jessore, Comilla, Sylhet, and the Chittagong Hill Tracts. The command in the east declared that a war had commenced, that India had invaded, and that operational orders in both East and West Pakistan should be activated.[24] Communications between the two wings from this point on were almost exclusively by telex, given the reluctance of general headquarters to use telephones; after the declaration of war on 3 December communication became intermittent and delayed, with the meaning of messages open to misinterpretation and confusion. The commander in chief and his closest advisers estimated that India's move on 21 November was a limited action, but felt it must be dramatized by Pakistan to the international community to impress upon the superpowers the necessity of imposing severe constraints on India. Pakistan would not benefit by declaring war; its strategy all along had been to avoid war and to contain India diplomatically.

There was reportedly strong sentiment among officers in west and east alike, however, to engage India in battle. When reviewing troops at the Sialkot front on 22 November, Yahya was greeted by chants of "Allah-O-Akbar!" and while he cautioned that war could not settle anything between Pakistan and India, he declared that if war were forced upon it, Pakistan would fight and "liquidate the enemy."[25] Upon their return from the front that afternoon, Yahya and Hamid were met at the general headquarter's helicopter landing pad by the chief of the army general staff, Gen. Gul Hasan, and the commander of the Pakistani air force, Air Marshal Rahim Khan. They urged Yahya and Hamid to meet with their fellow officers at general headquarters for a briefing on the situation in East Pakistan. The officer corps was becoming uneasy—it had heard conflicting rumors about the situation in the eastern wing and found this terribly disturbing. Yahya and Hamid reluctantly agreed to do this and met with officers at the general headquarters later that evening as well. In both of these meetings, the officers assembled strongly pushed for a declaration of war on India as a matter of pride, prudence, and necessity. Such a decision, however, was rejected by Yahya and Hamid, who argued that India was merely continuing its border actions and that had they wanted an excuse for war, it had already existed for several months. Why, then, make a major, irreversible decision on escalation just because tanks and troops had moved across the border? They had moved across the border in the past, though not in such great strength, but without Pakistan giving serious consideration to declaring war. Instead of war, the president spoke of the need to "handle things on the political front," indicating that he was convinced that India could ultimately be dissuaded by the United States and the United Nations if need be. Yahya and Hamid viewed this continued strategy as prudent, but other general officers present viewed it as numbness and paralysis.[26]

A few days after the Indian incursions General Hamid called the chiefs of the air force and navy and the chief of the army general staff, advised them that a war with India appeared inevitable, that preparations for war must be made, and that he would soon let them know the date.[27] The seriousness with which the high command viewed the situation became evident in the declaration of a national emergency, the recall of all officers up to the rank of major, as well as of all junior commissioned officers and other ranks on leave pending retirement, and a call for all reserves to report immediately to active duty. An announcement also went out over national radio that physicians were urgently needed for short service commissions.[28] The air force was put on a "phase two" alert, mandating that ten aircraft at all bases be put in an around-the-clock state of readiness.[29] In Lahore division a requisition for civilian trucks was also announced, with the stipulation that they be delivered to the Lahore cantonment by noon on 26 November.[30] The commitment to prepare for battle and actively resist was reflected in the exchange between Generals Hamid and Niazi during the last days of November. Hamid's message, received by Niazi in East Pakistan on 30 November, commended the Eastern Command "in meeting the latest challenge posed by the enemy in East Pakistan. The whole nation is proud of you and you have their full support. The gallant deeds of your soldiers in thwarting the enemy's evil designs have earned the gratitude of all countrymen. Keep up the noble work till the enemy's spirit is crushed and they are completely wiped out from our sacred soil. May ALLAH be with you." General Niazi replied: "Reassuring you and pledging afresh at this critical juncture of our history we will INSHALLAH fully honour the great confidence that has been reposed in us and no sacrifice will be considered too great in defending our sacred fatherland. By grace of ALLAH, initial Bharati onslaught has been blunted. GOD willing, we will take the war onto Indian soil to finally crush the very spirit of non-believers through the supreme force of ISLAM. Pray and believe that ultimate victory will be ours. INSHALLAH."[31]

Pakistan's decision to declare war derived from three considerations. The military command's sensitivity to the adverse publicity Pakistan was receiving in the Western press—an image of "nit-wits" and "idiots" being rendered powerless by India, as two principals in the conflict described it—had reached a breaking point.[32] The incongruity between declarations that the occupation of Pakistani soil by India would mean war and the actuality of tolerating what had been declared intolerable was itself becoming intolerable. Second, even this aggression by India against Pakistan, however limited, had not evoked an international response to force India to desist. War was necessary to hasten the process. Third, the timing of the decision was reportedly influenced by the caustic advocacy of Bhutto, who in a meeting with Yahya at the end of November reportedly described in rather graphic and primitive detail what Mrs. Gandhi was doing to the military leaders of Pakistan and declared that if Yahya did not react forcefully to India's outright aggression against Pakistan he would be "lynched by the people."[33] On 30 November the decision was made to declare war on India, with 2 December fixed as D day. Military chiefs were convened and so informed, except that officers in East Pakistan learned about it after the fact, much as Air Marshal Rahim Khan had learned of the military crackdown in the east eight months before. The date was postponed to 3 December in order to allow for additional preparation.[34]

THE DECISION TO SURRENDER

The war was planned and pursued with a lack of coordination and foresight not dissimilar to that of 1965—but in a different set of circumstances and with a woefully different outcome. Pakistan's air strike on 3 December had only limited effectiveness. The Indian airstrips were rapidly repaired. India's two-to-one advantage in aircraft was soon apparent in the air, and India completely controlled the skies above East Pakistan by 6 December. Pakistani troops moved in the Sind sector without air cover—without air force knowledge and coordination according to some sources; left unsupported by an air force fearful of losing planes and unsympathetic to the military's cause according to others.[35] The Pakistani air force was also reportedly reluctant to test a sophisticated missile defense system that India had acquired and put in place since the 1965 war. While the air force reportedly felt comfortable extending support on the Sialkot front, projecting into the Jammu sector of Kashmir, the strike force massed there did not become a factor in the war given the rapid movement of Indian troops in the east and concern about an Indian strike toward Lahore.[36] The military was also reluctant to commit armored units because of successful Indian attacks on oil storage facilities and the disruption of the railway system, which slowed movement of heavy equipment early in the war and left an assured fuel supply for only twelve days of military operations. Given the rapid collapse of Pakistani forces in the east and of diplomatic efforts in the United Nations, the government feared that the army would become overextended and vulnerable to both air strikes and well-fueled Indian armored units.[37]

While the information available was confusing in terms of specifics, it had become clear by 7 December that the defense of East Pakistan was collapsing. There were two channels of communication between East and West Pakistan, "inefficiently workable" even in situations short of war, and "completely unworkable" once "all out war" commenced.[38] One channel was through Governor Malik and his military adviser, Gen. Rao Farman Ali Khan; the other was through the commanding general of the Eastern Command and martial law administrator, General Niazi. Three centers of authority in West Pakistan concerned these offices in East Pakistan—the President's House, the office of the chief martial law administrator, and general headquarters. After India launched its "lightning campaign" against East Pakistan following the outbreak of war on the western front, communication and cooperation among these three centers of authority in the west were as intermittent as they were with their counterparts in the east.

On 9 December Governor Malik telexed the president impress-

ing upon him the urgency of the situation and the need to pursue
a political settlement. In his reply the next day Yahya indicated that
he had full faith in the authorities in Dhaka and that he was far
from the scene and left East Pakistani affairs to Malik's "good sense
and judgment."[39] A parallel message from Hamid to Niazi indicated that the president had authorized Malik to seek a political
settlement and to do what was necessary, keeping in mind that the
enemy had superior forces, and suggested that the maximum
amount of equipment be destroyed. This was locally perceived as
permission to surrender.[40]

As a consequence of these exchanges, a proposal for a cease-fire
was drafted with the concurrence of the governor, in whose name
it was sent, and Generals Niazi and Farman Ali, the latter taking
the lead in preparing and forwarding the message through Paul
Marc Henry, assistant secretary of the United Nations in charge of
relief in East Pakistan, to the U.N. secretary-general. The message
recommended a cease-fire and the creation of a civilian government
in Dhaka composed of the elected representatives from East Pakistan.

> As the conflict [in East Pakistan] arose as a result of political causes it
> must end with a political solution. I [Malik] therefore having been
> authorized by the President of Pakistan do hereby call upon the
> elected representatives of East Pakistan to arrange for the peaceful
> formation of the government in Dacca. In making this offer I feel
> duty bound to say the will of the people of East Pakistan would
> demand the immediate vacation of their land by the Indian forces as
> well. I therefore call upon the United Nations to arrange for a
> peaceful transfer of power and request. One: An immediate cease-
> fire. Two: Repatriation with honour of the Armed Forces of Pakistan
> to West Pakistan. Three. Repatriation of all West Pakistan personnel
> desirous of returning to West Pakistan. Four: The safety of all per-
> sons settled in East Pakistan since 1947. Five. Guarantee of no
> reprisals against any person in East Pakistan. In making this offer, I
> want to make it clear that this is a definite proposal for peaceful
> transfer of power. The question of surrender of Armed Forces will
> not be considered and does not arise and if this proposal is not
> accepted the Armed Forces will continue to fight to the last man.[41]

Reports from within his coterie of advisers in West Pakistan
indicate that Yahya "hit the roof" when he was informed of the
proposal from East Pakistan. It did not provide firm guidelines for
the maintenance of a united Pakistan, and it was unclear who the
elected representatives were supposed to be. In any event, the

authors of the proposal had exceeded their authority.[42] Yahya stated that the sections dealing with a political solution would have to be deleted. This was communicated to the United Nations and made known to the authorities in East Pakistan. The proposal, which authorities in the east were convinced was workable and had reason to believe was acceptable to the Soviet Union, was thus stillborn, as was the Polish resolution submitted to the Security Council subsequently, which contained essentially the same provisions—all much to the relief of the Indian leadership, who were aware of the difficulties acceptance of either would present.[43]

From this time on, officers in the east received messages alternating between "fight" and "cease-fire."[44] On 13 December, for example, a message in Pushto, the language of the North-West Frontier Province, was received from general headquarters advising that support was in the offing—"yellow from the north and white from the south"—and was immediately broadcast to the troops in an effort to bolster their flagging morale. It also did wonders for the spirit of the eastern commander, who, in response to his inquiries about the promised assistance, was instructed to hold on for thirty-six hours since diplomatic moves were under way. A sense of buoyancy continued until it was learned that neither the Chinese nor the American consulate knew anything about forthcoming assistance and that no wireless frequencies had been given for the purpose of contacting those whom the message implied were coming to the rescue.[45]

From this point on the will of central authority to defend East Pakistan collapsed. Messages from the Eastern Command pressing the urgency of the situation went unanswered. The governor, his cabinet, and some thirty senior civil servants formally severed their ties with the regime and sought refuge with the Red Cross at the neutral Hotel Intercontinental rather than in the Dhaka cantonment, many jumping over the fence into the hotel grounds to hasten their escape.[46] On 14 December, General Niazi received the following unclassified message from Yahya implying that the armed forces in East Pakistan should surrender:

> You have fought a heroic battle against overwhelming odds. The nation is proud of you and the world full of admiration. I have done all that is humanly possible to find an acceptable solution to the problem. You have now reached a stage where further resistance is

no longer humanly possible nor will it serve any useful purpose. It will only lead to further loss of lives and destruction. You should now take all necessary measures to stop the fighting and preserve the lives of armed forces personnel, all those from West Pakistan and all loyal elements. Meanwhile I have moved U.N. to urge India to stop hostilities in East Pakistan forthwith and to guarantee the safety of armed forces and all other people who may be the likely target of miscreants.[47]

Generals Niazi and Farman Ali immediately prepared plans for surrender; their intention was signaled to the Government of India through the U.S. diplomatic service.[48] The terms of the surrender were initiated by General Manekshaw, presented to General Niazi by General Jacob on 16 December, and signed by Generals Niazi and Aurora at the Ramna Race Course, the scene of Sheikh Mujibur Rahman's most significant political moments. Ironically, it was here too that General Niazi, commander of the forces of Muslim Pakistan, surrendered his arms to three generals of "Hindu" India—one a Parsi, another a Sikh, and the third a Jew.

THE TRANSFER OF POWER

In the wake of his acceptance of the cease-fire in West Pakistan on 17 December, only one day after a vow to carry on the war against India until victory was achieved and after the announcement and withdrawal of the constitution from public view, Yahya was faced with dissent not only in the streets of major cities in West Pakistan but in the headquarters of military installations. According to several sources, on 19 December the head of the Pakistani air force, Air Marshal Rahim Khan, received a call from the army chief of staff, Gen. Gul Hasan, requesting that he come immediately to GHQ, where a number of officers were in an agitated mood.[49] In particular, two colonels, the chiefs of staff of their respective divisions, had come to headquarters as representatives of, or, more accurately, as negotiators for an infantry division and an armored division stationed at Qadian, near Jhelum in the Punjab. They stated that their divisional commanders were being held under "house arrest" and would continue to be held until certain demands were met. They demanded that Yahya step down as president, chief martial law administrator, and commander in chief of the Pakistani army and warned that if he did not younger officers in their divisions were prepared to force him to. They were adamant that a transfer of power take place immediately, that it be arranged that very day, and that power be transferred to a general, not to a civilian, arguing that it was essential that the Pakistani army be able to take credit for removing Yahya, not Bhutto or some other politician.

The general officers whom the two colonels had approached were themselves committed to the transfer of power to a civilian elite, and they feared the consequences of a military coup in a situation where the military, which had become fractious during the Yahya interregnum, had grown even more distrustful and divided during the civil war and, now, the breakup of the country. These officers feared, however, that unless something were done, some other officer would feel compelled to lead a coup. They accordingly proposed to the colonels that Yahya declare immediately that he would resign the following day, and that they would then handle the situation.

After conferring with their fellow officers, the two colonels reported that this would be acceptable provided that Yahya resigned all three of his positions as they had requested. One of the general officers present then went directly to the house of Gen. Hamid Khan and told him that units in the army had threatened mutiny and that Yahya would have to go. A meeting was set with the president for 7:30 that evening, at which time a small group of officers presented the essence of the situation to Yahya, who seemed prepared for it, quiet and even-tempered, even relieved. His statement of resignation, drafted by one of the generals involved, was read out over the eight o'clock news.

At this meeting the generals also informed Yahya that the government had to be handed over to Bhutto, since otherwise some other general might attempt to grab power.[50] Yahya reportedly inquired when Bhutto was coming back. The response was "immediately"—an air vice marshal having been despatched to Rome with a PIA plane to hasten the future president's return. Bhutto returned to Pakistan on 20 December and arrived with several of his associates at the President's House at approximately half past ten in the morning. In the course of their discussions Yahya told Bhutto that he should assume the presidency in the transference of power to a civilian regime. Bhutto demanded the position of chief martial law administrator as well. Yahya and one adviser insisted that it would be inappropriate and possibly illegal to transfer that position to a civilian, and another argued that the position could only be acquired by the exercise of power. Bhutto indicated that this was precisely what he was doing. Yahya conceded in a manner reminiscent of his assumption of complete martial law authority nearly two years before. With this decision, another era in the political agony of Pakistan drew to a close.

12

Soviet, Chinese, and American
Policies in the 1971 Crisis

The major world powers were vocal commentators on the conflicts and wars of South Asia during 1971, and both India and Pakistan were deeply concerned with attracting their attention and support. None of the great powers wanted to see the breakup of Pakistan, but none could prevent it, even though each enjoyed an important presence in at least one of the warring states. The literature on both the international relations and the domestic politics of the South Asian states is, of course, replete with detailed analyses of the crucial role of the major external powers in the subcontinent since 1947, with most of the emphasis placed upon the intrusive policies of the Soviet Union, China, and the United States. While the importance of these powers in regional developments may well have been exaggerated, it is readily apparent that they have had a substantial impact upon decision making in the South Asian states. And by the mid 1950s the three major external powers had developed reasonably well defined, if not always consistent, policies toward South Asia that the regional states could not easily ignore.

The 1965 Indo-Pakistani war and the Tashkent Conference in February 1966 had led to some interesting innovations in Soviet, Chinese, and American policies in South Asia, based primarily on their perceptions of the political and strategic environment in the subcontinent in the post-Tashkent period. The most apparent changes in regional policies during 1966 to 1971 were made by Moscow and Washington, but Beijing also began subtly and indirectly redefining its role and policies south of the Himalayas.

THE SOVIET UNION

The Soviet Union had initially become involved in South Asia in the mid 1950s in order to forestall and counteract U.S. "intervention" in that region through Pakistan's membership in U.S.-sponsored military alliance systems and through massive American economic aid programs to India. Moscow expanded its policy objectives in the region over the next decade, in particular by using India as a channel to noncommunist states in Asia and Africa, with which it had established only the most tenuous connections during Stalin's rule. It was hoped that this would serve Soviet strategic and political interests in the Middle East and, to a lesser extent, Southeast Asia—areas in which Moscow was already involved in various ways. India was the critical state in the subcontinent in Soviet calculations, and giving primacy to India in Moscow's policy considerations made good sense; thus, it had become a basic objective of Soviet policy to prevent any serious disjunctures in its relationship with India.

At the Tashkent Conference, however, the Soviet Union began to modify its "support India" policy in South Asia in favor of a somewhat more nonpartisan position. This first became evident in the Soviet offer to mediate the settlement of the 1965 war and in Moscow's professedly neutral (in practice, however, slightly pro-Pakistani) role as the host power at Tashkent.[1] Its new, more balanced policy was continued in the post-Tashkent period, during which the U.S.S.R. made a concerted effort to expand its economic, political, and security relations with Pakistan, while at the same time seeking to maintain a close and friendly relationship with India. Moscow inaugurated a major program of economic assistance to Pakistan, including an agreement to construct its first modern steel mill, and in 1968 introduced a military assistance program that was initially relatively modest, but involved extensive negotiations between the two states on a much more substantial arms aid program.[2] The first Soviet-Pakistani arms aid agreement, signed in July 1968, provided for approximately $30 million in military equipment, including medium tanks, rocket launchers, artillery, and helicopters, but given the discount rates the U.S.S.R. charges for surplus military supplies, this was the equivalent of $50 to $60 million in U.S. military sales.[3]

As might be expected, the Government of India was greatly distressed by these changes in Soviet policy, and it quietly but forcefully made its views known to Moscow through diplomatic channels.[4] The Soviet Union sought to mollify New Delhi by arguing that its military and economic aid to Pakistan provided it with the capacity to counter the influence of "unfriendly" states—specifically, China—in that country, and that this served both Indian and Soviet interests.[5] The Soviets portrayed their objectives as being both a more balanced relationship with India and Pakistan and the curbing of Chinese influence in South Asia.

By mid 1969, however, the Soviet Union was once again reconsidering its assertively nonpartisan position in South Asia and began to move back, rather tentatively and cautiously, toward support for India over the next two years. Several factors influenced Soviet decision makers on this issue. The political crisis in Pakistan that led to the overthrow of the Ayub Khan regime in early 1969 had demonstrated the basic instability of the Pakistani political system and made a close working relationship with Pakistan seem an uncertain and possibly expensive gamble. Moreover, Moscow was disappointed that Islamabad had refused to moderate its alliancelike relationship with China, even while eagerly accepting Soviet economic and military aid.

In contrast, political developments in India from 1969 to 1971 made that country again appear to be the better bet. The 1969 split in the Congress party in India, with the so-called progressive wing of the party (which included most, but not all, of the pro-Soviet factions and leaders) lining up behind Prime Minister Indira Gandhi, seemed to hold some promise for the U.S.S.R. But probably of most importance to the Soviet Union was the receptivity of Mrs. Gandhi's government to Moscow's proposal for a treaty between the two states if, in response, the Soviets terminated, or at least reduced, their military aid to Pakistan.[6] Moscow considered such a treaty an important step in the direction of an Indian endorsement of Brezhnev's June 1969 "Asian mutual security" proposal, which was an integral part of the Soviet Union's "containment of China" policy. A broad agreement on the proposed Indo-Soviet treaty was reached during negotiations conducted by the Indian ambassador to Moscow, D. P. Dhar, in mid 1969, and it is probable that the treaty would have been signed in the first half of 1970 if the political situation in India had permitted.[7] For its part Moscow informed New Delhi in April 1970 that Soviet military aid to Pakistan was being "suspended," though in fact some arm shipments to Pakistan continued through 1970 and into 1971.[8]

All these negotiations with India had been conducted quietly and with no public announcements by either side. In form, then, the Soviet Union maintained its "balanced" policy in South Asia and even expanded its economic aid to Pakistan: a nuclear cooperation agreement was signed in Karachi on 20 May 1970, and the steel mill agreement was formally concluded during President Yahya's visit to Moscow in June. There were also reports in the Indian press in May—that is, before Yahya's Moscow trip—that the U.S.S.R. intended to offer SU-7 bombers and missile boats to Pakistan.[9] That this was given wide publicity in several pro-Soviet papers and journals in India (usually an unlikely source for unpalatable news about the U.S.S.R.) suggests that the reports may have been deliberately leaked by Soviet sources to pressure *both* India and Pakistan on Brezhnev's Asian mutual security proposal. New Delhi never endorsed the proposal as such, but it did indicate its receptivity to the concept of some kind of Asian security system that excluded China; Rawalpindi, in contrast, maintained a strongly pro-Chinese position on the Sino-Soviet dispute and indicated that it was disinclined to cooperate with Brezhnev's anti-Beijing policies. The Soviet "tilt" toward India thus had begun to reemerge by late 1970—that is, before the political crisis that later led to the third Indo-Pakistani war—but Moscow had by no means given up on its efforts to attain a more influential role in Pakistan as well.

The Soviet government was the first of the major external powers to respond publicly to the 25 March crackdown in East Pakistan. On 2 April 1971, President Podgorny sent a letter to President Yahya on behalf of the Supreme Soviet appealing "for the adoption of the most urgent measures to stop the bloodshed and repression against the population of East Pakistan and for turning to methods of a peaceful political settlement." He also asked Yahya to "correctly interpret the motives by which we are guided in making this appeal," that is, the "generally recognized humanitarian principles recorded in the Universal Declaration of Human Rights and by concern for the welfare of the friendly people of Pakistan."[10]

Yahya did what he was asked—he "correctly interpreted" Soviet motives. He was furious and considered it ludicrous that a government with the record of the Soviet Union on human rights had the gall to preach to him on the subject. In his reply, dated 6 April,

Yahya asserted that no country, including the U.S.S.R., could allow "anti-national and unpatriotic elements to proceed to destroy it or to countenance subversion" and also noted that any interference by outside powers would constitute a violation of the U.N. charter.[11] Yahya's response apparently had some impact in Moscow, as the Soviet press toned down its coverage of Pakistani developments, and a mid-April letter from Premier Kosygin to the Pakistani government was much milder in tone than Podgorny's— and was also not publicized, perhaps for that reason.[12] Moscow also reiterated publicly on several occasions thereafter that East Pakistan was an "internal affair" of Pakistan's. Throughout 1971, moreover, the U.S.S.R. continued to refer to "East Pakistan" in its statements, refusing to follow the practice adopted by India in mid 1971 of using "East Bengal."

The Soviet Union was also rather slow, or perhaps inefficient, in halting its military aid to Pakistan. Soviet arm shipments— primarily spare parts for equipment that had been supplied earlier—were received in Pakistan in late April 1971 and, according to Pakistani sources, even thereafter in small quantities. According to a Soviet embassy note to the Government of India on 7 July 1971, these arms had been contracted and shipped before 25 March; all military aid, according to the note, had been halted on 25 March.[13] The few cases of "leakage" in the shipment of arms, it was explained privately to the Indian authorities (but not publicly), were cases of bureaucratic inefficiency and not of government policy.[14] Perhaps; but it would seem reasonable to expect the Soviet bureaucracy to have been able to prevent arms shipments to Pakistan a month or more after the crackdown in East Pakistan.

Soviet policies and objectives immediately after the 25 March crackdown stressed peace and stability, both internal and international, in South Asia and looked upon developments in East Pakistan as a serious obstacle to the U.S.S.R.'s basic Asian policy—the creation of a Soviet-sponsored collective security system directed at the containment of China.[15] The U.S.S.R. sought to expand and strengthen its ties with India without, in the process, completely alienating Pakistan. Indeed, in the early stage of the struggle in East Pakistan, the Soviet Union indicated an interest in serving once again as mediator—this time between the two wings of Pakistan. But the Soviets quickly abandoned such aspirations when the complexities of the situation became clearer and when new opportunities presented themselves for exploitation.

It was only after the signing of the Indo-Soviet Treaty of Peace, Friendship, and Cooperation on 9 August 1971 that the U.S.S.R. began to abandon even the pretence of a relatively balanced position. According to most reports, the Soviet government was surprised and initially rather hesitant when the Government of India dispatched D. P. Dhar to Moscow in late July to propose the immediate conclusion of a treaty between the two governments based on the draft prepared in 1969, but expanded to include a "consultation clause" (article nine).[16] While Moscow was still enthusiastic about a treaty with India, it was concerned about what the Indians would expect in exchange. When Dhar made it clear, however, that New Delhi did not want a formal (or secret) Soviet commitment to come to India's assistance in the event of Chinese intervention in another Indo-Pakistani war, Moscow agreed.[17] Premier Kosygin was then sent to New Delhi to sign the treaty, the text of which had been agreed upon in Moscow.

Thereafter, Soviet policy began to show a clearer pro-India tilt, though not immediately. Pakistan's foreign secretary met with what was described as a "stiff Soviet attitude" when he visited Moscow in late August to ascertain the full significance of the Indo-Soviet treaty;[18] and in early September, Kosygin publicly characterized Yahya's policies in East Pakistan as "indefensible," the kind of language the Soviet Union had refrained from using previously. To New Delhi's irritation, however, the Soviet delegation to the Interparliamentary Union Conference in Paris in the latter part of September voted for two Arab resolutions that were interpreted as supportive of Pakistan.[19]

The total shift in Moscow's position on "Bangladesh" occurred only after Mrs. Gandhi's visit to Moscow from 27 to 29 September, during which she was given an unprecedentedly warm reception—including an invitation to stay at the Kremlin, a privilege usually reserved for "heads of state."[20] According to American sources, the Soviet Union continued to press for a "peaceful political solution" in the Moscow talks, but received a coldly negative response from Mrs. Gandhi. In any case, by the time she left Moscow, the Soviet government had concluded that India intended to use military force in East Pakistan. Apparently it took about two weeks for the U.S.S.R. to decide on its policy response, but finally in mid October Moscow suddenly informed the Government of India that Soviet Deputy Foreign Minister Nikolai Firyubin would be sent to New Delhi shortly for what the Soviet Union (but not the Indians) termed "consultations" under article nine of the Indo-Soviet treaty.[21] India tried to have Firyubin's visit delayed, as Mrs. Gandhi was scheduled to set off on important visits to Western Europe and the United States, and it was considered a bit embarrassing to have a high-level Soviet delegation come to India just two days prior to her departure.[22] But Moscow insisted, and Firyubin flew into New Delhi on 22 October as scheduled, presumably because Moscow wanted to make its offers to Mrs. Gandhi before she began her tour of the West.

During her visit to Moscow in September, Mrs. Gandhi had requested immediate and substantial military assistance. The Soviet government reportedly agreed to one billion dollars in military and economic aid, but with no specific programs designated.[23] By the time Firyubin came to New Delhi, the Soviet leaders were ready to talk about providing the specific weapons systems the Indian army wanted. On 30 October, Soviet Air Marshal P. S. Koutakhov arrived in New Delhi to arrange for the immediate transfer of some military equipment on an emergency basis. The result of all this was a step-up in the tempo of Soviet military shipments to India in November: three shiploads of arms were dispatched and an emergency airlift was launched to provide a limited quantity of specialized equipment and spare parts the Indian army and air force had requested.[24]

Thus, by late October it was clear that Moscow had decided on all-out support for India if another war broke out and had begun to implement its decision in ways that would be immediately appreciated in New Delhi. This was not an easy decision for Moscow, as there were persuasive arguments for continuance of a balanced policy—or at least the pretence of such a policy. The "support India" posture was certain to antagonize most of the Islamic states in the Middle East and North Africa, and Moscow was already experiencing serious difficulties in its relations with several of these governments. Moreover, the Soviet government was not sure that an Indian victory in the projected hostilities with Pakistan would be in Moscow's interest, as the eventual result would be the emergence of India as the unchallenged dominant power in South Asia and, concomitantly, the reduction of Indian dependence on Soviet support in meeting the threat of a Pakistan-China "axis." Apparently, however, Mrs. Gandhi had made it clear in Moscow that India intended to intervene militarily in East Pakistan no matter what the Soviet Union decided and that Moscow's failure to hew to a "support India" line would, of course, be considered in future decision making in New Delhi. In the Soviet view, this would constitute "unacceptable damage" to Indo-Soviet relations, and the decision was made accordingly.[25]

By early November there was a notable change in the tenor of Soviet press reporting on East Pakistan, with *Izvestia* and *New Times* publishing articles strongly criticizing the Pakistani government's efforts—or lack thereof—at a political settlement of the civil war. A *New Times* article specifically stated that Mujib and the Awami League must be involved in any political negotiations, though it also continued to insist that a settlement should preserve the territorial integrity of Pakistan. This was the general line in Soviet press and official statements through November. Following the formal declaration of war on 3 December, however, the Soviet press adopted a staunchly pro-India line, blaming the war on Pakistan's "cruel repressions" in East Pakistan, calling for a "representative"—that is, independent—government in East Pakistan, and asking other governments to avoid involvement in the conflict in what Tass called "the Hindustan peninsula"—a term that must have provoked the Bangladeshi Muslims nearly as much as the Pakistani Muslims.[26]

The principal focus of Soviet government attention immediately after the outbreak of hostilities was not on the "Hindustan peninsula," however, but on the United Nations in New York. The primary task of the U.S.S.R. in terms of its friendly relationship with India was to make sure that the U.N. Security Council did not act expeditiously in ordering a cease-fire before India had achieved its basic objectives in East Pakistan. And this the Soviet Union achieved through the veto power bestowed on it as a permanent member of the Security Council.

As the war progressed, India and the U.S.S.R. decided that it would be useful to establish regular lines of communication and discussion above the embassy level. This was accomplished by sending D. P. Dhar, the policy planning chairman and a close confidant of Mrs. Gandhi's, to Moscow on 11 December, while Soviet First Deputy Minister Kuznetsov arrived in New Delhi the same day. It may be an indication of the ways in which its pro-India policy embarrassed Soviet relations with a number of important states that in December—in contrast to October—it was India that defined this exchange of high-ranking officials as falling under article nine of the Indo-Soviet treaty, while Moscow did not acknowledge that the consultation process had been invoked. Just what Dhar and Kuznetsov actually did on their respective assignments to earn their keep has never been clarified, since the two governments did not really have that much to "consult" about at so high a level. But presumably it was a useful symbolic gesture for both sides.

Probably the most highly publicized aspect of Indo-Soviet relations during the war involved Soviet military support, both direct and implicit. The U.S.S.R. had stepped up the tempo of military deliveries to India in November, but there were no further deliveries by sea in December and because of the closure of the main air route between the two countries, probably none, or at least very few, by air. Unofficial reports in the Indian press noted that Soviet military personnel had been directly involved in combat operations aboard Indian aircraft and naval units. On 13 December, however, Tass issued an authorized denial of such reports.

Given far wider publicity in India was the claim put forward by pro-Soviet elements in India that the Soviet naval units in the Indian Ocean had been the effective deterrent to the U.S. naval task force that, allegedly, would otherwise have attacked Indian forces either there or somewhere else (the scenarios differed widely). The Soviet naval forces on regular assignment in the Indian Ocean by 1971 had been lightly reinforced in the fall and then more substantially after the outbreak of the war in December by a detachment of the Soviet Pacific fleet, normally based in eastern Siberia. The United States noted the dispatch of this Soviet detachment, and this was one factor in its decision to send the *Enterprise* task force into the Indian Ocean, though it was a minor one, as the United States saw no function for Soviet naval forces in the Indian Ocean in this particular conflict. Nor was Washington concerned about the possibility of a U.S.–Soviet naval clash. Neither side considered the issues involved worthy of a confrontation, and they had made their respective views clear to each other. It was mildly irritating to the United States to have the Russians claiming to have forestalled an American naval action that had never been projected; but then Washington was playing its own little public relations games with the Islamic states and, later, with China.[27]

Since both knew what the results would be on that front before the war began and did not strongly object to them, the most important issue for both Washington and Moscow in the 1971 conflict was not East Pakistan, but rather the fate of West Pakistan. On this subject there was a broad congruence of Soviet and American perceptions and interests. These interests were seen, for different reasons, as being best served by maintaining the integrity of West Pakistan, including the Pakistani-held areas of Kashmir, and by encouraging New Delhi to limit its military actions on the western front.[28] This had not been an easy decision for the Soviet leaders, as there were persuasive arguments favoring the disintegration of West Pakistan. King Zahir Shah of Afghanistan made a sudden uninvited visit to Moscow 12–14 December, reportedly to argue for the "Balkanization" of West Pakistan—in particular, the separation of the Pakhtoon area (the North-West Frontier Province) from Pakistan and its inclusion in Afghanistan. But Moscow was unimpressed, and on 17 December the U.S.S.R. quickly endorsed India's unilateral cease-fire order on the western front, which in effect ended the war. The U.S.S.R. moved almost immediately to attempt to improve relations with Pakistan, the Islamic states, and those members of the nonaligned movement that had been critical of India, while still maintaining a close relationship with an India that was much less dependent upon Soviet support than it had been before the 1971 war. The Soviet Union was on the winning side in the war, but there were almost no payoffs anywhere. Perhaps the most frustrating development for Moscow later was the virtually total exclusion of a Soviet role in Bangladesh after the overthrow of Mujib's one-party authoritarian regime in 1975.

CHINA

Since the formal establishment of the People's Republic of China (PRC) in October 1949, Beijing has tended to waver between several policy options in South Asia. This ambivalence has been reflected in China's perception of India and the policies the PRC has adopted toward the major power in the subcontinent. In 1949 the Chinese used the same denunciatory language as the Soviet Union in their commentaries on India, labeling the "bourgeois" Nehru government a "lackey of the Western imperialists" and demonstrating little interest in a friendly relationship with New Delhi. Beijing's attitude toward Nehru and India began to change earlier than Moscow's, however, in part because New Delhi assumed a "nonaligned" position on two critical issues for China— Korea and Tibet. Moreover, by 1950 Nehru had clearly defined India's basic foreign policy objectives, in particular the isolation of Asia from the Cold War through a cooperative relationship with China that would be directed at limiting the capacity of both the United States and the Soviet Union to intervene in Asian developments. While it is doubtful that Mao Zedong and Zhou Enlai shared Nehru's "utopian" objectives, they saw some advantages for China in a friendly relationship with India.

Negotiations between an eager India and a somewhat less enthusiastic China were carried on between 1952 and 1954, finally culminating in the 1954 treaty on Tibet that included the famous "five principles" (Panchshila) of "peaceful coexistence." Thereafter a tacit alliance evolved between the two powers in which China used India, with Nehru's enthusiastic concurrence, as a channel of communication to the still wary noncommunist states in Asia and Africa, offering to establish diplomatic relations with them on Panchshila terms. "Hindi-Chini, bhai-bhai" ("Chinese and Indians are brothers") was the slogan used by both New Delhi and Beijing to describe their relationship, and in the 1950s China carefully arranged its policies toward the other South Asian states to avoid giving umbrage to the Indians.

"Hindi-Chini, bhai-bhai" became "Hindi-Chini, bye-bye" with the outbreak of a bitter dispute over the Sino-Indian border in 1959, which coincided with the steady deterioration in Beijing-Moscow relations and culminated in the brief, but intense, Sino-Indian war of October–December 1962. From that point on China's policy objectives in South Asia fundamentally changed—from a generally supportive position toward India to one in which New Delhi became the primary target of Chinese policy in the region. Beijing's

basic operating principles under this new policy were (1) to undermine India's relations with the other South Asian states by supporting them in their disputes with New Delhi and encouraging them
to reject Indian terms for the settlement of disputes; (2) to complicate Soviet policy in South Asia by projecting an image of Moscow
as a "client" of the Indians in the other states in the region; and (3)
to extract a heavy price from India for its allegedly pro-Soviet
policies by periodic pressure upon disputed areas on the border
and by support of "revolutionary" and "separatist" movements in
India. Whether India, the Soviet Union, or China paid the higher
price for this Chinese policy is questionable; a good argument can
be made that the PRC's policies toward South Asia in 1960–71 were
counterproductive, as they obligated Beijing to invest much more
heavily in the region than it could afford, while extracting few
tangible gains from this investment. But whereas the anti-Indian
policy achieved few positive results for China, it did make the
Indian elite and public almost paranoid on the China question, and
India's tendency to overreact to perceived challenges from China in
turn reduced the effectiveness of New Delhi's regional policy.
Whether even this served China's long-range interests in the region is doubtful, however, since the principal consequence was to
enhance the value of the Soviet and the American "connection" for
the Indians, hardly an objective of Chinese policy.

The simultaneous crises in China's relations with India and the
Soviet Union in the early 1960s induced Beijing to undertake a
concerted campaign to improve and expand its relations with
Pakistan. This had three positive aspects for China. First, it encouraged the Pakistanis to reconsider their security relation with the
United States, at that time still "Enemy No. 1" for Beijing. Second,
it provided Pakistan with an alternative source (to the United
States) of support against Soviet pressure, thus allowing Rawalpindi to reject—politely but firmly—Moscow's proposals for an
accommodation at the expense of both the United States and
China. Third, and probably most important in the 1960s, it raised
the specter of Chinese-Pakistani "collusion" against India, thus
limiting the political and strategic options available to New Delhi in
dealing with either or both of its hostile neighbors. When the
United States terminated its military aid program to Pakistan during the 1965 Indo-Pakistani war, China became the primary exter-

nal source of military assistance to the beleaguered Pakistanis. As noted earlier, the Soviet Union attempted to compete with China in this capacity in the late 1960s, but eventually abandoned the effort. By 1965 China was thus seen in Pakistan as the country's only reliable friend among the major powers. Indeed, despite Beijing's failure to do anything substantial except make loud threats during the 1965 Indo-Pakistani war, Pakistanis tended to greatly exaggerate both China's capabilities and its willingness to serve as a source of support. By this time China was beginning to reevaluate the usefulness of Pakistan to Chinese policy objectives, as became increasingly clear in the 1971 crisis in South Asia and thereafter.

China's post–Tashkent Conference policy toward South Asia changed less on the surface than that of either the United States or the U.S.S.R., but there were some modifications in Beijing's role in the region. The 1965 war had clearly demonstrated the high price China might have to pay for its support of Pakistan if this had to be extended from the provision of military and economic assistance to actual military intervention against India. China sought to maintain and even expand its close relationship with Pakistan, but quietly rejected Rawalpindi's requests for specific security commitments that would obligate the Chinese to intervene in another Indo-Pakistani conflict. The period of the Cultural Revolution (1966–69) in China was marked by a high degree of ethnocentricity and a predilection for an isolationist foreign policy. Chinese foreign policy in general, and more specifically policy toward some Asian and African states that had previously been classified as friendly, became increasingly antagonistic and denunciatory. This was less evident in South Asia, where Beijing maintained good relations with Pakistan and, with one short exception, Nepal throughout the Cultural Revolution, but the internal strife and disorder that accompanied the Cultural Revolution did have some effect upon how governments in South Asia perceived China. The 1969 crisis in Sino-Soviet relations, involving large-scale clashes on the Chinese–U.S.S.R. border, also had repercussions on China's South Asian policy. India was depicted by Beijing as strongly supportive of the Soviet Union and, indeed, as an integral part of Moscow's "encirclement policy." Some quiet overtures from New Delhi in the late 1960s suggesting the commencement of a process of "normalizing" Sino-Indian relations—which might have been seriously considered under other circumstances—were rudely rejected by Beijing, which retained its basic anti-Indian policy in South Asia.

Of the three major external powers China was probably placed in the most difficult position by the events of 25 March 1971 in East Pakistan. Beijing concluded that it had nothing to gain, but much to lose, from these developments, no matter what the outcome might be. China was clearly unenthusiastic about the military crackdown in East Pakistan, which after all was directed against pro-Chinese political factions there as well as against the Awami League. China also faced the problem of defining a response that did not violate its general policy of endorsing "national liberation movements," including several that had more doubtful credentials than the Bangladesh movement in their claims to represent a "people."

On balance, however, Beijing was far more concerned with avoiding any actions that would weaken or alienate its "ally," Pakistan, or that would encourage India to "resolve" the East Pakistani crisis militarily. The first public notice of the crackdown by China was a *New China News Agency* report on East Pakistan on 4 April that merely mentioned that the Pakistani army had taken action to suppress "secessionist elements." The first editorial comment, which appeared on 11 April in the *People's Daily*, criticized Indian interference in Pakistan's domestic affairs, but abstained from any specific comments on the developments in East Pakistan.[29] A letter of the same date from Zhou Enlai to Yahya Khan was a masterpiece of evasion and subterfuge; it did not criticize *either* the Pakistan government *or* the Bangladesh movement, but noted "that of late the Indian government [has] been carrying out gross interference in the internal problems of your country. And the Soviet Union and U.S. are doing the same, one after the other." The letter ended with a pledge of Chinese support to the "Pakistani people"—but not specifically to the Yahya Khan government.[30]

At the same time that China was taking a public position seemingly supportive of the Pakistani government, however, it was also informing the Pakistani embassy in China and the foreign ministry in Islamabad *privately* that it would not intervene directly in hostilities, either internal or international, on the subcontinent. Thus, by mid April the core group in the Yahya Khan government—but not the Pakistani public—had learned that they could not expect Chinese military support in the event of another war with India and had acted accordingly thereafter in the Yahya regime's decision-making process.[31] According to several authoritative Indian and Bangladeshi sources, New Delhi was also cognizant at least by early June of the position China had taken in April, and India's policy and military decisions were based on the assumption that China would not intervene in another Indo-Pakistani war.[32]

China continued its economic and military aid to Pakistan after 25 March and even allowed the unloading of a large shipment of arms consigned to the Pakistani army in East Pakistan that had been shipped before 25 March, but did not reach Chittagong harbor until April.[33] But while China honored its previous arms aid commitments, it has been reported that Beijing was reluctant to approve new arms aid through the spring and summer of 1971. Pakistan made a specific appeal for some equipment, in particular aircraft, but China did not agree to the request until several months later.[34] Some small arms and ammunition were delivered to Pakistan in the latter half of 1971, but most of the fighter aircraft requested reached Pakistan only after the war was over.[35] But whether this was a policy decision or was because of the nonavailability of the equipment requested or other such factors is unclear.

In any case, throughout most of 1971 the Chinese government was discreetly silent on developments in East Pakistan and only occasionally referred to the situation there indirectly in its standard denunciations of Indian intervention in neighboring states. By the fall of 1971, however, it had become increasingly evident that India intended to resort to force if a satisfactory political solution was not achieved in East Pakistan reasonably quickly. The Pakistani government therefore decided to approach Beijing once again with a request for assistance—to reverse its April policy position—and a deputation consisting of Bhutto, Air Marshal Rahim Khan, and Gen. Gul Hasan was sent to Beijing on 7 November. In a meeting with Zhou Enlai, Rahim asked the Chinese to provide thirty fighter planes, as well as sundry other military supplies on an emergency basis, while Bhutto sounded out the PRC premier on whether China would consider coming to the assistance of Pakistan in the event of war with India. Zhou replied that war was unlikely, but that if it occurred Chinese military forces would not intervene directly in support of Pakistan, although China would support Pakistan politically and provide material assistance.[36]

This was a discouraging, but not surprising, response. What did surprise his colleagues on their return to Pakistan was Bhutto's public statement asserting that China had assured Pakistan of its support in the event of an Indian attack. This has aroused speculation in some of the literature on the 1971 war that the Pakistani government, and Yahya Khan in particular, was confused about Beijing's policy. This was not the case, as the president had been thoroughly and correctly briefed on Zhou Enlai's position.[37] What the Pakistani government had hoped to do was raise uncertainties in New Delhi about China's response to Indian intervention in East Pakistan. On 1 November—before the Pakistani delegation had even been sent to China—Yahya had been quoted by Radio Pakistan as having told a CBS interviewer that China would intervene in the event of an Indian attack on Pakistan.[38] Presumably Bhutto's public statement after his return from China was part of this same effort to raise the stakes in another Indo-Pakistani war. According to Pakistani sources, the Chinese were not pleased with Bhutto's statement but did not contradict it, as Beijing also had an interest in deterring India from taking military action.[39]

This minor exercise in game-playing had no impact on New Delhi, however, which remained confident that China would limit itself to vocal denunciations of India in the event of another war. Indeed, India doubted that China had the capacity to intervene effectively even if it wanted to. The Chinese military forces in Tibet had not been reinforced and resupplied on the scale that would have been required for anything more than a minor border incident.[40] Perhaps even more important in New Delhi's calculations was the September 1971 "coup" attempt by Mao's designated successor, Lin Biao, supported by some elements in the Chinese air force and army. This had led to the grounding of the PRC air force for some time, and there were still serious strains within the Chinese military establishment in late 1971. All this reinforced New Delhi's conclusion that China would do exactly what it did—vigorously denounce India in public statements, but carefully avoid any involvement, even a minor border clash, in the conflict over East Pakistan.

China behaved exactly as Pakistan and India expected during the 1971 war. In Beijing on 29 November, Chinese Vice Premier Li Hsien-Nien—in the presence of Premier Zhou Enlai—said that

China resolutely supported Pakistan in its "just struggle against foreign aggression," but then called for "peaceful consultations" and mutual withdrawal of forces. In the U.N. Security Council proceedings after 3 December, China demonstrated its unfamiliarity with the nuances of bargaining (the People's Republic had just replaced Taiwan in the "China seat" at the United Nations), always voting with the majority, supporting the resolutions calling for a cease-fire and opposing the Soviet resolution.

There were no incidents on the long Chinese-Indian border during the war. China did attempt to replay one of its 1965 Indo-Pakistani war stratagems at the tail end of the 1971 war when on 15 December Beijing protested the alleged incursion of Indian troops across the Sikkim-Tibet frontier on 10 December. During the 1965 war China had also waited until a tentative cease-fire date had been set and had then issued a strong ultimatum to India demanding the withdrawal of Indian forces from disputed points on the Sikkim border by a certain date—two days after the cease-fire was scheduled to go into effect. To Beijing's embarrassment in 1965 the Indo-Pakistani cease-fire was delayed, and China had to extend the date for the expiration of its ultimatum as well. The subject was dropped after the Indo-Pakistani cease-fire finally went into effect, and the same thing happened in 1971 to the more modest Chinese complaint on the Sikkim border. That was the only effort by Beijing to provide at least a touch of substance to the rather strong rhetoric used in its support of Pakistan, which obviously neither the Indians nor the Pakistanis paid much attention to at the time. Later, however, the Pakistanis used this verbal support to prove that the Chinese were always true friends, while the Indians used it to prove they were implacable enemies—when this was convenient.

THE UNITED STATES

In the view of the regional states, U.S. policy in South Asia has been even less consistent, and hence less predictable, than either Soviet or Chinese policy. The primary reason for this, it has been suggested, has been the relatively low priority assigned to South Asia by American decision makers, and the resultant propensity to use U.S. involvement in the subcontinent to support what have been considered more important American political and strategic interests in West Asia and Southeast Asia. This has been apparent in such diverse American policies in South Asia as the decision in the mid 1950s to incorporate Pakistan into the "containment of communism" military alliance systems sponsored by the United States in West Asia and Southeast Asia and the somewhat contradictory policy in regional terms that sought to recruit India into the American "containment of China" policy after the 1962 Sino-Indian war. Another fundamental reversal in policy objectives occurred in 1971, when in the context of the Nixon administration's efforts to "normalize" relations with Beijing, the "containment of China" policy was suddenly modified. Islamabad had interpreted the post-1962 shift in U.S. policy in South Asia as a violation of American security commitments to Pakistan, whereas New Delhi viewed the 1971 shift in Washington's "containment of China" policy as a threat to India's strategic interests.

The U.S. government usually sought to maintain a balanced role in South Asia, or at least to be perceived that it was doing so, but with no success with either Pakistan or India over the long run. In the 1950s the United States had tried to balance its arms aid to Pakistan with massive economic aid to India. But New Delhi never saw this as a trade-off, and instead usually characterized American policy in the subcontinent as pro-Pakistani—directed supposedly at achieving military "parity" between the two principal states in the region. The Pakistanis, in contrast, interpreted American economic assistance to India as an indirect form of military aid that threatened Pakistan's security. The switch in U.S. policy in 1962 with the introduction of an arms aid program to India during the 1962 Sino-Indian war merely enhanced Pakistani resentment. Pakistanis felt that they had been sold out by Washington for short-term strategic considerations.[41] New Delhi perceived U.S. arms aid to India as too small to be of much use, but the Pakistanis viewed it—when combined with the much greater Soviet military aid to India—as upsetting the relative balance of military power. It is not surprising, therefore, that the United States came to be viewed as basically unreliable by both India and Pakistan and that both countries generally felt uncertain about what the United States would do in any regional crisis or confrontation. It can be argued that U.S. policy in South Asia served its broader Asian or global interests, but this did not make it any less perplexing to the governments in the region that had to try and make sense of American policy decisions, which often defied comprehension in South Asian terms.

The 1966 Tashkent Agreement between India and Pakistan had a substantial impact upon U.S. policy toward both states, primarily characterized by an effort by the United States to assume a lower profile in the region. The primacy of the U.S. commitments to Vietnam in the 1965–75 decade did not permit major commitments elsewhere in Asia except where "vital" American interests were seen as involved. Moreover, Washington was piqued at the failure of both Pakistan and India to endorse its support of the integrity of the noncommunist regimes in Indochina, and the U.S. government was not inclined to respond sympathetically to overtures for greater economic or military assistance from either state.[42] There was also a sense of disillusionment in Washington with its pre-1965 policy, which had resulted in India and Pakistan using American economic and military assistance to conduct a war against each other on a larger, more sophisticated scale than would otherwise have been possible. During the 1965 conflict, the United States suspended military and economic assistance to both states; following the war it renewed bilateral economic assistance on a somewhat reduced scale, but terminated military aid except on a limited "one-time" basis under specific conditions.[43] The consequence was a much-reduced role for the United States in South Asia, and thus a self-perception in Washington of a greatly reduced capacity to influence either India or Pakistan.

America's reduced involvement in South Asia also reflected a somewhat more tolerant attitude in Washington toward the Soviet role in the region after the 1962 Sino-Indian war. There was, indeed, some degree of complementarity between U.S. and Soviet policy objectives in South Asia in the post-1962 period. This was limited to specific issues, but was nevertheless important to the policies of both states in the region, as was evident in Washington's support of Moscow's offer to serve as a mediator between India and Pakistan at the Tashkent Conference in 1966; the United States advised the rather hesitant governments in both New Delhi and Islamabad to attend the conference and then supported the agreement that resulted. Two factors appear to have been operative here. In the 1960s both the United States and the U.S.S.R. primarily emphasized their separate, but mutually supportive, "containment of China" policies in defining their objectives in South Asia, and the Indo-Pakistani dispute was seen as providing China with opportunities to expand its influence and role in the region. It followed, therefore, that Washington and Moscow were interested in discouraging regional conflicts in South Asia and sought to help resolve international disputes in the region and to discourage internal destabilization. Moscow came to terms first with Ayub and then with Yahya in Pakistan; Washington was generally supportive of Indira Gandhi in India.[44]

The crackdown on 25 March 1971 came as a surprise to Washington, as it apparently also did to Moscow and Beijing; none of them had a prepared policy position, and the response in all three capitals was marked by uncertainty, hesitation, and confusion. The flow of rhetoric from Moscow and Beijing, as we have noted, followed predictable lines, but in fact neither government did anything more than talk for several months. The only major power substantive policy decision in the immediate post-crackdown period came from Washington, and it concerned the U.S.–Pakistan agreement that had been announced on 7 October 1970 under which Pakistan could purchase some lethal weapons and "essentially unsophisticated" military equipment[45]—300 armored personnel carriers, seven "replacement" B-57s and six F-104s (to replace losses owing to attrition but not losses in the 1965 war), four maritime reconnaissance aircraft, and some "nonlethal" equipment, with a total estimated sales value of approximately $90 million—under the "one-time exception"rule.[46]

None of the armored personnel carriers or aircraft had been supplied by 25 March 1971, but licenses valued at about $35 million had been issued, and others were being negotiated.[47] On 27 March the Office of Munitions Control queried the South Asia desk in the Department of State concerning the pending licenses and arms deliveries to Pakistan and was instructed by the official in charge to hold all new licenses until a policy decision had been made. A decision was reached on 6 April under which the State Department ordered a total embargo on new licenses (retroactive to 25 March) but stipulated that equipment under old licenses—valid for one year—that had already been "delivered" should not be stopped.[48] A Department of Defense directive, issued on 23 April, added a stipulation that certain categories of shipments to Pakistan should be "held" until approved by the deputy secretary of defense. Thus, under this order only spares for nonlethal items and equipment already in the hands of the Pakistani government or its agents could be shipped.

This was the policy of the U.S. government in June 1971 when the fact that some "military" equipment was still being shipped to Pakistan was made public. The administration's explanation was that the items shipped in June were already "in the pipeline," that is, they had been purchased prior to 25 March, and legal title to the equipment had been transferred to agents of the Government of Pakistan before that date. These shipments thus did not constitute a violation of the 6 April suspension of military aid to Pakistan.[49] While the explanation was technically correct, it did not, of course, satisfy critics of the government's policy toward Pakistan in Congress, in the press, among the public, and even among some officials in the Department of State—not to mention the Indians. Nevertheless, President Nixon, in a memorandum dated 25 June, decided "to continue present policy as it is" for the time being, but place it under review.[50] According to a State Department report of 14 July, items "in the pipeline" to Pakistan totaled $14.9 million in value, but the licenses for nearly two-thirds of these items were about to expire and, under the 6 April regulation, could not be renewed.[51] By late August the value of actual shipments to Pakistan after 25 March totaled $3.6 million; these were primarily spare parts for equipment provided to Pakistan before the 1965 war. The licenses that had not yet expired covered goods worth $2.6 million.[52] Thus, "military" sales to Pakistan for the period up to December 1971, when a total embargo was imposed, amounted to less than $5 million, but they were nevertheless the subject of intense criticism by the American and Indian press, which vastly exaggerated the amount, type, and value of the equipment transferred to Pakistan.[53] The Government of India had been informed of the actual figures, but had no interest in making these public.

In July 1971, under strong congressional pressure, American economic aid of about $75 million to Pakistan for the fiscal year 1971 was also "suspended," but a food aid program for East Pakistan was introduced that totaled $90 million—$54 million in P.L. 480 food assistance and $36 million in cash.[54] On 1 October, President

Nixon requested an additional appropriation of $250 million for both refugee assistance to India and relief work in East Pakistan. Thus, by late summer 1971 the U.S. government had suspended virtually all economic and military aid programs to Pakistan except for a food aid program directed at preventing a serious famine in East Pakistan. At the same time, normal economic assistance and military sales (under the 1966 and 1967 "exceptions") to India continued; they were only suspended with the outbreak of war in December. Thus, if there was a "tilt" in U.S. aid policy up to December 1971, it was toward India rather than Pakistan.

The political response of the U.S. government to the crackdown in East Pakistan had been to repeat the warning to President Yahya prior to 25 March against a military solution in East Pakistan. But this was done privately in both Washington and Rawalpindi, and no threats of U.S. counteraction were appended to the advice. In early April the Pakistani government was reminded of the restrictions imposed on the use of U.S. arms by Pakistan under the 1959 Ankara agreement between the two powers, including a ban on their use in domestic disturbances.[55] Washington knew that previous reminders on this point had been ignored by the Pakistani army in the 1965 Indo-Pakistani war and in several operations in the frontier provinces of West Pakistan and assumed that it was unlikely that these restrictions would be honored in the East Pakistani civil war or in another conflict with India. But neither were the warnings to restrict usage totally ineffective; Rawalpindi made an effort to use arms produced in Pakistan or supplied by other sources—primarily China, but also France and the U.S.S.R.— rather than U.S. equipment in East Pakistan to avoid unnecessary complications in its relations with Washington.[56]

Washington's *public* position from 25 March and throughout 1971 was that the conflict in East Pakistan was an internal affair in which direct intervention by foreign powers should be avoided. The stated objectives of the United States were (1) to prevent another Indo-Pakistani war; (2) to provide the humanitarian relief required in East Pakistan; and (3) to encourage a political settlement of the Pakistani civil war—preferably one that would maintain at least the facade of a unified Pakistan. If that were impossible, then the United States wanted to help arrange a peaceful separation of the country into two sovereign states.[57]

The differences within the U.S. government—primarily between most of the South Asia section of the State Department and the National Security Council (NSC) and White House—were not over the objectives of U.S. policy but over the public position taken by the government. More specifically, the dispute focused on the question of whether the United States should *publicly* criticize the Yahya government for its repressive actions in East Pakistan. This assumed the format of a minor civil war within the State Department in the context of a cable from the U.S. consulate general in Dhaka that urged Washington to issue a strong protest to the Pakistani government on the crackdown in East Pakistan. This stance was endorsed by a substantial group of State Department officials on the South Asia desk, but was rejected by an interdepartmental committee under directions from the White House/NSC. A U.S. official statement of 6 April referred to the people killed in East Pakistan as "victims," but no other announcements included any criticism of the use of military force in East Pakistan.

The logic behind this approach was outlined in a Kissinger report to the Washington Special Action Group (WSAG) on South Asia in early September.[58] In discussing the 6 April decision on arms shipments to Pakistan, Kissinger stated that the administration had had a choice between two courses of action:

> *First,* it could have condemned the government in Pakistan and cut off all assistance. The purpose of such a stance would have been to rely on the political "shock effect" to change Pakistani policy. A secondary purpose would also have been to take distance from a government that, in much of the world's eyes, was responsible for a great deal of human suffering.
> *Or, second,* it could have expressed concern and restricted the actual flow of assistance but stopped short of an act of open condemnation. The purpose of such a stance as this would have been to try to maintain effective communication with Islamabad while making clear that a normal US–Pakistani assistance relationship could not be resumed as long as the present disruption in Pakistan continued."[59]

Kissinger said the U.S. government had chosen the second course, "not with any illusions about being able to shift sharply the course of events," but because it "would offer the best chance of conserving our limited ability to influence" Pakistani policies, as well as offering "the best chance that the United States could take effective action to help meet the human needs of the people of East Pakistan."[60]

In any case, the impact of U.S. public actions and private advice on Rawalpindi was negligible. The question remains whether Yahya would have responded to a strong public condemnation of the crackdown by moderating his repressive policy in East Pakistan. The general consensus, even among the critics in the government, was probably not. Projected U.S. military and economic aid to Pakistan in 1971 was not of a magnitude to provide Washington with much leverage to pressure the leadership in Rawalpindi to change policies in East Pakistan to avoid the loss of aid. The reputation of the United States as a "guarantor" of Pakistani security had also been seriously damaged by what Pakistanis interpreted as Washington's "pro-India" policy in the 1965 war. By 1971 Washington lacked much clout in Rawalpindi, particularly on issues that, in West Pakistani eyes, struck at the very basis of their national existence. The critics of American policy inside the U.S. government argued that it was immoral not to criticize the Yahya regime and that, moreover, no vital U.S. interests would have been seriously affected by a public condemnation of it. They were, however, less sanguine about the effect this would have on the Pakistani government's repressive policies.[61] Kissinger, in contrast, apparently considered moral condemnations that have no effect upon another government's behavior as irresponsible, albeit perhaps emotionally satisfying.

Thus, while the U.S. government continued to advise Pakistan to seek a political, rather than military, solution in East Pakistan until the outbreak of war in late 1971, it did this quietly and informally, usually in private discussions between Yahya and various American officials. The United States offered its services as a mediator between the Government of Pakistan and the Awami League in late summer 1971, but backed off in September because of the strongly unfavorable response in New Delhi and a seeming lack of interest in Rawalpindi.[62] On several occasions American officials also told Yahya that no political solution in East Pakistan was viable unless Mujib was part of the process, but the impression they received was that Yahya was unwilling even to consider this seriously.[63] In its efforts to prevent another Indo-Pakistani war, therefore, Washington depended more on international pressure and enticement intended to deter India from initiating a conflict than on American pressure on Pakistan to resolve the crisis through major concessions to the Bangladesh movement. This strategy failed to have the effect desired, but because of the limited capacity of the United States to influence either India or Pakistan on an issue vital to both powers, it is very doubtful whether a reversal of tactics would have been any more successful.

The termination of all U.S. military sales to Pakistan on 8 November and the cancellation of all unused valid export licenses issued before 25 March ended the debate in the U.S. government on that issue, but just in time for an even more intense debate on the war that erupted in South Asia a couple of weeks later. On 23 November, Yahya sent Nixon a letter detailing the Indian incursions (quite accurately, according to later Indian publications) and expressing the hope that some initiatives might be taken to prevent an outbreak of hostilities.[64] On 26 November, U.S. Ambassador Farland suggested to Yahya that a meeting be arranged between one of the "cleared" Awami Leaguers and Mujib as a first step toward a political settlement that might be acceptable to India.[65] But it was already much too late for such "first steps" to have any effect, and the Indian invasion, behind a Mukti Bahini screen, continued.

In an attempt to pressure the Indians into exercising some restraint in East Pakistan, the U.S. government announced on 1 December that it would not issue new Munitions List export licenses or renew existing Munitions List licenses for military sales to India. Valid licenses covering the export of about $2 million worth of components and machinery for the manufacture of ammunition were ordered cancelled, but outstanding licenses covering items valued at approximately $11.5 million remained valid (this latter figure was for assistance in the development of India's air defense system against China). Then on 6 December the United States announced that "general economic assistance in the pipeline for India has been suspended to the extent it is not firmly committed to suppliers and banks." The amount of economic aid affected was $87.6 million.[66]

For the U.S. government India's intentions toward West Pakistan were critical. East Pakistan was presumed to be lost, and there was not much sympathy for Pakistan or concern over U.S. interests there in Washington. But given Pakistan's membership in the CENTO alliance system in the Middle East and the very difficult position of the United States in that region between the 1967 and 1973 Arab-Israeli wars, the preservation of West Pakistan's national integrity and political viability was considered important to the United States. In Kissinger's words: "There was no question of "saving" East Pakistan. Both Nixon and I had recognized for months that its independence was inevitable; war was not necessary to accomplish it. We strove to preserve *West* Pakistan as an independent state, since we judged India's real aim was to encompass its disintegration."[67] But if no serious debate raged within the U.S. government over East Pakistan, a bitter controversy still remained within the inner circle, including the intelligence community, over India's objectives in West Pakistan.

The dialogue on this subject became particularly vigorous in the context of a "clandestine report" from the CIA in New Delhi that, citing a high Indian government official as the source, stated that Mrs. Gandhi intended to launch a major offensive into West Pakistan in order to destroy the Pakistani armored forces and seize some sections of Pakistani-held Kashmir. This report was first raised at a National Security Council meeting on 6 December and subsequently at a Washington Special Action Group meeting on 8 December. Most of the intelligence community had disagreed with this report, and even the New Delhi CIA office had downplayed it subsequently, but apparently this was not clearly stated to the NSC, which concluded that the report had been accepted.[68] As one high State Department official later noted, while there were doubts about the accuracy of the controversial CIA report, there was nothing then to prove it was wrong, and the government felt obliged to act on the assumption that the "worst possible" appraisal of India's intentions might be correct. The Indian ambassador, the highly respected L. K. Jha, was asked to provide "categorical assurances" on India's objectives in West Pakistan, but never gave a satisfactory response.[69] The public statements by Indian officials, including the prime minister, on this subject were usually reassuring, but ambiguous, which was only to be expected in a wartime situation.

Probably the single most controversial action by the Nixon administration during the 1971 war was the dispatch of the *Enter-*

prise—Task Force 74, or "Oh Calcutta" as it was called by some cynics—into the Indian Ocean. On 10 December the *Enterprise* and four escorts were ordered to sail from their station in the Gulf of Tonkin toward Singapore. On 12 December they met another naval detachment off the Singapore coast and on 14 December, after two days' unexplained delay, sailed down the Strait of Malacca during the daylight hours into the northernmost section of the Bay of Bengal. Task Force 74 then turned south and was operating in the Indian Ocean to the southeast of Sri Lanka when Dhaka surrendered on 16 December and the war ended the next day with the cease-fire on the western front. It remained in this general area until 7 January, when it rejoined the Seventh Fleet off the Vietnam coast.

A number of explanations and accusations have been made concerning the objectives of Task Force 74, none of which are very persuasive.[70] One that received considerable attention at the time, particularly in India, was the report that the *Enterprise* was to be used to rescue Americans trapped in Dhaka. But as the Americans who wanted to leave Dhaka had already been flown out on 12 December, two days before the task force left Singapore, a rescue mission made no sense, and nothing in the orders to the task force referred to this subject. Indeed, the orders to the *Enterprise* were ambiguous and all-inclusive—namely, to conduct "naval, air and surface operations as directed by higher authority in order to support U.S. interests in the Indian Ocean area"—not specifically in the Bay of Bengal.[71]

Kissinger and Nixon have generally tended to explain and justify the *Enterprise* episode in broader geopolitical terms, primarily the supposed impact of this symbolic gesture of support for our Pakistani "ally" on China, just at the time when the United States was beginning the process of normalizing relations with the People's Republic. Some others in the State Department placed greater importance on the impact of American support of a Muslim state on the international Islamic community. Both were factors that were considered, but in and of themselves would not have been decisive.[72]

Another important consideration for the U.S. government was the presence of a Soviet naval force in the Indian Ocean. When the war began, the U.S.S.R. had only a small force on station—two destroyers, two minesweepers, and an oiler. But on 6 December a three-ship Soviet naval force, including a missile cruiser, left Vladivostok, and on 13 December a second task force, consisting of four ships, including a missile cruiser and missile destroyer, was dispatched to the Indian Ocean from Vladivostok—under immediate American surveillance, of course. The first task force entered the Indian Ocean only on 18 December and the second on 24 December, both after the war had ended: thus neither served as a deterrent to the *Enterprise* during the couple of days Task Force 74 was in the war zone while the war was going on. This also calls into question the frightening accounts in some American sources about how close the United States and the Soviet Union were to a naval confrontation during the war. Whether the *Enterprise* task force served any useful purpose is doubtful. But it can be safely assumed that it was basic American policy that, in any crisis in the Indian Ocean area in which the Soviet Union had a fleet immediately available (as happened again in the 1973 Arab-Israeli war), an American naval detachment would be sent in as well, even if there were no obvious tasks for it to perform.

All things considered, the United States came out of the Bangladesh war far better than it had any right to expect. There was an upturn in U.S. relations with the Islamic states, including eventually even Egypt, over the next few years, and Nixon's 1972 visit to China was a solid success. Whether U.S. policy in the Bangladesh war had a positive impact on these very important relationships is impossible to say. Probably not; but a clearly anti-Pakistan position, as advocated by some in the State Department, could well have been an obstruction. Pakistan's gratitude was as short-lived as such phenomena usually are in interstate relations, and before too long the Pakistani elite was again criticizing the United States as "unreliable" for not having come to the assistance of its "ally" either in 1971 or in 1965.

There was, of course, a bitter response from the Indian public to the U.S. role in the war, which is still evident in the products of Indian academics. But the Indian government, more aware of some of the mitigating factors, moved quickly to begin the process of improving relations with the U.S. government. As sometimes happens, New Delhi took out its grievances against the Nixon administration in policies directed at safe targets—American academics, even though most of them had fervently argued the Bangladeshi (and Indian) case in the United States. Most surprising, perhaps, was how quickly U.S.–Bangladesh relations were normalized and then, from about mid 1974 on, became quite close. When the war ended, the acting prime minister of Bangladesh stated that his government would not accept American economic assistance, but within a year the United States was the largest single donor of bilateral economic aid to Bangladesh, a status it has retained ever since.

13

Interpretations

In each of the conflicts discussed above, the major participants started without the expectation that it would end violently. All the participants, both within the region and outside it, pursued solutions they felt would accommodate the interests of others. Although at the outset none of the regional participants expected war, each at some juncture in each of the two conflicts became prepared for war and accepted it as a necessary and legitimate way to either achieve or defend its interests. In the case of the Bangladesh war, which terminated this process, the sole opposition to war came from the external powers, which were unwilling to or incapable of assuming the risks that the measure of involvement required to avoid war would have entailed.

NEGOTIATION AND CIVIL WAR

The negotiations toward a constitutional settlement and transfer of power in Pakistan in 1971 began with four sets of domestic participants, three major and one minor—the Awami League, the Pakistan People's Party, the government, and the smaller parties. The process ended in polarization between two coalitions and the outbreak of civil war. Three factors were critical in this transformation. First, participants mistrusted the intentions of their counterparts, which led to misperceptions about the meaning and rationale of actions others took in pursuing their avowed intentions. Second, participants took positions that were ambiguous, thus exacerbating the existing proclivity to distrust one another. Seemingly contradictory positions taken by each of the participants also frustrated trust, the fundamental problem being uncertainty about what could be trusted, with each participant, over time, accepting a worst-case scenario as the only basis for rational calculation. Third, each participant was fearful that its core interests could not be protected under any arrangement in the transfer of power of which it was not a part. The process of polarization was encouraged as well by the inability of the military regime to preserve its neutrality in the negotiations; ultimately it became a contestant with standing no different from that of the others. With the passing of time, divisive events, both "natural" and calculated, resulted in popular pressure within the constituency of each group and served to reduce the flexibility of the elite. The most powerful constraining forces, however, were stereotyping and distrust drawn from past political conflicts, the former serving to distort images of old actors in new situations, the latter resulting in the distortion of their purposes and intentions.

Each of the major participants at the commencement of the process was committed to a transfer of power and the creation of a liberal constitutional regime, although there were differences of opinion on acceptable conditions among their supporters. Gen. Yahya Khan, president and chief martial law administrator, was committed from the outset to turning power over to an elected civilian government. In preparation for the transfer of power, the president made two fundamental decisions that were unpopular with several of his key advisers, but that he deemed essential to establish the good faith of the government in the eyes of the major contestants: (1) a return to the four "natural" provinces in West Pakistan and (2) the introduction of a universal franchise with representation based on the regional distribution of populations. This commitment continued after the elections, but given the unexpected results of the polls, the transfer of power had to be conducted with caution. Sheikh Mujib and most of the Awami League were committed to a transfer of power in a decentralized, but united, Pakistan and were prepared to form a government that would include parties whose support was in West Pakistan in order to provide a sense of a national coalition. For Bhutto and the PPP, the displacement of the military regime was a basic objective, although they insisted that timing could not be allowed to work to their disadvantage. Neither Bhutto nor his closest supporters were prepared to voluntarily give up their demand to be included in any national government that would succeed the military regime. The smaller parties were no less committed than any of the other contestants to a negotiated settlement and transfer of power, though they assumed the role of a Greek chorus during most of the crisis.

The intention of the Awami League was to assert its right to govern by virtue of its majority and to create a decentralized political order in Pakistan that would rectify the inequalities of the past. The justification rested on the assumptions of voter equality, majority rule, and the necessity of constitutional engineering to eradicate regional inequalities. The intention of the PPP elite was to share power at the national level as an essential requisite to the maintenance of party integrity and popular support. Its justification derived from a belief in the political equality of regions, the need for a "concurrent majority" in any national government coalition (in which the PPP would have to be a participant), and the commonality of public problems among different provinces, views the Awami League did not share. The smaller parties, after recovering from their electoral trauma, became increasingly committed to supporting the intentions of the Awami League, thereby giving that party political standing in the west. The intention of the government was to transfer power to a government that could maintain domestic tranquility within the structure of a constitutional regime that enjoyed broad popular consensus. Such an arrangement would have to ensure the corporate interests of the military, however, which required assurances of financial autonomy for the central government, as well as adequate funding for the defense establishment and its freedom from political interference.

While all participants were committed to a common general objective and made both public and private commitments to that effect from the outset, each was mistrustful of the intentions of the others and was fearful that its core interests would not be furthered by others in power. No participant was prepared to compromise what present control it had in the creation of any new political arrangement, whether negotiated or imposed, without firm guarantees that its interests would be realized and protected. Each insisted upon and each achieved a veto over any solution that did not explicitly honor those conditions. While suspicious and distrustful, each participant commenced the prologue to negotiation with positive expectations, perceiving in the statements and commitments of other participants intentions and particular applications of them most amenable to its own interests. Mujib and the Awami League, for example, felt that Yahya's public reference to Mujib as the next prime minister of Pakistan and the absence of opposition to the six points in the January meetings between the presidential delegates and the Awami League was a commitment by the president to the transfer of power on the Awami League's terms. Questions raised in the meetings were perceived not as reservations but as requests for clarification, while suggestions that the PPP had to be convinced were seen not as conditions but as friendly encouragement. On the other hand, while uneasy with the idea of a government led by the Awami League, the president and his counselors sought comfort in Mujib's assertion that the six points were "not the word of God, but the word of man," and thus subject to negotiation and improvement.

Similarly, after the subsequent meetings between the Awami League and the People's Party, the former felt that Bhutto was committed to the prompt convening of the National Assembly, which would automatically result in the creation of an Awami League government. Bhutto's insistence in his talks with Mujib that the PPP had to be accommodated in a national government was seen by the Awami League as a natural effort to share in power, but as not essential given the PPP's commitment to the early convening of the Assembly and given its sanguine statements concerning the six points even after Mujib's rejection of Bhutto's request. The PPP leadership initially perceived the Awami League as amenable to accommodation on the six points and ultimately agreeable to the People's Party's participation in government given the Awami League's desire to assume power and see a constitution based on the six points adopted, and given the sentiment of the government that Mujib and the Awami League would have to come to terms with Bhutto and the PPP before provisions for the transfer of power would be made effective. Core interests of all could be realized simply by sharing power. The government felt that the PPP would have to come to terms with the Awami League and would perhaps have to sit in opposition. It perceived Bhutto as prepared to compromise to hurry the departure of the martial law regime. Bhutto and the PPP believed that the president and his advisers were committed to transferring power, but also that they could not comprehend political realities and were responsive to PPP pressure.

As the general principles initially articulated were made explicit and as conditions perceived as secondary were defined as essential by the people who had advanced them, participants evinced a sense of betrayal, of having been deceived. As a result the other participants, who were initially seen as competitors, were transformed into untrustworthy adversaries. Applications of principle were seen as assertions of new demands, which were in turn perceived as evidence of malevolent intent.

Thus the Awami League perceived Bhutto's activities after the January meeting in Dhaka as a betrayal of his avowed commitment to the transfer of power and as incongruous with his public profession that he would not stand in the way of a prompt meeting of the National Assembly. His declarations that there were "two majority parties" and that he was the sole representative of West Pakistan were seen as depreciating the standing of the Bengali population within the national community and as an effort to change the rules of the political game in a way that would transform the Awami League from the winner in the elections to loser in the Assembly. Likewise, the discussions at Larkana between the president and Bhutto were seen as indicative of collusion to deny the Awami League its right to govern and as indicative of reluctance on the part of the government to honor its intention to transfer power. They were also taken as a violation of the president's declared intention to play a facilitative, rather than active and partisan, role in the political process. The subsequent meeting of martial law administrators and the postponement of the Assembly were perceived as compelling evidence of suspected and feared West Pakistani collusion. The unresponsiveness of the government and the PPP to Mujib's signals that the Awami League would be receptive to suggestions on constitution making in the discussions the Awami League proposed be held before the Assembly was called into session was perceived as an indication of the insincerity of both.

The government perceived the Awami League's increasingly intense insistence on the six points as a violation of the party's assurances that these principles were flexible and that accommodations could be negotiated. It perceived Mujib's continual refusal to accept Yahya's invitations to visit West Pakistan, regardless of circumstances, and his alleged "softness" toward India as compelling evidence of a profound insensitivity to the national interest, if not hard evidence of secessionist intent. The PPP perceived the Awami League's resistance to a coalition as an arrogant and calculated effort to deprive the PPP of its overwhelming electoral victory in the west and to weaken Pakistan's position vis-à-vis India through the Awami League's domination of the center. The Awami League would, on the one hand, have autonomy in the region of its primary interest and, on the other, could take action inimical to the interests of the western region at the national level—the level of government in which the PPP felt the Awami League would ultimately be least interested. The Awami League was also seen as insensitive to, as its policy threatened, the PPP's most elementary interest—political survival—and the PPP feared that the president would capitulate to the Awami League or be seduced by assurances of political protection and gain. Agreement between the Awami League and any West Pakistani group had to be frustrated at any cost. The Awami League was seen as a party of novices that, given time, would collapse into its numerous anomic parts, but not before doing grave harm.

The strategies of confrontation with the Awami League pursued by the PPP and of toughness on the part of the government, culminating in the efforts to suppress dissent after the announcement of the postponement of the Assembly, did not have the expected effect of making Mujib "see sense," but rather intensified the conditions that the strategies were calculated to correct. The PPP strategy did, however, have the desired effect of encouraging its image in the west as a fearless advocate of West Pakistani interests, both among the public and within important military circles.

Shared distrust of the Awami League and fear that their core interests could not be assured under an Awami League regime encouraged the development of what was in essence an informal alliance between the military government and the PPP, which ultimately resulted in the government assuming the role of principal negotiator in the final negotiations. Given distrust of Awami League assurances and without a vehicle for controlling its actions once in power, there was an expanding consensus among influential general officers that military interests would be placed in jeopardy under an Awami League government. Cooperation with the Awami League might not have the desired results, and it would leave the military open to attack by the PPP; action against Bhutto would in all likelihood result in mass action in the west, which, based on past experience, would be more difficult to contain than its equivalent in the east. In the case of the PPP, Bhutto's position would probably collapse without power, and with it the party as well. The government's assurances on prior agreement on constitutional design and its decision to postpone convening the National Assembly provided Bhutto with the power of veto in the transfer of power both in principle and in fact.

The government was also unable to maintain its autonomy in the larger decision-making process, which was both symptom and cause of its incapacity to engage in long-range political planning. Core decision makers were not buffered from political intrusion; there was no autonomous group of decision makers charged with the development of government policy and strategy. Political intelligence was unrefined and that from the government and martial law authorities in East Pakistan was progressively discarded by those in Rawalpindi as suspect. The government tended to treat political advocacy as technical advice similar to that received from civil servants on less fundamentally important questions; it was not used as information to be weighed, processed, and incorporated in the development of policy alternatives. Bhutto was seen as an "expert" in the field of politics, just as, for example, M. M. Ahmed was seen as an expert in the area of economic planning and Gen. Hamid Khan as an expert in military operations. Selected position papers aside, a government position with respect to constitutional matters was never developed, and neither were areas of consensus and difference worked out with respect to the six points prior to the Dhaka negotiations, in which they were approached on an ad hoc basis. Increasingly the government itself became an exponent of a limited interest, with a single option, acting in informal coalition with a single interested party, the PPP, and ultimately serving as its proxy. Instead of remaining a neutral umpire or arbiter, the government became a partisan participant.

At the outset there was variance of opinion and interest among subgroups within each contesting party, just as there was preliminary communication and discussion about compromise and coalition formation between particular members of the different parties. As conflict became more intense, however, each contesting party tended to turn inward, with common commitment to a single position. Though this unanimity was desired by the core decision makers in the case of their own groups, the objective was to discourage the process among their adversaries, to seek to induce division, find allies, and thus mute the effectiveness of opposition to the objectives of their cause. These strategies induced the opposite effect, the strategies themselves being perceived by others as constituting an unacceptable threat resulting in greater effort to close ranks and prepare a "fortress defence."

This process occurred in a radically changed Pakistan. The structure of political elites and the level of mass political involvement were fundamentally altered by the 1970 elections. While the trend toward the provincialization of the party system and of mass political support had commenced within a decade of partition, it had become more pronounced and deeper under the 1969 martial law regime. The level of intensity of mass mobilization in the east was made evident by the ineffectiveness as a means of political control of state violence—a strategy that had met with quiet acquiescence in the past.

In this situation of mass political involvement, party elites focused on developing consensus and cohesion within their own partial constituencies rather than within a national constituency. The support base of each of the major contestants was divided and "soft" at the outset. The institutional bonds within each of the major political parties were fragile. Efforts on the part of the leaders of each party to galvanize support to force concessions from adversaries made leaders themselves prisoners of their own constituencies. The appearance of compromise, particularly on values used in the mobilization of party support, involved high risk of the collapse of support for party leaders.

The failure of negotiations and the outbreak of civil war are also instructive of the problems of military withdrawal from governance. Preparations for the transfer of power were filled with uncertainty and fear in the military about civilian retribution, a fear even more substantial after the military crackdown than before. Factions were augmented, particularly within the army, as various

officers and groups endeavored to protect their individual interests, as opposed to corporate military interests, through alliances
with parties and political groups. As this occurred, parties and
groups were able to penetrate and influence political decision
making through the information they provided, the deals they
could strike, and the expectations they could raise in particular
groups within the military. While party leaders feared political
collapse from below, military leaders were ever cognizant of the
possibilities of coups at the top. Indeed, power was ultimately
transferred in December 1971 in the form of an anticipatory military
mini-coup. Withdrawal, in short, induced division in the general
officer corps.

The process of negotiated withdrawal was also alien to the
culture of command. In the political discussions before the military
crackdown, military decision makers evinced discomfort in negotiation, oscillating between a sense of the importance of the quest
for a consensual settlement and an urge to resolve conflict through
imposition, command, and control. This was reflected in the discussions and preparation for military action in February, as well as
after the erosion of central authority in the east in early March.
Even though constitutional agreement was reached in the Dhaka
negotiations, it was not trusted. This distrust, together with a sense
of impotence on the part of the military in the face of effective
parallel authority in the east, caused a swing in preference from
uncomfortable political negotiation to command and drastic application of force. Stress and uncertainty of outcome induced by
negotiation and consequent threat to military cohesion were solved
by an assertion of control through force of arms, with those not
conforming either resigning or being unceremoniously relieved of
their commands.

INTERNATIONAL CONFLICT, WAR,
AND SECESSION

The conflict between Pakistan and India that culminated in the
Bangladesh war commenced with both sides attempting to avoid
conflict and each expecting Pakistan's problem in its eastern wing
to be resolved in a manner short of an internal war. At the outset of
the March crisis the Indian government felt that some kind of

settlement would be reached, perhaps depriving the Awami League of the full measure of its electoral victory, but certainly something less than civil war. The Pakistani government felt that India would be involved in East Pakistani affairs, just as it always had been, but believed New Delhi would be disinclined to interfere with Pakistan's efforts to restore order and certainly would not resort to military intervention. With the exodus of refugees from East Pakistan into India, however, the situation changed fundamentally for New Delhi. From the onset of the refugee flow, the situation was judged unacceptable; Rawalpindi had to understand that India could not tolerate such an influx of population into politically volatile areas; any rational actor would understand this. The refugees would have to return. As the severity of the refugee influx grew, and as Pakistan perceived India as interfering in Pakistan's internal affairs with armed support for the Bangladeshi insurgents, each prepared for the possibility of a third Indo-Pakistani war.[1]

Each side viewed the intentions and declarations of the other as fundamentally hostile. Possibilities of accommodation were not explored; instead, the probability of intent to do harm became the basis of inference, planning, and decision making. The perception at the outset of the predilection of others to do harm was a heavy and controlling weight derived from each side's understanding of "history" and contributed to the future as history in an even more forceful way. Each side perceived the intentions of the other in the present as it had perceived and understood them in the past. Neither India nor Pakistan accepted the other as acting in good faith, but rather in a way designed to do the greatest harm to the interests of the other. This, too, was a function of the powerful influence of the historical context.[2]

The decision-making groups in India and Pakistan during the crisis were uneven in experience and were structured in very different ways. The core group in India was clustered around the prime minister, centered in the prime ministerial secretariat, and included experienced and trusted civil servants. Selected members of the cabinet were kept informed and invited to comment, as were appropriate authorities in the military. Coordination of different agencies involved in decision making was considered paramount, and these various agencies had overlapping memberships, with coordination ultimately in the hands of the prime minister's office. This core group had also handled crises before and had long experience in foreign affairs. All members had held positions of power at the time of the 1965 conflicts with Pakistan, had experienced the crises of the Congress party in the elections of 1967, when the party had lost elections in eight of sixteen states, and had weathered the split of the party in 1969, after which the prime minister governed with a minority in parliament. Furthermore, senior members of the cabinet and senior members of the bureaucracy involved in 1971 had worked together in the same or equivalent positions for substantial periods of time. In short, decision making was institutionalized and was controlled by incumbents "who had been there before."

In the case of Pakistan, the decision-making elite was likewise small, but it was composed almost exclusively of uniformed military personnel, none of whom had held political positions before the 1969 coup. The failed negotiations for a constitutional settlement in Pakistan after the 1970 elections were the only crisis these men had faced. While the work of administration in India was broadly distributed and effectively coordinated, in Pakistan it was concentrated. The president by choice governed without a cabinet or council of ministers. He held the position of chief martial law administrator and also had original responsibility for defense and foreign affairs and supervisory responsibility for military operations in his role as supreme military commander. As the crisis with India intensified, Yahya spent less and less time in the President's House and more and more time in the company of fellow officers at the army general headquarters. He was thus largely sequestered from the civilian side of the state. Efforts to solicit political advice and cooperation were minimal, the president's feeling being that such advice could not be trusted, was not necessary, and had been useless at best in the past. In the terminal phase of the crisis before the outbreak of war with India, just as in the terminal phase in negotiations with the Awami League in Dhaka, decision makers in the martial law regime labored under severe and self-admitted stress. In each instance threats to the state were personalized as threats to the decision makers themselves—threats to their image, threats to the welfare of the military in a successor state, and threats in the way of charges that the military was prepared to barter away Pakistani sovereignty.

It may appear ironic that there was strong and consistent control in democratic India during the Bangladesh crisis, but relatively weak and inconsistent control in authoritarian Pakistan. Democratic India was the "hard" state; authoritarian Pakistan the "soft." Throughout the crisis, there was strong and incessant domestic political pressure in India for action against Pakistan, whether through recognition of Bangladesh or force of arms. These demands came not only from opposition benches but from the back benches of the ruling Congress party as well. The prime minister enjoyed political buffers that allowed for wide deliberation in policy planning and decision making. Mrs. Gandhi, of course, had a large parliamentary majority, with many newly elected MPs dependent upon her goodwill, and she did not have to appeal to public appetites in anticipation of an election. This dominant parliamentary majority coexisted with a divided opposition that did not constitute a political threat and that was kept informed by emissaries from various orbits around the prime minister, as were outer groups in her own party. Such emissaries provided limited information, suggested that prudent planning was taking place, and counseled restraint. Second, India possessed a tradition of prime ministerial autonomy in foreign policy, established by Nehru since the creation of the state. Third, the prime minister did not face pressure for precipitate action from within the bureaucracy, including the military, the latter being wary of Chinese intentions, of fighting a war on riverine foreign soil during the monsoons, and of becoming involved in a war without a period of what one principal described as "battle inoculation" for the troops.

Among decision makers in India, there was a conscious quest for information on the political situation in East Pakistan; appraisals were conducted of the capacity and will of the Bangladeshi forces and of the Pakistani government and its forces in the east, as well as of the interests and probable responses of external powers. There was close appraisal of the force requirements for different levels of military action. Indian policy-making also had the advantage of a long-term perspective in planning and a pattern of sequential reasoning—an "if, then" analysis in the adoption of options and consideration of consequences. On India's part the decision to go to war was deliberate, not taken under duress, or with a sense that immediate action was needed to stave off disaster.

The military elite in Pakistan asserted its autonomy to the point of closure after the failure of political negotiations and the military crackdown. The government did not seek out political leaders for advice until the threat of increased Indian military activity and an expanded insurgency as the monsoons started to recede prompted efforts at restoration of public order. Neither did political leaders attempt to influence the regime. Not until near the end were political groups invited to offer advice and exert influence. With the selection of Bhutto to serve as representative with plenipotentiary powers at the United Nations, the military decision makers surrendered political control, believing that political knowledge was necessary to save the day and that Bhutto possessed the greatest political skill of all.

While Pakistani decision making before the military crackdown of 25 March was unsystematic in design and insensitive to consequences, it subsequently became more ad hoc in structure, minimalist in terms of political reform, and dependent upon external events with respect to timing. Just as the military did not develop a strategy for dealing with contingencies in constitutional negotiations, neither did it develop a plan for the restoration of order after the military action. Movement toward a political settlement was intermittent, ambiguous in intent, and grudging. Policy was driven by an obsession with what India would or would not do and how political reforms, short of an accommodation with the Awami League, could be used to deprive India of justification for intervention. As in the negotiations for a constitutional consensus, the policy of the military decision makers was passive and reactive rather than active and assertive.

Ultimately, Pakistan's behavior in the crisis with India was the same as it had been with the Awami League and East Pakistan. Pakistani policy was reflexive and designed more to deny India satisfaction than to reach domestic accommodation. The sense of dependence and of being manipulated resulted in the perception of there being but one option available—to fight: first against the Awami League, next against India. In each case the decision was reached under severe time constraint, with a sense of being "forced" into war and in situations that the military decision makers found exhausting and fraught with uncertainty. In each case, buoyed by a sense of invincibility and contempt for the Bengalis, the military firmly believed that force would somehow succeed. With respect to India, however, there was contempt not so much for the Indian army as for the culture from which it sprang. Pakistan had never lost a war to India was the refrain; it had always been able to control East Pakistan by force before. However, in neither the first crisis that resulted in civil war nor the second that gave birth to Bangladesh did the Pakistani military elite understand the interests of their enemies or the depth of their commitment to them in 1971. Neither did the military appreciate the limitations that a polycentric international system placed on the calculations of its major foreign patrons. Old perceptions and old patterns of behavior were judged valid and appropriate in a new and vastly changed international and regional situation.

Each side refused to negotiate or communicate with the other. Although Pakistan made overtures toward the end, India saw them as too late and insincere. Thus each side communicated with the other through public statements and occasionally the good offices of external powers. Perception of the meaning of signals and actions in the crisis became progressively intractable. Statements of resolve by one side were perceived by the other as a commitment to resist any resolution of the crisis. What one side saw as a concession and invitation to compromise or as a bona fide statement of its interests, the other perceived as a threat or as an intention to frustrate a resolution of the conflict. Pakistan's moves toward political settlement were seen as cause for alarm on the part of India, in that they were judged as merely encouraging an isolation of valid Bangladeshi political sentiment and representatives and as a continuation of the threat to Indian interests. India's observations that the refugees would have to return were perceived by Pakistan as threatening and unwarranted intrusions into Pakistan's affairs.

Each side had a different understanding of the international system, and these understandings were fundamentally important in the development of policy for coping with the crisis. The Pakistanis strongly expected international intervention to ultimately resolve the situation. Their perception was a function of precedent; conflicts between India and Pakistan had never been allowed to get out of hand before; both of the superpowers desired a strong and friendly relationship with Pakistan; secession had always been resisted by the international community, as had the conquest of one state by another.

New Delhi expended considerable time and effort in seeking to convince the world of the rightness of its cause and urging the major external powers to try to make Pakistan "see sense," but judged it unlikely that the international community would become directly involved or would be successful even if it were inclined to exert influence. India thus felt it necessary to prepare for independent action and to resist any international intrusion designed to end hostilities without solving the political problem in Pakistan.

The decisions made in New Delhi and Rawalpindi were not merely the result of the perceptions the two governments had of each other. They were also made on the basis of expectations. The escalating threat of war narrowed expectations of peacefully arranged outcomes as it reduced the tolerance of decision makers for "dissonant" information and cues. Indeed, the field of expectation became so narrow that it excluded the contemplation of alternatives. Richard Smoke had generalized this type of process as follows:

> As escalation proceeds . . . a double gap is likely to open up between the two sides. Each finds it cognitively more dissonant to make a significant new offer, and cognitively more difficult to "hear" any hints of a new offer from the other—which the other is also finding cognitively more difficult to make. As the escalation sequence goes on, this double gap will widen. As time passes and events become more threatening, each side may, so to speak, gradually retreat into its own universe.[3]

The crises of 1971 in South Asia brought to a close the first phase of modern interstate relations in this region of the world. Regional as well as international actors now accept India as the regional hegemon. Without the eastward pull of its eastern province, however, Pakistan has more noticeably and articulately turned its attention to West Asia. Rid of a two-flank Pakistani threat, India is now confronted with claims from each of its neighbors. Relations between India, Pakistan, and Bangladesh in the post-1971 period have been characterized by attempts at peaceful resolution of disputes, but intergroup hostility and violence continue to be a matter of domestic politics for each.

Notes

1. PROLOGUE AND OVERVIEW

1. These wars have attracted numerous analyses, interpretations, compilations, and participant observations, though no thorough overall analysis. See the Bibliography for a listing of the principal publications on the Bangladesh crisis and the 1971 war.

2. Reprinted in Government of Pakistan, *White Paper on the Crisis in East Pakistan* (Islamabad, 5 August 1971).

3. Ibid., appendix B.

4. Interviews, Pakistan, 1979.

5. See chap. 6 for a detailed analysis.

2. PAKISTANI POLITICS

1. Maj. Gen. Fazal Muqueem Khan, *The Story of the Pakistan Army* (Lahore: Oxford University Press, 1963), chaps. 11, 12. In this informative review Fazal describes military operations used to control smuggling and black-marketeering in East Bengal. Military perceptions of Bengali ineptitude and weakness in the face of force were still strikingly evident in our interviews in Pakistan in 1979. For a useful study of the army that includes an examination of religious symbolism, see Stephen P. Cohen, *The Pakistan Army* (Berkeley and Los Angeles: University of California Press, 1984), especially chaps. 2 and 4.

2. *Dawn*, 16 November 1947.

3. For a review of the "language" riots and the rise of student political activism, see Talukder Maniruzzaman, *The Bangladesh Revolution and Its Aftermath* (Dakha: Bangladesh Books, 1980), chap. 4. For an early analysis of the problems in East Bengal, see Richard D. Lambert, "Religion, Economics, and Violence in Bengal," *Middle East Journal* 4 (July 1950): 307–28. East Bengal was the province created by the partition of the united province of Bengal at the time of independence.

4. The constitution of Pakistan until 1956 was an amended form of the Government of India Act, 1935, which provided for a governor-general as the head of state who enjoyed authority to appoint and dismiss the governments at the national level and whose appointees, governors, enjoyed the same authority in the provinces. For a detailed analysis of the constitutional background of Pakistan's creation, see Keith Callard, *Pakistan: A Political Study* (London: Allen and Unwin, 1957). An authoritative analysis of the ideological and political problems in framing the constitu-

tion is in Leonard Binder, *Religion and Politics in Pakistan* (Berkeley and Los Angeles: University of California Press, 1961. See also Sir Ivor Jennings, *Constitutional Problems in Pakistan* (London: Cambridge University Press, 1957).

5. Ralph Braibanti, "Public Bureaucracy and Judiciary in Pakistan," in *Bureaucracy and Political Development*, ed. Joseph La Palombara (Princeton: Princeton University Press, 1963), 360–440. See also Richard D. Lambert, "Factors in Bengali Regionalism in Pakistan," *Far Eastern Survey* 28 (April 1959): 49–58; and Henry Frank Goodnow, *The Civil Service of Pakistan: Bureaucracy in a New Nation* (New Haven: Yale University Press, 1964), chap. 4.

6. Lambert, "Factors in Bengali Regionalism," 54.

7. National Assembly of Pakistan, *Debates*, vol. 1, no. 1 (1963), 29–30; no. 19 (1963), 1223–28.

8. *Dawn*, 1 November 1950; emphasis added. For expanded discussions of regional conflict over representation, cf. Keith Callard, *Pakistan*, 77–113, 135–93; and Binder, *Religion and Politics*, 116–34, 200–208, 241–58, and 307–14.

9. See Callard, *Pakistan*, 134–38, for a general discussion of the dismissal. For discussion of the other points, see Richard Sisson, "Pakistan and U.S. Foreign Policy Formulation: Interest, Perception, and the Context of Choice," in Leo E. Rose and Noor A. Husain, eds., *United States–Pakistan Relations* (Berkeley: University of California, Institute of East Asian Studies, 1985), 110–27; and Richard L. Park and Richard S. Wheeler, "East Bengal under Governor's Rule," *Far Eastern Survey* 23 (September 1954): 129–34.

10. Callard, *Pakistan*, 57. Some saw Indian involvement in the elections. Firoz Khan Noon, for example, a scion of the landed gentry, member of the Muslim League from the Punjab, and prime minister at the time of the 1958 military coup, called the election results a "victory of the Calcutta Communists" (*Dawn*, 5 April 1954).

11. See John Broomfield, *Elite Conflict in a Plural Society: Twentieth-Century Bengal* (Berkeley and Los Angeles: University of California Press, 1968); and Khalid Bin Sayeed, *Pakistan: The Formative Phase*, 2d ed. (New York: Oxford University Press, 1968).

12. Richard L. Park, "East Bengal: Pakistan's Troubled Province," *Far Eastern Survey* 23 (May 1954): 70–74. For a general discussion of East Bengali politics at this time, see F. M. Innes, "The Political Outlook in Pakistan," *Pacific Affairs* 26 (December 1953): 303–17.

13. Park, "East Bengal," 71–72. The Lahore Resolution, adopted by the Muslim League on 24 March 1940, constituted the first demand on the part of the league for separate "independent states" in Muslim majority areas.

14. *The Hindu*, 10 May 1954, as quoted in Park and Wheeler, "East Bengal under Governor's Rule." For a review of the development of Bengali political regionalism, see M. Rafique Afzal, *Political Parties in Pakistan, 1947–1958* (Islamabad: National Commission on Historical and Cultural Research, 1976), chaps. 4 and 5; for a critical view of the chief minister's activity, see K. K. Aziz, *Party Politics in Pakistan, 1947–1958* (Islamabad: National Commission on Historical and Cultural Research, 1976), 15–20.

15. See Stanley Maron, "The Problem of East Pakistan," *Pacific Affairs* 28 (June 1955): 132–44.

16. Park and Wheeler, "East Bengal under Governor's Rule," 132.

17. Charles Burton Marshall, "The Military in Pakistan" (typescript, n.d.), 13.

18. See Constituent Assembly of Pakistan, *Debates,*1954, nos. 17, 18, 20, 30.

19. Ibid., 1956, no. 1, 1816. See also *Dawn,* 23 October 1955; Callard, *Pakistan,* 186–90.

20. *Dawn,* 7 October 1958.

21. Ibid.

22. Ibid. For a review of the coup, see Wayne Ayres Wilcox, "The Pakistan Coup d'Etat of 1958," *Pacific Affairs* 38 (Summer 1965): 142–63; and K. J. Newman, "Pakistan's Preventive Autocracy and Its Causes," *Pacific Affairs* 32 (March 1959): 18–33.

23. *Dawn,* 16 October 1958.

24. Khan, *Story of the Pakistan Army,* 202; *Dawn,* 28 October 1958.

25. *Report of the Constitution Commission, Pakistan* (Karachi: Government of Pakistan Press, 1962), 1. In a major statement of his conception of the Pakistani political malaise, Ayub proposed that the form of government adopted was crucial and that perhaps the formal political institutions had been more conducive to political instability prior to 1958 than the inadequacies of politicians. See Mohammed Ayub Khan, "Pakistan Perspective," *Foreign Affairs* 37 (July 1960): 550.

26. Cf. Richard S. Wheeler, "Pakistan: New Constitution, Old Issues," *Asian Survey* 3 (February 1963): 107–15; Khalid Bin Sayeed, "Pakistan's Constitutional Autocracy," *Pacific Affairs* 36 (Winter 1963–64): 365–77.

27. Mohammed Ayub Khan, "A Short Appreciation of Present and Future Problems of Pakistan," in Col. Mohammed Ahmad, *My Chief* (Lahore: Longmans, 1960), 86–93. The work of the Constitution Commission and the results of its inquiry into public opinion concerning a constitution are reported in Edgar A. and Kathryn R. Schuler, *Public Opinion and Constitution Making in Pakistan, 1958–1962* (East Lansing: Michigan State University Press, 1966).

28. Ibid., 111–13.

29. *Pakistan Times,* 5 and 17 April and 5 October 1962.

30. Ralph Braibanti, "Pakistan: Constitutional Issues in 1964," *Asian Survey* 5 (February 1965): 79–87.

31. Sharif-al-Mujahid, "Pakistan's First Presidential Elections," *Asian Survey* 5 (June 1965): 280–94, and "The Assembly Elections in Pakistan," *Asian Survey* 5 (November 1965): 538–51.

32. A key leader in this opposition was the president's erstwhile foreign minister, Zulfiqar Ali Bhutto, who was to be important subsequently in Pakistan's continued search for a consensual political order.

33. Sheikh Mujibur Rahman, *Bangladesh, My Bangladesh* (New Delhi: Orient Longman, 1972), 129–48.

34. Khalid Bin Sayeed, "Pakistan: New Challenges to the Political System," *Asian Survey* 8 (February 1968): 97–104.

35. See Rounaq Jahan, *Pakistan: The Failure of National Integration* (New

York: Columbia University Press, 1972), chap. 4; and Khalid Bin Sayeed, *Politics in Pakistan: The Nature and Direction of Change* (New York: Praeger, 1980), chaps. 3 and 4.

36. Talukder Maniruzzaman, "Crises in Political Development and the Collapse of the Ayub Regime in Pakistan," *Journal of Developing Areas* 5 (January 1971): 221–28; see also Rehman Sobban, "East Pakistan's Revolt against Ayub: Old Resentments and New Needs," *Roundtable* no. 235 (July 1969): 302–7.

37. Jahan, *Pakistan*, 106–7.

38. Cf. M. Rashiduzzaman, "The Awami League in the Political Development of Pakistan," *Asian Survey* 10 (June 1970): 574–87.

39. Shahid Javed Burki, "Ayub's Fall: A Socio-Economic Explanation," *Asian Survey* 12 (March 1972): 201–12. See also Babafemi Adesina Badejo, "From Growth Philosophy to Social Justice: Politics and Planning in Pakistan under Ayub" (Ph.D. diss., University of California, Los Angeles, 1982); and Khalid Bin Sayeed, "Mass Urban Protests as Indicators of Political Change in Pakistan," *Journal of Commonwealth and Comparative Politics* 17 (July 1979): 111–35.

40. Cf. Anwar H. Syed, "The Pakistan People's Party: Phases One and Two," in Lawrence Ziring, Ralph Braibanti, and W. Howard Wriggins, eds., *Pakistan: The Long View* (Durham: Duke University Press, 1977), 70–116.

41. For a discussion of this crisis, see Lawrence Ziring, *The Ayub Khan Era: Politics in Pakistan, 1958–1969* (Syracuse: Syracuse University Press, 1971), chap. 5.

42. Interviews, Pakistan, 1979.

43. Ibid.

44. Ibid.

45. Ibid.

46. Ibid. A review of the organization and style of the Yahya regime is found in Lawrence Ziring, "Militarism in Pakistan: The Yahya Khan Interregnum," in W. H. Wriggins, ed., *Pakistan in Transition* (Islamabad: University of Islamabad Press, 1975), 198–232.

47. Interviews, Pakistan, 1979.

48. Although the provinces of West Pakistan assumed their old names—Baluchistan, North-West Frontier Province, Punjab, and Sind—after the coup, East Pakistan did not assume its former name of East Bengal. During the Bangladesh crisis Mrs. Gandhi's reference to "East Bengal" (the leaders of the Awami League urged her to use "Bangladesh") was perceived by Pakistani leaders as evidence of India's commitment to destroy Pakistan. Ironically, the Awami League's use of "Bangladesh" was considered similarly disruptive in intent.

49. Interviews, Pakistan, 1979. Yahya's comment was remembered by one of the key figures in the drafting of the LFO. This reconstruction of the drafting of the LFO derives from interviews other than those with Yahya, although his recollection of matters was congruent.

50. Ibid. The Legal Framework Order was published on 30 March 1970. Government of Pakistan, *White Paper on the Crisis in East Pakistan*.

51. Interviews, Pakistan, 1979.

52. Ibid. Also see Herbert Feldman, *The End and the Beginning: Pakistan,*

1969–1971 (London: Oxford University Press, 1975), chap. 8, for a discussion of this and other aspects of the election; and G. W. Choudhury's excellent study *The Last Days of United Pakistan* (Bloomington: Indiana University Press, 1974), chap. 5.

53. Craig Baxter, "Pakistan Votes: 1970," *Asian Survey* 11 (March 1971): 197–218.

54. *Dawn*, 14, 16 November 1970.

55. Interviews, Pakistan, 1979.

56. *Dawn*, 3 November 1970.

57. *Dawn*, 26 September 1970.

58. *Dawn*, 10 November 1970.

59. Election statements of party leaders made over Pakistani television were reprinted in *Dawn*, October through November 1970.

60. *Dawn*, 15 September 1970.

61. *Dawn*, 5 December 1970. Maulana Bhashani and the other candidates of the eastern National Awami Party withdrew from the elections after the cyclone, reportedly because the party sensed that the voters were shifting toward the Awami League in a pronounced fashion. Several political figures both inside and outside the regime have reported that the government encouraged and financially supported Maulana Bhashani in his radical stance in an effort to draw Mujib and the Awami League to extremer positions, thus leaving greater space in the center and to the right for more "national" parties (interviews, Pakistan, 1979).

62. *Dawn*, 1, 21 September 1970.

63. Ibid., 4 September 1970.

64. Interview, Pakistan, 1979.

65. Interviews, Pakistan, 1979.

66. Ibid. Interviews, Bangladesh, 1978.

67. Interviews, Pakistan, 1979.

68. One leader of the Council Muslim League (CML) reported that during the early stages of ticket allocation, Bhutto proposed a no-contest agreement in the Punjab if the Pakistan People's Party were to receive twenty seats. The offer was declined, since the CML leadership knew that the PPP could not raise enough money to win that many seats. This leader further observed that this had been a gross miscalculation: when the government moved in May 1970 to support the PPP as a counterbalance to the Awami League, the funds CML candidates had traditionally received from business houses went to parties opposing the Awami League in the east and to the People's Party in the west (interviews, Pakistan, 1979).

69. See Baxter, "Pakistan Votes," 216–17, for consideration of this observation. For an analysis of the social and economic origin of the East Pakistan representatives elected in 1970, see Rounaq Jahan, "Members of Parliament in Bangladesh," *Legislative Studies Quarterly* 1 (August 1976): 355–70.

3. INDO-PAKISTANI RELATIONS

1. For what are typical recent Indian and Pakistani comments on the "two nation" theory, see G. S. Bhargava, *South Asian Security after Afghani-*

stan (Lexington, Mass.: Lexington Books, 1983), 10–11, and Anwar Hussain Syed, *Pakistan: Islam, Politics, and National Solidarity* (New York, Praeger: 1982), 86–91.

2. See, for instance, Sharif al-Mujahid, *Quaid-i-Azam Jinnah: Studies in Interpretation* (Karachi: Quaid-i-Azam University Press, 1981), 256–67, for a lucid discussion of the rejection of the concepts of both "secularism" and "theocracy" by the leaders of Pakistan in the post-1947 period.

3. See V. P. Menon, *The Story of the Integration of the Indian States* (New York: Macmillan Co.), 1956, for the definitive work from the Indian perspective on the "princely states" question; and Chaudhri Muhammad Ali, *The Emergence of Pakistan* (New York: Columbia University Press, 1967), 222–36, for a Pakistani view on the same subject. See also Wayne Ayres Wilcox, *Pakistan: The Consolidation of a Nation* (New York: Columbia University Press, 1963).

4. The large body of literature on the Kashmir issue in the 1947–49 period is divided on the question of the dominance of the pro-Indian National Conference, headed by Sheikh Abdullah, in Kashmir valley. The limited amount of solid data that is available, however, supports the contention that the National Conference had a much larger and more solid popular support base in the Kashmiri Muslim community in 1947 than its principal Muslim organizational rival—the Muslim Conference.

5. Interviews, India, 1966.

6. Interviews, India, 1978.

7. For background information on the enclaves issue, see R. N. Banerji, "Indo-Pakistani Enclaves," *India Quarterly* 25 (July–September 1969): 254–57.

8. In 1978 a high official of the Bangladesh government who had served on the prosecution team in the Agartala conspiracy trial insisted that there was ample evidence of Mujib-Indian contacts at Agartala in India. What remains unclear from his verbal descriptions of the evidence is whether it proved that the objective of either side in this relationship was, as charged, the division of Pakistan through an armed separatist movement.

9. Interviews, India, 1978. Indeed, Indian decision makers wanted to keep Awami League leaders at arm's length and saw them as "third-raters," who without Mujib would not be able to either negotiate or govern, thus increasing the risk of political turmoil on India's eastern borders.

10. One of the bonuses for India in the 1971 war was the elimination of these camps and the capture or dispersal of the Nagas and Mizos undergoing training. This seriously disrupted the rebel movements in the northeast, since it took several years to reestablish support lines into China through southeastern Bangladesh and Burma. By this time, moreover, China had begun to reconsider its policy and by 1978 had halted aid to the rebels as part of its efforts to "normalize" relations with India (interviews, India, 1980, 1981).

11. Interviews, India and Pakistan, 1978, 1979, 1981.

12. See, for instance, the statement by Acharya Kripalani, Congress party president in 1947, that "the freedom we have achieved cannot be complete without the unity of India," that is, the reunification of India and

Pakistan (quoted in Michael Brecher, *Nehru: A Political Biography* [London: Oxford University Press, 1959], 378).

13. *The Hindu,* 24 August 1950.

14. There is also, of course, the post hoc fact that New Delhi never seriously considered incorporating Bangladesh into the Indian Union after the 1971 war as many Pakistanis had charged it would do. Indeed, India withdrew its forces as quickly as possible after the cessation of hostilities.

15. See Margaret W. Fisher and Joan V. Bondurant, *Indian Views of Sino-Indian Relations* (Berkeley: Institute of International Studies, 1956), for several official Chinese comments on the Kashmir dispute.

16. Shirin Tahir-Kheli, *The United States and Pakistan: Evolution of an Influence Relationship* (New York: Praeger, 1982).

17. Leo E. Rose, "India, China, and the Afro-Asian Bloc," in Allan A. Spitz (ed.), *Contemporary China* (Pullman: Washington State University Press, 1967), 23–24.

18. For discussions of this transformation, see Richard Sisson, "The Military and Politics in Pakistan," in John Lovell, ed., *The Military and Politics in Five Developing Nations* (Kensington, Md.: Center for Research in Social Systems, 1970), 86–142.

19. DOS, "Report on U.S. Military Obligations to India and Pakistan," 15 October 1971 (FOI document).

20. See S. M. Burke, *Mainsprings of Indian and Pakistan Foreign Policies* (Minneapolis: University of Minnesota Press, 1974), 177–83. See also Mohammed Ayub Khan, *Friends Not Masters: A Political Autobiography* (London: Oxford University Press, 1967).

4. A CULTURE OF DISTRUST

1. Government of Pakistan, *White Paper,* especially Article 20, paras. 1 and 4.

2. Interviews, Pakistan, 1979.

3. Interviews, Pakistan and Washington, 1979. Reports were made through Gen. Akbar Khan, head of the Inter-Services Intelligence Division, through the civilian intelligence division, and through Gen. Ghulam Umar, head of the National Security Council. Two different reports were customarily submitted, one for the cabinet and one for the martial law authorities.

4. See chap. 2.

5. See Mujib's statements of 17 and 19 December 1970. Reprinted in *The Bangladesh Papers* (Lahore: Vanguard Books, n.d.) 131–32; also Rahman, *Bangladesh, My Bangladesh,* 20–24.

6. Interviews, Bangladesh, 1978; Pakistan and England, 1979.

7. For useful discussions of the People's Party, see Khalid Bin Sayeed, "How Radical Is the Pakistan People's Party?" *Pacific Affairs* (1975): 42–59; Syed, "Pakistan People's Party," in Ziring, Braibanti, and Wriggins, eds., *Pakistan: The Long View,* 70–116; and Khalid Bin Sayeed, "Political Leadership and Institution Building under Jinnah, Ayub, and Bhutto," in ibid., 241–70.

8. These points were made to the authors by erstwhile leaders of the PPP as well as the martial law regime (interviews, Pakistan, 1979).

9. Ibid.

10. *Morning News*, 10 December 1970, reprinted in Rahman, *Bangladesh, My Bangladesh*, 21–22.

11. In his reflective autobiographical appraisal of his experience in the Yahya regime, G. W. Choudhury refers, however, to his work on guidelines for a constitution that he submitted to Yahya on 11 December. The president replied on 21 January in a short note, duplicated in Choudhury's book, that he generally agreed with the points made and referred the author to his comments in the file; with the exception of aid and trade, the points were congruent with those of the Awami League (Choudhury, *Last Days*, pp.143–45).

12. The president's emissary was a general officer in the martial law administration; public statements started to reflect these discussions soon after (interview, Pakistan, 1979).

13. Interviews, Pakistan, 1979.

14. *Bangladesh Papers*, 299.

15. *Pakistan Times*, 21 December 1970. The People's Party had started to make its strategy public on 15 December, when Bhutto announced that he was establishing a commission within the party that would have full authority to negotiate with the Awami League on behalf of the PPP on constitutional matters. At the same time he also sounded a more solemn and prophetic note, observing that the road to constitutional democracy in Pakistan was paved with danger.

16. Ibid., 22 December 1970.

17. *Dawn*, 25 December 1970.

18. *Pakistan Observer*, 22 December 1970. Tajuddin Ahmed was an important contributor to Awami League doctrine and strategy and a leader of a loosely clustered left-wing group within the party; he was to become prime minister of the Bangladesh government in exile in India and at independence.

19. Ibid., 4 January 1971. Ironically, in an event distant and unforeseen, it was at the Ramna Race Course that Lt. Gen. A. A. K. Niazi, commanding general of the Eastern Command, signed the instruments of surrender before Lt. Gen. Jagjit Singh Aurora, commander of the Indian and Bangladesh Forces, Eastern Command on 16 December 1971.

20. Rahman, *Bangladesh, My Bangladesh*, 29–30.

21. *Dawn*, 4 December 1970.

22. Interview, Pakistan, 1979.

23. *Pakistan Times*, 11 January 1971; Radio Pakistan, newscast, 11 January 1971.

24. Interview, Pakistan, 1979. The reconstruction of the meetings between martial law and Awami League representatives is based upon newspaper reports and news broadcasts, as well as on interviews with five principals in the discussions.

25. It will be recalled that Mujib had first enunciated the six points in March 1966 and later forcefully articulated them at the All-Parties Round Table Conference in 1969, a move that divided the Awami League, with West Pakistani members of the league opposing the points (interview, England, 1979). Also see Rounaq Jahan, "Elite in Crisis: The Failure of Mujib-Yahya-Bhutto Negotiations," *Orbis* 17 (Summer 1973): 575–97.

26. Interviews, Pakistan, 1979.

27. The exchanges summarized here are based upon interviews with four of the principals involved.

28. The discussions reported here are based upon interviews with seven of the principals involved.

29. We were unable to interview either Bhutto or Mujib; the former had been hanged a few hours before we landed in Karachi in April 1979, and the latter had been assassinated before the study commenced. The exchanges reported here are reconstructed from reports and interviews with advisers and confidants of each.

30. Interviews, Pakistan and England, 1979.

31. Interviews, Pakistan, 1979.

32. Ibid. and *Pakistan Times*, 31 January 1971.

33. Interviews, Pakistan, 1979; England, 1979; Bangladesh, 1979. Awami League leaders were surprised at how little attention and thought PPP leaders had given to the constitutional issues. They saw themselves as far more advanced and as setting the agenda without contest on this count.

34. *Pakistan Times*, 31 January 1971.

35. Interview, Pakistan, 1979.

36. These discussions were reported in the press. Meetings were at the same time being held among leaders of the various smaller parties as well.

37. *Pakistan Times*, 15 February 1971. The symbolism of the venue was important, since before the famed Lahore Resolution had been adopted there by the All-India Muslim League just under thirty-one years.

38. *Pakistan Times*, 4 February 1971.

39. Interviews, Pakistan, 1979.

40. Ibid.

41. Interviews, Bangladesh, 1978; England, 1979.

42. Interviews, Pakistan, 1979.

43. *Dawn*, 15 February 1971.

44. *Pakistan Observer*, 16 February 1971.

45. *Dawn*, 16 February 1971.

46. *Pakistan Times*, 16 February 1971.

47. *Pakistan Observer*, 16 February 1971.

48. *Dawn*, 18 February 1971.

49. Interview, Pakistan, 1979.

50. Radio Pakistan, newscast, 19 February 1971.

51. *Pakistan Times*, 20 February 1971.

52. Interview, Pakistan, 1979.

53. Based upon interviews with three principals present.

54. Interview, Pakistan, 1979.

55. Ibid.

56. *Pakistan Times*, 22 February 1971.

57. Ibid., 21 February 1971.

58. Ibid., 22 February 1971.

59. The following reconstruction is based on interviews with five of the principals present.

60. Interviews, Pakistan, 1979.

61. *Pakistan Times*, 22 February 1971.

62. Two important leaders of opposition parties, for example, told us

that they had been unable to meet with Yahya to report on talks with Mujib, but they believed that Bhutto had had unencumbered access.

63. *Pakistan Times,* 25 February 1971.
64. Interview, Pakistan, 1979.
65. Ibid.
66. Interviews, Pakistan, 1979; Bangladesh, 1978.
67. Interviews, Pakistan, 1979.
68. Ibid. Some of Bhutto's primitive and evocative language was often lost in translation.
69. Ibid.
70. Ibid.

5. CRISIS BARGAINING

1. Interview, Pakistan, 1979.
2. Radio Pakistan, newscast, 5 March 1971.
3. Interviews, India and Bangladesh, 1978; Pakistan and England, 1979.
4. *The People,* 2 March 1971.
5. *The People,* 3 March 1971.
6. Ambulances, hospitals, pharmacies, press cars, and electricity and water supplies were exempt from the *hartal* rules, Ibid.
7. His use of such terms as *hartal* and *satyagraha* (literally "soul force") was a source of extreme irritation to some officers, since these had been symbols and terms used by Mahatma Gandhi and the Congress party in their nationalist confrontations with the British Raj; it was taken as yet another indication of Bengali affinity for India and of Indian involvement in the Awami League (interviews, Pakistan, 1979).
8. *Dawn,* 4 March 1971. The exact number of casualties is not known.
9. People who visited Mujib on the morning of his 7 March speech also indicated to us that he was fearful for his life (interviews, Bangladesh, 1978).
10. Awami League directives were issued intermittently until the military crackdown of 26 March.
11. *Pakistan Times,* 3 March 1971.
12. Ibid.
13. For some insightful observations on Bhutto's political calculus and style, see Anwar H. Syed, "Z. A. Bhutto's Self-Characterizations and Pakistani Political Culture," *Asian Survey* 18 (December 1978): 1235–66.
14. Yahya and Gen. Hamid even threatened to court-martial certain general officers in the east. Nearly a decade later several former general officers still wondered why Gen. Yaqub Khan had been kept in positions of great public trust and felt he should have been brought before the military bar for what they perceived as gross errors of judgment in his position as martial law administrator and governor (interviews, Pakistan, 1979).
15. Ibid.
16. Ibid. The analysis here is based upon interviews with senior army officers both at the center and in East Pakistan.
17. Officers interviewed who had been posted in East Pakistan and had attended the meeting of the martial law administrators spoke of the enor-

mous change in "social temperament" that had occurred between the time that they left and returned to Dhaka; after the announcement of the postponement, resistance was such that the restoration of central authority with limited force was impossible (interviews, Pakistan, 1979).

18. *Dawn*, 6 March 1971

19. Interview, Pakistan, 1979. Although curfews that had been ordered were lifted in several provincial towns, they were subsequently reimposed (Radio Pakistan, newscasts, 5–10 March 1971). It is not known whether or not Yaqub briefed his superiors upon his return to the west. When his predecessor as governor, Admiral Ahsan, had returned to West Pakistan and had attempted to contact Yahya and his principal staff officer to report on the situation in the eastern province, he had found the former unavailable and the latter "otherwise engaged" (interview, Pakistan, 1979).

20. *Pakistan Times*, 3 March 1971. A less formal meeting of political leaders was planned in February if Mujib accepted the president's invitation to visit the west (interview, Pakistan, 1979).

21. *Pakistan Times*, 4 March 1971.

22. *Dawn*, 4 March 1971. Mujib reportedly initially indicated openness to attending an all-party conference, but declined after consulting with other leaders of his party (interviews, Pakistan, 1979).

23. Interviews, Bangladesh, 1978; England, 1979.

24. Interview, Pakistan, 1979.

25. Ibid.

26. Ibid. When Mujib had told Bhutto that the presidency had already been offered to someone else (Yahya), Bhutto urged Mujib to at least extend him the courtesy of being permitted to nominate Yahya. Reflecting on this request later, Mujib humorously noted that if Bhutto had been given this authority, he would have appointed himself president one day and fired Mujib as prime minister the next.

27. Ibid.

28. Ibid. Two other senior general officers serving in West Pakistan also expressed this sentiment to us.

29. Ibid.

30. *Dawn*, 7 March 1971.

31. *Dawn*, 8 March 1971. It has been reported from different sources that Mujib was under extreme pressure from some quarters to declare independence in this speech (interviews, Pakistan, 1979; and Bangladesh, 1978).

32. In his initial statement Mujib referred to seven different demands, but he later distilled them to four.

33. *Dawn*, 8 March 1971.

34. Ibid.

35. Interviews, Pakistan, 1979. This sense of things was shared elsewhere. Both the BBC and Radio Hilversum had suggested the possibility of secession in broadcasts on 5 March.

36. The process and timing of consensus on Bangladeshi independence is disputed. Some members of the martial law regime, at least in retrospect, believe that a consensus on independence had developed even before the 1970 elections; others propose that it occurred after the announcement of the postponement of the National Assembly; and still others say that a

consensus did not develop until after most of the Awami League high command were in exile. Although leaders of the Awami League had discussed the idea of independence, the evidence available suggests that they were commited to maintaining the territorial integrity of Pakistan until after the military crackdown on 26 March and that they put their creative energies into constitution drafting and preparation for the convening of the Assembly. By 20 March both the government and the Awami League negotiating teams felt that they had found a solution to the political impasse.

37. Interview, Pakistan, 1979.

38. *Pakistan Times,* 8 March 1971.

39. *Dawn,* 10 March 1971; Radio Pakistan, newscast, 9 March 1971.

40. *Dawn,* 9 March 1971. Khan Abdul Qayyum Khan, head of the Muslim League (Qayyum) called on Maulana Mufti Mehmood to hold a broader meeting of parties and then negotiate with Mujib; after this was found to be unacceptable, the Muslim League (Qayyum) refrained from participating in the Lahore meeting (Radio Pakistan, newscast, 11 March 1971).

41. Interviews, Pakistan, 1979. Those in attendance were Maulana Mufti Mehmood (Jamiat-ul-Ulema-i-Islam), Mian Mumtaz Daultana and Shaukat Hayat Khan (Council Muslim League), Jamal Mohammad Koreja (Convention Muslim League), Maulana Shah Ahmed Noorani (Jamat-ul-Ulema-i-Pakistan), Prof. Abdul Ghafoor (Jamiat-i-Islami), and Maulana Zafar Ahmed Ansari and Sardar Maulana Soomro (independents). The chair of the meeting, Maulana Mufti Mehmood, indicated that although the National Awami Party (Wali Khan) was not represented at the meeting, the conference enjoyed that party's backing.

42. *Dawn,* 14 March 1971.

43. Ibid.

44. Radio Pakistan, newscast, 11 March 1971.

45. Interview, Pakistan, 1979.

46. Radio Pakistan, newscast, 12 March 1971.

47. Interview, Pakistan, 1979.

48. *Dawn,* 15 March 1971. Two seasoned leaders of smaller political parties saw Bhutto's demand as political melodrama, not to be taken too seriously, although one observed that Bhutto had a penchant for floating propositions that he did not take seriously initially, but pursued them with vigor when others took them seriously.

49. *Dawn,* 16 March 1971.

50. Interview, Pakistan, 1979.

51. *Dawn,* 16 March 1971.

52. Ibid.

53. For an extended exposition of Bhutto's position after the fact, see his *The Great Tragedy* (Karachi: Pakistan People's Party, 1971).

54. Interviews, Pakistan, 1979.

55. Ibid.

6. CONSTITUTIONAL CONSENSUS AND CIVIL WAR

1. Siddiq Salik, *Witness to Surrender* (Karachi: Oxford University Press, 1977), 59.

2. Interviews, Pakistan, 1979. This did not allay the fears that military activity in East Pakistan had already aroused. This is clearly evident, for example, in an interview with Mujib by the journalist Michael Clayton. In a response to Clayton's question, "If the present state of uncertainty continues, is it possible that the slogan of independence might lead to a stage where there is no scope for a negotiated solution to the crisis?" Mujib replied:

> Western armies are being rushed to East Pakistan. They are busy in building fortifications. What is the purpose behind this? East Pakistanis are unarmed. We want to wage a peaceful struggle. It is not a war. But I want to make it clear that no power can suppress seventy million people. It is possible that there might be bloodshed for one or two years. It is quite possible that some of the leaders might have to sacrifice their lives. But the determination of the people is firm and resolute and they cannot be suppressed. New history will be created.
>
> (BBC newscast, 16 March 1971).

3. Interviews, Pakistan, 1979.

4. Ibid.

5. *Dawn*, 19 March 1971.

6. Interviews, Pakistan, 1979. Some officers were convinced that the broader inquiry would reveal Indian involvement in the affair and could be used not only to discredit the Awami League leadership but also those in the military considered "soft" on the situation in East Pakistan.

7. Studies and reports that have addressed the negotiations and have proved helpful in our analysis include Bhutto, *Great Tragedy*; Choudhury, *Last Days*; David Dunbar, "Pakistan: The Failure of Political Negotiations," *Asian Survey* 12 (May 1972: 444–61; Feldman, *End and the Beginning*; Jahan, "Elite in Crisis"; Khan, *Story of the Pakistan Army;* Salik, *Witness to Surrender;* Rehman Sobhan, "Negotiating for Bangladesh: A Participant's View," *South Asian Review* 4 (July 1971): 315–26; and Government of Pakistan, *White Paper*. Dates and times in the sequence of events were initially established through Radio Pakistan newscasts and reports in *Dawn* and the *Pakistan Times*. The bulk of the analysis, however, derives from interviews with both military and civilian members of the presidential negotiating team, members of the Awami League team, several general officers present in Dhaka during the negotiations, and even leaders of West Pakistani political parties who met with both the government and Awami League teams during the final negotiations in Dhaka.

8. Interview, Pakistan, 1979.

9. Government of Pakistan, *White Paper*, 18–20.

10. Interviews, Pakistan, 1979. To add to the PPP's sense of isolation and vulnerability, Bhutto had his pocket picked even while being so closely protected. His comments about the incident reportedly reflected deep sentiments other than amusement.

11. Interviews, Pakistan, 1979.

12. Bhutto, *Great Tragedy*, p. 43.

13. Interviews, Pakistan, 1979; England, 1979; and United States, 1979.

14. Bhutto, *Great Tragedy*, p. 45.

15. Interviews, Pakistan, 1979.
16. Interviews, Pakistan, 1979.

7. THE INDIAN RESPONSE

1. While the Awami League publicly supported a settlement of the Kashmir dispute on the basis of the various U.N. resolutions—the official Pakistani position—the party was unhappy with the way in which the Kashmir issue had been used in Pakistan's domestic politics. After the 1970 elections, for instance, Mujib told an Iranian correspondent that "the Kashmir dispute" had been exploited by the "military caste" and "the capitalists as an excuse for dictatorship and heavy expenditure on armament"; but he added: "and yet we have not done our duty towards the people of Jammu and Kashmir"—an ambiguous remark to be sure, and one not likely to arouse enthusiasm in New Delhi (*Dawn*, 20 February 1971).

2. Interviews, India, 1978. Lars Blikenberg obtained a similar impression in his interviews with Indian officials on developments in Pakistan during February and March 1971 (see his *India-Pakistan: The History of Unsolved Conflicts* [Munksgaard: Dansk Udenrigspolitisk Institut, 1972], 314).

3. Pakistani officials criticized the hijackers for the destruction of the plane (*Pakistan Times*, 3 February 1971), but granted them asylum and permitted them to address public meetings in which they strongly criticized Indian policy in Kashmir.

4. Interviews, India, 1978.

5. India had banned military overflights on 2 February and then extended this ban to all Pakistani overflights on 4 February. The ban was initially described as temporary, that is, until the Pakistani government accepted the Indian demand for compensation for the plane (*Asian Recorder* 17 [19–25 February 1971]: 10018–23). If Islamabad had accepted responsibility before 25 March, it is *possible* that New Delhi would have lifted the ban; after that date, however, there was no question but that India would continue the ban until the East Pakistani crisis had been settled to its satisfaction.

6. These points were forcefully made to us by the prime minister as well as by several of her key advisers (interviews, India, 1978).

7. The section that follows is based primarily on interviews in India in 1978 and 1979, but several publications have also discussed this subject at some length. One of the more useful for 1971 is G. K. Reddy, "Crisis Diplomacy and Decision Making," *The Hindu*, 8 June 1971.

8. A National Defence Council had also been established by Nehru after the 1962 war to associate the chief ministers of the state governments with defense and foreign policy decision making. While the council had not been formally abolished, it was never summoned by Mrs. Gandhi during the 1971 crisis.

9. Interviews, India, 1978.

10. Ibid.

11. See, for instance, Mrs. Gandhi's statement to the Lok Sabha on 27 March, in which she expressed her government's intention "to follow proper international norms" on East Pakistan (Indira Gandhi, *India and*

Bangladesh: Selected Speeches and Statements, March to December 1971 [New Delhi: Orient Longman, 1972], 11). Four Awami League leaders visited New Delhi in early April to solicit Indian support, but they received a rather cold reception and, to their surprise, no solid guarantees of support (interviews, India, 1978, and *Amrita Bazar Patrika*, 5 April 1971.

12. India also granted political asylum to two East Bengali diplomats assigned to the Pakistan High Commission in New Delhi, but there was no effort to seize the High Commission's offices by pro-Bangladesh elements.

13. There were several resistance forces operating under a variety of names, but the group officially recognized by the Indians was the Mukti Fauj (later Mukti Bahini), the force affiliated with, though not effectively controlled by, the Awami League. To simplify matters, we have called all Bangladeshi resistance forces Mukti Bahini, even though it was late summer before most of them had been brought within its fold under strong pressure from India.

14. Interviews, India, 1978. Some Mukti Bahini were later sent to Indian military institutions for "specialized training," but this was not considered necessary by the BSF in the early stages of the struggle in East Pakistan.

15. Interviews, India and Bangladesh, 1978.

16. For example, it was reported in early April that two BSF battalions "who had infiltrated" across the West Bengali border into the Jessore area of East Pakistan had been "wiped out" (Radio Pakistan, newscast, 12 April 1971). Neither side subsequently recalled such levels of engagement that early in the conflict (interviews, India, 1978; Pakistan, 1979).

17. Interviews, Pakistan, 1979. A number of the clashes between the BSF and the Pakistani army occurred in disputed enclave areas on the border that had never been demarcated. Unintentional troop movements across these borders were common, but of course on such occasions both governments accused the other of aggression. See *Asian Recorder* 17, no. 27 (2–8 July 1971): 10233–35, for a long list of charges and countercharges by the two governments in April–May 1971.

18. Interviews, India, 1978, 1979.

19. Interviews, India and Pakistan, 1978, 1979. An American official who was a close observer of the 1971 developments noted in an interview that the Indian army did not start moving heavy equipment to the East Pakistani border area until October, which would appear to support the Indian position on this issue (Carnegie Endowment files).

20. Interviews, India, 1978.

21. According to the Indian minister of labour and rehabilitation, there were 119,566 refugees as of 17 April; 536,308 by 24 April; 1,672,200 by 7 May; 2,669,226 by 14 May; and 3,435,243 by 21 May (Government of India, *Bangladesh Documents*, vol. 1, 675).

22. There is some disagreement among Indian officials on the refugee policy question. Several of those interviewed insisted that there was no policy decision as such. However, several others in a more authoritative position around the prime minister stated that the decision to establish camps for the refugees and, as far as possible, to resolutely inhibit their resettlement outside the camps had been made in mid April, when the refugee inflow began to reach substantial proportions. On this subject Mrs.

Gandhi told newsmen on 4 May that her government had no intention of rehabilitating the refugees from East Pakistan on a permanent basis, an assertion of the basic policy (*India News* 11: 7, 14 May 1971). This may be yet another case in which the informality of the Indian decision-making process in 1971 explains the different perceptions among officials on this issue. Apparently, the decision was taken by the core group around Mrs. Gandhi and became policy without being referred to one of the formal decision-making institutions—the Political Action Committee or the cabinet. It should also be noted that by no means did all of the refugees from East Pakistan end up in Indian camps. Many of them had family ties in India and moved directly into their homes, since, under the circumstances, it was impossible for the Border Security Force or the police to channel the massive flow across the border entirely into camps.

23. In a statement to the Lok Sabha on 24 May, for instance, Mrs. Gandhi said that the three and a half million people who had sought refuge in India "belong to every religious persuasion—Hindu, Muslim, Buddhist and Christian. They come from every social class and age group. They are not refugees in the sense we have understood this word since partition" (a justification for the different Indian policies toward them and earlier "real" refugees, that is, Hindus fleeing a Muslim-dominated society?) (*Foreign Affairs Record* [Government of India], May 1971, 75–78). Mrs. Gandhi was literally correct, but by mid May about 80 percent of the "refugees" entering India were Hindus according to official Indian sources.

24. It should be noted, however, that there was some inconsistency on this matter in public statements by Indian officials. Samar Sen, India's representative to the United Nations, termed the developments in East Pakistan a "domestic affair" in a note to the U.N. secretary-general dated 29 March, which presumably had New Delhi's approval (*Times of India*, 31 March 1971). Mrs. Gandhi and Foreign Minister Swaran Singh also made statements to the Lok Sabha on 27 March that, implicitly at least, reached the same conclusion. On 4 April, however, Mrs. Gandhi reportedly told the All-India Congress Committee that she rejected Pakistan's contention that East Pakistan was an internal matter (*Hindustan Times*, 5 April 1971). There was, thus, some confusion on this question within the Government of India, but its tendency during the first couple of months was to downplay any Indian involvement in the Pakistani civil war.

25. See the 15 May note from the Government of India to the Government of Pakistan (*Washington Star*, 19 May 1971).

26. Mrs. Gandhi met with opposition party leaders on 27 March and informed them that her government would not support the secessionist movement in East Pakistan at that time, as this would have "international repercussions" (*The Statesman*, 28 March 1971). The *public* response of most of the opposition parties was to urge the government to extend diplomatic recognition to Bangladesh, but reportedly their *private* response was to accept the government's position (interviews, India, 1978; see also *Motherland*, 28 March 1971, and *Times of India*, 8 April 1971).

27. Interviews, India, 1978.

28. Interviews, Pakistan, 1979.

29. Interviews, New Delhi, 1978.

30. Peter Hazelhurst, *The Times* (London), 13 July 1971.

31. *The Hindu,* 30 March 1971.
32. Interviews, India, 1978; also more informal discussions with several Indian officials in the summer of 1981.
33. Interviews, India, 1978, 1979.
34. Interviews, India, 1978.
35. Ibid.
36. *Lok Sabha Debates,* (Government of India) 24 May 1971, 187. The size of the refugee population was a matter of dispute between India and Pakistan. On 1 September, for example, Pakistan's ambassador to the United States, General Hilaly, maintained that the refugee figure was a bit over two million. India at this time maintained that the figure was somewhat over eight million. The USAID deputy administrator, Maurice Williams, who spent time in both India and Pakistan during the year for discussion of relief operations and attendant matters, reported to Washington from New Delhi in October that Indian refugee registration appeared effective and that the Indian refugee totals were thus probably fairly accurate (U.S. Department of State, *Situation Report,* 27 October 1971 [hereafter these documents are referred to as DOS, *Sitrep,* with the appropriate date. Those designated by a number were prepared for the India-Pakistan Working Group, those without a number were prepared as memoranda for the Secretary of State]).
37. *Lok Sabha Debates,* 5 June 1971, 122; 26 July 1971, 58; *New York Times,* 30 September 1971.
38. Interviews, India, 1978. Similar observations are found in DOS, *Sitrep,* 13 October 1971, in which it was reported that "violent incidents within the refugee camp and tensions outside the camp appear to have increased. The former probably resulted from the monotony of camp life and administrative problems, while the latter stem from unhappiness of the local populace with the guaranteed ration of the refugees and the pressures they place on the local market."
39. *Lok Sabha Debates,* 24 May 1971, 187.

8. PAKISTAN, 25 MARCH–OCTOBER 1971

1. Emphasis added. The speech has been reproduced in various places, for example, Government of Pakistan, *White Paper on the Crisis in East Pakistan,* appendix A., 11–13; and *Bangladesh Papers,* 275–77.
2. This was purposely designed as an evocative echo to Mujib's statement on 1 March after the postponement of the National Assembly, in which he declared: "We are the representatives of the majority people and we cannot allow it [the postponement] to go unchallenged" (*Bangladesh Papers,* 190). This report derives from an official involved in drafting the presidential statement (interview, Pakistan, 1979).
3. The Pakistani government's allegations of criminal, antistate, and antisocial activity, which were to be crucial in the subsequent disqualification of Awami League National and Provincial assembly members, are included in "Terror in East Pakistan," Government of Pakistan, *White Paper on the Crisis in East Pakistan,* 29–44. See also Salik, *Witness to Surrender,* chap. 7. These charges were later repeated in the president's

speech of 28 June announcing plans for approaching a political settlement (*Bangladesh Papers*, 276).

4. Interviews, Pakistan, 1979.

5. One senior military officer in the east remarked that strange faces started to appear at political meetings after the 1970 monsoons. Another reported that in 1970 an unusually large amount of Hindu-owned property came on the market; the suspicion being that part of the proceeds were used to subsidize the Awami League (interview, Pakistan, 1979).

6. Ibid.

7. Ibid.

8. Ibid.

9. Salik, *Witness to Surrender*, chaps. 9 and 10, provides a detailed account of the military action, which the officers directly involved whom we interviewed described as substantially correct. The orders for "Operation Searchlight" are included as appendix 3 of Salik's book.

10. Interview, Pakistan, 1979. This officer also observed that the armed forces would have been unable to identify leaders of the Awami League because of the military's physical and cultural distance from Bengali society.

11. In his statement of 3 January, for example, Mujib had referred to a conspiracy to undo the election results and said that subordinates of the president were committed to this, but that "the people of Bengal would confront those elements with bamboo sticks"; he repeated this in another statement a week later (*Bangladesh Papers*, 137–40, 142–43).

12. Interviews, Bangladesh, 1978; Pakistan, 1979.

13. Interviews, Pakistan, April 1979.

14. See Radio Pakistan, "Newscast Transcripts," in English, Urdu, Punjabi, Pushto, Dari, Sindi, and Bengali, located in the archives of the Indian Institute of Defence Studies and Analyses.

15. Interview, Pakistan, 1979.

16. Ibid. Pakistan received expressions of support from Muslim states as well as from many other countries during the course of the drama. Those countries that extended support were catalogued in successive issues of *Pakistan Horizon* during the year. India, on the other hand, experienced enormous difficulty in soliciting international condemnation of the Pakistan government's action in East Pakistan (see, for example, *Lok Sabha Debates*, 17 June and 19 July 1971).

17. Interviews, Pakistan, 1979.

18. Ibid.

19. The information on the recreation of public and police services in East Pakistan was derived from interviews with those involved in martial law administration in East Pakistan and in the central government.

20. Interview, Pakistan, 1979.

21. The following reconstruction of the decision-making process derives from interviews conducted in Pakistan in 1979 with the principals involved.

22. Cf. broadcast of the president of Pakistan, 18 June 1971, and *aide-mémoire* of the permanent representative of Pakistan to the secretary-general of the United Nations, 13 August 1971, reprinted in *Pakistan Horizon* 24 (Third Quarter 1971): 111, 133.

23. Reprinted in ibid., 111–23. This statement coincided with a message from President Yahya to President Nixon stressing the importance of clarifying the attitude of Pakistan's principal aid donors toward future economic assistance to Pakistan and seeking Nixon's help in the matter (U.S. Department of State, memorandum for Mr. Henry A. Kissinger, 1 July 1971).

24. *Pakistan Horizon*, 24 (Third Quarter 1971): 111–23.

25. Interview, Pakistan, 1979.

26. *New York Times*, 20 July 1971. Also DOS, *Sitrep*, 4 August 1971.

27. Interview, India, 1978.

28. Press release reprinted in *Pakistan Horizon* 24 (Fourth Quarter 1971): 148. Mujib was given a choice of defense lawyers and chose A. K. Brohi, an eminent Pakistani advocate, who was assisted by Ghulam Ali Memon, Akkar Mirza, and Ghulam Hussain.

29. Interviews, Pakistan, 1979.

30. *New York Times*, 8, 19, and 20 August 1971. As of late August no "cleansed" member had come out publicly in support of the government, which resulted in a pessimistic view on the part of the U.S. State Department concerning prospects for a political settlement (DOS, *Sitrep*, 25 August 1971). By mid September, after the appointment of Malik as governor and the appointment of two Awami Leaguers as members of his Council of Advisers, only fifteen Awami League MPAs had reportedly come forward to support the government (DOS, *Sitrep*, 22 September 1971).

31. *New York Times*, 20 September 1971.

32. Interviews, Pakistan, 1971.

33. DOS, *Sitrep*, 5 August 1971.

34. Ibid., 11 August 1971.

35. Ibid., 25 August 1971.

36. Ibid., 25 August 1971. In these discussions on 19 August, Yahya indicated that A. K. Brohi would represent Mujib and also said that he had given consideration to Ambassador Farland's suggestion that a civilian governor be appointed in East Pakistan to replace Gen. Tikka Khan. He noted that even though Tikka Khan had done a good military job, he had nevertheless acquired a reputation not conducive to a return to normalcy. Yahya had thus decided to appoint Dr. A. M. Malik, a Bengali with a career of public service, to replace him. Malik would have the authority to appoint a cabinet, all of whom Yahya indicated he hoped would be Bengali (letter from American Embassy, Islamabad, to secretary of state, 20 August 1971), made available to us under the Freedom of Information Act (hereafter referred to as FOI documents).

37. DOS, *Sitrep*, 30 September 1971. It was also reported that serious cleavages had developed in Mujibnagar between factions supporting Khondikar Mushtaq and Tajuddin Ahmed. Secret talks were held between representatives of the government and Awami League National Assembly members who had stayed behind in East Pakistan. These forty-six all indicated that they were prepared to go to West Pakistan for the convening of the National Assembly (interview, Pakistan, 1971).

38. Radio Pakistan, newscast, 12 October 1971.

39. Interviews, Pakistan, 1979.

40. Ibid.
41. *New York Times,* 9 September 1971.
42. Ibid., 23 September 1971.
43. Interviews, Pakistan, 1971.
44. Radio Pakistan, newscast, 22 October 1971.
45. Ibid., 27 October 1971.
46. Radio Pakistan, newscast, 27 October 1971.
47. Ibid., 9 November 1971.
48. Interview, Pakistan, 1979.

9. INDIA AND THE PRELUDE
TO WAR, JUNE–OCTOBER 1971

1. Interviews, India, 1978.
2. During Mrs. Gandhi's visit to Washington in mid October, Nixon offered to have the United States assume full responsibility for all refugee camp expenses, but she displayed no interest. By then, of course, New Delhi had already made the decision to take military action and dump ten million refugees back on a destitute Bangladesh by the end of 1971.
3. The Indian government announced plans in late May to move fifty thousand refugees to Mana, a camp in Madhya Pradesh; eventually about twenty-five thousand were sent to Mana, but this was an exception to India's general policy of keeping the refugees in the border states (statements by Labour and Rehabilitation Minister R. D. Khadilkar in the Rajya Sabha, 24 May 1971, Government of India, *Bangladesh Documents,* vol. 1, 675).
4. Four U.S. air force C-130s transported 13,165 refugees from Tripura to Assam and 1,750 tons of rice to Tripura from mid June to mid July, when the project was terminated at India's request on the grounds that the monsoons made it uneconomical (USDOS, *Sitrep,* 21 July 1971, and secret memorandum to Henry Kissinger, 13 July 1971 [FOI document], The White House, p. 3 (henceforth, "Secret Memorandum to Kissinger"). Presumably this was because of India's decision in early July to keep the refugees where they were. Figures on the Soviet air force's participation in these exercises are not available, but reportedly it was at about the same level as that of the Americans.
5. Ibid.
6. *Indian Express,* 10 June 1971.
7. Interviews, India, 1980.
8. During the 1971 crisis the Bengali-dominated Communist Party (Marxist) in Tripura was able to establish effective working relations with broad segments of the traditional tribal leadership in that state, leading eventually to a CPM state government in Tripura.
9. Interviews, India, 1978; Pakistan, 1979.
10. Interviews, India and Bangladesh, 1978; U.S. Government records, in particular a CIA internal memo dated 12 October 1971 (FOI documents). The change in the name of the Indian-recognized Bangladeshi military units from Mukti Fauj (liberation army) to Mukti Bahini (liberation force) was of more than symbolic significance. One of India's problems was that a high proportion of the Bengali Muslim refugees, who constituted over 80

percent of the various resistance forces (most East Pakistani Bengali Hindu refugees were disinclined to get involved), were young students susceptible to more radical political appeals than those of the Awami League.

11. Interview, India, 1978.

12. Interview, Pakistan, 1979.

13. Ibid. The Pakistani army was aware of the location of these camps, just as the Indian army was aware of the positioning and status of forces of the Pakistani army in areas close to the border.

14. Ibid.

15. One of Mrs. Gandhi's closest confidants referred to the "Mujibnagar people" (i.e., the Bangladesh government in exile) as "third rate types" and maintained that a settlement that did not restore Mujib to leadership in the Bangladesh movement and government would not have been worthy of consideration by India (interview, India, 1979).

16. The three other members were Maulana Bhashani (the head of the pro-China faction of the National Awami Party), Manoranjan Dhar of the Bangladesh National Congress (the "token" Hindu on the committee), and Khondikar Mushtaq Ahmad, foreign minister in the Awami League government in exile.

17. *National Herald*, 21 June 1971.

18. *The Hindu*, 26 June 1971.

19. Indira Gandhi, *India and Bangladesh*, 18.

20. *The Hindu*, 22 June 1971.

21. Secret memorandum to Kissinger, 13 July 1971 (FOI document). According to American sources, U Thant was distressed by an Indian allegation that he was acting on the advice of the U.S. government in taking this initiative and strongly denied that this was the case.

22. *India News* (Indian Embassy, Washington, D.C.), 13 August 1971, 10:20. The usual Indian practice in public statements in this period was to refer to East Pakistan as "East Bengal," but in this statement Swaran Singh also used "Bangladesh"—possibly a slip of the tongue.

23. U.S. Department of State document (secret), 27 November 1971 (FOI records).

24. *New York Times*, 19 November 1971; *India News*, 3 December 1971, 10:36.

25. Interviews, India, 1980.

26. *The Patriot* (pro-Soviet daily, New Delhi), 29 June 1971.

27. Foreign Minister Swaran Singh's address to the National Press Club in Washington on 17 June, as cited in the *Hindustan Times*, 18 June 1971.

28. *Foreign Affairs Record* 17, no. 6 (June 1971):107–8.

29. The Government of India had long been one of the most vocal critics of the use of economic *and* military aid by donor governments to extract political or economic concessions from recipients—the "aid without strings" line. In 1971, however, New Delhi was espousing exactly the opposite position in the case of foreign aid to Pakistan, demanding that it be terminated if Pakistan did not change its policies on East Pakistan.

30. "U.S. Policy in the Indian-Pakistani Crisis, March-December 1971," Historical Studies Division, Bureau of Public Affairs, Department of State, Research Project no. 1033 (rev.), March 1973, 16–17 (FOI document).

31. Secret memorandum to Kissinger, 11 August 1971 (FOI document).

302 Notes to Pages 194–199

32. DOS, *Sitreps*, 15 and 29 September 1971 (FOI document).

33. Lawrence Lifschultz, *Bangladesh: The Unfinished Revolution* (London: Zed Press, 1979), 163–68, presents a collection of allegations against Kissinger, Harold Saunders (National Security Council), George Griffin (a consular officer at the U.S. consulate general in Calcutta), and Khondikar Mushtaq Ahmad (the Bangladesh government in exile foreign minister), based according to Lifschultz on "independent Washington sources and Carnegie sources." We have no idea of who the "independent Washington sources" may be, but our own careful reading of the Carnegie files on Bangladesh do not support any of Lifschultz's imaginative conspiracy theories; indeed, in several places he distorts the substance of the comments made by the interviewees by selective quotation or by omitting qualifying phrases.

Nor do the State, Defense, and CIA secret records obtained under the Freedom of Information act substantiate Lifschultz's charge that Kissinger and Saunders were directly involved in the comparatively low-level contacts with the government in exile or that there were any significant U.S. policy objectives involved other than arranging a *peaceful* separation of the two wings of Pakistan if possible (by early fall 1971 there was broad agreement at all levels within the U.S. government that there was virtually no chance of preserving a unified Pakistan). Lifschultz's allegation that the U.S. ambassador in New Delhi and consul general in Calcutta were kept in the dark about the negotiations with the government in exile is also incorrect. Reports from both missions in August and September (FOI records) make it clear that there was no confusion on that issue. While the ambassador and the consul general doubted (along with virtually everyone else) that a peaceful settlement was possible, they were certainly not opposed to efforts to attain one.

34. DOS, *Sitrep*, 3 November 1971.

35. Carnegie Endowment files.

36. Ibid.

37. Interviews, India, 1980.

38. That the Soviet Union supplied Pakistan with tanks and artillery under its military aid program was bad enough, but New Delhi was even more unhappy with the program under which the Soviets also supplied spare parts for the *Chinese* tanks and planes, based on Soviet models, that had been provided to Pakistan by the PRC.

39. For the best detailed analysis of these developments, see A. G. Noorani, *Brezhnev Plan for Asian Security* (Bombay: Jaico Publishing, 1975), chaps. 1–3.

40. According to U.S. government sources, at the Indo-Soviet talks in Moscow of May 25–29, 1970, Soviet leaders assured India that they were "finishing" military deliveries to Pakistan (FOI documents). Some Indian sources give the date as a month earlier or a month later, but all agree that by mid 1970 Moscow had agreed to its part of the deal with India (interviews, India, 1978, 1980).

41. Interviews, India, 1978.

42. Ibid.

43. According to authoritative Indian and American sources, Kissinger made no such statement to Indian officials during his visit to New Delhi in

July. Later, after his return to Washington, he did inform the Indian ambassador to the United States, L. K. Jha, that the 1963 security commitment applied only in the event of Chinese aggression against India and not in circumstances under which India initiated military action against Pakistan. Rather curiously, both Americans and Indians usually discuss the July 1963 Indo–U.S. agreement in terms of an American commitment to provide military assistance to India in the context of another conflict with China. But in fact, the July 1963 U.S.–Indian Air Defense Agreement (the only one there is) merely calls for consultations between the United States and India on possible measures to strengthen India's air defenses in the event of renewed Chinese aggression and makes no specific U.S. commitments of assistance.

44. The sources for this information include one former official of the Pakistani foreign service who provided copies of the Sino-Pakistani correspondence to the Indian intelligence service at the home of a well-known Indian journalist in New Delhi.

45. Interview, India, 1978.

46. Interviews, India, 1978, 1980.

47. Interviews, India, 1978, and FOI documents. The fullest newspaper account of the Indian efforts to reassure Washington on this matter was published in the *Times of India*, 10 August 1971.

48. Noorani, *Brezhnev Plan*, 142.

49. Tass report, 10 October 1971.

50. *Foreign Affairs Record*, October 1971, 249.

51. Noorani, *Brezhnev Plan*, 145.

52. See *Pakistan Times*, 13 April 1971, for the text of the Zhou Enlai letter as circulated by the Pakistani government.

53. Interviews, Bangladesh, 1982; Pakistan, 1979. Anwar Hossain, the Bengali foreign language expert at Peking Radio from 1966 to 1972, claimed that he had translated Zhou's letter into Bengali for Peking Radio and that it had included the last sentence that was omitted from the Pakistani version of the text ("A Bangali Grandstand View," *Far Eastern Economic Review*, 11 October 1974).

54. The Pakistanis did propose bilateral negotiations, suggesting a "summit meeting" between Mrs. Gandhi and Yahya Khan in July, and in September during Yahya's visit to Iran, and in October at the U.N. General Assembly. But the subject for discussion was in each case narrowly defined as the refugee problem rather than broader political issues, such as the role of the Awami League in any future political settlement. New Delhi rejected the Pakistani overtures, stating that the situation in East Pakistan that was causing the refugee influx into India was not, in Mrs. Gandhi's words, "an Indo-Pakistan problem" (*India News*, 29 October 1971, 1).

10. WAR: INDIA

1. Interviews, India, 1978, 1981.

2. American intelligence reports noted that India's prime concern was the prospect of a prolonged struggle in East Pakistan, in the course of which the extreme leftist factions in the Bangladesh movement would eventually gain dominance (FOI document, "The 1971 Indo-Pakistani

Conflict: A Study in Escalation," Defense Intelligence Agency, September 1971). Similar views were also expressed, usually quite clearly, in our interviews with some responsible Indian officials.

3. See D. P. Dhar's interesting comments on this subject in an interview with a *Washington Post* correspondent published on 13 November 1971. In our interviews several Indian leaders who held critically important positions in 1971 invariably expressed their doubts about the capabilities, and in some cases the integrity, of Awami League leaders other than Mujib.

4. Interviews, India, 1978, 1981.

5. It was particularly irritating to the Indians that some Indian units sent into Sri Lanka to help the government suppress a "Maoist" uprising were operating the air communication system at Colombo airport. Indian air control officers thus had to provide directions to Pakistani military aircraft transporting troops and supplies between West and East Pakistan.

6. Nepalese rebel forces had used bases in India in the 1950–51 revolt against the Rana family regime and again in 1961–62 against King Mahendra, so a degree of sympathy existed for Pakistan facing a similar situation in 1971.

7. See the useful discussion on the "debate" within the Government of India on the East Pakistan issue in Pran Chopra, *India's Second Liberation* (Delhi: Vikas, 1973), 80–118.

8. Interviews, India, 1978.

9. The main points made by Mrs. Gandhi in her meetings with Nixon are listed in "Indira Gandhi Visits Washington," NESA report, 10 November 1971 (FOI document).

10. Interviews, Pakistan, 1979; India, 1978.

11. On the involvement of Indian military personnel in Mukti Bahini raids, see Sasthi Bratha, "Big Brother Goes to War," *Guardian*, 18 September 1971, which quotes a Bangladeshi "liberation fighter" who admitted that all the big operations in East Pakistan were carried out by Indians. The extensive literature by Indian army and Border Security Force officers, published long after the war in most instances, is quite clear about the Indian involvement in the East Pakistani resistance from mid 1971 on.

12. According to one of the leading Pakistani military officers in Dhaka in 1971, the destruction of vital bridges by Indian-aided Mukti Bahini units confused the Pakistanis as to Indian objectives. Some Pakistanis argued that the Indians would not have allowed this if they were planning an all-out invasion, for which they, too, would need the bridges. This was one factor in the decision to follow a "defend the borders" strategy devised to forestall the establishment of a "liberated zone" rather than a "defense line around Dhaka" strategy. Apparently it never occurred to the Pakistanis that the Indians were simply being shortsighted—pursuing short-run objectives whose accomplishment might run counter to their long-term needs.

13. The conclusion reached by the U.S. government was that India was escalating its support of the Mukti Bahini to force the Pakistani government to make a difficult choice, that is, either to seek an accommodation with the Bangladesh movement or, if opting for war, to take the initiative in opening hostilities (FOI document, "Intelligence Support in Political-

Military Crises: A Case Study of the India-Pakistan Crisis of 1971," 1972).

14. Indian sources stated on 7 November that Indian troops had crossed into East Pakistani territory on 31 October in retaliation for Pakistani shelling of an Indian border town. This was the first time that "unimpeachable Indian sources had admitted crossborder actions by Indian forces" (*New York Times*, 8 November 1971).

15. In an official Indian source, Mukti Bahini forces in a "liberated area" are described as having been overrun by Pakistani tanks advancing *toward* the Indian border. The Indian forces allegedly intervened to stop the advance and in the process destroyed or damaged thirteen Pakistani tanks (Ministry of Defence, *Annual Report: 1971* [New Delhi: GOI Press, 1972], 7). According to more reliable Indian sources, however, Indian troops had quietly occupied the area several days earlier and then repelled Pakistan's efforts to throw them out.

16. The Indian strategy is clearly described and analyzed in publications by Indian military officers who served in command positions in 1971, who make it clear that the "war of liberation" started for their units on or about 21 November. In particular, see Maj. Gen. Lachhman Singh, *Indian Sword Strikes in East Pakistan* (New Delhi: Vikas, 1979); Maj. Gen. Sukhwant Singh, *The Liberation of Bangladesh* (New Delhi: Vikas, 1980); Brig. H. S. Sodhi, *"Operation Windfall": Emergence of Bangladesh* (New Delhi: Allied Publishers, 1980); and Vice Admiral N. Krishnan, *No Way but Surrender: An Account of the Indo-Pakistan War in the Bay of Bengal, 1971* (New Delhi: Vikas, 1980).

17. Interviews, India, 1978; Singh, *Indian Sword*, 89–92; Chopra, *India's Second Liberation*, 174.

18. It was indicative of the noncrisis approach to decision making that characterized the Government of India in this "crisis period" that on 3 December, when the Pakistani air force attacked several Indian air bases, three of the key ministers in the cabinet were out of New Delhi. Mrs. Gandhi was in Calcutta, Defence Minister Ram was in Bihar, and Finance Minister Chavan was in Bombay—all on business that had nothing to do with Pakistan (*Asian Recorder* 18, no. 1 [January 1–7, 1972]: 10535).

19. Interviews, India, 1978, 1981.

20. When the Soviet Union volunteered to serve once again as a "nonpartisan mediator" between India and Pakistan in early 1972, New Delhi politely rejected the offer. According to several Indian officials, their experience at Tashkent had influenced the Indian government to reject any third-party mediation and to insist upon a bilateral settlement with Pakistan under which India would retain the strategic points in Kashmir seized in the 1971 war.

21. In a significant comment on 12 November, Defence Minister Ram stated that Bhutto had returned from China "empty-handed" and that Mao had advised Pakistan to seek a political settlement with the Bangladesh movement (*The Hindu*, 13 November 1971). Since Bhutto and the Pakistani press were claiming (quite misleadingly, if not disingenuously) that China had agreed to come to Pakistan's support if India attacked, it is evident that New Delhi knew the facts immediately.

22. According to one Indian Defence Ministry source, New Delhi had sent an "observer" to Singapore in September to check on the expected

movement of a Seventh Fleet detachment into the Indian Ocean in the event of an Indo-Pakistani war. No one else we interviewed mentioned this, however, and it is unclear why an observer would have been considered necessary, since this source also indicated that India knew the dispatch of the fleet would be a highly publicized, symbolic action by the U.S. government.

23. According to Tariq Ali, in an interview in mid 1984, Mrs. Gandhi stated that immediately after the fall of Dhaka several of her colleagues in the cabinet had "insisted that the war be fought to the finish" and that she "was alone in demanding a unilateral ceasefire on our part." She also said the military had wanted to finish the job, but that she had "lectured them on [her] position," and they "saluted and said they would carry out our instructions" (quoted in the *Sunday Observer* [Bombay], 14 November 1984, 5). In our own interviews with Mrs. Gandhi and other officials, they noted the debate in *early* December over the policy on West Pakistan, but none mentioned a serious difference of opinion on the unilateral cease-fire decision of 18 and 19 December.

24. India set the number of victims of Pakistani atrocities at three million, and this is still the figure usually cited. We interviewed two Indian officials who had held responsible positions on the issue of Bangladesh in 1971. When questioned about the actual number of deaths in Bangladesh in 1971 attributable to the civil war, one replied "about 300,000." Then when he received a disapproving glance from his colleague, he changed this to "300,000 to 500,000." Regardless of the figure, this is a horrifying loss of life, but it is still impossible to get anything like reliable estimates as to (1) how many of these were "liberation fighters" killed in combat, (2) how many were Bihari Muslims and supporters of Pakistan killed by Bengali Muslims, and (3) how many were killed by Pakistani, Indian, or Mukti Bahini fire and bombing during the hostilities. One thing is clear— the atrocities did not go just one way, though Bengali Muslims and Hindus were certainly the main victims.

25. The source for U.N. Security Council resolutions, debates, and voting is the U.N. Security Council, *Official Records*, Twenty-sixth year, Supplement for October, November, and December (1971), and in particular meetings 1606, 1607, 1608, 1611, 1613, 1614, and 1621.

26. The source for the General Assembly resolution and debate is U.N. General Assembly, *Official Records*, Twenty-sixth session (1971), and in particular plenary meetings 2002 and 2003, 7 December 1971.

27. Indeed, several key figures in India could not understand why Pakistan did not readily agree to the proposal, since it would have left India in a most difficult and compromising position (interviews, India, 1978).

28. In our interviews with him in 1979, Yahya Khan related a rather curious account of his experience with Bhutto on the Polish resolution. Yahya had been talking to Bhutto—who was at the U.N. meetings in New York—by telephone about several matters. At one point Yahya said that he was far away, of course, but that the Polish resolution looked good, and "we should accept it." Bhutto replied, "I can't hear you." Yahya repeated himself several times, and Bhutto kept saying, "What? What?" The operator in New York finally intervened and said, "I can hear him fine," to

which Bhutto replied "Shut up." Yahya seemed still bemused and bewildered by all this in 1979. The Polish resolution and Bhutto's action that ended its consideration, though a matter of concern to the general officers still in power in 1971, never became a political issue in Pakistan until the spring of 1986, when Bhutto's daughter Benazir returned to Pakistan to assume leadership of the People's party's campaign against President Zia ul-Haq. Progovernment sources raised the question of Bhutto's motivations in sabotaging the Polish resolution. Benazir Bhutto replied that it had not been the Polish resolution her father tore up but some other papers. She may be right, but Bhutto's walkout from the Security Council did halt all consideration of the Polish resolution.

11. WAR: PAKISTAN

1. Who formally "started the war" on 3 December is difficult to establish. Prime Minister Gandhi reported on national radio that "Some hours ago, soon after 5:30 P.M. on the 3rd of December, Pakistan launched a full-scale war against us." Pakistan's Inter-Services Intelligence Directorate declared that India had launched simultaneous attacks on Pakistan at Sialkot, Chamb, Jessore, and Rahimyar Khan between 3:30 and 4:00 P.M. on the third. Pakistan reported that its air strikes on Indian airfields in Amritsar, Pathankot, Srinagar, Awantipur, Uttarlai, Jodhpur, Ambala, and Agra were in response to Indian aggression (e.g., see DOS, *Sitreps*, nos. 17 and 18, 3 December 1971).

2. Interview, Pakistan, 1979.

3. See letters from President Richard Nixon to President Yahya Khan, 1 July 1971 and 28 October 1971. Communications within the U.S. government and between it and Pakistan were couched in restrained language. In mid July, for example, the United States noted that it was going to approach Pakistan "to express our concern at any action which would reflect adversely on Pakistan's international image and set back the prospects for political accommodation" (DOS, *Sitrep*, 21 July 1971). Later, in reporting plans for an upcoming meeting between Deputy USAID Administrator Maurice Williams and Ambassador Farland with President Yahya, it was indicated that the U.S. emissaries would "weave into the discussion suggestions that in order to make the humanitarian relief effort more effective, the GOP *might* consider an offer of amnesty, expansion of the list of 'cleared' Awami League members of the National Assembly, dealing with the Awami League (under that label or otherwise), the effects of the trial of Sheikh Mujib, and the desirability of having a civilian Bengali governor of East Pakistan" (DOS, *Sitrep*, 17 August 1971).

4. Interviews, Pakistan, 1979. The Pakistani government realized that the Soviet Union had a special relationship with India, but was also confident of Soviet interest in developing closer relations with Pakistan. Yahya's discussions with Podgorny at the celebration held by the shah of Iran at Persepolis and the explanation of Firyubin's visit to New Delhi immediately prior to Mrs. Gandhi's departure for Western capitals satisfied the Pakistanis that the Soviet Union was committed to the preservation of a united Pakistan and to restraining India from launching a war.

5. The Chinese did not commit to intervention. In their visit to Beijing

in November, Pakistani delegates were told by Premier Zhou Enlai that there would be no war in South Asia, since it was to no one's interest to go to war. The question of Chinese military involvement was, therefore, moot, as was the necessity for assistance in the way of aircraft. One member of the delegation suggested to the premier that planes be sent to Pakistan anyway; if there were no war, they would be returned without damage; if war broke out, their availability would make a great difference and would be acknowledged as the assistance of a trustworthy friend. Zhou reportedly did not find this argument compelling, though the Chinese continued throughout to extend moral and verbal support to Pakistan and provided some arms and tanks. Yet Pakistan hoped that the Chinese would somehow act or threaten to act, and nearly a decade later Pakistanis were still disappointed that they had not done so (interviews, Pakistan and United States, 1979).

6. As late as October, Egypt, Libya, and Saudi Arabia extended strong support to Pakistan.

7. Interviews, Pakistan, 1979.

8. Ibid.

9. Ibid.

10. Ibid.

11. USDOS, *Sitrep*, 25 August 1971. It was reported that the Mukti Bahini claimed to have thirty trained and equipped frogmen whose purpose was to discourage shipping in Chittagong port. In late September mines damaged a number of ships, prompting seven shipping lines, representing 25 percent of shipping to East Pakistan, to suspend their service (DOS, *Sitrep*, 30 September 1971).

12. There were reportedly at this time three divisions of Indian troops and a brigade of Mukti Bahini forces operating against Syhlet, Brahman-baria, and Chandpur; an Indian infantry brigade and Mukti Bahini brigade against Tura-Mymensingh; two Indian divisions against Pachagarh-Rangpur and the Hilli sector; and two divisions against the Jessore sector from the west, in addition to nineteen engineer battalions. It was reported to us that the Pakistani GHQ was not prepared to counter this massing of forces by raising new battalions or by supplying the necessary matériel to augment Pakistan's defensive capacity. Two divisions added after the political troubles in the east commenced were intended and required to suppress the insurgency.

13. Interviews, Pakistan 1979. U.S. government sources also reported at the time that "a senior officer told an assembly of general officers in Rawalpindi on September 28 that on a just-completed visit to East Pakistan he found the situation 'bleak' and not improving. He reportedly stated that the activities of the guerrillas are hurting the Army; provincial administration is almost non-existent; Bengalis are afraid to venture out in the presence of the Army; and the razakars (pro-GOP local militiamen) are deserting in growing numbers" (DOS, *Sitrep*, 5 October 1971).

14. Radio Pakistan, newscasts, 12 October 1971.

15. Ibid., 13 October 1971, 0740 hours.

16. *New York Times*, 22 October 1971.

17. Radio Pakistan, newscasts, 31 October 1971.

18. Ibid., 1 November 1971. See *Newsweek*.

19. DOS, *Sitrep*, 3 November 1971.
20. See, e.g., DOS, *Sitrep*, 28 November 1971.
21. *New York Times*, 13 November 1971; and Radio Pakistan, newscasts, 16 and 19 November 1971.
22. Radio Pakistan, newscast, 20 November 1971.
23. Interview, India, 1978.
24. Interview, Pakistan, 1972.
25. Radio Pakistan, newscast, 23 November 1971.
26. Interviews, Pakistan and United States, 1979.
27. Interview, Pakistan, 1979.
28. Radio Pakistan, newscast, 24 November 1971.
29. CIA, *Sitrep*, no. 2159/71, 24 November 1971.
30. Ibid., 25 November 1971.
31. Quoted from copies of communications made available in an interview, Pakistan, 1979.
32. Interviews, Pakistan, 1979.
33. Interviews, Pakistan and United States, 1979.
34. Ibid.
35. Ibid. For more detailed reviews of the progress of the war, see Robert W. Jackson, *South Asia Crisis: India, Pakistan, and Bangladesh, a Political and Historical Analysis of the 1971 War* (New York: Praeger, 1975), chap. 5; Singh, *Indian Sword;* and Singh, *Liberation of Bangladesh*, vol. 1.
36. Interview, Pakistan, 1979.
37. Ibid. Within a few days of the outbreak of war, India had destroyed about 40 percent of Pakistan's total oil supplies, leaving the country with an estimated maximum of two weeks of essential petroleum products (DOS, *Sitrep*, 9 December 1971).
38. Interviews, Pakistan, 1979.
39. Salik, *Witness to Surrender*, 196.
40. Interviews, Pakistan, 1979.
41. Salik, *Witness to Surrender*, 198. The message was given to the British, French, and Soviet representatives in Dhaka as well as to the American consul general (DOS, *Sitrep*, no. 32, 10 December 1971).
42. Interview, Pakistan, 1979. Also DOS, *Sitreps*, nos. 33 and 34, 10 December 1971. The authors of the proposal wanted to leave the referent vague. If a cease-fire were arranged, they could decide which of the "elected representatives" were indeed the legitimate ones. After all, those in Mujibnagar in India would have come back to claim their seats (interviews, Pakistan, 1979).
43. Interviews, India, 1978.
44. Interviews, Pakistan, 1979.
45. Interviews, Pakistan, 1979; United States, 1979. An officer who was at GHQ when the message was being sent asked the officer transmitting the message why in the world he was authorizing it. The latter indicated that they would understand on the other end. The Government of India intercepted this message as it did others. (Interview, India, 1978). Several officers indicated the emotional vacillation experienced in the face of impending military defeat; cut off from the rest of the country and caught between the desire to fight and the prudence of surrender, there was a tendency to "grasp at straws" (Interview, Pakistan, 1979).

46. CIA, *Sitrep*, no. 2173/71, 14 December 1971.

47. Reprinted in Salik, *Witness to Surrender*, 207.

48. The proposal was made at 6 P.M. on 14 December in a letter from General Niazi to the American consul general in Dhaka, countersigned and delivered by Gen. Farman Ali with a request that it be sent to Bhutto and the Indian representatives at the United Nations. The cease-fire was in fact a surrender in verbal disguise. It proposed (1) a regrouping of Pakistani armed forces in "designated areas" to be mutually agreed upon between the commanders of the opposing forces; (2) a guarantee of safety to all military and paramilitary forces; (3) a guarantee of safety to those who had settled in East Pakistan since 1947; and (4) no reprisals against those who helped the East Pakistani regime since 1947. The letter also indicated General Niazi's promise to abide by a U.N. Security Council decision providing for a permanent settlement of the conflict (CIA, *Sitrep*, no. 2173/71; DOS, *Sitrep*, no. 43, 14 December 1971).

49. The transfer of power is reconstructed from interviews of both military officers and leaders of the Pakistan People's party involved in the process (interviews, Pakistan, 1979; United States, 1979).

50. Shortly after the outbreak of war, Nurul Amin had been named prime minister and Bhutto had become deputy prime minister and foreign minister. It was reported that a civilian government under Amin would be instituted before the meeting of the National Assembly. It was also reported that Bhutto had been included in the government so that he would be easier to control (CIA, *Sitrep*, no. 2159/71). Before his departure for the United Nations, Bhutto informed the U.S. embassy in Pakistan that he expected to be installed in office after his return (DOS, *Sitrep*, no. 30, 9 December 1971).

12. SOVIET, CHINESE, AND AMERICAN POLICIES IN THE 1971 CRISIS

1. At Tashkent, Premier Kosygin had pressured a reluctant—and ailing—Prime Minister Shastri of India into accepting the reestablishment of the 1949 cease-fire line in Kashmir as part of the agreement, thus obligating the Indian army to withdraw from several strategic positions in that state, which had been seized at considerable cost of life during the 1965 war. This rankled in Indian official and military circles and was one factor in New Delhi's decision in 1972 to reject a Soviet offer to mediate after the 1971 war. Apparently the Indians preferred to settle these matters directly with Pakistan on a bilateral basis—accomplished in the 1972 Simla agreement, which defined a new "line of control" for the old cease-fire line in Kashmir and allowed India to retain several key posts captured during the 1971 war that had been restored to Pakistan in the Tashkent Agreement.

2. Kosygin visited Pakistan in April 1968 and offered military aid (DOS, intelligence memorandum, 3 May 1971 [FOI document]), but reportedly the agreement was actually signed in July (*Asian Recorder* 16, no. 28 [9–15 July 1970]: 9633). New Delhi was particularly upset with the provisions in the Soviet aid program under which spare parts for *Chinese*

military equipment (e.g., MIG-19s) based on Soviet models would be provided to Pakistan (DOS records, June 1970 [FOI document]).

3. According to U.S. government sources, Soviet arms deliveries in 1968 included sixty T-54 and T-55B tanks (DOS, INR report, 10 November 1971 [FOI document]).

4. Indian President Dr. Zakir Hussain and then Minister of Foreign Trade Dinesh Singh visited Moscow in June–July 1968 and strongly protested the Pakistani arms aid program at the highest levels of the Soviet government (interviews, India, 1978).

5. Interviews, India, 1978. One Indian source noted in conversations with Western diplomats in Moscow that the Soviet Union had assured India that Moscow's policy toward India had not changed and that, in any case, the amount of military aid to Pakistan was small (DOS note, 16 September 1971 [FOI document]). This did not, of course, ease Indian anxieties.

6. Interviews, India, 1978, 1980.

7. Ibid., 1978.

8. Interviews, Pakistan, 1979, 1982.

9. *The Statesman* (Calcutta), 29 May 1970.

10. *New York Times*, 5 April 1971. A few days earlier, on 28 March, the Soviet ambassador to Pakistan had conveyed an oral message to Yahya from Kosygin urging the Government of Pakistan to use moderation in dealing with East Pakistan (DOS, intelligence memorandum, 3 May 1971 [FOI document]).

11. *Pakistan Times*, 6 April 1971. Yahya was particularly indignant that the Soviet government had "leaked" the text of Podgorny's letter to the press before it was presented to him, and he did the same with his reply to the Soviet president (interview, Pakistan, 1979).

12. *Pakistan Times*, 24 April 1971. Kosygin had reassured the Pakistani ambassador on 12 April that Moscow did not intend to take sides in the dispute (DOS, intelligence memorandum, 3 May 1971 [FOI document]). This was also the general line taken by the Soviet press until fall 1971. And indeed Indian Foreign Minister Swaran Singh complained about the coverage of East Pakistan by the Soviet press in his June 1971 visit (interviews, India, 1980).

13. *Times of India, Hindustan Times, The Hindu*, 8 July 1971. See also Foreign Minister Singh's statement in *Foreign Affairs Record* 17, no. 7 (July 1971): 131. There were also two North Korean ammunition shipments to Pakistan after 25 March that presumably—though not necessarily—originated in the Soviet Union (DOS, INR, "Arms Flows to India and Pakistan: More Continuity Than Change since Bangladesh," 10 November 1971 [FOI document]).

14. According to Indian sources, during President V. V. Giri's visit to Moscow in mid 1970 Soviet officials had stated that they would "suspend" the flow of arms to Pakistan, but apparently the U.S.S.R. continued to honor the commitments made to Pakistan in 1968–70.

15. This is the general appraisal of Soviet policy objectives in 1971 in Pakistani, Indian, and American official sources. One exception was a former Pakistani diplomat with long experience in the foreign service, who had a quite different view. According to him, by 1971 the U.S.S.R. was

looking for a reliable and compliant client state in South Asia. India was too large and independent minded, accepting Soviet assistance for the achievement of New Delhi's objectives, but unwilling to follow Moscow's directives. Pakistan, Nepal, and Sri Lanka were excluded because they had closer ties to Beijing than to Moscow. But a Bangladesh that had won its independence with Soviet assistance might prove more responsive to Soviet dictates. Moscow assumed (correctly) that Bengali Muslims would soon shift their denunciations from West Pakistani "colonialism" to India's "Hindu hegemonism" and would look for an outside source of support as a balance to New Delhi—support that the U.S.S.R. could provide (interview, 1981). There are some serious problems with this scenario, primarily the inconsistency in Soviet policy on East Pakistan during 1971. But it is true that India and the U.S.S.R. were subtly competing for the preeminent role in Bangladesh in 1972–75. This ended with Mujib's assassination in 1975 and the eventual emergence of a government in Dhaka that sought to curtail relations with both India and the U.S.S.R. and to expand relations with the United States and China. To the victor belong the spoils?

16. Interviews, India, 1978; interviews with various American officials as cited in the Carnegie Foundation files.

17. Interviews, India, 1980.

18. DOS, INR, "Soviet Role in Indo-Pak Conflict," (FOI document), February 1972.

19. *Times of India*, 3 October 1971. Yahya stated in an interview that he had received assurances from Podgorny when they met in Iran in mid October that the Indo-Soviet treaty "was not directed against us and that his country was not encouraging Indian aggression" (*Le Monde*, 18 October 1971).

20. DOS, intelligence report, 19 October 1971 (FOI document).

21. Ibid.

22. *Hindustan Times*, 28 October 1971.

23. DOS, intelligence report, 19 October 1971 (FOI document). According to this report, the Indian foreign secretary, T. N. Kaul, had cited the one billion dollar figure to a journalist as early as 6 October. It should be noted, however, that Soviet economic assistance to the Bengali refugees in India totaled only $11 million through 13 September—$10 million for rice and $1 million for smallpox vaccine—compared to $124 million contributed by the U.S. government and private American sources (memorandum to Kissinger, 15 September 1971 [FOI document]).

24. Memorandum to Kissinger, 17 November 1971 (FOI document). According to one Pakistani source, Soviet aircraft used the Lahore airport as a refueling stop on the airlift to India. The Pakistani government knew the Soviet planes were carrying military equipment for the Indian army, but felt it could not prevent the use of the Lahore facilities for this purpose (interview, Pakistan, 1979). This has not been verified through documentation or confirmation by other Pakistani sources, but 1971 was crazy enough that it could have happened. The alternative route to India, it might be noted, was through Iran, an ally of Pakistan's and a reluctant source of cooperation in the Soviet airlift.

25. DOS, INR, "Soviet Role in Indo-Pak Crisis," 11 February 1972 (FOI document).

26. Tass statement, 5 December 1971. It should be noted, however, that the U.S.S.R. only recognized the Bangladesh government on 24 January 1972, and that Soviet press reports usually referred to "East Pakistan" throughout the war.

27. A propensity to project minor, but highly publicized, issues in U.S.–Soviet relations as crises in which World War III has just barely been averted by the noble restraint and/or brilliant leadership of Soviet and/or U.S. leaders is a regular feature of superpower politics. Perhaps the most amusing sally between the two superpowers in 1971 was an article in *Pravda* on 16 December in which the commentator, Konstantine Geivandov, asked, "What business has an American naval squadron in the Indian Ocean?" The same question could, of course, be asked about the Soviet naval squadron, which had been there first and also for no apparent reason.

28. This congruence of views was reflected in Nixon's "State of the World" address to the U.S. Congress in February 1972, in which he specifically praised the Soviet Union for having helped dissuade India from launching a major offensive against West Pakistan. While this has usually been dismissed as an effort on Nixon's part to exonerate himself from some of the policies followed by his administration in 1971, the extensive exchange of correspondence between the Soviet and U.S. governments on this issue in December 1971 clearly demonstrates that both sides were concerned (FOI data).

29. *Pakistan Times*, 13 April 1971.

30. Ibid., 23 April 1971, contains the full text of the letter.

31. Interviews, Pakistan, 1979; Bangladesh, 1978, 1980, 1982; Carnegie Foundation files. Washington (and presumably Moscow) also had received intelligence reports of Beijing's policy by at least mid 1971, although this is not evident in Kissinger's account of the Bangladesh crisis (see his *The White House Years* [Boston: Little, Brown, 1979], 842–918).

32. Interviews, India, 1978, 1979. This was never stated directly by the Indian sources, but several Indians in positions that gave them access to intelligence data emphasized that they were confident by July that China would not intervene in another Indo-Pakistani conflict. According to a responsible Bangladeshi source who had participated in this exercise, copies of the Chinese letters were provided to the Indian intelligence services by "East Pakistanis" in Pakistan's Foreign Service during May and June of 1971, usually shortly after their receipt by the Pakistani government.

33. Interviews, India, 1978. An American ship with $350,000 in arms aid was in Chittagong harbor on 25 March. The U.S. authorities tried to prevent the unloading of the shipment, but the Pakistani officials refused to allow the ship to depart until the supplies had been unloaded. The captain of the vessel finally complied with the Pakistani demand (Carnegie Foundation files). It is doubtful, however, that the Chinese exhibited the same reluctance to deliver their shipload of arms.

34. Interviews, Pakistan, 1979; Bangladesh, 1980.

35. Defense Intelligence Agency, "The 1971 Indo/Pakistani Conflict: A Study of Escalation," September 1972 (FOI document).

36. Interviews, Pakistan, 1979, 1980.

37. Ibid. G. W. Choudhury, a close confidant of Yahya Khan's in 1970–71, makes it quite clear that there was no confusion in the Pakistani government on Chinese policy (*Last Days*, 216–19).

38. DOS, "Chronology of Events in the 1971 Bangladesh Crisis" (FOI document).

39. Interviews, Pakistan, 1981.

40. In mid 1971 there were three Chinese infantry divisions in Tibet, two deployed along the eastern border and one near Lhasa, as well as one reinforced infantry regiment in the Chumbi valley opposite Sikkim and one regiment on the Nepal border north of Kathmandu. There was another division in Xinjiang, opposite Ladakh, which made a total of about 60,000 troops on the entire Himalayan frontier (Defense Intelligence Agency, "Sino-Indian Border Troops Dispositions," 15 June 1971). This force would have had to be substantially reinforced to hold its own in a conflict with India, much less launch a major military action, and according to both Indian and American sources, no expansion of the Chinese force occurred prior to December 1971.

41. In the U.S. government's view, however, it was Pakistan that had opted out of the U.S. security system in 1961–62, when Islamabad began to develop a very close relationship with Beijing, which undermined American strategic policy in Asia.

42. The literature on U.S.–Pakistani relations in the mid 1960s has not noted one irony. Pakistan, supposedly a U.S. ally in SEATO, refused to even nominally support American involvement in Vietnam, presumably to avoid any strains in Sino-Pakistani relations. India, a nonaligned nation on everything but China at that time (as Nehru put it after the 1962 war), quietly accepted the U.S. decision to intervene in Indochina, which New Delhi saw as a deterrent to *Chinese* expansionism. It was only in the latter half of 1967, following Mrs. Gandhi's visit to Moscow, when the Soviet leaders made it clear that their decision on arms aid to Pakistan would be linked to the Indian position on Vietnam, that New Delhi began to become more critical of U.S. policy in Vietnam (interviews, India, 1967–68, 1981).

43. In 1966 the embargo on arms aid was modified to permit the sale to both India and Pakistan of "nonlethal" items (communication, medical, and transportation equipment). In 1967 the embargo was further modified to allow the sale to both countries of spare parts and ammunition for military equipment that had been provided to them prior to the 1965 war.

44. Several Indian commentators have alleged that the U.S. government was antagonistic to Prime Minister Gandhi from the time she first took office in 1966, and that the CIA and other American agencies were involved in financing opposition parties in their efforts to remove her from power. During his stint as ambassador to India in the early 1970s, however, Daniel Patrick Moynihan received a report on a search through the files of the various U.S. government agencies that revealed that the only American financial assistance to any Indian party, organization, or political leader was given on two occasions to the Congress party—once directly to Mrs. Gandhi in her capacity as its president—to support it in contests against the Communist party in Kerala and West Bengal (Daniel P. Moynihan, Susan Weever, *A Dangerous Place* [Boston: Little, Brown, 1978], 41).

45. *New York Times*, 8 and 11 October 1970.

46. There appears to be some confusion in U.S. government sources on the definition of "nonlethal." One State Department source commented that bullets are defined as nonlethal if they are sold without guns; Defense Department sources deny this, however, and presumably are more knowledgeable on this particular subject.

47. The information on U.S. arms aid policy toward Pakistan is based largely upon interviews in 1972 with approximately one hundred American officials (State, Defense, CIA, National Security Council) and journalists conducted by a team from a project sponsored by the Carnegie Endowment for International Peace in Washington, D.C. The files are confidential, hence we do not cite the sources by name.

48. Reportedly, the DOS and DOD also had different interpretations of what "delivery" meant (apparently the question had never come up before in this form). To Defense delivery meant "handing over the title of purchase," but State interpreted delivery as the actual shipment of the goods outside U.S. territorial waters. The DOS, including the secretary of state, had assumed that the 6 April policy decision would prevent any further shipments to Pakistan; it was greatly embarrassed when it became evident in June that this was not the case.

49. DOD, "Military Supply Policy for Pakistan: Status Report," 29 July 1971 (FOI document).

50. Ibid.

51. Ibid.

52. DOS, confidential report, 2 September 1971 (FOI document).

53. Carnegie Endowment files.

54. See U.S. Congress, Senate Committee on the Judiciary, *Relief Problems in East Pakistan and India*, pt. 3, *Hearings before a Subcommittee to Investigate Problems Connected with Refugees and Escapees* (Washington, D.C.: Government Printing Office, 1971) for details on the food aid program to India and Pakistan.

55. Carnegie Endowment files.

56. According to one Indian source, the Indian army captured more Soviet than American equipment in East Pakistan in the December war (interview, India, 1981). But this has not been documented and seems rather unlikely. What is worth noting, however, is that official Indian publications never even mentioned the Soviet arms, while loudly complaining about the Chinese and American arms that were seized.

57. A separate Bangladesh was viewed as an unfortunate precedent in international relations that could lead to similar separatist movements elsewhere (including India), but not as a disaster. The disintegration of West Pakistan, in contrast, would have been considered a catastrophe by Nixon, Kissinger, and most State and Defense department officials (Carnegie Endowment files).

58. The Washington Special Action Group on the 1971 crisis was chaired by Kissinger, the president's assistant for national security affairs. The following officials—or their deputies—were the usual participants in the meetings on South Asia: (1) the under secretary of state for political affairs; (2) the assistant secretary of state for the Near East and South Asia; (3) the deputy assistant secretary of state for South Asia; (4) the deputy secretary of defense; (5) the assistant secretary of defense for international

security affairs; (6) the chairman of the Joint Chiefs of Staff; (7) the director of the CIA; and (8) the deputy administrator of USAID.

59. DOS, Kissinger statement to the Washington Special Action Group dated 2 September 1971 (FOI document; the date of the meeting is not indicated in the records made available).

60. Ibid.

61. See, for instance, the critique of Kissinger's interpretation of the 1971 crisis in his *White House Years* by Christopher Van Hollen—in 1971 the deputy assistant secretary of state for Near Eastern and South Asian affairs—in "The Tilt Policy Revisited: Nixon-Kissinger Geopolitics and South Asia," *Asian Survey* 20, no. 4 (April 1980): 339–61.

62. For example, in a meeting between Yahya and U.S. Ambassador Farland on 19 August, in a response to a suggestion that Yahya deal with at least the eighty-eight members of the Awami League who had been "cleared" by the Pakistani government, Yahya "refused to deal with any group, however cleansed, under [the] name of [the] Awami League" and said he had been strongly criticized in West Pakistan for "having cleared as many as 88 former AL members." However, according to one high Department of State official, Yahya eventually agreed to meet any *"bona fide* Awami Leaguers"* (Carnegie Endowment files).

63. Carnegie Endowment files and various FOI records. However, according to one Pakistani source close to Yahya in 1971, Yahya was prepared to have Mujib included in negotiations with the Awami League and even asked the shah of Iran to assist in the negotiation of a political solution with the Awami League during Yahya's visit to Tehran in September (interview, Pakistan, 1981).

64. DOS, *Sitrep*, no. 2, 23 November 1971.

65. Ibid., no. 8, 27 November 1971.

66. Ibid., no. 24, 6 December 1971.

67. Kissinger, *White House Years*, 842–918.

68. CIA "Intelligence Support in Political-Military Crises: A Case Study of the India-Pakistan Crisis of 1971," mid 1972 (FOI document). According to this report, Prime Minister Gandhi stated at an Indian cabinet meeting late on the night of 3 December that India had no interest in annexing any part of West Pakistan, but that it hoped to destroy the Pakistani army. Mrs. Gandhi was quoted by the Indian source as having said on 6 December that after the liberation of Bangladesh, India would occupy the southern section of Pakistani-held Kashmir for strategic reasons and would destroy the Pakistani army's "striking power" ("Indian Military Intentions toward West Pakistan," summary of CIA reports, 1971 [FOI document]).

69. Carnegie Foundation interview with a State Department official usually considered a critic of the Kissinger policy.

70. This would all have been rather academic were it not for the vehement denunciation of the Nixon-Kissinger "tilt toward Pakistan" policy after the war, much of it based on "investigative reporting" on the subject by Jack Anderson and George Clifford published in *The Anderson Papers* (New York: Ballantine Books, 1973), 255–326. As is sometimes the case in investigative reporting, in Washington and elsewhere, the investigators obtained *some* documents relevant to the subject and used these to

"prove" conclusions that evidently had already been determined. In any case, our reading of these same documents, as well as of some apparently not made available to Anderson by his in-house sources, has led us to a less simplistic analysis of the 1971 Bangladesh events.

Moreover, the section on the Bangladesh crisis in *The Anderson Papers* is so loaded with basic factual errors about South Asia that we can only presume that no specialist on the area read it prior to publication. Most of these errors have little or no reference to the main theme of the book—the defamation of Nixon and Kissinger. Still, one might have expected greater care as regards some of the basic geopolitics of South Asia, since the book expounds on this subject at considerable length. It was surprising, for instance, to read that by 1971 the old caravan trail over the Karakoram Range between Xinjiang in China and Pakistan had been "widened and hardened to provide a modern all weather road" down which "motorized caravans roared over the mountains, carrying the tools of war to Pakistan" (269). In fact, it was a decade later before an unpaved road over the difficult 16,000 ft. pass on the border was opened, and only in 1985 that it was completed. Virtually all Chinese arm shipments to Pakistan in 1971 were sent via the long sea route from China around the subcontinent to the port of Karachi in West Pakistan.

71. Lt. Commander Kenneth R. McGruther, "The Role of Perception in Naval Diplomacy," *Naval War College Review*, 5.

72. In subsequent statements and publications, Kissinger has placed almost all the emphasis on the China factor in the *Enterprise* taskforce—and other—decisions made by the U.S. government in December 1971, but this is not evident in the Washington Support Action Group or other documents of that period. Whether it is a matter of afterthought or that he merely did not bother to discuss these matters with the State Department at the time is unclear. For the most thorough and informed critique of Kissinger in the 1971 conflict from within the State Department establishment, see Van Hollen, "Tilt Policy Revisited," 339–61.

13. INTERPRETATIONS

1. The general theoretical literature on international crisis decision making is substantial. Particularly useful for our purposes are Charles F. Hermann, ed., *International Crises: Insights from Behavioral Research* (New York: Free Press, 1972); Glenn H. Snyder and Paul Diesing, *Conflict among Nations: Bargaining, Decision Making, and System Structure in International Crises* (Princeton: Princeton University Press, 1977); and, more recently, Michael Brecher and Patrick James, *Crisis and Change in World Politics* (Boulder, Colo.: Westview Press, 1986).

2. Alternative models of crisis decision-making processes are reviewed in Ole Holsti, "Theories of Crisis Decision Making," in Paul Gordon Lauren, ed., *Diplomacy: New Approaches in History, Theory, and Policy* (New York: Free Press, 1979). See in the same volume, Samuel R. Williamson, Jr., "Theories of Organizational Process and Foreign Policy Outcomes," 137–61. See too Robert Jervis, *Perception and Misperception in International Politics*

(Princeton: Princeton University Press, 1976), especially chaps. 1–2, 4, and 8–9.

3. Richard Smoke, *War: Controlling Escalation* (Cambridge, Mass.: Harvard University Press, 1977), 289. Also see his more abbreviated "Theories of Escalation," in Lauren, *Diplomacy*, 162–82. For a suggested treatment of decision under conditions of risk, see Amos Tversky and Daniel Kahneman, "Judgment under Uncertainty: Heuristics and Biases," *Science* 185 (September 1974): 1124–31.

Participants Interviewed

We conducted a large number of interviews with people in India, Pakistan, Bangladesh, and the United States who were either involved in decision making in their countries or were knowledgeable about the course of events in 1970–71. We held most of these interviews jointly, which resulted in near-verbatim accounts and more broadly based inquiries than would otherwise have been the case. Many of the principals were interviewed at least twice and several four or five times, usually in sessions that lasted from one to over two hours. In addition to these formal interviews, from 1978 to 1987 we had more informal discussions on the subject of this study with many other Indians, Pakistanis, Bangladeshis, and Americans (and some Soviet and Chinese specialists) who are not listed here.

We should also note that we assured our interviewees that we would not cite them by name in our analysis, a principle we have adhered to except in a couple of instances in which the interviewees informed us that anonymity was not required.

Most of the principal leaders of the Awami League had been assassinated or were in prison when we began our study in 1978. Later we were able to meet with a few of the surviving league members, as well as some academics and journalists well informed on the events of 1971, in Bangladesh, England, India, and the United States.

In the United States we met with several members of the U.S. Foreign Service who had key roles in the events of South Asia. Under the sponsorship of the Carnegie Endowment for International Peace, a series of interviews had been conducted in Washington, D.C., with a large number of U.S. government officials in various departments and agencies who had been involved in some way with the 1971 Bangladesh developments. We were granted permission to use the transcripts of these interviews on condition that we not quote directly from them or specifically cite an interviewee. We were informed, however, that we could list the officials whose interviews we had found most useful in expanding our understanding of U.S. policy and objectives in the 1971 South Asian crisis.

Unless otherwise indicated, the positions and offices given are those held by the interviewees in 1971.

PAKISTAN

Office of the President and Chief Martial Law Administrator
(CMLA): Officers and Advisers

Gen. Agha Mohammed Yahya Khan, president and CMLA

Lt. Gen. S. G. M. Peerzada, principal staff officer to the CMLA

Gen. Abdul Hamid Khan, commander in chief of the Pakistani army and a member of the CMLA's staff

Air Marshal Rahim Khan, commander of the Pakistani air force

Air Marshal Nur Khan, member of the Council on Administration and a leader of the Council Muslim League

Maj. Gen. Ghulam Umar, secretary of the National Security Council

Col. M. A. Hasan, judge advocate general and martial law and constitutional adviser to the CMLA

Justice A. R. Cornelius, former chief justice of the Supreme Court and an adviser to the CMLA on constitutional matters

M. M. Ahmed, deputy chairman, Planning Commission, and economic adviser to the CMLA

G. W. Choudhury, member of the cabinet and constitutional adviser to the CMLA

Gen. Sher Ali Khan, member of the cabinet

A. K. Brohi, prominent constitutional lawyer and attorney for Sheikh Mujibur Rahman in his 1971 treason trial

Pakistani Officials in East Pakistan, 1970–71

Vice Admiral S. M. Ahsan, governor of East Pakistan until March 1971

Gen. A. A. K. Niazi, general officer commanding, the eastern command (East Pakistan), 1971

Maj. Gen. Rao Farman Ali Khan, in charge of civil affairs in the East Pakistan martial law administration and adviser to the governor of East Pakistan

Lt. Gen. Sahabzada Yaqub Khan, martial law administrator, East Pakistan

Political Party Leaders and Members

Pakistan People's Party
Mumtaz Bhutto
Dr. Mobhashar Hasan
A. H. Kardar
J. A. Rahim

Hafeez Pirzada
M. B. Naqvi
Council Muslim League
  Mian Mumtaz Daultana
  Sardar Shaukat Hayat Khan
Pakistan Muslim League
  Khan Abdul Qayum Khan
Jamiat ul-Ulema-i-Pakistan
  Maulana Shah Ahmad Noorani
  Zahoor Bhopali

Ministry of Foreign Affairs, Pakistan

Sultan Mohammad Khan, foreign secretary
Safqat Khan
Tamiur A. Khan
Ali Sarwara Naqui
Zahid Said
Nazimuddin Sheikh

INDIA

Prime Minister's Office, Cabinet, and Secretariat

Indira Gandhi, prime minister
Jagjivan Ram, minister of defence
K. C. Pant, minister of state for home affairs (responsible for states bordering on East Pakistan)
Ram Niwas Mirdha, minister of state for home affairs (responsible for states bordering on West Pakistan)
P. N. Haksar, secretary, prime minister's secretariat (until August)
P. N. Dhar, secretary, prime minister's secretariat (after August)
Dinesh Singh, minister of external affairs (until March 1971)
G. Parthasarthy, vice-chancellor of Jawaharlal Nehru University; a close confidant of Mrs. Gandhi's.
L. K. Jha, ambassador to the United States

Government and Military Officials

T. N. Kaul, secretary, Ministry of External Affairs
K. B. Lal, secretary, Ministry of Defence

Lt. Gen. Jagjit Singh Aurora, commanding general, Eastern Command.
Khushro Rustamji, director, Border Security Force
P. R. Chari, joint secretary, Ministry of Defence
K. Subrahmanyam, director, Institute of Defence Studies and Analyses,
    New Delhi

Ministry of External Affairs

Kewal Singh
Shankar Bajpai
Dr. I. P. Singh
Peter Sinai
J. N. Dixit
K. P. S. Menon
U. S. Bajpai
Romesh Bhandari
Eric Gonsalves
A. K. Damodaran
Salman Haider
Jagat Mehta
I. J. Gujral
M. K. Rasgotra
V. H. Coelho
Natwar Singh
S. K. Singh
Juscaran Teja
Ashok Chib

Journalists, Academics, and Politicians

Dilip Mukherjee
Kuldip Nayar
Girilal Jain
Inder Malhotra
V. P. Ramachandran
Pran Chopra
Satish Kumar
Jaswant Singh
Subrata Roy Chowdhury (Calcutta)
Jibanlal Banerjee (Calcutta)

Bhabani Sen Gupta
H. K. Dua
Subramanian Swamy
A. G. Noorani (Bombay)
S. P. Sheth (Bombay)

BANGLADESH

Kamal Hossain, member of the Awami League negotiating team in early 1971 and adviser to Sheikh Mujibur Rahman on constitutional matters

Rehman Sobhan, economic adviser to the Awami League

Gen. M. A. G. Osmani, military adviser to the Awami League and commander of the Mukti Bahini forces

Azaduzzaman Khan, Awami League member of parliament in 1971 who remained in East Pakistan

A. M. A. Muhith, civil servant in 1971 who joined the government in exile

Rashid Choudhury, Pakistan's deputy high commissioner in New Delhi (April 1971), who retained his position through most of the year but assisted the Bangladesh movement in India

Ghulam Kibria, East Bengali serving in the Pakistani embassy in Moscow in 1971

Shafiul Azam, chief secretary in the East Pakistani government in 1971

Mainul Hussain, editor of *Ittefaq* (a pro–Awami League paper) in 1971

Shahidul Huq, *Bangladesh Times*

M. Rashiduzzaman, Political Science Department, University of Dhaka

Rounaq Jahan, Political Science Department, University of Dhaka

THE UNITED STATES

Foreign Service

Christopher van Hollen, deputy assistant secretary, South Asia, 1971

Craig Baxter, Pakistan Desk, Department of State, Washington, D.C.

Harold Saunders, assistant secretary of state, Near East / South Asia, 1971

George Griffin, U.S. Consulate-General, Calcutta

Archer Blood, U.S. Consulate-General, Dhaka

W. Dean Howells, Intelligence and Research, South Asia, Department of State, Washington, D.C.

Thomas Thornton, Policy Planning Section, Department of State, Washington, D.C.

Howard Schaeffer, India Desk, Department of State, Washington, D.C.

Donald Gelber, FSO aide to chief of naval operations, Admiral Zumwalt

Carnegie Endowment for International Peace

Joseph Carr, public safety program director for Near East / South Asia, 1971

Eric Griffell, director, U.S. Agency for International Development, Dhaka, 1971

Maurice Williams, deputy director, U.S. Agency for International Development, 1971

Don Grand Pre, Sales Negotiation, International Security Agency, Department of Defense, 1971

Lt. Col. Woolf Gross, Pakistan Desk officer, Department of Defense, 1971

W. Dean Howells, Intelligence and Research, South Asia, 1971

Joseph Sisco, assistant secretary of state, Near East / South Asia, 1971

Samuel de Palma, assistant secretary of state, International Organizations, 1971

Winston Lord, National Security Council staff, 1971

Joe Johnson, member, Presidential Commission on Bangladesh (private body appointed August 1971)

Richard Wilson, economic officer, Dhaka, 1971

Joseph Vaughn, chief of Licensing Division, Office of Munitions Control, 1971

Thomas Thornton, Policy Planning Section, Department of State, 1971

Edmund Finegold, Arms Transfer Division chief, Department of Defense, 1971

Louis Fields, Chief Legal Adviser's Office, South Asia Section, Department of State

William F. Spengler, country director, Pakistan, Department of State (until 1 July 1971)

John W. Sipes, Office of Munitions Control, Department of Defense, 1971

Howard Schaeffer, India Desk, Department of State, 1971

Bruce Laingen, country officer for Afghanistan and Pakistan, Department of State (from July 1971)

Craig Baxter, political officer for Pakistan and Afghanistan, Department of State, 1971

Archer Blood, consul-general, Dhaka 1971

Douglas Cockran, Pakistan Desk, Department of State, 1971

Christian Chapman, military sales & assistance officer for South Asia, Department of Defense, 1971

Clyde Bryant, chief intelligence officer (Office of Munitions Control), Bureau of Politico-Military Affairs, Department of State, 1971

Charles Bray III, press spokesman, Department of State, 1971

Scott Butcher, political officer, Consulate-General, Dhaka, 1971

Herbert Gordon, U.S. consul-general, Calcutta, 1971

Lee T. Stull, political counsellor, American Embassy, New Delhi, 1971

John Foster, South Asia, Central Intelligence Agency

Angus Thuermer, special assistant to R. Helms, Central Intelligence Agency, 1971

Select Bibliography

Afzal, M. Rafique. *Political Parties in Pakistan: 1947–1958*, Islamabad: National Commission on Historical and Cultural Research, 1976.

Ahmad, Akhtarruddin. *Nationalism or Islam: Indo-Pakistan Episode*. New York: Vantage Press, 1984.

Ahmad, Kabir Uddin. *Breakup of Pakistan: Background and Prospects of Bangladesh*. London: Social Science Publishing, 1972.

Ahmad, Kamruddin. *The Social History of East Pakistan*. Dhaka: Pioneer Press, 1967.

Ahmad, Moudid. *Bangladesh: Constitutional Quest for Autonomy, 1950–1971*. Wiesbaden: Steiner, 1978; Dhaka: University of Dhaka Press, 1979.

Akhtar, Jamna Das. *The Saga of Bangla Desh*. Delhi: Oriental Publishers, 1971.

Ali, Chaudhri Muhammad. *The Emergence of Pakistan*. New York: Columbia University Press, 1967.

Ali, Mohammed Abbas. *Salvation of East Pakistan*. Lahore: Ilmi Printing Press, 1971.

Ali, S. M. *After the Dark Night: Problems of Sheikh Mujibur Rahman*. Delhi: Thomson Press, 1973.

Ali, Tariq. *Pakistan: Military Rule or People's Power*. New York: Morrow, 1970.

al-Mujahid, Sharif. *Quaid-i-Azam Jinnah: Studies in Interpretation*. Karachi: Quaid-i-Azam University Press, 1981.

Anderson, Jack, with George Clifford. *The Anderson Papers*. New York: Ballantine Books, 1973. Pages 255–326 deal with the Bangladesh crisis.

Appadorai, A. *Select Documents on India's Foreign Policy and Relations, 1947–1972*. Vol. 1. New Delhi: Oxford University Press, 1982.

Ayoob, Mohammed, and K. Subrahmanyam. *The Liberation War*. New Delhi: S. Chand, 1972.

Ayoob, Mohammed, et al. *Bangladesh: A Struggle for Nationhood*. Delhi: Vikas, 1971.

Aziz, K. K. *The Making of Pakistan: A Study in Nationalism*. London: Chatto and Windus, 1967.

———. *Party Politics in Pakistan, 1947–1958*, Islamabad: National Commission on Historical and Cultural Research, 1976.

Ball, Nicole. *Regional Conflicts and the International System: A Case Study of*

Bangladesh. Brighton: Institute for the Study of International Organisations, University of Sussex, 1974.

The Bangladesh Papers. Lahore: Vanguard Books, n.d.

Baujyan, Md. Abdul Wadud. *Emergence of Bangladesh and Role of Awami League.* New Delhi: Vikas, 1982.

Beeck, Louis. *Van Pakistan tot Bangla Desh.* Antwerp: De Nederlandsche Boekhandel, 1972.

Bhutto, Zulfikar Ali. *The Great Tragedy.* Karachi: Pakistan People's Party, 1971.

————. *If I Am Assassinated . . .* New Delhi: Vikas, 1979.

Binder, Leonard. *Religion and Politics in Pakistan,* Berkeley and Los Angeles: University of California Press, 1961.

Bindra, S. S. *Indo-Bangladesh Relations.* New Delhi: Deep and Deep Publishers, 1982.

Blikenberg, Lars. *India-Pakistan: The History of Unsolved Conflicts.* Munksgaard: Dansk Udenrigspolitisk Institut, 1972.

Brecher, Michael and Patrick James. *Crisis and Change in World Politics.* Boulder, Colo.: Westview Press, 1986.

Burke, S. M. *Mainsprings of Indian and Pakistan Foreign Policies.* Minneapolis: University of Minnesota Press, 1974.

Callard, Keith. *Pakistan: A Political Study.* London: Allen and Unwin, 1957.

Chakrabarti, S. K. *The Evolution of Politics in Bangladesh, 1947–1978.* New Delhi: Associated Publishing House, 1978.

Chatterjee, Sisir. *Bangladesh: The Birth of a Nation.* Calcutta: Book Exchange, 1972.

Chopra, Pran. *India's Second Liberation.* Delhi: Vikas, 1973.

Choudhury, A. K. *The Independence of East Bengal: A Historical Process.* Dhaka: Jatiya Grantha Kendra, 1984.

Choudhury, G. W. *The Last Days of United Pakistan.* Bloomington: Indiana University Press, 1974.

Chowdhury, Najma. *The Legislative Process in Bangladesh: Politics and Functioning of the East Bengal Legislature 1947–1958.* Dhaka: University of Dhaka Press, 1980.

Cohen, Stephen P. *The Pakistan Army.* Berkeley and Los Angeles: University of California Press, 1984.

Das, Mitra. *From Nation to Nation: A Case Study of Bengali Independence.* Calcutta: Minerva Associates, 1981.

Dreyfus, Paul. *Du Pakistan au Bangladesh.* Paris: Arthaud, 1972.

Feldman, Herbert. *The End and the Beginning: Pakistan, 1969–1971.* London: Oxford University Press, 1975.

————. *From Crisis to Crisis: 1962–1969.* London: Oxford University Press, 1972.

————. *Revolution in Pakistan: A Study of the Martial Law Administration.* New York: Oxford University Press, 1967.

Franda, Marcus. *Bangladesh: The First Decade.* New Delhi: South Asian Publishers, 1982.

Gandhi, Indira. *India and Bangladesh: Selected Speeches and Statements, March to December 1971.* New Delhi: Orient Longman, 1972.

Goodnow, Henry Frank. *The Civil Service of Pakistan: Bureaucracy in a New Nation,* New Haven: Yale University Press, 1964.

Haque, Azizul. *Trends in Pakistan's External Policy, 1947–1971: With Particular Reference to People's China.* Dhaka: Asiatic Society of Bengal, 1985.

Hermann, Charles F. *International Crises: Insights from Behavioral Research.* New York: Free Press, 1972.

India, Government of. Ministry of External Affairs. *Bangladesh Documents.* Vols. 1, 2. 1971–73.

Jackson, Robert W. *South Asia Crisis: India, Pakistan, and Bangladesh, a Political and Historical Analysis of the 1971 War.* New York: Praeger, 1975.

Jahan, Rounaq. *Pakistan: The Failure of National Integration.* New York: Columbia University Press, 1972.

Jennings, Sir Ivor. *Constitutional Problems in Pakistan.* London: Cambridge University Press, 1957.

Jervis, Robert. *Perception and Misperception in International Politics.* Princeton: Princeton University Press, 1976.

Kapur, K. D. *Soviet Strategy in South Asia: Soviet Policies towards the Indian Subcontinent and Afghanistan.* New Delhi: 1983.

Karim, A. K. Nazmul. *The Dynamics of Bangladesh Society.* New Delhi: Vikas, 1980.

Khan, Mohammed Ayub. *Friends Not Masters: A Political Autobiography.* London: Oxford.

Khan, Fazal Muqueem. *Pakistan's Crisis in Leadership.* Islamabad: National Book Foundation, 1973.

———. *The Story of the Pakistan Army.* Lahore: Oxford University Press, 1963.

Khan, Zillur R., and A. T. R. Rahman. *Autonomy and Constitution Making: The Case of Bangladesh.* Dhaka: Green Book House, 1973.

Kissinger, Henry. *White House Years.* Boston: Little, Brown, 1979. Pages 842–918 are on Bangladesh.

Krishan, Vice Admiral N. *No Way but Surrender: An Account of the Indo-Pakistan War in the Bay of Bengal, 1971.* New Delhi: Vikas, 1980.

Kumar, Satish, ed. *Documents on India's Foreign Policy, 1972.* New Delhi: Macmillan Co. of India, 1975.

Lauren, Paul Gordon, ed. *Diplomacy: New Approaches in History, Theory, and Policy.* New York: Free Press, 1979.

Lewis, Stephen R. *Pakistan: Industrialization and Trade Policies.* London: Oxford University Press, 1970.

Lifschultz, Lawrence. *Bangladesh: The Unfinished Revolution.* London: Zed Press, 1979.

Malek, Abdul. *From East Pakistan to Bangladesh: A History of Exploitation and Repression.* Manchester: Independent Commission for Human Rights, 1973.

Maniruzzaman, Talukder. *The Bangladesh Revolution and Its Aftermath.* Dhaka: Bangladesh Books International, 1980.

Mansingh, Surjit. *India's Search for Power: Indira Gandhi's Foreign Policy, 1966–1982.* New Delhi: Sage Publications, 1984.

Mascarenes, Anthony. *The Rape of Bangladesh.* New Delhi: Vikas, 1971.

Maswani, A. M. K. *Subversion in East Pakistan.* Lahore: Amir Publishers, 1979.

Mishra, P. K. *India, Pakistan, Nepal, and Bangladesh.* New Delhi: Sundeep Prakashan 1979.

Momen, Nurul. *Bangladesh: The First Four Years.* Dhaka: Bangladesh Institute of Law and International Affairs, 1980.

Moraes, Dom. *The Tempest Within: An Account of East Pakistan.* New Delhi: Vikas, 1971.

Noorani, A. G.. *Brezhnev Plan for Asian Security.* Bombay: Jaico Publishing, 1975.

O'Donnell, Charles Peter. *Bangladesh: Biography of a Muslim Nation.* Boulder, Colo. Westview Press, 1984.

Pakistan, Government of. *White Paper on the Crisis in East Pakistan.* Islamabad, 5 August 1971.

Palit, D. K. *The Lightning Campaign.* Salisbury, England: Compton, 1972.

Papanek, Gustav F. *Pakistan's Development: Social Goals and Private Incentives.* Cambridge, Mass.: Harvard University Press, 1967.

Rahman, Matiur. *The Role of India and the Big Powers in the East Pakistan Crisis of 1971.* London: Razia Rahman, 1984.

Rahman, Mizanur. *Emergence of a New Nation in a Multi-Polar World: Bangladesh.* Washington, D.C.: University Press of America, 1978.

Rahman, Sheikh Mujibur. *Bangladesh, My Bangladesh.* New Delhi: Orient Longman, 1972.

Rampal, S. N. *India Wins the War.* New Delhi: Army Education Stores, 1971.

Rashid, Colonel. *The Road to Freedom.* Dhaka: Syed Ataur Rahman, 1984.

Rashiduzzaman, M. *Pakistan: A Study of Government and Politics.* Dhaka: Ideal Library, 1967.

Rizvi, Hasan Askari. *Internal Strife and External Intervention: India's Role in the Civil War in East Pakistan (Bangladesh).* Lahore: Progressive Publishers, 1981.

Salik, Siddiq. *Witness to Surrender.* Karachi: Oxford University Press, 1977.

Schuler, Edgar A. and Kathryn R. *Public Opinion and Constitution Making in Pakistan, 1958–1962.* East Lansing: Michigan State University Press, 1966.

Samasujjamana, Kaji. *Amara Svadhina Halama* (History of the 1971 Bangladesh freedom struggle). Dhaka: Nargisa Jamava, 1985.

Sayeed, Khalid Bin. *Pakistan: The Formative Phase.* Oxford: Oxford University Press, 1968.

———. *Politics in Pakistan: The Nature and Direction of Change.* New York: Praeger, 1980.

Sen, Rangalal. *Political Elites in Bangladesh (1940–1970)*. Dhaka: University of Dhaka Press, 1986.

Sen Gupta, Jyoti. *Eclipse of East Pakistan*. Calcutta: Renco, 1963.

———. *Bangladesh in Blood and Tears*. Calcutta: Naya Prokash, 1981.

Sharma, Shri Ram. *Bangladesh Crisis and Indian Foreign Policy*. New Delhi: Young Asia, 1978.

Siddiqui, Kalim. *Conflict, Crisis, and War in Pakistan*. New York: Praeger, 1972.

Singh, Maj. Gen. Lachhman. *Indian Sword Strikes in East Pakistan*. New Delhi: Vikas, 1979.

Singh, Maj. Gen. Sukhwant. *The Liberation of Bangladesh*. New Delhi: Vikas, 1980.

Smoke, Richard. *War: Controlling Escalation*. Cambridge, Mass.: Harvard University Press, 1977.

Snyder, Glenn and Paul Dieslag. *Conflict Among Nations: Bargaining, Decision Making, and System Structure in International Crises*. Princeton: Princeton University Press, 1977.

Sodhi, Brig. H. S. *"Operation Windfall": Emergence of Bangladesh*. New Delhi: Allied Publishers, 1979.

Subrahmanyam, K. *Bangladesh and India's Security*. Dehra Dun: Palit and Dutt, 1972.

Syed, Anwar Hussain. *Pakistan: Islam, Politics, and National Solidarity*. New York: Praeger, 1982.

Tahir-Kheli, Shirin. *The United States and Pakistan: Evolution of an Influence Relationship*. New York: Praeger, 1982.

Tharoor, Shashi. *Reasons of State: Political Development and India's Foreign Policy under Indira Gandhi 1966–1977*. New Delhi: Vikas, 1982.

Upadhyaya, Anjoo S. *Self-Determination in World Politics: Emergence of Bangladesh*. Allahabad, India: Lokbharati Prakashan, 1984.

Umar, Badruddin. *Politics and Society in East Pakistan and Bangladesh*. Dhaka: Mowla Brothers, 1974.

Wilcox, Wayne Ayres. *Pakistan: The Consolidation of a Nation*. New York: Columbia University Press, 1963.

Williams, L. F. Rushbrook. *The East Pakistan Tragedy*. London: Tom Stacey, 1972.

Ziring, Lawrence. *The Ayub Khan Era: Politics in Pakistan, 1958–1969*. Syracuse, N. Y.: Syracuse University Press, 1971.

———, Ralph Braibanti, and W. Howard Wriggins. *Pakistan: The Long View*. Durham: Duke University Press, 1977.

Index

Abdullah, Sheikh, 39, 286
Afzal, M. Rafique, 282
Aga Khan, Sadruddin, 189
Agartala conspiracy, 22, 42, 71, 286
Ahmad, Khondikar Mushtaq, 131, 299, 301, 302
Ahmed, M. M., 55, 119, 124–25, 272
Ahmed, Muzzafar, 185
Ahmed, Tajuddin: and intraparty conflict, 288, 299; in mass movement, 98, 102, 105; on military authorities, 89; in negotiations, 131; on political settlement and governance, 61, 78, 98, 102, 114
Ahsan, Vice Admiral S. M.: dismissal of, 90, 108, 291; as minister and governor, 24, 64–65, 76–77; and Mujib, 87, 89; and political settlement, 84–85, 89–90
Ali, Chaudhri Muhammad, 286
All-Parties Round Table Conference, 22–23, 29, 288
al-Mujahid, Sharif, 283, 286
Amin, Nurul, 79, 176, 310
Anderson Papers, The, 316–17
Ankara agreement, 50–51
Asian collective security, 197, 240, 241
Aurora, Gen. Jagjit Singh, 225, 234, 288
Awami League: in constitutional negotiations, 116–27; in elections, 3, 15, 29–30, 32–33; governmental ban and "cleansing" of, 154–55, 169–70, 172–73; organizational cohesion, problems of, 56, 62, 78, 92–93, 100–101, 272; origins of, 12, 14–16. *See also* Perception/misperception; Rahman, Sheikh Mujibur; Six-Point Demand
Ayub Khan, Gen. Mohammed: and constitution, 170–71, 283; as coup leader, 16–17; governance of, 17–20; political demise of, 21–24
Aziz, K. K., 282

Badejo, Babafemi Adesina, 284
Banerji, R. N., 286

Bangladesh, government of: and India, 181–86, 303, 304; and military regime, 173–74; organization of, 142–43, 183–84. *See also* Mukti Bahini; Perception/misperception
Bargaining. *See* Negotiations
Baxter, Craig, 32, 285
Bhargava, G. S., 285
Bhashani, Maulana, 30, 103, 285, 301
Bhutto, Mumtaz Ali, 67, 96
Bhutto, Zulfiqar Ali: and Awami League, 68–71; Dhaka negotiations of, 120–22, 128–29; in elections, 3, 33–34; and military regime, 66–68, 80; and Mujib, 67–68, 70–71, 122; personality of, 57–58, 59–60; political strategy of, 56, 60–61, 72, 74–76, 78–80, 88–89, 95, 105–7; and PPP, 56–57, 71–72, 88–89; in transfer of power, 235–36; in U.N. Security Council and Polish resolution, 220, 306–7. *See also* Pakistan People's Party
Biharis, 146, 163, 165
Binder, Leonard, 282
Bizenjo, Ghaus Bux, 119, 131
Blikenberg, Lars, 294
Bogra, Mohammed Ali, 11
Bondurant, Joan V., 287
Border Security Force (India), 143–45, 184
Braibanti, Ralph, 282, 283, 284, 287
Bratha, Sashti, 304
Brecher, Michael, 287, 317
Brezhnev, Leonid, 40, 197, 240
Broomfield, John, 282
Burke, S. M., 287
Burki, Shahid Javed, 284

Callard, Keith, 281, 282
Cariappa, General, 150
Central Reserve Police (India), 144
Central Treaty Organization (CENTO), 39, 49, 217, 262
Chavan, Y. B., 139, 215, 305

Tahir-Kheli, Shirin, 287
Tandon, B. N., 138
Tashkent agreement: domestic conflict about, 40–42; in Indo-Soviet relations, 196–97, 215, 238, 305, 310; and 1971 Indian strategy, 215, 224; and U.S. policy, 255
Thant, U, 189–91, 301
Transfer of power: in 1971, 234–36; at partition in 1947, 38; preparation for, in 1969, 25–26
Tversky, Amos, 318
Twenty-one points, 12
Two-nation theory, 35–36

Umar, Maj. Gen. Ghulam, 24, 89, 108, 287
United Front, 12
United Nations: General Assembly, 219; Security Council, 210, 218–20; UNESCO, 188; United Nations High Commission for Refugees (UNHCR), 189, 191
United Progressive Party, 15
United States. *See* India; Pakistan

Van Hollen, Christopher, 316

Washington Special Action Group, 259, 262, 315–16
Weever, Susan, 314
Wheeler, Richard, 282, 283
Wilcox, Wayne Ayres, 286
Williams, Maurice, 174, 297, 307
Williamson, Samuel R., Jr., 317
Wriggins, W. Howard, 284, 287

Yahya Khan, Gen. Agha Mohammed: assumption of power, 2, 23; and Awami League, 63–66; and Bhutto, 66–68, 80, 119–20, 122; on ceasefire, 233–34; and mass movement, 98–100; in military action and aftermath, 154–56, 167–71; and Mujib, 63–64, 67–68, 76–77, 81, 112–16, 154; on war, 226–29. *See also* Negotiations

Zhou Enlai, 203–4, 250, 251, 252, 303, 308
Ziring, Lawrence, 284, 287

Printed in the United States
3574